Exploring
the
BC Coast
by Car

Exploring the BC Coast by Car

Diane Eaton
Allison Eaton

HARBOUR PUBLISHING

We acknowledge the financial support of the Government of Canada through the Book Publishing Industry Development Program.

Published by **HARBOUR PUBLISHING** P.O. Box 219, Madeira Park, BC Canada V0N 2H0

Cover, page design, composition, maps by Martin Nichols, Lionheart Graphics.
Project editing by Peter A. Robson and Derek K. Fairbridge. Additional research, writing and editing by Peter A. Robson, Derek K. Fairbridge, Diane McKay, Ann Macklem, Patricia Wolfe and Amanda Amaral.
Map on p. 10 courtesy BC Ferries. The section on 4-wheeling was written by Mark Bostwick.

Printed in Canada.

PHOTO CREDITS
All photos not listed below are by the authors
Interior photos: Alberni Valley Museum/John Taylor, 212 (left); Wilfred Atleo, 155; British Columbia Archives and Records Service, 98 (top, F-02163), 103 (F-5229), 110 (F-01220), 229 (HP7931), 335 (41054), 363 (G-00822); British Columbia Ferry Corporation, 334, 345; British Columbia Mining Museum, 53; Butchart Gardens, 113, 114; Mary Cain, 44; Campbell River Museum, 280 (9993); Leslie Ann Cass, 39; City of Vancouver Archives, 12 (TR.P.37.N.26); Cumberland Museum, 271; Steve Dennis, 233; Ian Douglas, 140 (bottom), 162 (bottom), 170, 180, 273, 274 (left), 297, 328, 341; Jennifer Echols, 16 (left), 19, 20 (both), 23, 25 (bottom), 26, 27 (bottom), 32, 33 (bottom), 36, 40 (top), 43 (both), 48, 51; Horne Lake Family Campground, 258; Hummingbird Inn Pub, 174; Chris Jaksa, 10, 140 (top), 331, 352; Lynn Katy, 194 (left), 270, 274 (right), 275; Fred/Debbie King, 173; James LaBounty, 42; Derrick Lundy/Gulf Islands Driftwood, 130, 131, 135, 136; Mandelbrot, 10, 35, 38, 70, 74, 123; National Film Board/John Dugh, 282; Martin Nichols, 225; Katie Nielsen, 285, 286; North Island Forestry Centre, 306; Oak Bay Marine Group, 276, 279; Ocean Adventures Charter Co., 218 (right), 333, 358, 360, 364, 373, 381, 382, 384, 385, 386, 388, 389; Marie O'Connor, 102; Peter A. Robson, 57, 58 (right), 60, 62, 75, 81, 133, 134 (top), 184, 222 (all), 223 (all), 257, 325, 348, 367; Linda Rowbotham, 377; Royal British Columbia Museum, 100; Seaside Adventures, 154, 156, 157, 210, 234, 235; J. Duane Sept, 119; Shearwater Marine Group, 339; David A.E. Spalding, 16 (right), 25 (top), 148 (right); Stubbs Island Whale Watching, 313; Keith Thirkell, 45, 46, 47, 52, 55 (both), 58 (left), 68, 70, 71, 73, 76 (both), 78, 82, 84 (both), 86, 168 (right), 170, 215, 314, 391; Tourism BC, 30, 31, 49 (top); Tourism Vancouver, 18, 21, 22, 24, 27 (top), 29, 34, 37 (bottom, Albert Normandin), 40 (middle); Nancy J. Turner, 133 (bottom two); Ucluelet Chamber of Commerce, 226, 232, 248; Dean van't Schip, 85, 170; Vesuvius Inn, 146; Wickaninnish Inn, 230.

Canadian Cataloguing in Publication Data

Eaton, Diane F.
  Exploring the BC coast by car

  Includes bibliographical references and index.
  ISBN 1-55017-178-X

  1. Pacific Coast (B.C.)—Guidebooks.   2. Automobile travel—Pacific Coast (B.C.)—Guidebooks.   I. Eaton, Allison, 1971–   II. Title.   III. Title: Exploring the British Columbia coast by car.
FC3845.P2A3 1999   917.11'1044   C98-910221-1
F1089.P2E27 1999

Second printing, 2001

CONTENTS

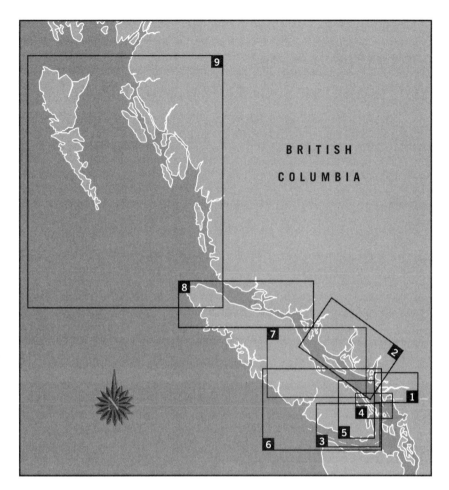

Area Map Index

Chapter

Road and Ferry Travel in BC

Road and Highway Information
The British Columbia Ministry of Transportation and Highways operates a "charge-to-caller" road report information service for all of the province. **1-900-565-4997** or **1-800-550-4997**.

Using Forest Service/Logging Roads; The public generally has free access to these gravel-surfaced roads, however, use may be restricted. Watch for the signs and remember, *always* give logging trucks the right of way on logging roads.

For information on construction progress of the Inland (Vancouver) Island Highway, 250-953-4949.

BC Ferries

BC Ferries
1112 Fort Street
Victoria, BC V8V 4V2
website: **www.bcferries.bc.ca**

Ferry Schedules, Fares and Information. Recorded information 24 hours a day. Agents available 7 a.m.–10 p.m. daily, Pacific Standard Time.

From outside BC **250-386-3431**
Fax **250-381-5452**
Toll-free in BC **1-888-BCFERRY (1-888-223-3779)**

On most BC ferry routes, bikes, cars, trucks and RVs can be carried. Foot passengers are welcome on all routes.

Cash and travellers cheques can be used for payment on all routes. Credit cards (VISA and MasterCard) can be used to pay for fares on most routes and must be used for most telephone reservations.

ATMs are available aboard the ferries plying the major routes, such as the Vancouver—Vancouver Island routes, and at the major terminals. Debit cards cannot be used to pay fares at this time.

If you plan on driving onto the ferry, you should be at the terminal at least 30 minutes before the scheduled sailing time, and even earlier during the busy summer months and on weekends. On holiday weekends, peak traffic volumes occur on Friday afternoon and evening, Saturday morning and Monday afternoon. On regular weekends, Friday and Sunday afternoons are the busiest. Walk-on passengers must buy their tickets at least ten minutes before the scheduled sailing time.

Reservations *are available* for your car, truck or RV on the three major routes between the Vancouver area and Vancouver Island. Reservations *are recommended* for travel between Vancouver (Tsawwassen) and the Southern Gulf Islands. Vehicle reservations *are required* for the Discovery Coast Passage, Inside Passage and Queen Charlotte Islands routes. Reservations are not available on other routes. Passenger sales representatives are available to reserve passages from 7 a.m. to 10 p.m (Pacific Time) daily, toll-free in BC **1-888-724-5223**, outside BC **604-444-2890**.

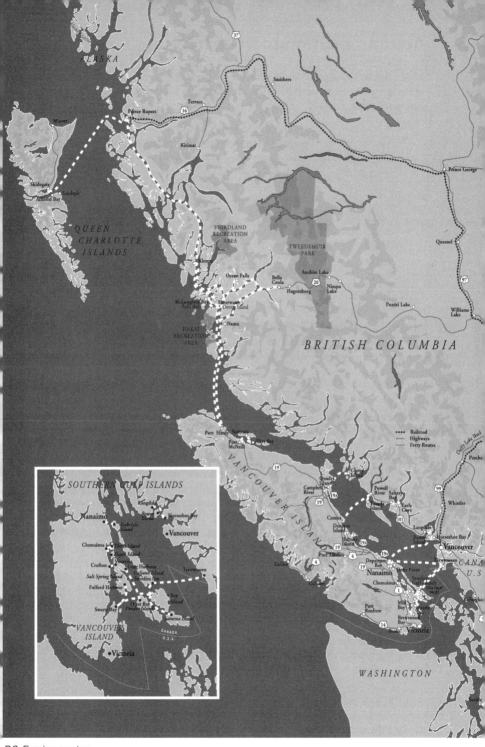

BC Ferries routes

Accommodation in British Columbia

Super, Natural British Columbia Reservation and Information Service is a central agency for planning travel in BC and arranging accommodation. Services include:

- Information packages on visiting British Columbia
- Information and reservations for Tourism BC approved accommodation from hotels and B&Bs to guest ranches and resorts
- Listings of regional B&B registries
- City sightseeing tours of Vancouver and Victoria
- Information and reservations for honeymoon or golf getaways, ski packages, live theatre packages, adventure packages, including whale watching tours
- Bus and ferry transportation information
- Float plane and helicopter flights between Vancouver and Seattle or Victoria and Seattle
- Reservations for the West Coast Trail (Pacific Rim National Park Reserve) and Gwaii Haanas National Park Reserve and Haida Heritage Site (Queen Charlotte Islands)

Greater Vancouver **604-663-6000** or toll-free **1-800-663-6000**
(Agents available 7 a.m.–6 p.m. weekdays and 9 a.m.–5 p.m. weekends, Pacific Standard time)
For direct hotel bookings through the website: **www.snbc-res.com**

Discover Camping Reservation Service

At most BC Provincial Parks and Parks Canada Parks, campsites are available on a first-come, first-served basis. However, 50 parks in BC do accept reservations. In 1999, reservable campgrounds on coastal BC include Englishman River Falls Provincial Park, Goldstream Provincial Park, Gordon Bay Provincial Park, Cowichan River Provincial Park, Miracle Beach Provincial Park, Montague Harbour Provincial Park, Saltery Bay Provincial Park, Porpoise Bay Provincial Park, Porteau Cove Provincial Park, and Pacific Rim National Park. The list of participating parks is updated yearly. Campsite fees and a non-refundable reservation service fee are charged. Campsites may be reserved up to 3 months in advance and 2 days prior to your arrival. The earliest reservable arrival date is March 15 and the latest is September 15. Reservations may be changed before 2 days prior to your arrival date. An additional reservation service fee will be charged for changes. Party size and number of vehicles are subject to restrictions. Reservations fill up quickly, so book early.

To reserve a campsite:
Greater Vancouver **604-689-9025**
Toll-free **1-800-689-9025**
(Agents available 7 a.m.–7 p.m. weekdays and 9 a.m.–5 p.m. weekends, Pacific Standard Time)
website **www.discovercamping.ca**
BC Parks **250-387-4550**
website **www.elp.gov.bc.ca/bcparks**
Pacific Rim National Park Reserve **250-726-4212**
website **http://fas.sfu.ca/parkscan/pacrim**

INTRODUCTION

Since 1592, when the old Greek pilot Juan de Fuca scurried back to Europe excitedly trying to convince his countrymen he had discovered an earthly paradise on the far side of the New World, the BC coast has been known as one of the world's most rewarding places to explore.

Occupying the 500-mile space between the 49th parallel and Alaska, the BC coast complicates itself into some twenty thousand miles of intricately entwined inlets, islands and channels. It boasts the busiest seaport on North America's west coast and a maritime wilderness beyond measure, as well as the world's most treacherous ocean graveyard and its most enchanting inland sea. It is a land of ancient, crumbling totem poles and humming high-speed ferries, of towering, desolate fjords and vibrant, modern resorts.

To experience the full magnificence of the coast you might assume that you would, like Juan de Fuca, require a well-appointed caravel and the backing of the Spanish Crown, or at least a pricey ticket on a cruise ship. But this book proves that you can explore the BC coast just as enjoyably and far more cheaply—thanks to the world's most highly developed ferry system—in the comfort of your family car.

The book is divided into eight chapters covering the coast's main geographic regions. Each begins with a brief overview, then takes you through the area from one end to the other.

Like each region it describes, *Exploring the BC Coast by Car* is unique. It is first of all a thorough and practical travel guide, carefully organized and laid out in an easy-to-use format. But it is much more than that. Despite the efforts of Captain Juan and the many explorers who followed in his footsteps, this coast of wonders is still relatively undiscovered territory on the world's travel map, and it needs some explaining. The authors have spared no effort to make sure you have all the background information you need to make the most of your coastal explorations. Even for those who know the coast well will find the book worth having for its overall portrait of coastal history and contemporary life.

Whether you want to burn up the territory or simply relive great sights by the fireside, we know *Exploring the BC Coast by Car* will prove an indispensable travelling companion.

A Brief History of the BC Coast

When Captain Vancouver imagined habitation for this beautiful coast in the late 1790s, he was thinking of Europeans. Human settlement on the BC coast had actually begun thousands of years before the white wings of European sailing ships hovered on the horizon, and at one time the BC coast was one of the most densely populated places in all of the Americas.

Even the Coast Salish, who met Vancouver's expedition, were relative newcomers to the seacoast. Smaller groups had made their way out of the colder, harsher BC interior about four hundred years before Vancouver's arrival—perhaps drawn by rumours of a mild seacoast with abundant food. They had spread north as far as Bute Inlet and south as far as the Columbia River in Washington state and developed a culture that was a blend of Interior Indian traditions and Northwest Coast ways. Some Coast Salish took up lands near present-day Vancouver, Victoria and southern Vancouver Island. Their descendants still live on or near their ancestral lands—including the X'muzk'i'um (Musqueam), Tsawwassen and Squamish First Nations of Vancouver, the Lekwammen of Victoria (today's Songhees and Esquimalt First Nations), and the Malahat, Cowichan, Chemainus and Sne ney mux (Nanaimo) peoples of southern Vancouver Island.

Over the millennia other First Nations groups had also established their own territories along the BC coast, including the Haida, Tsimshian, Kwakwaka'wakw (Kwakiutl), Heiltsuk (Bella Bella), and Nuu-chah-nulth (Nootka). The peoples of the Northwest Coast spoke many different languages but all had similar lifestyles. Blessed by an abundance of natural riches—salmon and cedar in particular—Northwest Coast Native culture was so rich, complex and distinctive that it is considered to have been monumental. For most Northwest Coast peoples, including the Coast Salish, hunting and food gathering expeditions on land and sea occupied the warm months, and social gatherings and ceremonials the winter months. These communal celebrations were full of pomp and pageantry. Huge feasts and potlatches took place, splendid gifts of jewelery, blankets, foods and furnishings were heaped on guests to celebrate important occasions and to affirm the roles played by both giver and receiver in their community. In some villages, complex rituals with music and storytelling dramatized by masked dancers revealed the interplay between human affairs and the spirit world. Ritual items that survive today, including masks, capes, feasting bowls, coppers and totems, still hum with spirit power. As more and more Europeans moved to BC, the potlatch and the rest of this "monumental" Northwest coast culture came under strong and sustained attack, but many languages, skills and traditions have survived and evidence of dynamic aboriginal cultures can be felt all along the coast.

Europeans had begun to explore the BC coast by the mid-1700s. The famous explorer Captain Cook sailed into Nootka Sound on Vancouver Island in the spring of 1778 with officers George Vancouver and the infamous William Bligh on board. Cook and his crew spent a month resupplying the ship and trading with the Hesquiat, the Nuu-chah-nulth people of Nootka Sound. The next year James Hanna sailed his brig into Nootka Sound to trade iron bars for sea otter furs. Hanna sold the furs in China at an enormous profit, and soon European traders of a half-dozen nationalities began making calls on the coast to barter for the luxurious furs so highly prized by Chinese mandarins. However, it was not until the nineteenth century, when the British fur trading company began to establish outposts in the region, that Europeans began to be felt as a day-to-day presence along the BC coast.

Loggers start falling a large fir tree in Vancouver, circa 1885. BC's largest city was once heavily forested with giants like this.

A sprinkling of Europeans turned into a tidal wave when the Cariboo Gold Rush of 1858 drew 25,000 gold seekers to what is now British Columbia. After the gold dust settled, Vancouver and Victoria began to carve out their respective roles. In 1868 Victoria became the provincial capital. The city built the resplendent Parliament Buildings to nail down its claim as the capital and then settled into its identity as a staid outpost of the British empire. Victoria's residents were long known as "more English than the English."

Victoria was chosen as the capital city, but it was Vancouver that became the real seat of economic and political power in the province. When the cross-country railway stretched across the nation and, in 1886, came to a halt at what is now Vancouver, the city's ascendancy was assured. The America-born general manager of the Canadian Pacific Railway, Sir William Cornelius Van Horne, declared that the place where the CPR established its western terminus was destined to be a great city. If he had his way, Van Horne declared, that new city's name would be Vancouver. And Vancouver it was. Victoria quietly settled into its identity as a small, dignified city and Canada's western gateway to the world. Wheat, lumber and minerals began flowing from the port of Vancouver, and people began flowing in to the city.

Natural resources, especially trees, fish and minerals, drew other newcomers to the region. Soon little settlements began to dot the whole coast. At first small coastal steamers were the major links between BC's coastal settlements and the outside world. Later roads, railroads, airplanes and BC Ferries routes knit up the coastal transportation system. Some of the early settlements withered away, while others blossomed into towns and small cities. Duncan, Ladysmith, Chemainus and Nanaimo on Vancouver Island are just a few places where a colourful coastal history blends with contemporary life.

CHAPTER 1
VANCOUVER & AREA

City lights from Stanley Park

Vancouver may have started life as a minor British fur trading post but today it is a quintessentially North American west coast city. The daily rhythms of life are easy, and even the city's downtown is surprisingly laid-back. Eavesdrop on a lunchtime conversation between serious business types and you'll most likely hear the talk turn to outdoor fun. Fitness is a way of life, and Vancouverites are always out and doing: **golfing, hiking, cycling, jogging, rollerblading,** or **skiing** in the nearby North Shore mountains or at the world-class Whistler/Blackcomb ski resort. With "water, water, everywhere," any time the sun shines locals pull out **scuba** gear, **swimsuits** or deck shoes, grab their **fishing** gear, stick their **canoes** or **kayaks** or **sailboards** on the roof rack, slap on the sunscreen and head for the wet stuff. Vancouver is a vast outdoor playground that attracts visitors from around the province, country and the world.

Vancouver is also a thoroughly cosmopolitan city. Since the turn of the century wave after wave of immigrants have swept into the city. Italian, East Indian, Latin American, Greek, Japanese, Chinese, Vietnamese, Lebanese, Iranian—the list goes on. Some Vancouver neighbourhoods have a distinctive ethnic slant. Main Street south of 49th Avenue is known as "**Little India**," Commercial Drive is distinctly **Italian**, Kingsway has a **Southeast Asian** flavour, West Broadway has its **Greek** community, Richmond is the new **Chinatown**. But the old ethnic boundaries are fading fast as the whole city opens up to newcomers—even the staunchly "Whites only" British Properties in wealthy West Vancouver has lost its colour sensitivity. Ethnic food shops, stores and restaurants abound right across the city. And visitors reap the harvest of Vancouver's ethnic mix in a windfall of fine restaurants. Take your pick from Thai, Chinese, Italian, Jamaican, Indian, Dutch, Spanish, Japanese, Ethiopian, Persian, or eclectic "fusion" restaurants where fresh local ingredients are melded with exotic cuisines. Taste sensations run the gamut from lemon grass, garam masala and hot chili oil to balsamic vinegar, asiago cheese and shiitake mushrooms. Take your choice—it's all there to please your palate. (Pick up the free *City Food* magazine in local bookstores and cafés for the latest tips on Vancouver restaurants.)

VANCOUVER

Vancouver Aquarium

The Greater Vancouver area is big enough to offer all kinds of attractions for visitors (we've listed our favourites on pp. 40–52), but Vancouver's downtown core is still the heart of the action. If time is short, head for the city centre, located on the peninsula ringed by False Creek, English Bay and Burrard Inlet, with beautiful Stanley Park at its tip. Once there you can explore different areas of downtown as personal whim and weather dictate.

During the last twenty years, Vancouver has experienced a huge population boom as newcomers came from all directions to enjoy the picture-perfect setting, kind climate,

Vancouver Art Gallery

Highlights

1000 acres of
magnificent parkland

Lively public beaches and
seaside walks

Public markets

Vibrant night life

Cuisine from around the world

Wide variety of cultural
events and performances

Professional hockey,
basketball and football

What to See Downtown

- ☐ **1** Stanley Park
- ☐ **2** Vancouver Aquarium
- ☐ **3** Seawall Promenade
- ☐ **4** Canada Place
- ☐ **5** Vancouver Art Gallery
- ☐ **6** Gastown
- ☐ **7** Chinatown
- ☐ **8** Library Square
- ☐ **9** Vancouver Maritime Museum
- ☐ **10** Vancouver Museum/ Planetarium
- ☐ **11** Granville Island
- ☐ **12** BC Place/GM Place
- ☐ **13** Science World

easy-paced lifestyle and cosmopolitan atmosphere. Vancouver exudes an urbane self-confidence, in part because more young professionals are not only working downtown, but living there, in condos and apartments that are springing up all around the city core. In fact the city's downtown residential population is growing faster than any other city in

Vancouver Harbour

North America. New pubs and clubs, shops and markets, espresso bars and streetside cafés all swing to the upbeat rhythms of a younger crowd who work and play downtown. Developers have been quick to locate condos and "artist's lofts" in what were once the city's meaner streets in Yaletown, Gastown, Strathcona (just east of Chinatown) and Mount Pleasant (near Broadway and Main). These areas have been home to Vancouver's poorer and more transient residents, but this is a city in which gentrification has never been accepted without an argument. Vancouver's long tradition of social awareness is especially visible in the Downtown Eastside, where residents transformed a heritage building into the Carnegie Community Centre, and where bright new housing cooperatives have begun to appear.

Meanwhile, development continues, especially along the waterfront. The Vancouver skyline is latticed with construction cranes, and the smell of freshly poured concrete wafts over the city.

Around Library Square: Vancouver's Theatre and Sports District

All that construction has been a bonanza for theatregoers and sports fans. You can't miss Library Square, Vancouver's newest landmark on Georgia Street between Homer and Hamilton. Architect Moshe Safdie's masterpiece looks as if the outer skin was peeled off the Roman Coliseum and curled loosely around the taut glass-and-concrete skeleton of the **public library**. A glass-covered atrium bridging the two segments is one of Vancouver's liveliest indoor people places. On a rainy day the atrium is a welcome spot for pizza munching and people watching as folks from all walks of life converge on the library's dazzling new digs. And right across Georgia Street is the grand dame of Vancouver theatre, dance and opera, the **Queen Elizabeth Theatre** complex.

For those who like their live entertainment fast-paced and sweaty, the big new **General Motors Place**—affectionately known to sports fans as "the Garage"—is just the ticket. Two professional sports teams, the **Vancouver Canucks** hockey team and the **Vancouver Grizzlies** basketball team, split the action at GM Place. Just west at the foot of Cambie Street bridge, is **BC Place Stadium** where Vancouver's third pro sports team, the **BC Lions** football team, puts on its show. BC Place is sometimes called "the Giant Pincushion" for its trademark huge white inflatable dome. When the athletes are on the road, the Garage and the Giant Pincushion rock to the music of **live concerts**, including recent performances by two famous ain't-dead-yet entourages, the Rolling Stones and The Three Tenors.

Vancouver Public Library

Georgia Street from Granville to Burrard: Downtown Vancouver

Just three blocks north of Library Square on Georgia is the longtime heart of downtown shopping. Canada's two venerable department stores, **Eaton's** and the **Hudson's Bay Company** ("the Bay") are still locked in a turf war for Vancouver shoppers' dollars at the intersection of Georgia and Granville. (In front of Eaton's is a little kiosk that serves up handy tourist information.) Just a few paces north of the intersection is the glass dome of the two-hundred-store underground **Pacific Centre Shopping Centre**, where you'll find the predictable rainbow of mall fare from fashion wear to a food fair. (Another tourist information booth is just inside the Pacific Centre's glass dome.) On the fourth corner is the new flagship store of the longtime Vancouver bookseller, **Duthie Books**. For a great collection of Canadiana, specialized BC guide books or a serendipitous browse, just step through the big brass doors into book lovers' heaven. On your way out, pick up a *Georgia Straight* magazine. It's Vancouver's all-time favourite freebie, a weekly that has the scoop on everything that's shaking in the city "entertainment-wise," and a trusty restaurant guide. (The *Straight* is also available at bookstores, record and video stores, and some cafés.)

Just a block north on Georgia between Howe and Hornby is the **Vancouver Art Gallery** (VAG) (604-662-4719 or 604-662-4700). If it looks more like a courthouse to you, you're right—the building used to be Vancouver's provincial courthouse. Justice no longer hangs in the balance here, but paintings certainly do. VAG has mounted exhibitions by **Edvard Munch, Andy Warhol, Bill Reid** and **Jack Shadbolt**, among many others, and

Harbour Centre

has the largest permanent collection in Canada of paintings by **Emily Carr**. The gallery gift shop is a neat place for just-so gifts, and the upstairs café with its breezy outdoor terrace is a popular lunchtime meeting place.

At night a platoon of mobile dressing rooms often line the curb at the VAG's Howe Street entrance. Vancouver is known as **"Hollywood North"** (or "Brollywood" to a few rain-cursing California actors), thanks to a big new North Shore studio, experienced film crews, a favourable US dollar exchange rate, and a plethora of potential film sets from mountains, beaches and forests to sleek downtown towers, warehouse districts both old and new, streets bristling with historic storefronts, a medley of residential architectural styles from gaudy Gothic to streamlined steel-and-glass, with giant cruise ships and an old steam train thrown in for good measure. The VAG is just one of a dozen downtown sites popular for film shoots. Vancouverites have gotten used to stumbling upon film crews and spotting stars like **Robin Williams, Gene Hackman, Sharon Stone, Sean Penn, Sean Connery, Glenn Close, Richard Gere, Brad Pitt** and **Demi Moore** in local hangouts. Only Los Angeles produces more TV episodes than Vancouver, and new stars have been born in Vancouver-based TV series, including **Johnny Depp** ("21 Jump Street") and **Gillian Anderson** and **David Duchovny** ("The X-Files"). So keep your eyes peeled. Who knows when **Arnold Schwarzenegger** or **Mel Gibson** will make a repeat appearance?

The **Hotel Vancouver**, doyen of downtown hotels, dominates the block north of the VAG on Georgia and Howe streets. Connoisseurs of Canadian railway hotels will instantly recognize the monumental Canadian Pacific chateau style that draws its architectural inspiration from French and Scottish castles. Its steep-pitched copper roof and resident gargoyles have hovered over passers-by since 1939. Recently the hotel was given a multimillion-dollar facelift that's taken off the tarnish and returned it to its former glory. The cozy lobby bar is a great place for libations before heading out to city sights.

Before you leave the neighbourhood, take a closer look at **Cathedral Place** straight across Georgia Street from the Hotel Vancouver. It's one of Vancouver's most people-friendly postmodern buildings. A few years

Hotel Vancouver

ago the Art Deco Georgia Medical Dental Building stood on this spot. It is gone now, despite protests by heritage protectionists including pop singer **Bryan Adams**, having been dramatically "imploded" with a barrage of strategically placed explosives. Cathedral Place has risen in its place. The new building's playful Art Deco-inspired details pay homage to the former Medical Dental Building, including its replicas of the old building's three signature nurses, affectionately known as the Rhea Sisters ("Pyo," "Gono" and "Dia"). Cathedral Place is also an architectural tip-of-the-hat to the Hotel Vancouver. Its roof and the gargoyles were inspired by their elegant counterparts across the street. Walk through the lobby to the cloistered garden courtyard just beyond. Here you'll find a quiet sanctuary that's just steps from the busy street. Across the courtyard is Vancouver's little-known gem, the **Canadian Craft Museum**. This is the first public art gallery in Canada devoted to fine handicrafts, and its exhibits range from intriguing to exquisite (604-687-8266).

Granville and Robson Streets

Granville Street was the city's main drag and major movie district in the 1950s. It was a dazzling showplace of some of North America's first and finest neon signs. But by the 1960s it was sliding into seediness, and a stodgy city council pointed the finger of blame at Granville Street's "neon jungle." Big signs were banned, and the bright lights faded. But Granville is still Vancouver's downtown **movie district**, some of those great old neon signs are reappearing, and a couple of old movie theatres have been rescued from the wrecking ball. The wonderful 1927 Spanish baroque-style **Orpheum Theatre** at

Robson Street

Granville and Smithe, with its ornate coffered ceiling, marbled Moorish arches and crystal chandeliers, has been meticulously restored. It was once the biggest vaudeville theatre in Canada where Charlie Chaplin had 'em rolling in the aisles. Later patrons pressed into the gilded hall to gape at the new "talkies." Now it's home to the **Vancouver Symphony Orchestra** as well as touring dance groups and concerts. For a taste of Granville's glory days, check out what's playing at the Orpheum (604-684-9100).

Like the two ends of a teeter-totter, when Granville Street's fortunes fell, Robson Street's soared upward. In the 1960s "Robsonstrasse" was full of knackwurst-and-beer-style German restaurants, specialty meat and cheese delis, European pastry shops and foreign-language newsstands. It

Orpheum Theatre

was funky and lovable, but could not survive the visions of developers through the 1980s. The new **Robson Street** is sheer froth, beaten into airiness by massive lashings of upscale spending. If you can order a tall-nonfat-double-shot-mocha-cappuccino-no-sprinkles without coming up for air, this is your place. Day and night, crowds of people drive down the street, weave past each other on the sidewalks, or lounge under big umbrellas at **outdoor cafés**. A huge new **Virgin Mega Store** anchors one end of the Robson Street experience, on the site of the old Vancouver Public Library building at Georgia and Robson. Just around the corner in the same building is a **Planet Hollywood** restaurant courtesy of **Bruce Willis**, **Arnold Schwarzenegger** and company. Two Starbucks **coffee houses**—Vancouverites *love* their coffee around the clock!—oversee the action at Robson and Thurlow streets. Robson Street is a magnet for young **fashion-conscious shoppers**, and several outlets cater to **Asian tourists**, including a quadrant of opulent gift shops for **Japanese visitors**, known as "little Ginza." Robson Street restaurants also attract an eclectic clientele. At a half dozen new sushi restaurants waiters greet every new arrival with a warm *Irashaimase!* On a single square block you can also enjoy **Mexican, Chinese, Italian, French, Californian** or **Korean**, or just plain family food from deli to deep-pocket prices.

> ### Gateway to Asia

Poised on the Pacific Rim, the port of Vancouver has long been considered Canada's gateway to Asia. Recently it has become a major gateway from Asia as people from Taiwan, China, the Philippines, Japan, South Korea, Malaysia and Singapore immigrated during the 1980s and 1990s. Most new Vancouverites are from Hong Kong, and they are an integral part of the city's character: one in seven Vancouver residents is of Chinese descent. Asian immigrants—and Asian investment capital—have been big factors in the city's recent growth spurt. In spite of the recent Asian market "correction" ("downturn" is just too negative for this Pacific Rim city) millions of dollars in Asian real estate investment have transformed the city.

The West End and English Bay Beaches

North and west from Robson Street is the longtime residential neighbourhood known as the West End. Near the turn of the century it was once home to Vancouver's rich and powerful, who wanted to distance themselves from the rough-edged industrial neighbourhood nearer the port. More than three quarters of the families listed in the 1908 *Elite Directory* lived here, and many sent their daughters to nearby Granville School, a private establishment for the privileged classes with the intimidating motto *Rien sans Peine* (Nothing without Pain). Most of their substantial Edwardian residences were squeezed out by the building boom of the 1960s, when a wall of high-rise apartment buildings sprang up. Pockets of former residential splendour remain, however, including the park known as **Barkley Square** with its nine **heritage houses** in period landscaping. **Roedde House**, built in 1893 by Vancouver's first bookbinder, Gustav Roedde, is now a **museum**. This charming Queen Anne house complete with verandah and cupola was home to Roedde, his wife Matilda, six offspring and a passel of St. Bernards. (For hours and guided tours, phone 604-684-7040.) To get to Barkley Square, go north on Robson Street to Broughton Street and then left for one block. The square is bounded by Broughton, Barclay, Nicola and Haro streets.

Eight blocks north of Burrard Street, Robson intersects **Denman Street**, a longtime see-and-be-seen **pedestrian promenade**. Here, you'll find plenty of upmarket **coffee bars** and lively street vibes. For many West End apartment dwellers, the street is their hometown and the **sidewalk bistros** are as familiar as backyards. Denman is the soul of the West End, centre of Vancouver's **gay community**, and—with over **fifty restaurants in seven blocks**—the last outpost of good food and drink before you submerge yourself in not-to-be-missed Stanley Park just north of Denman. A favourite watering hole is the Edwardian-style, classically vine-covered **Sylvia Hotel** just north of Denman on Gilford Street. The Sylvia looks over English Bay and one of Vancouver's favourite beaches. The famous **Stanley Park Seawall Promenade** just behind **English Bay beach** runs south to **Sunset Beach** where—you guessed it—the sky lights up in evanescent shades of orange, mauve and deep purple when the sun goes down. It also runs north into Stanley Park to two more popular English Bay beaches, **Second Beach** and **Third Beach**. (That English Bay Beach is first and foremost apparently goes without saying.) At Second Beach is a huge aquamarine **swimming pool** perched on the lip of the ocean with nearby **picnic tables, playgrounds and concession stand**. This is a perfect **family spot** to while away a summer's day.

Evening view across English Bay

Stanley Park

Stanley Park is the crown jewel of Vancouver's many beautiful parks. With a foresight astonishing for the times, Vancouver's first city council set aside this 400-hectare wooded peninsula as parkland as its very first act in 1886. Stanley Park was officially dedicated to the "Use and Enjoyment of People of All Colours, Creeds and Customs For All Time" by Canada's Governor General Lord Stanley in 1889. There are lots of ways to enjoy Stanley Park—**on foot** or **rollerblades**, on a **bike**, in a **horse-drawn carriage**, or by **car**, **public bus** or **tour bus**. In 1998 the Vancouver Parks Board started a **free daily Stanley Park shuttle bus** service that runs every 15 minutes with stops at 14 park attractions from mid-May to mid-September. (Schedules and maps are available at Vancouver tourist information centres.)

Stanley Park Seawall, a must for every visitor.

The centre of the park is a loamy green wilderness of cedar, hemlock and fir trees, and the deep forest is crisscrossed with old logging skid roads now used as **walking paths**. But, most visitors stick to the outer edges of the park to enjoy unbelievably beautiful panoramas of city, ocean and mountains. A **perimeter drive** takes car traffic around the park. (Entrances are off Georgia Street and Beach Avenue.) The delightful 9-km **Stanley Park Seawall** built of hand-hewn granite blocks takes pedestrian traffic. And a new bike and rollerblade path lets faster traffic circle the park in style. (Look for bike and rollerblade rental outlets near the Georgia Street entrance.)

Stanley Park has plenty to offer besides drop-dead gorgeous scenery. You'll find an **aquarium, children's petting zoo, a miniature train, a water park, playgrounds, a swimming pool, beaches** with **washrooms** and **concessions, a cricket pitch, a par-three golf course, a putting green, tennis courts, a cricket and rugby oval, lawn** bowling facilities, picnic areas, two **waterfowl sanctuaries** (Lost Lagoon and Beaver Lake), **totem poles and statues**, and **sweeping lawns** and **formal English gardens** by Frederick Law Olmstead, the same landscape architect who designed New York City's Central Park. Several concession stands serve up standard fast food, and two **fine restaurants**, the Fish House at Stanley Park and the Ferguson Point Tea House, offer great upscale fare. Ferguson Point was the site of a gun emplacement and military command centre in the Second World War. One of Canada's best-known artists, **Jack Shadbolt**, was the young recruit assigned to paint the tea house camouflage green, but according to the *Vancouver Book*, he hated the drab green colour so much that he painted the building sky blue and then added some clouds for good measure.

A killer whale at the Vancouver Aquarium

The **Vancouver Aquarium**, with its curvilinear bronze killer whale by Haida artist **Bill Reid** out front, is Stanley Park's stellar attraction. You can watch sleek black-and-white **killer whales** (orcas) and playful white **beluga whales** from dramatic subsurface viewing areas. Kids love to watch the **seals and sea otters** spinning and diving in nearby tanks. You can also enjoy (through glass) the menace of circling **sharks** in the Tropical Pacific Gallery or stalk the steamy jungle of the **Amazon Rain Forest gallery** where slow-moving sloths hide in the tree canopy above displays of reptiles and amphibians. The Vancouver Aquarium is also an internationally recognized **research facility** with ongoing animal breeding and rehabilitation programs. (For information, phone 604-659-3474.)

The other big draw is the dramatic grouping of **totem poles** near **Brockton Oval**. These poles pay tribute to the diversity of BC First Nations cultures, including

Stanley Park totem poles

Kwakwaka'wakw (Kwakiutl), Nuu-chah-nulth (Nootka) and Haida groups. Many Northwest Coast First Nations groups are organized into clans that trace their lineage back to supernatural beings. The Nisga'a's main clans, for example, are Eagle, Wolf, Killer Whale and Raven. The totems are essentially outlines of stories associated with the pole. The pole created by Nisga'a artist Norman Tait tells the story of how the Beaver family persuaded the Eagle family to stop killing all the beavers. You can pick it out by finding the figure of a man of the Eagle people (Tait's family crest) holding a raven. Other mythic figures carved into these poles include Sea Bear, Sky Chief, Thunderbird, White Owl, Fog Woman, Humpback Whale, Wolf, Lightning Snake, Kingfisher, Moon, Cannibal Bird and Mountain Goat. (For more information on totems, see Hillary Stewart's *Looking at Totem Poles*.)

The Downtown Waterfront

From Brockton Oval in Stanley Park you can look south across the water to **Deadman's Island**—by turns a Coast Salish burial ground, site of a smallpox hospital, a squatters' community, and finally HMCS *Discovery*, a naval cadets' training school. Just beyond Deadman's Island are the boatsheds and wharves of the Royal Vancouver Yacht Club in Coal Harbour. Farther off is Canada's global gateway, the port of Vancouver. Three thousand ships flying the flags of ninety nations sail into the port of Vancouver every year. **Canada Place** is the newest waterfront landmark with its soaring five-sailed white roof modelled on the Sydney (Australia) Opera House. It houses the **Vancouver Trade and Convention Centre**, the five-storey CN **IMAX theatre**, a seafront restaurant, a food court, retail shops and the cruise ship terminal.

A cruise ship in front of Canada Place

The **cruise ship** business in Vancouver is booming. Every year more than 600,000 passengers board the sleek white ships of the Cunard Lines, Holland America, the Royal Caribbean, the Princess cruises and others to cruise from Vancouver up the beautiful Inside Passage to Alaska. Two sparkling new luxury hotels, the Pan Pacific Hotel and the Waterfront Centre Hotel, have located just beside Canada Place for the pleasure of well-heeled cruise ship passengers and convention-goers. The developments at Canada Place are just the start of changes planned for Vancouver. The Canadian Pacific Railway's real estate subsidiary Marathon Realty is planning a massive twenty-year redevelopment of the railway yards north along the waterfront to Coal Harbour.

A block north of the Waterfront Centre Hotel at Burrard Street is a large **Vancouver Travel InfoCentre** where you can get lots of information and travel trips, including public transit information. Just south down West Cordova Street at the foot of Seymour Street is the old Canadian Pacific Railway station, now a terminus for **Skytrain** (Vancouver's light rapid transit system) and **SeaBus** (Vancouver's passenger ferries that shuttle across Burrard Inlet between downtown and North Vancouver). This elegantly restored building is well worth a side trip to gaze at its white-pillared, high-ceilinged lobby with original paintings depicting scenes along the CPR route when train travel was a romantic adventure. Better yet, hop aboard a SeaBus to North Vancouver for a quick, scenic, inexpensive cruise across Burrard Inlet. After a twenty-minute Seabus ride you'll land at **Lonsdale Quay Market**, an eye-catching (and mouth-watering) potpourri of fruit and vegetable stalls, specialty food shops, boutiques, craft carts, restaurants, an exotic food fair and a hotel all under one roof. A colourful industrial waterfront extending east from the Quay has a fascinating jumble of tugboats, trains, shipyards and grain elevators as well as views across the water to the Port of Vancouver. If you enjoy the sight of raw industrial power at work, this is the place to go.

False Creek

Lonsdale Quay and harbour tugs

Gastown

Just south of the old CPR station at the intersection of West Cordova and Water streets is Gastown, the historic heart of Vancouver. In the 1850s, after the California Gold Rush had faded, new gold fields were discovered up the Fraser River, and hordes of "Forty-niners" dusted off their dreams and headed for British Columbia. Victoria (on Vancouver Island) and Fort Langley (upriver from present-day Vancouver) boomed as thousands of prospectors rowed, paddled and/or steamed up the Fraser River. When the gold petered out, most miners just drifted away again. But some stayed and joined the lumberjacks who had discovered that the real gold on the BC coast didn't glitter at all. It was tall timber.

The deep forests of cedar and fir kick-started the city of Vancouver. An irascible Englishman, Captain Edward Stamp, built the first sawmill known as Hastings Mill in 1865 near the mouth of Burrard Inlet. (The old Hastings Mill Store building has been moved to the foot of Alma Street at Jericho and restored as a museum.) One old-timer recalled the hectic days of Vancouver's early lumber industry when a huge fleet of ships—barques, brigs and schooners, as many as forty-two vessels at one time—anchored off Captain Stamp's mill to load spars, lumber and shingles destined for the four corners of the world.

"Gassy Jack" Deighton was just one step behind Captain Stamp. In 1867 Gassy Jack floated a whiskey barrel ashore at the foot of Carrall Street, not far from Hastings Mill, where he found some thirsty millworkers. They agreed to build a makeshift saloon in return for the keg of whiskey, and Gassy Jack was in business. Deighton's near-legendary talkativeness earned him the moniker "Gassy," and the rough-and-tumble little townsite around his saloon, officially called Granville, was known far and wide as Gastown. A great fire swept through in 1886 and destroyed the area. But a makeshift settlement of tents and

▶ Vancouver Annual Events

January
Polar Bear Swim (Jan 1)

February
Chinese New Year Festival

April
Vancouver Sun Run

May
VanDusen Flower and Garden Show
Vancouver International Marathon
Vancouver International Children's Festival
(late May-early June)

June
International Dragon Boat Festival
International Jazz Festival (late June)
Bard on the Beach Shakespeare Festival
(June–Sept)

July
Vancouver Folk Music Festival
Vancouver International Comedy Festival
Vancouver Chamber Music Festival
Symphony of Fire

August
Pacific National Exhibition

September
Molson Indy Vancouver
Vancouver Fringe Festival
Terry Fox Run
Vancouver International Film Festival

October
Vancouver International Writers Festival

November
Christmas at Hycroft

December
Christmas Carol Ship Parade
Christmas at Canada Place
Festival of Lights (VanDusen Botanical Garden)

For more information, Vancouver, Coast and Mountains Tourism Region **604-739-0823** or **1-800-667-3306**

lean-tos soon sprang up, and thirsty upcoast lumberjacks and local mill-hands were bellying up to the bar once again.

The completion of the railway and discovery of another rich gold field—this time in the Klondike—helped to revive Gastown's fortunes after the fire. Most of the area's finest buildings date from its commercial heyday from 1898 onward. Gradually the centre of the city shifted away from the waterfront, however, and Gastown became Vancouver's Skid Road. Now its fortunes are rising once again, thanks to the Vancouver's Community Arts Council's heritage renovation project. The old **cobblestone streets** have been accented with **antique street lamps** and new plantings of maple trees. Many historic buildings have been given spiffy retrofits. Water Street is the centre of Gastown and a favourite stroll for visitors. You'll find a lively if occasionally startling mix of outlets, including **touristy souvenir stores** and **upscale boutiques**, plenty of pubs and cafés, Canadian **Native art galleries** and furniture stores, **clubs** with **live music** from jazz to rock, funky secondhand stores, the occasional down-on-its-luck commercial hotel, and lots of people taking in the sights.

Gastown and its famous steam clock

Don't miss the huge window with views of the North Shore mountains inside **The Landing** at Water Street and West Cordova. This 1905 building, originally a warehouse for a wholesale grocer, has been converted to a chic two-level mall with designer-label clothing stores and stylish eateries. Across from The Landing on the triangle of land between Water and Cordova streets is the wonderful Holland Block with its San Francisco-style bay windows. If you like this building, go down Water Street to Maple Square to see the flatiron-shaped **Hotel Europe** in the triangle between Powell and Alexander streets. This was the first reinforced concrete structure in Vancouver and the first fireproof hotel in the Canadian West. Other favourites are the brick-paved **Gaoler's Mews** with its ivy-covered walls, and behind it **Blood Alley Square** with its original cobbled yard and iron stairways. To sample a bit of the rough-hewn saloon culture that started Gastown, try Lamplighters in the Dominion Hotel at Water and Abbott streets. This brick and stone pub with wooden pillars and a restored tin ceiling harks back to the brawling days of

Gassy Jack. The most-photographed object in Gastown is the world's first **steam-powered clock**, at the corner of Water and Cambie streets, which plays the Westminster chimes at every quarter hour. It's not an antique—it was erected in 1977—but it runs on a century-old technology using an underground steam source and weights on a chain to keep the time.

Be aware that Vancouver's Skid Road is located adjacent to the east end of Gastown, so be street smart as you head south and east through this part of town.

Need a break? Take a few minutes to visit **Portside Park**, along Burrard Inlet at the foot of Main Street. Downtown Eastside residents persuaded the City of Vancouver to establish this waterfront park—first called CRAB (Create a Real Alternative Beach)—in 1987, on former Harbours Board land. Visit the pavilion marking the site known as luk'luk'i by Coast Salish, and rest your feet while enjoying panoramic views of the busy seaport and the splendid backdrop of the North Shore mountains.

Chinatown

Vancouver's Chinatown, with some 150,000 residents, is Canada's largest Chinese community. It's just a few blocks away from Gastown in the area bounded by Abbott, Powell, Heatley and Prior streets. The first Chinese arrivals in British Columbia—almost all of them men—came from California to prospect during the gold rush of 1858. By 1863 more than 4,000 Chinese people had settled in BC and were doing whatever work they could get, often as labourers, laundrymen, servants, cannery workers or cooks. A second wave of Chinese labourers—about 17,000 in total—arrived between 1881 and 1885 to build Canada's transcontinental railway, and many of them settled in BC. They were the pioneers of the dynamic community that still gives Chinatown its unique character. Many other Chinese communities thrive in Greater Vancouver today, but local and offshore investments are also driving the commercial and residential redevelopment of Chinatown. The centerpiece is the seven-storey, $22-million Chinatown Plaza shopping

The Chinese Cultural Centre

mall with its 1,000-car parkade. Meanwhile, the historic Chinatown is still alive and well in the Pender Street area. **Chinese restaurants**, Chinese grocery stores with **barbecued pork** hanging in the windows and brightly-coloured **vegetable stands** line the sidewalks, along with **gift shops** laden with jade, lacquerware, bamboo furniture and blue-and-white patterned porcelain. Bright red pagoda-roofed phone booths and street signs in both English and Chinese add to the flavour.

"Today Vancouver's Chinese Canadians can best be seen as a community of communities. They are a monolithic unit only to outsiders who persist in viewing all Chinese Canadians as the same. In reality, there are those who speak no Chinese and others who speak no English; there are the rich and the working class; there are the fifth-generation Chinese Canadians, and there are newcomers speaking many languages and dialects. These natural divisions intersect the community. But ultimately, it is like any other Canadian community. The people work, pay taxes, raise families, and hope that the future will shine brighter on everyone."—from *Saltwater City: An Illustrated History of the Chinese in Vancouver* by Paul Yee.

Chinatown market scene

Two favourite stops for visitors are the Sam Kee building and the Dr. Sun Yat-Sen Classical Chinese Gardens. The Sam Kee building is on the corner of Pender and Carrall streets. When Pender Street was widened about seventy-five years ago, Chang Toy of Sam Kee Company was left with only a tiny sliver of land. But among Chinatown's early merchants, land was a highly prized asset. This building with its big bow windows and under-the-sidewalk basement with a glass-panelled ceiling was Chang Toy's inspired response. At just 30 metres long and 2 metres wide, the **Sam Kee Building** has made the *Guinness Book of Records* as the **world's thinnest office building**. The **Dr. Sun Yat-Sen Classical Chinese Garden** is just south of Pender at 578 Carrall Street. Opened in 1986, this quiet garden enclave is the first authentic Ming Dynasty-style garden to be built outside China since 1492. Working with traditional materials, fifty-two craftsmen from China's famous garden city of Suzhou have created a fascinating miniature landscape of limestone rocks, twisting trees and tiled pavilions surrounding a man-made pond that recreates a scholar's garden of the Ming period. It was named for the Chinese revolutionary leader Dr. Sun Yat-Sen (1866-1925) who came to Vancouver several times in the early 1900s seeking help in overthrowing the Manchu dynasty and founding the first Chinese Republic. (For information or tours, 604-662-3207.)

False Creek and Yaletown

South and west of Chinatown is False Creek. This long and narrow saltwater inlet is the eastward extension of English Bay. It was named False Creek because it looked temptingly like the mouth of the Fraser River to early explorers but turned out to be just more salty ocean water. The three bridges into downtown Vancouver—Cambie, Granville and Burrard bridges—all arch over the 5-km long False Creek.

For years False Creek was nothing but a marshy, muddy industrial wasteland. Then it was chosen as the site for **Expo 86** and everything changed. Two Expo legacies—**Science World**, the huge silver geodesic dome with its impressive **Omnimax Theatre** at Quebec and Terminal streets, and the Plaza of Nations just west of Science World—still grace False Creek's downtown shoreline. Li Ka-Shing, a Hong Kong billionaire, bought up much of the former Expo lands for the Concord Pacific development, a multibillion-dollar waterfront office, retail and residential complex now under way. Rows of giant new wedding-cake condos with floor-to-ceiling windows look out over False Creek. The **seawall** edging the water runs clear up to **English Bay** where it joins the **Seawalk Promenade**.

Science World

Soon it will hook round the end of False Creek near Science World and join the walkway circling past Granville Island and up to Kitsilano Beach. Already Vancouver's Sunday **cyclists** and **roller bladers** are happily whipping up and down this stretch of shoreline.

Yaletown is just behind the former Expo lands between Davie and Smithe on Homer, Hamilton and Mainland streets. Yaletown was first settled by CPR railway workers, then it became a warehouse district, then fell on hard times. In recent years Yaletown has been resuscitated as Vancouver's newest in-place with an attitude. Its solid old warehouses are becoming urban lofts for young downtown types and up-and-coming commercial and professional enterprises. Yaletown has a popular microbrewery and pub, lots of **"billiard bars"** where pool players can drink beer or sip lattés, Euro-trendy **furniture stores**, **galleries** and design shops, and several of Vancouver's best new **restaurants**. Even the old railway loading bays on Hamilton and Mainland have taken on a new look as outdoor patios. It's lots of fun, especially if you're looking for the mildly outrageous. And slowly it's also getting to have that neighbourhood feel as more folks hang their hats in Yaletown.

Granville Island

Granville Island, just across False Creek from Yaletown, is Vancouver's biggest and best revitalization project and the highlight of many a visitor's trip. Granville Island was created by dredging the muck out of False Creek and loading it on top of two seaweed-laden sandbars corseted with wooden pilings. Originally named Industrial Island, it was the dirty milling and manufacturing heart of Vancouver right through the 1940s. Out of its corrugated tin factory buildings poured wire ropes, barrels and drums, anchor chains, concrete, paint and steel rivets—as well as plenty of thick smoke. But gradually, company after company closed or moved away, and by 1963 Granville Island was grimy and dilapidated, on the verge of ruin.

But visionary urban renewal plans changed all that, and in 1979 **Granville Island Public Market** opened its doors. The public market is Granville Island's showcase attraction. It's a huge **farmers' market** with great **fresh produce** and **seafood**, **ethnic takeout** food counters and **gourmet food** shops, yummy **bakeries**, **jewellery** and **pottery** shops and other art works. In summer, wandering **buskers** and **street performers** delight the crowds.

But the market is just the beginning. More than 260 other businesses have staked out territory on the island. There's the **Granville Island Brewing Company**, where great lager is brewed with simply malt, hops, water and yeast. And there's the **Emily Carr**

Granville Island

Institute of Art & Design where students in paint- and clay-splashed jeans master their craft. There are three **live theatres** with performances ranging from revue to experimental, and a fistful of **studios where artisans blow glass, weave, paint, make prints or make paper** right in front of your eyes. There's the **Granville Island Hotel**, a half dozen good **restaurants** and loads of fascinating locally owned **galleries** and **specialty stores**, including a **toy store** "just for kids." (Grown-ups are welcome, too, as long as they're kids at heart.) There's a glorious marina chock full of powerboats and sailboats, and even a **sport fishing museum and model ship museum**. And, of course, the water-front views from Granville Island are spectacular. The scene is so lively that lots of visitors just settle along the water and gaze to their heart's content.

If you're not content to be shorebound, rent a canoe or kayak and get out on the water. False Creek is a good, safe place for a paddle. Want someone else to supply the oomph? Hop aboard one of the little **mini-ferries** that beetle around False Creek from drop-off points on the water side of Granville Island Market. Both **False Creek Ferries** and **Aquabus** offer on/off adventure passes around False Creek, so you can stop at several major attractions including Science World and the **museums at Vanier Park**. You can also ride these ferries from downtown to Granville Island.

Granville Island Public Market

Vanier Park, Museums and West Side Beaches

The English Bay beaches aren't the only great beaches close to downtown. From Vanier Park west a pearl necklace of sandy beaches runs along the north shore of Vancouver's West Side. (The West Side stretches from Cambie Street across Point Grey peninsula to the University of British Columbia at the far west tip. It is different from the West End, the downtown high-rise district bordering English Bay and Stanley Park.) **Vanier Park**, at the south end of Burrard Bridge, is just a seven-minute walk (or a two-minute drive) north and west along False Creek from Granville Island. It's a fine place for kite flying, scenery slurping and culture mongering. In late May many-coloured canvas tents pop up like mushrooms as the famous **Vancouver Children's Festival** swings into action at Vanier Park. By summertime Shakespeare is all the rage with **Bard on the Beach** taking over the big tops. Vanier Park is also home to three of Vancouver's prime attractions—the Vancouver Museum, the Planetarium Theatre, and the Vancouver Maritime Museum. The **Vancouver Museum** is Canada's largest civic museum with displays on Vancouver history and First Nations cultures (1100 Chestnut Street, 604-736-4431). You'll find a Canadian Pacific Railway passenger car from the 1880s as well as re-creations of a trading post and an immigrant ship. This complex is also home to the **H.R. MacMillan Planetarium Star**

The Vancouver Museum, with its distinctive roof

Theatre, which features everything from family star shows and "virtual voyages" to high-energy laser/rock concerts (604-738-7827). The nearby **Vancouver Maritime Museum** has colourful displays on BC maritime history, including interactive displays using telescopes, computer games and an underwater robot. It also houses the historic two-masted schooner the *St. Roch*. This was the first ship to travel the treacherous Northwest Passage from west to east. Step aboard the restored *St. Roch* to experience shipboard life on an RCMP patrol boat (604-257-8300).

The big sandy curve of **Kitsilano Beach** is just west of Vanier Park. A heated beachside **saltwater pool** is a major draw for sociable splashers. More hardy types prefer the

Kitsilano Beach

chilly wake-up of an ocean dip. Lots of "Kits Beach" visitors just lie on the beach and watch the passing parade. Dog owners towed by lively pooches and parents hanging onto excited children mingle near the concession stand with taut-muscled beach volleyballers and, occasionally, a tattooed man with a boa constrictor wrapped over his shoulders. Sun worshippers turn their backs to the crowd and squint at the soaring North Shore Mountains across Burrard Inlet. Non-sun worshippers have it made in the shade. A wide ribbon of grass and ornamental trees makes a leafy buffer zone between beach and street.

The apartment-packed hillside behind Kits Beach is the neighbourhood of choice for university students and young city professionals. Social life for Kitsilano denizens alternates between the beach scene and the lively shops and restaurants of **Fourth Avenue** just a few blocks south of the beach. For a big choice of eateries—most moderately priced and some satisfyingly cheap—head for Fourth Avenue. The shops, too, are well worth browsing for their slightly quirky edge. Buy a whodunit at a **mystery book shop**, find out about the latest in adventure touring in a youth-minded travel store, or pick up a gift for your favourite TV addict at a couch-potato gift shop.

You've got your spandex and want a cardio workout? Then join the neon-clad joggers and cyclists heading west from Kits Beach along the well-marked **cycle route** to Spanish Banks Beach some 8 km away. If that sounds strenuous, just drive along the water till a beach strikes your fancy, and settle in for a peaceful day. **Jericho Beach** at the corner of Point Grey Road and Alma Street has a wide grassy park where the old **Hastings Mill Store** has been given a new home. On the waterfront beyond the mill is the Royal Vancouver Yacht Club. Look past the yacht club for a swarm of tacking white sails out in Burrard Inlet. Sailing regattas are big events among west coast yachters, and Jericho Beach is a popular place for small-boat race starts. The annual **Vancouver Folk Music Festival** is held here on the third weekend each July. It's a must-hear!

Spanish Banks

Locarno Beach and **Spanish Banks** are west of Jericho. To get there by car, head south from Jericho Beach on Alma Street and take a right at the stoplight onto Fourth Avenue. Where Fourth Avenue forks, take the right fork to NW Marine Drive, which loops around the tip of Point Grey (and changes to SW Marine Drive on the southern shore). The heavily treed residential neighbourhood of Point Grey is the turf of some of Vancouver's well-to-do. Point Grey is known for its deep, well-manicured gardens and sizable homes, many with fantastic views of Burrard Inlet and the North Shore mountains.

Locarno Beach and Spanish Banks Beach are on NW Marine Drive. Either one is just right for a relaxed family picnic and swim. You'll find parking, change rooms, concession stands, picnic tables and wide, sandy tidal flats. The incoming water is nicely sun-warmed, and at low tide you can wade through knee-high water way out toward the shipping channel markers to size up those giant freighters anchored off the beach. And, of course, the North Shore mountains make a perfectly splendid backdrop.

Cyclists won't want to miss the most popular mountain-biking area in greater Vancouver. The 763-hectare **Pacific Spirit Regional Park** straddles Point Grey just east of the University of British Columbia campus. A trailhead across the road from Spanish Banks connects with more than **35 km of trails** winding through fir and cedar forests brightened with ferns and berry bushes and atwitter with birdsong. **Pedestrians, dog walkers, birdwatchers** and **horseback riders** all share the trails with cyclists. You might even run into a film crew at work in the park, a favourite set for deep-woods shots. (Trail maps are available at the park information centre at 4915 W. 16th Ave or at trailheads on Chancellor Boulevard and elsewhere.)

Tucked well out of sight around the cliff west of Spanish Banks is Canada's only legal "clothes-optional"—i.e. nude—beach. **Wreck Beach** wraps all the way around the cliffs at the western tip of Point Grey. In the mid-sixties flower children and free spirits—many of them UBC students from the nearby campus—clambered down the cliffs to strip and sun on this lovely natural beach. A few outraged Vancouver city council members tried for years to get them back into their trousers. But in 1991 the council voted to forget the whole thing and let the chips (or clothes) fall as they may. Today all sorts of people from toddlers to grannies scramble down haphazard trails to enjoy clothes-free suntanning. Vendors descend to sell everything from T-shirts, suntan lotion and cheeseburgers to tarot readings and body painting. The easiest trail to find begins just behind the Museum of Anthropology.

UBC Museum of Anthropology

Perched on the cliff above Wreck Beach is UBC's Museum of Anthropology (6393 NW Marine Dr, 604-822-3825). Step into the soaring glass-walled Great Hall, designed by architect **Arthur Erickson**, and fall under the spell of the monumental art of the Northwest Coast. Ancient cedar totem poles stand against a backdrop of cliff and ocean. **Giant potlatch bowls, cedar canoes, bentwood boxes, elaborate rattles and ceremonial masks**—Raven, Bear, Thunderbird and more—exude an eerie power. The spirit of Northwest Coast Native cultures is almost palpable.

The museum also houses works of **contemporary Native master artists** who have breathed new life into ancient art forms. The centrepiece is Haida artist **Bill Reid**'s massive cedar sculpture *Raven and the First Men* in the specially-designed rotunda off the main gallery. The sculpture of a raven perched atop a giant clamshell represents the Haida story of the creation of humankind when Raven dropped a clamshell onto the beach and out spilled the first men on earth. Even this momentous work sings with Reid's humanity and wit. He jokingly told his friend Arthur Erickson that the naked little fellow trying desperately to scramble back into the clamshell was Reid himself.

In the **Research Collection** just across the hall from Reid's sculpture, visitors can poke through drawers full of cultural artifacts from around the world, including stone and bone tools, body ornaments, masks, weapons and carved figures. Changing displays, performances, workshops, a European ceramics collection, a small café (summer only) and a fine little gift shop specializing in First Nations crafts, round out the museum's offerings. Behind the museum

Native carving

are more totems and two Haida longhouses—one for the living and one for the dead—set in a tangled planting of native grasses. If you go to just one museum in Vancouver, make it the UBC Museum of Anthropology.

The University of British Columbia

The University of British Columbia is one of western Canada's oldest and most prestigious universities. UBC was established in 1915 and moved to its present Point Grey location in 1925. The university has grown steadily since World War II and now has over 50,000 students enrolled in degree programs each year. If you like architecture, you'll be fascinated by the campus' wide range of building styles, from the neo-Gothic Main Library to the thoroughly modernist War Memorial Gymnasium. And make sure to visit the impressive **First Nations House of Learning**, an enormous modern day longhouse that contains several specially commissioned Salish totem poles. Interested in gardening? The UBC Botanical Garden has an enormous range of native and exotic plant species. Of particular interest are the **David C. Lam Asian Garden**, the **E.H. Lohbrunner Alpine Garden**, and the **Nitobe Memorial Garden**. UBC is also home to the **Chan Centre for the Performing Arts**. Built in 1997, this beautiful concert hall has thrilled music lovers and architectural critics alike with its warm acoustics and innovative design. Fans of the arts can also visit the **Morris and Helen Belkin Art Gallery** or take in a play at the **Fredric Wood Theatre**.

Commercial Drive

Back across town from UBC, and ten minutes east of downtown Vancouver, is one of its funkiest areas, the stretch of Commercial Drive running from Venables Street south to Broadway. "The Drive" is one of the oldest neighbourhoods in Vancouver, the longtime heart of the **Italian and Portuguese communities**. Once known as Little Italy, the Drive is much more ethnically diverse now with visible influences from Asian and Caribbean cultures, and a hip young student population. A summer evening stroll along the Drive will

Commercial Drive market

take you past a wonderful and unassuming jumble of **ethnic restaurants, old-style Italian coffee bars, retro clothing stores, left-wing book shops, organic food stores, galleries** and even a laundromat/café with attitude. The street's alive day and night, so join the throng for a steaming espresso or a plate of tapas with live salsa music on the side.

In September the **Fringe Theatre Festival** brings together dozens of actors and hundreds of theatregoers in performance spaces all over the Drive, and just down the street is the **Vancouver East Cultural Centre.** Known locally as "the Cultch," this cozy performing arts theatre in a refurbished turn-of-the-century church attracts music, dance and offbeat theatre from all over the city. Audiences are friendly, acoustics and sightlines are great, and performances are predictably high calibre.

Punjabi Market

No visit to Vancouver would be complete without a trip to the Punjabi Market, located on Main Street between 48th and 51st avenues. The area was originally settled by Indian immigrants who came to Vancouver at the turn of the century. Today, the Punjabi Market is one of the most prosperous South Asian shopping areas in North America, housing over 50 retail businesses, including fabric, jewellery and **specialty food stores.** If you're looking for **fine silks** or **gold ornaments** this is definitely the place to go. The market also provides visitors with a unique taste of South Asian culture: pictures of gurus and Indian entertainers hang in store windows and exotic music floats through the air. The market is also at the centre of several festivals including the Basakhi Day Parade, the Sikh sports festival, and November's Festival of Lights. The **Ross Street Temple**, located just east of the market, is also worth visiting. Considered one of Vancouver's most beautiful religious buildings, the temple was designed by Arthur Erickson, who used the geometry of Indian religious symbols as his inspiration. The Ross Street Temple is a central house of worship for Vancouver's large Sikh community.

Deer Lake Park

Deer Lake Park serves as a cultural centre for the city of Burnaby. The park is home to the **Burnaby Art Gallery**, the **Shadbolt Centre for the Arts** and the 1967 **Century Gardens.** The park also houses the **Burnaby Village Museum**, a working replica of a turn-of-the-century village that is popular with both families and school groups. Although it is an urban park, Deer Lake boasts 5 kilometres of **beautiful wooded shoreline** as well as a **sandy beach. Birdwatchers** will be impressed by the large variety of waterfowl that live on Deer Lake. If you're visiting the park on a nice day, try renting a **pedal boat** and touring Deer Lake from the water. And make sure to keep your eyes open for film crews: Deer Lake Park has been showcased in many films and television shows, including "Cousins" and "MacGyver."

Punjabi street signs

OUTINGS FROM VANCOUVER

Highlights

Rich fishing history

Nearby mountains

Hiking

Downhill and
cross-country skiing

Scenic rail and boat tours

Swimming, diving and
other water sports

Bike touring

Dyke walking

Westminster Quay

Visitors who are interested in catching a glimpse of Greater Vancouver's history can take the SkyTrain to New Westminster, the oldest incorporated city in western Canada. Established in 1860, New Westminster was a bustling port city supported by fishing, logging, shipbuilding and commercial trade. Paddlewheelers and sailing ships routinely fought for space along the city's waterfront. By the turn of the century, New Westminster was so prosperous that its main street, Columbia Street, was dubbed "Miracle Mile." Over the course of the twentieth century the city was eclipsed by Vancouver, which gradually replaced New Westminster as the region's primary port of trade. New Westminster is no longer considered a major

The New Westminster waterfront

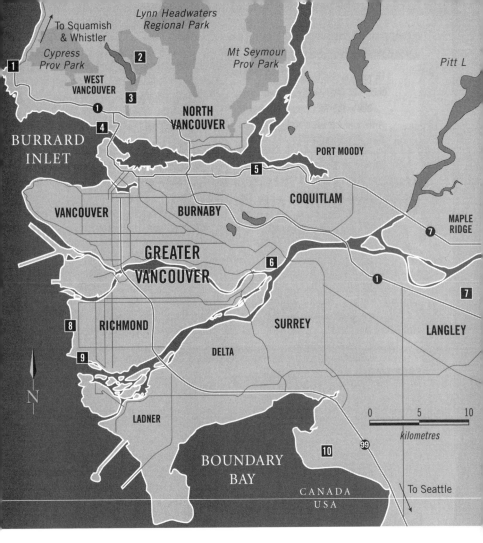

To Squamish & Whistler

Lynn Headwaters Regional Park

Cypress Prov Park

1

2

WEST VANCOUVER

3

1

Mt Seymour Prov Park

NORTH VANCOUVER

4

BURRARD INLET

PORT MOODY

5

Pitt L

VANCOUVER

BURNABY

COQUITLAM

MAPLE RIDGE

7

GREATER VANCOUVER

6

1

7

RICHMOND

8

SURREY

LANGLEY

9

DELTA

N

0   5   10

kilometres

LADNER

10

99

BOUNDARY BAY

CANADA USA

To Seattle

What to See

- ☐ **1** Horseshoe Bay
- ☐ **2** Grouse Mountain Skyride
- ☐ **3** Capilano Suspension Bridge
- ☐ **4** Ambleside Village and Park
- ☐ **5** Burnaby Mountain/SFU
- ☐ **6** Westminster Quay
- ☐ **7** Fort Langley
- ☐ **8** Richmond Dyke Trails
- ☐ **9** Steveston
- ☐ **10** White Rock

industrial centre, but visitors can still see remnants of the port's heyday in the **heritage homes** and **Edwardian buildings** that line the city's streets. Just a few blocks south of the New Westminster SkyTrain Station lies the **Westminster Quay Public Market**, a unique marketplace that sits on the edge of the Fraser River. The Quay features a wide range of **food, craft and clothing shops**. Visitors can also **walk along a scenic boardwalk** or **take a ride up the Fraser River on a paddlewheeler**. Those interested in the history of the area will want to see the *Samson V* **Maritime Museum**, a floating museum housed in an old paddle wheeler that is moored next to the market. The Quay hosts several festivals each year, including the Hyack Festival, the Philippine Festival, Fraserfest, Oktoberfest and Winterfest.

Simon Fraser University/ Burnaby Mountain Park

If you truly want a breathtaking view of Greater Vancouver, make your way to Simon Fraser University on the top of Burnaby Mountain. On a clear day, the university offers a **panoramic view** of Burrard Inlet, the Fraser River and Vancouver Harbour. Visitors who are interested in architecture will revel in SFU's **unique modernist design**. The university was designed by Arthur Erickson who took his inspiration from classical Greek structures and from ancient mountain villages in southern Europe. Built in 1965, the campus is a collection horizontal concrete terraces that culminate in an enormous outdoor courtyard called the Academic Quadrangle. SFU is surrounded by Burnaby Mountain Park and the **Burnaby Mountain Conservation Area**. With their large swaths of **pristine forest**, these two wilderness areas are home to a **wide range of wildlife** and are excellent places for **hiking and outdoor recreation**. Burnaby Mountain Park also has an impressive collection of **Salish and Japanese totem poles**, created to celebrate Burnaby's native heritage and its close ties with its sister city, Kushiro, Japan. You can reach SFU by turning onto Gaglardi Way from the Lougheed Highway. To see Burnaby Mountain Park, simply turn north up Centennial Way from Gaglardi Way.

Simon Fraser University's unique modernist design

Fort Langley National Historic Site and Fort Langley

Fort Langley town

Walk through the big wooden palisade at Fort Langley National Historic Site into the heyday of BC's fur trade. The **Hudson's Bay Company fort** on the mighty Fraser River was built in 1827 to supply foodstuffs to other Company **fur trading** posts, and the site has been restored as a "living museum" of the 1950s when furs, farm produce and salmon were the lifeblood of the fort. Visit the Big House (built for Chief Factor James Douglas, who became BC's first governor) where HBC officers enjoyed a social elegance surprising in so remote a posting. See demonstrations by **blacksmiths** making tools at the forge and **coopers** crafting the barrels once used for shipping cured salmon to San Francisco, Hawaii and Australia. Stop by the outdoor ovens for a taste of bannock, the traditional bread of the Sto:lo First Nations people of nearby MacMillan Island. Many Sto:lo men worked as trappers, fishermen and farmhands for the HBC. You can watch **Native carvers** build the canoes that were the HBC's all-important wilderness transportation. During **Brigade Days** in early August costumed paddlers reenact the arrival of the HBC canoe brigade from the interior of BC.

The historic village of Fort Langley with its many original buildings is charmingly quaint without being too cute. **Antique lovers** will find happy hunting grounds. Fort Langley is steeped in history, and two more museums record its past. **The Langley Centennial Museum & National Exhibition Centre** has displays on **Coast Salish culture** and the **pioneer world** of BC's early **miners, farmers and loggers** (corner of Mavis and King streets, 604-888-3922). The **British Columbia Farm Machinery and Agricultural Museum** has a big collection of farm machines from mowers and stump pullers to buckboards and early diesel tractors. Look for the **Tiger Moth** airplane, the first crop duster at work in BC (9131 King St next to Langley Centennial Museum. 604-888-2272).

Fort Langley National Historic Site is about an hour (40 km) east of Vancouver off Hwy 1 at 23433 Mavis Ave, Fort Langley (604-888-4424, email fort_langley@pch.gc.ca, website fas.sfu.ca/parkscan/fl). You can also get to the fort by taking your car aboard the free Albion Ferry that connects Hwy 7 and Hwy 1. It crosses the Fraser River between the south end of 240th St and the village of Fort Langley every 15 minutes (604-467-7298). Or you can take **"The Fraser**

Fort Langley National Historic Site

River Connection," an all-day return sailing from New Westminster to Fort Langley aboard a replica nineteenth-century paddle wheeler (Fraser River Cruises 604-525-4465, fax 604-525-5944).

White Rock/Crescent Beach

Sunny White Rock and Crescent Beach were Vancouver's favourite seaside resorts for decades. Now, the little clapboard cottages where families settled in for the summer are mostly gone, but summer fun is still the name of the game.

White Rock's famous "white rock" and pier

White Rock's wide, wide **sandy beach** is a magnet for sand castle builders, volley-ballers, and lie-back-and-tan-it sun worshippers. Watch for migrating **gray whales** from the old White Rock Pier where coastal steamship passengers disembarked at the turn of the century. Just behind the beach is a spanking-fresh 2-km **pedestrian promenade**. And just behind the promenade is Marine Drive, with blocks full of great little restaurants, beach boutiques and ice cream shops. Locals and visitors loll under a dazzle of streetside patio umbrellas sipping Margaritas and eating tapas or sushi. "The Beach" has gone upscale but keeps its friendly, low-key profile.

Crescent Beach at the end of Crescent Road is another popular beach with a more old-time beach community feel. Don't overlook **Elgin Heritage Park** on Crescent Road just after the exit from Hwy 99. It includes the **Stewart family heritage house and pole barn** dating from the 1880s on the Nicomekl River and the **Hooser Weaving Centre** specializing in traditional weaving and spinning.

The White Rock/Crescent Beach area is about 50 minutes (56 km) south of Vancouver near the US border. Follow signs from Hwy 99 to White Rock (Marine Dr) or Crescent Beach (Crescent Rd). A summer InfoCentre is located next to the **White Rock Station Museum and Archives** at Station Centre (a restored 1913 Great Northern Railway Station) near the White Rock Pier. Or contact the White Rock and South Surrey Chamber of Commerce, 15150 Russell Ave (604-536-6844).

Steveston/Richmond Dyke Walks

Steveston is the oldest surviving community in Greater Vancouver. By 1890 this **historic fishing port** had a population of 10,000 people. More than a dozen canneries were going full blast during fishing season, and workers' wages disappeared fast in the town's saloons, gaming houses, opium dens and bordellos. The Fraser River had the biggest salmon run in North America, and at one time more than fifty Steveston canneries packed the delicious pink salmon flesh into tins. The canneries are gone, but the new **Gulf of Georgia Cannery National Historic Site** keeps cannery-day memories alive (12138 4th Ave, 604-664-9009). So do Steveston's rustic boatsheds and net lofts and the hundreds of commercial fishing boats in the port. Go down to the **public fish sales dock** to bargain for sea-fresh **prawns, salmon, tuna, crab and halibut** straight from the boat deck. Enjoy the new waterfront boutiques and restaurants at **Steveston Landing** and longtime Steveston establishments on Moncton St. Great fish and chips are a Steveston specialty. For outdoor fun head for **Garry Point Park**, a 44-ha park just a 5-minute walk west from "downtown" Steveston where you can **fish, fly kites, picnic or take a stroll or bike ride** on the **Richmond Dyke Trails**. The 50 km of trails run along perimeter dykes and through public parks, commercial and historical areas all around Richmond.

For history buffs two little-known treasures are just east of Steveston. **Britannia Heritage Shipyard** on the Fraser River at the foot of Railway St preserves **turn-of-the-century shipyards, canneries, stores, houses and boardwalks** (604-718-1200). The weathered grey buildings stand in a natural 3-ha park above a tidal marsh. The Japanese worker's home is a poignant reminder of Steveston's many Japanese Canadians who helped build the community but were forcibly removed from the coast during World War Two. The First Nations House harkens to the days when Coast Salish paddled in from all over BC's southwest coast to harvest and pack the Fraser River salmon run. **London Farm Heritage Site** (1877) just east of Britannia Heritage Shipyard on the Fraser River at 6511 Dyke Rd (604-271-5220), invokes the days when Richmond was checkerboarded with dairy, vegetable and fruit farms. The graceful yellow farmhouse has been restored to

Steveston's historic cannery

the 1880–1914 period, and the surrounding gardens and berry patch are a delight. Take a picnic and enjoy.

Steveston is a half-hour drive (32 km) south of downtown Vancouver. Take Hwy 99 south to the Steveston Hwy exit just before the George Massey Tunnel. Follow Steveston Highway right to No. 2 Rd, turn left and then take a right onto Moncton St and follow Moncton to Steveston village.

The North Shore Mountains: Skiing and Hiking

Do those steel-blue mountains across Burrard Inlet on the North Shore look tempting? The North Shore mountains are the place for year-round outdoor recreation. In winter downhill skiers and snowboarders swoosh through the moguls at the North Shore's three night-lit ski areas—Grouse Mountain, Mount Seymour and Cypress Bowl (see below). Cross-country skiers glide over well-marked **cross-country trails** at Mount Seymour and Cypress Bowl. And **hikers and mountain bikers** head for dozens of trails that criss-cross the North Shore Mountains. Thanks to Vancouver's mild climate, trails on the lower slopes are often open all year. Some hikes are easy strolls and others are killer day-long or overnight treks. There's something for every ability on the North Shore. (P.S.:These mountains are rugged and dangerous for the unwary. Every year dozens of hikers and skiers have to be rescued by the forty-three-member North Shore Rescue Team. So be prepared for hazardous conditions as well as bears and occasionally cougars. This is true wilderness, right at Vancouver's doorstep.)

A good half dozen hiking books that can point you in the right direction are available at local bookstores and outdoor equipment stores, or pick up a free North Shore Hiking Trails Map at North Shore InfoCentres, weekdays at 131 East 2nd St, or seasonally at the junction of Capilano Rd and Marine Dr and Lonsdale Quay (604-987-4488, website: www.cofcnorthvan.org). Here are a few of the North Shore's most popular outdoor recreation areas:

A snowboarder kicks loose

Mount Seymour Provincial Park/Seymour Ski Country

A 3,508-ha park in North Vancouver offers **mountaineering, day hiking, and moderate to easy shorter walks**. Four main trails. The easiest is **Goldie Lake Trail** (1 1/2 hrs), running around the lake and through a forest with 250-year-old Douglas fir trees. Maps available on site. Ski area has four double chairlifts, two rope tows, 25 runs, cross-country skiing and snowshoeing. Ski and snowshoe rentals and ski school. **Night skiing**. Day lodge, cafeteria. Take Mt. Seymour Parkway exit from Hwy 1 and follow signs to Mt. Seymour Rd, North Vancouver (Seymour Ski Country 604-924-1056 or snow phone 604-718-7771).

Cypress Provincial Park/ Cypress Bowl Ski Area

This 3,012-ha park is one of BC's busiest day parks. Excellent hiking for all levels, including wheelchair-accessible **Yew Lake Trail**. Great panoramas of Howe Sound, the Lions and

Cypress Bowl ski area overlooks Vancouver

Vancouver. The Friends of Cypress Provincial Park are battling to save an old-growth "snow forest" of **1,000-year-old yellow cedars** (yellow cypress), western hemlock and mountain hemlock. To see these ancient giants, follow the **Baden-Powell trail** east (right) from behind the ski service buildings. (Watch out for bears.) Maps available at the park. Ski area has 4 double chairlifts, 2 rope tows, 25 runs, cross-country trails, ski and snowshoe rentals, ski school, day lodge, cafeteria, lounge, ski shop. **Night skiing**. Take Cypress Bowl exit from Hwy 1/99 Cypress Bowl Ski Area and follow Cypress Bowl Rd up 15 km to ski area parking lot (Cypress Bowl Ski Area 604-926-5612, or snow phone 604-419-7669).

Lynn Canyon Ecology Centre/Lynn Headwaters Regional Park

250-hectare Lynn Canyon Park has an **ecological centre** with nature films, hands-on displays, summer nature programs, rainforest trails and wonderful stands of timber. (Lynn Valley was known as Shaketown in the 1860s for all the shakes and shingles produced from the North Shore's giant cedars.) The big draw is a **75-metre high suspension bridge** straddling spectacular Lynn Canyon. In 1912 it cost 5 cents to cross the 68-m long bridge, but now it's free!

The 4,685-ha **Lynn Headwaters Regional Park** is in a long U-shaped river valley surrounded by rugged mountains. It has 20 km of developed trails for a range of abilities. There is an easy walk beside Lynn Creek along historic Cedars Mill Trail. Look for artifacts from historic logging operations. The challenging hike up Lynn Peak—a favourite subject for the famous Canadian artist Frederick Varley (1881-1969)—pays off with great views of Lynn Valley and Seymour Valley. There is also access to Seymour Demonstration Forest (see next page) from this park. Take Hwy 1 to Lynn Valley Rd exit. Follow Lynn Valley Rd and watch for park signs. For Lynn Canyon Ecology Centre, turn right at Peters St (604-981-3103. For Lynn Headwaters Regional Park, continue up Lynn Valley Rd 4 km to park entrance (604-432-6350).

Lower Seymour Conservation Reserve

This area is part of a 5,600-ha Greater Vancouver watershed once off-limits but opened in 1987. More than 40 km of trails ranging from easy **Ecology Loop Trail** around pretty **Rice Lake** to 22-km round-trip hike to huge concrete Seymour Dam. Some gravel and paved sections. **Cycling** and **rollerblading** on weekends. Visit the **fish hatchery**, walk the **interpretive trails** or take a Sunday tour (604-987-1273). Educational emphasis on how to manage working forests. To get there, take Lillooet Rd exit from Hwy 1 and go past Capilano College and the cemetery onto a gravel road leading to the entrance. Self-guided maps available. North Vancouver (604-640-9690).

North Vancouver Attractions

Capilano Suspension Bridge

To the east of Lions Gate Bridge on the North Shore is North Vancouver, home to three of Vancouver's all-time favourite tourist attractions. The Capilano Suspension Bridge and Park has been drawing crowds since the turn of the century when a Scotsman named George Grant Mackay suspended the first plank bridge a dizzying 70 metres above the rushing Capilano River. Every year nearly a million visitors pluck up their courage to swing and sway across the 137-m plank bridge. (Margaret Thatcher—always up for a challenge—crossed it twice!) On the far side is a nature park with **easy walking trails** through **old-growth forest**. Return across the bridge to the recently revamped gardens with sproutings of **totem poles**, a **Native carving demonstration centre**, a classy little display on the bridge's history, and a humungous Canadian **gift shop**. 3735 Capilano Rd, North Vancouver (604-985-7474, fax 604-985-7479).

"George Mackay's original suspension bridge was built with the help of two Squamish Nation men—August Jack Khahtsahlano, a handlogger, spirit dancer and respected Native leader, and his older brother Willie. They used a horse team to haul two heavy hemp ropes across the ravine. Once the ropes were anchored to huge cedar posts on the far side, they laid cedar-shake boards between the ropes. The Squamish called it the laughing bridge for the sounds the boards made when the wind down the canyon set the ropes to dancing."—from *The Laughing Bridge*, by Eleanor Dempster.

Capilano Suspension Bridge

Grouse Mountain and Skyride

At the top of Capilano Rd is another popular tourist attraction that leaves some visitors gasping for breath— the Grouse Mountain Skyride. This **aerial tram** whips more than 1,000 metres up Grouse Mountain to the **ski and entertainment area** at the top—in eight short minutes. And don't forget your camera. At the top you can snap incredible panoramic photos for the folks back home. Grouse Mountain's bar and restaurant are famous for the **night-time spectacle** of Vancouver's lights sweeping around Burrard Inlet. In winter the night-lit **ski area** with its dozen runs is a big-time favourite with the younger set. In summer duck into the multimedia **Theatre in the Sky** featuring near-3D films about BC. See loggers test their skill in **logger sports**, and join **First Nations' celebrations and feasting** in the Híwus Feasthouse. Watch **hang gliders** fly with the eagles and then drop into the terrifyingly small landing site at the base of the ski area. **Hike** off toward Crown

Grouse Mountain Skyride

Mountain or Lynn Valley (with due caution and all the right gear!). Or pedal down the peak on a **mountain bike** tour (Velo-City Cycle Tours, 604-924-0288, fax 604-929-8822, website www.velo-city.com). By the way, you *can* hike from the parking lot up to the Grouse Mountain summit. The infamous Grouse Grind is not a pretty hike, and was the site of an avalanche disaster in early 1999, but it sure is steep—and that's why lots of super-fit types "grind" their way up. They like the challenge and the bragging rights—"I did the Grind this weekend. No sweat." To ride down the Grouse skytram, bring money. This once-free service now has its price. 6400 Nancy Greene Way (604-984-0661, snow phone 604-986-6262).

The Royal Hudson Scenic Rail/Boat Tour

Huge puffs of drifting white smoke and the musical whooo-whooo of a steam whistle mark the Royal Hudson's summer season. Old Engine 2860 is the last of the sixty-five steam trains that once shuttled across Canada. In 1939 King George VI was so delighted by his cross-country train trip to Vancouver aboard Hudson 2860 that he officially dubbed the Hudson engines "Royal." Today the Royal Hudson chugs along spectacular Howe Sound from BC Rail's North Vancouver station to Squamish. The rail line winds between forest and ocean, treating some 70,000 passengers a year to kaleidoscopic views of snowy peaks and deep fiordland dotted with islands. A layover in the logging town of Squamish allows time for leg-stretching and a choice of entertainment, like a visit to the **Logging Show**, the **West Coast Railway Heritage Museum** or **Shannon Falls**. Take the train back or switch to **Harbour Cruises' MV Britannia** and cruise to Coal Harbour in

The Royal Hudson

downtown Vancouver. Ask about the new **Pacific Starlight Dinner train** combining sunset ocean views and west coast cuisine. The Royal Hudson runs Wednesday through Sunday and holiday Mondays from early June to late September. Train leaves from 1311 W. 1st St, North Vancouver (BC Rail, 631-3500, 1-800-663-8238). Harbour Cruises, north foot of Denman Street, Vancouver (604-688-7246).

West Vancouver Attractions

Scenic Marine Drive

The North Shore has the best seaside drive in Greater Vancouver, not to mention beaches, restaurants and upscale shopping and antiquing. Take the West Vancouver exit from the Lions Gate Bridge, and you're on Marine Drive. West Vancouver is the richest municipality in Canada, and sprawling multimillion-dollar waterfront homes have almost squeezed out the holiday cottages that once dotted the shoreline. West Vancouverites believe they live in a West Coast Eden—see for yourself as you wind along Marine Dr to postcard-pretty Horseshoe Bay. On the way you'll pass through a pleasantly villagey shopping district called **Ambleside Village**, just past Park Royal Shopping Centre, with lots of coffee bars, clever little restaurants, chic clothing stores and gilt-edged antique shops. On the waterfront is **Ambleside Park** and the North Shore's most popular swimming beach, where you can watch wedding-cake cruise ships slide under the Lions Gate Bridge. And don't forget the family pooch—at the far end of the beach dogs can run free and it's one big doggy pow-wow on weekends. Stretch your legs on the **West Vancouver Seawalk** that runs along the shore from **Ambleside Beach** to **Dundarave Pier** (with a sideways skip onto Bellevue St just beyond Ambleside Park). You can also get to Dundarave Pier by driving along Marine Dr through the block-long **Dundarave village** and turning left at 25th St. Dundarave Beach is a picturesque little gem, and the hamburgers in the summer

Water sculptures at Ambleside Park

concession stands are great. Watch for **Capers**, an upmarket whole-earth food emporium (and a super place for gourmet picnic stuff), and **Jim's Hardware**, an old-style hardware store with some great quirky buys. Beyond Dundarave, Marine Drive winds close to the coast through another village, **Caulfeild**, whose meandering roads (and peculiar spelling) were the products of English gentleman William Caulfeild, who laid out the village "according to the contours of nature." There is no prettier residential area in all of Vancouver, with its Tudor Revival residences and soaring cedar-and-glass contemporary homes perched on dramatic rock outcroppings. Keep a sharp eye out for **Lighthouse Park** just past the firehall at Tiddley Cove where you can traipse through towering **400-year-old Douglas fir** trees to the 1912 **Point Atkinson lighthouse**, an easy 20-minute walk from the parking lot. Settle onto a rocky ledge under a sundance of shade and light from an overhanging arbutus and watch all the boats heading up the Strait of Georgia.

Horseshoe Bay

At the end of Marine Drive is the village of Horseshoe Bay tucked in a deep U-shaped cove beneath the towering Coast Mountains. This is the departure point for BC Ferries bound for Vancouver Island, the Sunshine Coast and Bowen Island. For information, pick up the BC Ferries Mainland/Vancouver Island/Sunshine Coast schedule or phone anywhere in BC 1-888-BCFERRY (1-888-223-3779). Grab a cool ice cream or a salty packet of fish and chips and head for the foreshore park to watch the big white ferries sucking up and spitting out their cargos of cars and passengers.

Ferry arriving in Horseshoe Bay

Bowen Island

For a unique adventure from Horseshoe Bay, buy a foot passenger ticket and ride the ferry across Howe Sound to the charming little village of **Snug Cove** on Bowen Island. Bowen is the rugged ever-green-clad shoulder of land at the entrance to Howe Sound. The trip takes about 20 minutes and the spiffy Bowen Island ferry sails through an inlet so beautiful that even commuters don't take it for granted. When you step off in Snug Cove, you're in another world. Bowen Island was once a holiday destination for Vancouverites, and it still radiates the peaceful cheeriness that earned it the nickname "Happy Isle." In the 1920s the coast's famous Union Steamship Company built a resort with a hotel, a general store and nearly 200 cottages, and happy vacationers flocked aboard the steamship *Lady Alexandra* to picnic and swim by day and dance the night away. The Union Steamships' historic Tudor-style general store still stands at the top of the BC ferry dock, and so do a handful of the old cottages in the heritage Davies Orchard just back of Snug Cove. One cottage is now a museum/visitor centre, another has been restored as an interpretive cottage of the Union Steamship period, and a couple more are still rented out! Snug Cove is a pleasing jumble of old and new buildings with idiosyncratic little shops, boutiques and food outlets, including favourites like **Dunfield & Daughters Whole Foods Market, Books on Bowen**—with titles by Bowen's many writers, including Nick Bantock of *Griffin & Sabine* fame—and Doc Morgan's Inn pub/restaurant, at the site of a cottage built in 1918 for Doc Morgan, a pioneer Vancouver barber. Idle away a happy hour or two on a shopping-and-snacking promenade of "the Cove." Then pick up a free map of adjacent **Crippen Regional Park** (604-432-6350) and walk those calories off. This 240-ha park was carved out of the old Union Steamship property after Bowen Islanders stood in front of bulldozers to save it from development. The 4-km (2-hr.) **Killarney Lake Trail** loop is a local favourite, but you can take longer or shorter jaunts.

The Sea to Sky Highway to Whistler

The Sea to Sky Highway (Hwy 99) winds north from Horseshoe Bay, along precipitous mountains jutting out of Howe Sound and through glacier-hung peaks for 120 km (1 1/2 hrs) to Whistler. This is the path to heaven for outdoor recreationists. It's all there somewhere along the way—river rafting, rock climbing, hiking, windsurfing, camping, golfing, scuba diving, mountain biking, paragliding, sport fishing, snowmobiling, roller blading, swimming, nature-watching, kayaking and canoeing—and, of course, great skiing at **Whistler/Blackcomb**. And the scenery is BC at its dramatic best. At **Porteau Cove Provincial Park** (13 km north of Horseshoe Bay) **scuba divers** flutterkick around four shipwrecks, including a World War II minesweeper and a steam tug. Stop at **Furry Creek** to golf at oceanside or save your green fees for other great courses at Squamish, Pemberton and Whistler. Kids can dip into the wet stuff at picture-pretty **Murrin Lake Provincial Park** (35 km north of Horseshoe Bay) or munch their sandwiches below the much-photographed 335-m **waterfalls** at **Shannon Falls Provincial Park** (39 km north

The Sea to Sky Highway

of Horseshoe Bay). Adrenalin junkies can dangle from ropes on the **more than 250 climbing routes** on the monolithic **Stawamus Chief** (652 m) near Squamish (44 km north of Horseshoe Bay). "The Chief" is second only to the Rock of Gibraltar as the world's largest freestanding granite outcropping, and the truly scary **University Wall** is reputedly the most difficult rock climb in Canada. **Windsurfers** can get their kicks off **Squamish Spit** where winds sometimes gust up to 60 km per hour. (In the Coast Salish language Squamish means "mother of the wind," and the local breezes are real mothers!) Check out **whitewater rafting** excursions from Squamish and Pemberton

▶ Britannia

The BC Museum of Mining in Britannia Beach (33 km beyond Horseshoe Bay). The old Britannia Copper Mine is now a National Historic Site. Britannia's curious medical doctor-cum-prospector, Dr. Alexander Forbes, discovered rich copper deposits on Britannia Mountain in 1888 and the mine was born. An economic mainstay, the Britannia Copper Mine belched out copper ore for nearly seven decades. Revisit the days of hard rock mining in the original mining buildings staggered up the mountainside. Open seasonally May-early September. (In Britannia 604-896-2233, in Vancouver 604-688-8735.)

(north of Whistler) in summer and **eagle watching** at the **Eagle Run** viewing site near **Brackendale** (10 km past Squamish). From November through February hundreds of eagles descend on the Squamish Valley to feed on river gravel bars. (A world-record-breaking 3,769 eagles were counted in 1994.) Brackendale celebrates the great raptors' arrival with a Winter Eagle Festival. The world-famous 195,000 ha **Garibaldi Provincial Park** starts just north of Squamish and stretches past Whistler. **Black Tusk** (2315 m), a strikingly angular molten eruption from a now-inert volcano, is a favourite hiking destination. This big park has well-marked access routes and 196 wilderness walk-in campsites (604-898-3678). **Wildflower meadows, glacier-blue lakes, alpine tarns and snow-white peaks** are magnets for outdoor lovers. Whistler Resort (56 km beyond Squamish), one of the top five ski resorts in the world, has been rated number one in North America by *Snow Country* magazine and *Ski* magazine. With more than 200 runs and 30 lifts on Whistler and Blackcomb mountains, the longest continuous fall-line skiing in North America, and the only summer skiing in North America (on Blackcomb's Horstman Glacier), it's easy to see why throngs of skiers from Asia, Europe and North America head for Whistler. Don't overlook other snow sports like **heli-skiing, cross-country skiing, snowmobiling** and **snowshoeing**. **Whistler Village**, a faux-European village at the heart of the action, is alive with dozens of sidewalk cafés, elegant restaurants, lodges and condominiums and shops galore. The new **Chateau Whistler Resort** near the lift base is the biggest hotel built in Canada in this century, and a whole new village extension, **Whistler Town Plaza**, has opened its hundreds of doors. But Whistler doesn't stop humming when the snow melts. It is a true year-round resort with all the bells and whistles, including three **award-winning golf courses** designed by Jack Nicklaus, Robert Trent Jones Jr. and Arnold Palmer, a 15-km Whistler Valley trail for jogging, rollerblading and biking, five lovely lakes and six lakeside parks for **canoeing, windsurfing, boating, fishing, picnicking and swimming**, and oodles of great **hikes**. (Both mountains operate summer lifts.) And those are just the tip of Whistler's recreational iceberg. For more information call the Whistler Activity and Information Centre (604-932-2394), Whistler Resort Association (604-932-2394) or Whistler InfoCentre (604-932-5528), or visit the year-round InfoCentre at the junction of Hwy 99 and Lake Placid Rd (Whistler Creek gondola base) or summer InfoCentres at Village Square and Village Gate.

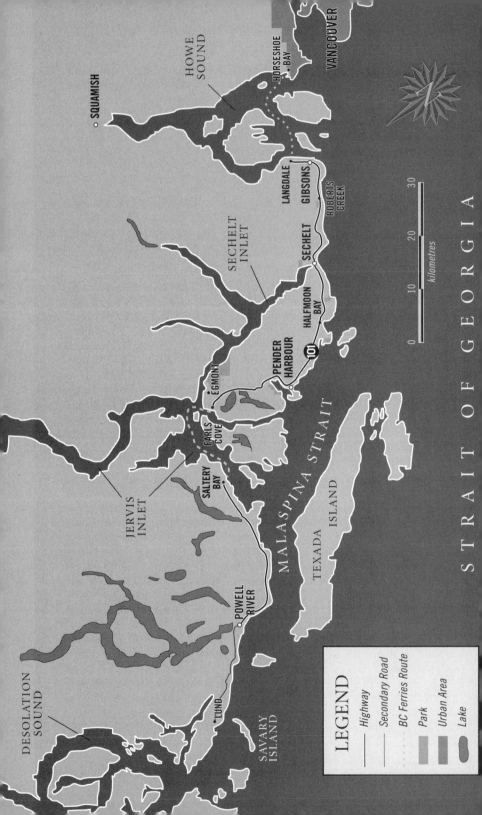

CHAPTER 2

THE
SUNSHINE COAST

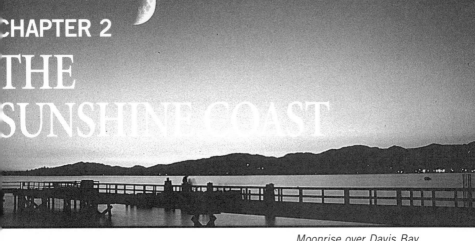

Moonrise over Davis Bay

The Sunshine Coast is a scenic 160-km stretch of shoreline beginning a short ferry ride north of Vancouver and running along the eastern side of the Strait of Georgia. A winding ribbon of road meanders its length and is dotted with small communities. The area's special geography—a layering of forest-clad mountains, glacier-carved fjords, quiet coves and beaches, ocean and lakes—makes it a natural for outdoor adventure, and for sitting back in the car or on the ferry deck and just enjoying the British Columbia coast.

Lund; start or end of the road

The Sunshine Coast has served as a favourite weekend and cottage getaway for Vancouverites for generations, boasting a slower pace of life and an abundance of outdoor recreation possibilities. There's Princess Louisa Inlet and Chatterbox Falls, which inspired one famous author to write: "Perhaps an atheist could view it and remain an atheist, but I doubt it." The 8,200-ha Desolation Sound is the largest, most spectacular and most popular marine park in the province. Then there's the legendary Skookumchuck rapids, one of North America's most awesome saltwater spectacles. See magnificent cedars up to 1,200 years old in the Caren Mountain range and hike or ski the 6,000-ha high-altitude alpine Tetrahedron Recreation Area. Read on, there are plenty more reasons to visit the Sunshine Coast.

Don't expect five-star hotels, luxury resorts, health spas and gourmet restaurants on every corner, but do expect hiking, biking, fishing, boating, camping, scuba diving and lots of forest and ocean at your fingertips. For those who want a simple, relaxed

Approximate Distances
From Langdale to Gibsons 5 km
From Gibsons to Sechelt 22 km
From Sechelt to Earls Cove 59 km
From Saltery Bay to Powell River 31 km
From Saltery Bay to Lund 55 km

Davis Bay near Sechelt

weekend getaway, there is good fare, plenty of beautiful beach and forest walks and cozy motels and B&Bs. Best of all, this picturesque piece of BC is just a short ferry ride from the Vancouver area, but worlds away from the hustle and bustle of the city. From the moment you leave the ferry terminal, you'll feel the area's special laid-back rural charm. This is a place where independent, inventive people have settled down and made their living any way they can just so they can live along this beautiful slice of seacoast.

Getting to the Sunshine Coast

From Vancouver *Drive aboard the BC ferry from Horseshoe Bay terminal.*

40-minute crossing to the Langdale terminal on the lower Sunshine Coast; 8 sailings daily year round.

Across Jervis Inlet *Drive aboard the BC ferry from either Earls Cove (lower Sunshine Coast) or Saltery Bay (upper Sunshine Coast). 45 to 55 minutes crossing time; 9 sailings daily year round.*

From Vancouver Island *Drive aboard the BC ferry from the Comox terminal. 1 hour and 15 minutes crossing time to the Westview terminal in Powell River; 4 sailings daily year round.*

Sunshine Coast CirclePac *The Sunshine Coast CirclePac is a special package of discounted BC Ferry fares for anyone travelling on all four of the following routes:*

- *Horseshoe Bay (Vancouver) to Langdale (Sunshine Coast)*

- *Earls Cove (lower Sunshine Coast) to Saltery Bay (upper Sunshine Coast)*

- *Powell River (upper Sunshine Coast) to Comox (Vancouver Island)*

- *Vancouver Island to Mainland (Vancouver)—from Nanaimo (Departure Bay) to Horseshoe Bay or Duke Point to Tsawwassen) or from Victoria (Swartz Bay to Tsawwassen).*

You must buy your CirclePac tickets when you start your trip, and some restrictions apply. Check with BC Ferries for details.

Ask about the Coastal Getaway plan for help in planning your itinerary and special discount packages everywhere CirclePac takes you. Call Vancouver Coast and Mountains Tourism Association for details: **1-800-667-3306**.

(For more information about travel aboard BC Ferries, see p. 8.)

To get to the Sunshine Coast from the Vancouver area, you'll take a BC ferry across Howe Sound, and to travel from there to the upper Sunshine Coast you'll drive up Hwy 101 and take another ferry across Jervis Inlet. So short sea voyages through BC's stunning coastal fjords are built right into your itinerary. Once you're there, take your time.

There are dozens of excellent hikes on the Sunshine Coast

THE LOWER COAST

Gibsons Marina

Highlights

Forests and ocean
close at hand

Lots of waterfront to explore

Secluded coves

Tranquil fishing villages

Beautiful hiking trails

Swimming, diving and
other water sports

Great mountain bike trails
and touring routes

Plenty of amenities

Walk, drive or bike onto the Langdale ferry at BC Ferries' Horseshoe Bay terminal, which is a 20- to 40-minute drive northwest of downtown Vancouver (depending on traffic). Then sit back and enjoy your first taste of BC's spectacular coastal fjords. From picturesque little Horseshoe Bay, the ferry sails past mountains rising almost straight out of **Howe Sound**. The rugged profiles of nearby islands, including **Bowen Island**, **Anvil Island** and **Gambier Island**, add dramatic swatches of dark green against the deep blue waters and snow-white peaks.

Gibsons

From the Langdale terminal it's just a 5- to 10-minute drive to Gibsons, one of the largest communities on the Sunshine Coast (pop. 6,000). Take the left turn at the traffic lights when you exit the Langdale terminal and head along Marine Drive. You'll avoid the ferry traffic heading upcoast and you'll get to enjoy a much more scenic oceanside route—a perfect introduction to the flavour of the Sunshine Coast. Gibsons is still famous to millions of fans worldwide as the setting for the TV series "The Beachcombers." You can still see **Molly's Reach** café with its yellow clapboard sidings just above the wharf where make-believe beachcombers swilled down buckets of Molly's coffee as the TV cameras rolled. It's no wonder this quaint old fishing village overlooking Shoal Channel and Howe Sound was once a film set. Gibsons' slightly down-at-the-heels wooden buildings and the authentic working harbour just below Molly's Reach are

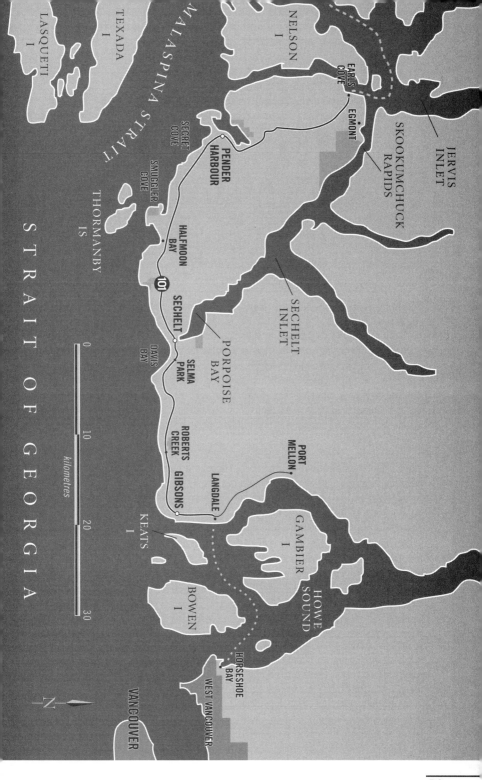

Molly's Reach café, of "Beachcombers" fame

charming legacies from Gibsons' pioneer past and well worth a stop. You can get a walking tour of the local historical buildings at the nearby **Elphinstone Pioneer Museum** (716 Winn Rd, 604-886-8232, daily May–Sept or by request) or just enjoy Gibsons' friendly, funky charm on your own. Don't miss outlying buildings like the fine old **Inglis House** (1913) on the hill above Molly's Reach. For nearly three decades Dr. Frederick Inglis was the area's sole physician. He made house calls on a horse named Paddy, then by motorcycle, and later in a Model-T Ford. Conditions were often primitive, and more than one patient was stitched up by the light of Dr. Inglis's flaring carbide headlights. The house is a private home and not open to the public, but do take a moment to admire it from a respectful distance.

Present-day Gibsons was founded by sheer accident in 1886. **George Gibson**'s jerry-rigged sloop was blown off course and he fetched up for the night on Keats Island near Gibsons. Next morning he sailed across to the mainland, liked what he saw, and blazed "witness trees" to claim a homestead. The first seed of the new village was sown. Gibson soon settled on his land with his family and built a "landing"—a wharf where **Union Steamship Company** ships could dock. These ships were the lifeblood of the coast for nearly seventy years, making calls at logging camps and tiny settlements huddled around wharves, to bring in mail, supplies and fresh faces, and to pick up products and outbound passengers on their way to Vancouver and the rest of the world. People lived with their faces turned toward the sea and their ears cocked for the distinctive "long-short-short-long" whistle of the Union ships. "Boat Day" was a big event when everyone gathered to watch the ship dock. In his delightful history of the Union steamships, *The Good Company* (Harbour), Tom Henry quotes a logger's description of the sight from shipside as a Union vessel eased into a wharf: "You'd all go out and hang over the rail, everybody'd be there on the dock, there'd

What to See

- ☐ **1** BC Ferries to Vancouver
- ☐ **2** Marine Drive
- ☐ **3** Government Wharf/ Molly's Reach
- ☐ **4** Elphinstone Pioneer Museum
- ☐ **5** Gower Point/Chaster Park

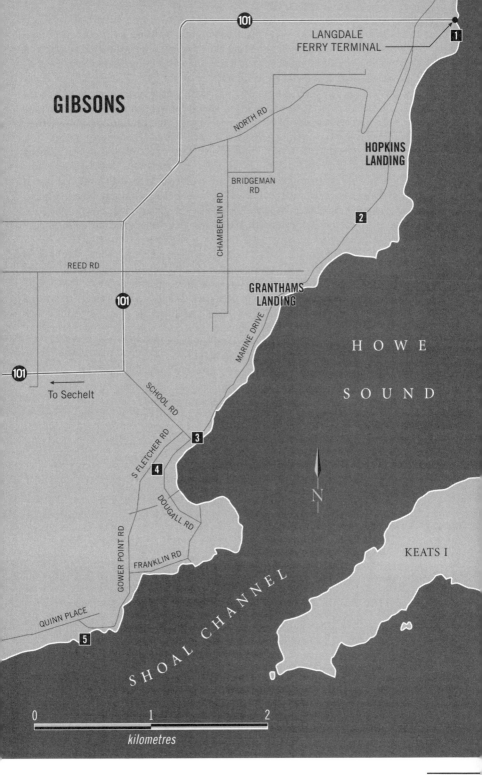

GIBSONS

LANGDALE
FERRY TERMINAL

1

101

NORTH RD

HOPKINS
LANDING

2

BRIDGEMAN
RD

CHAMBERLIN RD

REED RD

101

GRANTHAMS
LANDING

101

To Sechelt

MARINE DRIVE

H O W E

S O U N D

SCHOOL RD

3

S FLETCHER RD

4

DOUGALL RD

GOWER POINT RD

FRANKLIN RD

KEATS I

N

QUINN PLACE

5

S H O A L   C H A N N E L

0   1   2

kilometres

always be someone you'd know...women'd be screamin' back and forth, some gyppo [logger] maybe would be there catchin' freight and guys up on the boat would be after him about work...people'd be stumbling along still yappin' as the boat eased back, shouting and waving—and this would go on all the way up the line... That kinda kept things together, you see. The coast in them days was like a buncha people along a street seeing each other all the time on the way by." No wonder the Union steamships were sometimes called the "upcoast streetcars." Locals eventually began calling their community Gibsons, but old-timers still call the village Gibson's Landing—or just The Landing.

The new **government wharf** below Molly's Reach has replaced George Gibson's makeshift wood dock and George himself has been replaced by his bronze statue in nearby **Pioneer Park**. But go down to the wharf and you'll discover that the real face of Gibson's Landing is still turned out to sea. "The boats at the government wharf in Gibsons are the boats of the coast's real boat people," says local historian Howard White, "and a visitor can learn more about the authentic maritime culture of the region in a half-hour dock walk there than in weeks of haunting museums."

You can sometimes buy fresh fish and crabs straight off the fish boats. Fishing charters and boat and kayak rentals are available in the vicinity of the wharf. For an interesting stroll, take the **Seawalk** which follows the shoreline around portions of the harbour. If the tide's out, you can walk a long way back toward Langdale. Enjoy great ocean views, tangy salt air and the busy colourful motion of seabirds at the water's edge. You'll walk along the beach side of the Marine Drive buildings and see historic Gibsons from a whole new perspective. Watch for the marine ways where boats have been pulled up for repairs since 1947. Up on the street side of the same building is Coles Marine repair shop, where you'll discover that pioneer odd-jobbing enterprise persists in Gibsons. When business is slow in the machine shop, the owner turns his hand to crafting wrought-iron pieces ranging from elegant gates to whimsical iron-and-stone waterfowl.

Granthams Landing

The streetside village is another enjoyable stroll. You can browse in Gibsons' attractive little boutiques and specialty shops and explore a couple of old-time museums. And if you're hungry, you're in luck. There are several good restaurants and delis where you can get seafood, Tex-Mex, veggie stuff—a surprisingly large choice of good eats for a small place. In some of these spots you can enjoy great sea views, too. In summer, visit the **Tourist InfoCentre** just across the street from Molly's Reach for detailed area maps and friendly insider advice on more things to see and do. If you like arts and crafts, ask for the self-guided tour map to **artists' studios** on the Sunshine Coast. And if you're a hiker or mountain biker, ask for local **trail** maps or contact BC Forest Service at Wilson Creek (604-740-5005). There are numerous excellent walks and hikes in the area, many of them detailed in the book *Sunshine and Salt Air* (see box, page 57).

Before heading for the highway, you might also want to follow Gower Point Road, which begins at the intersection just above Molly's Reach, to **Chaster Provincial Park**. Captain George Vancouver came ashore here to camp for the night one cloudy Friday evening in 1792, and a cairn marks his arrival. A dour man on his fourth British surveying expedition in this remote region, Vancouver had been painfully disappointed to discover that Howe Sound was not the hoped-for opening to the Northwest Passage. But his spirits lifted a bit as he sailed past present-day Gibsons—a landscape with "a more pleasing appearance than the shores of Howe's Sound" and he named his night's resting spot **Gower Point** in honour of the British admiral Sir Erasmus Gower.

▶ Gibsons &
  Roberts Creek
  Annual Events

June
Gibsons Jazz Festival
July
Maritime History Weekend
Canada Day Celebrations
Sea Cavalcade
August
Roberts Creek Daze
Gambier Island Craft Fair
For more information,
Gibsons InfoCentre
604-886-2325

Vancouver's faint praise fails to do justice to one of the most prized summer resort areas on the lower Sunshine Coast. Go for a picnic at sunset and you'll see why it's such a special place.

Upper Gibsons (farther along Highway 101), with its suburbs and strip malls, lacks the charm of the Landing. But if you need supplies or a quick burger and fries, you'll find them here.

Roberts Creek

Once past Upper Gibsons, you can step on the gas and stay on Highway 101 for a few hours, driving through pleasant second-growth forest with the occasional glimpse of the ocean. But you'll discover more of the real Sunshine Coast if you take the turnoffs leading down to the water or up to the nearby lakes and mountains. If you have a night or two to stay in one of the lower Sunshine Coast's many first-rate B&Bs, you'll find an independent, creative, hospitable breed of people who love their patch of coastline and who will gladly share it with you.

Roberts Creek is a good starting point for your side-road adventuring. From Highway 101 on the outskirts of Gibsons, take the left turn marked Lower Roberts Creek Road and follow this scenic route for 6 km. At the stop sign you'll find the heart of the community, a small village known locally as "The Creek." It's nestled in what was once the old Roberts family homestead, near the spot where Roberts Creek tumbles into the ocean, and it's a tiny but charming collection of brushed-up heritage buildings and a scattering of modern ones, including a funky general store and post office, a couple of restaurants, a community hall, an old chapel and a school.

Harry Roberts, the village founder and longtime presiding spirit of Roberts Creek, was a witty and enterprising man, an artist and writer, a skilled craftsman, a dyed-in-the-wool nonconformist and above all a cheerful humanitarian. Harry was known for building ingenious boats, houses and stores, and he ran the post office—which meant, in pre-wharf days, risking his life a couple of dozen times a year to row through dirty weather to fetch the mail from the Union steamer. Once the wharf was built, vacationers began arriving in droves and the enterprising Harry built rental cottages to accommodate them.

Important Numbers

Emergencies **911**

Medical clinic (9 am–5 pm)
604-886-2221

Travel InfoCentre **604-886-2325**

Gibsons & Roberts Creek Recreation, Accommodations and Services

Recreation	Services
Bicycle rentals	Travel InfoCentres
Kayak/canoe rentals	Restaurants
Fishing charters	Pubs
Dive charters	Cafés
Golf courses	Banks (ATMs)
Major hiking trails	Art gallery
Parks	Marina
Accommodations	Post office
Bed & Breakfasts	Shopping malls
Motels	Gas/service stations
Inns	Medical clinic
Campground (R. Creek)	

Later he sold land for a summer camp for girls. Known as the Kewpie Kamp, it was one of a dozen children's camps operating on the lower Sunshine Coast. The Kewpie Kampers, who were togged out in khaki blouses and bloomers and bright red berets, were dubbed the "little tomatoes," and they were a familiar sight each summer as they swam, fished, hiked and marched in line to church on Sunday.

Roberts Creek remains a special place. The **public park** on the waterfront with its long community-built pier and wide driftwood-backed beach is a great place for fishing, picnicking or just lazing in the sun. You can enjoy fine dining at the Creekhouse Restaurant, a longtime favourite with locals and visitors. Or grab a bite at the Gumboot Garden Café—part laid-back 1960s-style café, part independent-minded art gallery, and home to the Acoustic Gumboot Society. **Artists' studios** tucked away here and there offer a chance to see the work of the area's many talented craftspeople.

Not far away is the 65-ha **Cliff Gilker Park**, an ideal place for a family hike. To get there from Roberts Creek, continue on Lower Roberts Creek Road until it loops back to Highway 101. Turn right (toward Gibsons) and backtrack to the signed turnoff. Next to it is the **Sunshine Coast Golf and Country Club**'s inviting 18-hole course with lots of sand

The ocean seems to stretch on forever from Roberts Creek Provincial Park

traps and water hazards to challenge duffers. Just up Highway 101 heading toward Sechelt from Cliff Gilker Park is the signed turnoff to **Roberts Creek Provincial Park**. Follow the signs to the 25 tree-shaded campsites (604-885-9019). The park also has a separate pebble swimming beach with picnic tables 1.5 km southeast of the campground on Beach Road. Roberts Creek is also known for its B&Bs, so if you're looking for tranquility and charming accommodations, look no further. (Gibsons InfoCentre, 604-886-2325 or Super, Natural British Columbia Accommodations 1-800-663-6000.)

The Sechelt Area

The next major stop up Highway 101 is the town of Sechelt (pop. 6,000), a 10- to 15-minute drive from Roberts Creek. Sechelt sits on the Sechelt isthmus, which separates the long Sechelt Inlet (to the right as you drive up the highway) from the Strait of Georgia (to the left). For hundreds of years that mile-wide strip of land was just nuisance—something to get past in travelling between the inlet and the ocean. In early times the people of the Sechelt Nation, who had some eighty villages along the Sunshine Coast, dragged their canoes across a skid that traversed the isthmus, to avoid a 120-km paddle up the Sechelt Inlet and back down the Strait of Georgia.

Sechelt Arts Centre

The first view of Sechelt as you approach from the south is **Davis Bay**, a tempting sweep of oceanfront dotted with motels. The view is delightful and a waterside stroll at sunset is a pleasure. There's a convenience store, an antique/crafts shop, art gallery and restaurants. The beach itself is a bit stony, but this is a popular seashore spot for all ages.

"Downtown" **Sechelt**, a few miles up the highway, serves up a full complement of facilities from banks, pubs, supermarkets, restaurants, laundromats, liquor store, pharmacy and hospital, to boat rentals, diving charters and scenic cruises. It's been a popular tourist destination for nearly a century. In fact, tourism took off at Sechelt at about the same time as at Roberts Creek. Like Harry Roberts, Herbert Whittaker was an entrepreneurial spirit, but he didn't have any of Harry's cheerful benevolence. "Bert" Whittaker charged money for mail delivery to lonesome loggers in isolated camps, watered down the milk he sold at his store, and faked breakdowns of the launch carrying Vancouver-bound loggers to Sechelt so they'd miss the steamer and have to pay for a night's lodging in his hotel.

Because or in spite of Whittaker's relentless greed, he managed to build a small empire in the Sechelt area. Beginning in 1904, he built a wharf on each side of the Sechelt isthmus to take advantage of the thriving logging trade on the Sechelt Inlet, and charged wharfage at both ends as well as cartage fees across the isthmus. Tourism was soon to

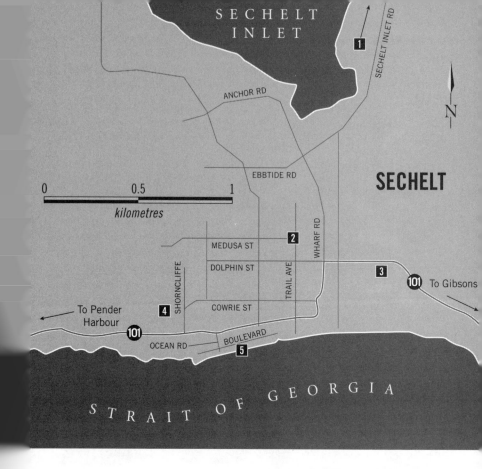

To Gibsons

To Pender Harbour

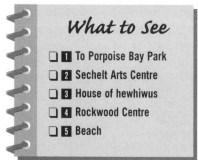

What to See

- [ ] **1** To Porpoise Bay Park
- [ ] **2** Sechelt Arts Centre
- [ ] **3** House of hewhiwus
- [ ] **4** Rockwood Centre
- [ ] **5** Beach

become big business at Sechelt, and Whittaker was in on the ground floor. He added stores, hotels and cottages to his holdings and then expanded some more to steamship companies, sawmills and logging camps. In 1912, according to local historian Helen Dawe, the new schoolteacher arrived to find that Bert Whittaker "owned practically all of Sechelt."

But a few other independent operators did manage to build hotels and lodges for the pleasure of summer visitors. Among them were Jessie and Bill Youngson, a Scottish couple who built Rockwood Lodge in 1936. This graceful heritage lodge is now **Rockwood Centre**, home to Sechelt's annual **Festival of the Written Arts**. The nationally known festival is a four-day celebration of Canadian writing held each August that brings together big-name authors (Mordecai Richler, Peter Gzowski and W. P. Kinsella have been guests), rising literary stars and an audience of enthusiastic readers and aspiring writers, for readings, lectures, barbecues, writers' workshops and light classical and jazz concerts. (For information, phone 1-800-565-9631.) In non-Festival times the

Rockwood Centre is a tranquil place to take a few minutes' break. The former lodge sits on a gentle slope amidst an inviting arboretum and gardens lush with rhododendrons and magnolias. Next door is **St. Hilda's Pioneer Cemetery** where tilting headstones scattered through the quiet churchyard are a picturesque reminder of Sechelt's former days.

The intriguing design of the **Sechelt Arts Centre** with its twining driftwood pieces and angular roofline is another pleasant surprise. Inside you can see a variety of exhibits by local artists. A well-shaded park kitty-corner from the Arts Centre offers a cool retreat for a picnic on a warm summer day.

Sechelt is also home to the shíshálh, or people of the Sechelt Nation. **The House of hewhiwus**, "House of Chiefs," located beside the Sechelt **Travel InfoCentre** toward the south edge of town, is an impressive cultural complex housing the Sechelt Indian District Government offices, Native gift shop, theatre and museum. The complex is the visible sign of band elders' determination to renew the Sechelts' heritage. At the **Raven's Cry Theatre**, films are shown and live performances of First Nations music and dances are held. (Phone 604-885-4597 for a schedule of events.) The by-donation **Tems swiya Museum** is a small but interesting entry into the world of the Sechelts, past and present. It includes displays on basketry, fishing and logging, as well as a brief history of the Sechelt community and photographs and stories of the elders. The four divisions of the Sechelt Nation—the sxixus (Skaiakos) of Pender Harbour, the tewankw (Tuwanek) of Sechelt Inlet, the xenichen (Kunechin) of Upper Jervis Inlet and the ts'unay (Tsonai) of Deserted Bay—officially amalgamated as the Sechelt band in 1920.

After years of struggle the Sechelt Nation became the first Native group to win self-government in Canada. When the Canadian Parliament passed the Sechelt Act (Bill C-93) in 1986, the 650 members of the Sechelt Nation moved out from under the federal government's Indian Act and formed an independent legal entity with the same rights over its reserve as other municipal governments across Canada. The band was also granted a mix of what are normally provincial powers and even federal powers over areas like social services, health, education and public order, and the band's laws can supersede BC provincial laws— making it, in the band chief's

▶ **Sechelt & Halfmoon Bay Annual Events**

June
Children's Festival
Annual Halfmoon Bay Triathlon

July
Canada Day Celebrations
Halfmoon Bay Country Fair

August
Festival of the Written Arts
Hackett Park Craft Fair

September
Fall Festival

For more information,
Sechelt InfoCentre
604-885-0662

Rockwood Centre, home of the writers' festival

Fishboats under a foreboding sky at Porpoise Bay

words, a "third order of government." On a bank near the House of hewhiwus is a group-ing of wooden figures that capture the changing prospects of the Sechelt Nation. Some of the figures are faceless, symbolizing the group's lack of self-determination under the Canadian Indian Act. "It represents when we as a people didn't have any say in our affairs," said former Sechelt Chief Thomas Paul. Other figures have fully detailed faces, symboliz-ing the Sechelt band's new identity under self-government. The Sechelt band is now a major entrepreneur in the Sechelt area, operating a real estate development, a local air-line, a gravel mine and several local businesses.

Porpoise Bay Provincial Park on Sechelt Inlet is a 61-ha park where you can swim in warm ocean water, relax on a beautiful (trucked-in) sand beach with a wide grassy area circled by trees, and stay a while at the many inviting camping and picnicking spots—including cyclist-only and group camping areas (604-898-3678). This is one of the most popular camping spots on the Sunshine Coast and reservations are accepted, so be sure to book early (Discover Camping reservations, March 1–September 15, 1-800-689-9025, from Vancouver 689-9025). To get there, turn right at Wharf Avenue (the first stoplight when entering Sechelt), right again at East Porpoise Bay Road, and follow the road 4 km to the park entrance.

The park is also a good base for marine adventuring along Sechelt Inlet (sometimes called the "Inland Sea") and its tributary arms, Salmon Inlet and Narrows Inlet. The provincial park system has established eight wilderness campsites along the inlet intend-ed mainly for small boats, kayaks and canoes. Charter boats will also take you up the Skookumchuck Rapids at the northern end of the inlet (see p. 74) or even farther afield to Princess Louisa Inlet and magnificent Chatterbox Falls (see p.75). Phone Sunshine Coast Tours (883-2456) or the Sechelt InfoCentre (604-885-0662).

The Sechelt Inlet is also a favourite with scuba divers. The best-known diving site is the wreck of the HMCS *Chaudière*. This old destroyer was scuttled 6 km north of Sechelt off Kunechin Point as a project of the Artificial Reef Society of BC. It now rests in the mud 35 metres below the surface of the water, where it has become home to all kinds of marine life.

About 5 km past Porpoise Bay Provincial Park is the 2,400-ha **Tetrahedron Recreation Area,** essentially a high-elevation (900–1,800 m) wilderness area which contains a network of hiking and cross-country skiing trails and several cabins for public use. Access is via logging road and permission is required to use the road. For further information, contact BC Parks (604-898-3678).

Sechelt & Halfmoon Bay Recreation, Accommodations and Services

Recreation	Services
Bicycle rentals	Travel InfoCentre
Kayak/canoe rentals	Restaurants
Fishing charters	Pubs
Dive charters	Cafés
Golf courses	Banks (ATMs)
Major hiking trails	Shopping mall
Community parks	Gas/service stations
Accommodations	Post office
Bed & Breakfasts	Hospital
Motels	Medical clinic
Inns	
Campground/RV park	

Back on Highway 101, just a few minutes from Sechelt, is the historic **Wakefield Inn**. This pub is a favourite with locals and boasts a panoramic deckside view of the Strait of Georgia and the Trail Islands. The "Wakey" began life in Depression days as the impressive log mansion of one Major Sutherland of the Provincial Police. Although it has been through half a dozen reincarnations, the Wakefield Inn is much the same as it was in the beginning—a delightful example of coastal architecture and a great place to while away a few hours.

Halfmoon Bay

Just a few minutes north of Sechelt, take the left turnoff from Highway 101 onto Redrooffs Road and you'll be in beautiful Halfmoon Bay country. At **Sargeant Bay Provincial Park**, 1.4 km along Redrooffs, is a pretty beach where you can try your luck at fishing, and also indulge in kayaking, canoeing, sailboarding and other ocean sports. Or walk along a grassy path to a creek complete with a small freshwater pond and fish ladders or the fall salmon run.

Another 1.3 km along Redrooffs is **Coopers Green Regional Park**, the site of the annual Halfmoon Bay Country Fair. This is a popular spot for scuba divers, snorkellers and boaters (there's a free launching ramp here), and a great place for a picnic. You can enjoy a friendly, tranquil setting with gorgeous ocean vistas, and the kids can let off some steam (at low tide) by poking around the kelp-strewn rocks for hermit crabs, clingfish and the occasional tiny octopus.

To get to the Halfmoon Bay town centre, turn left on Mintie Road, about 10 km from where you first turned onto Redrooffs. A general store (look for the sign), the **Anchor Rock Gallery** and a government wharf are located here. Just past this spot, Redrooffs Road loops back to Highway 101.

Smuggler Cove

Next you'll come to what may be the most picturesque cove on the whole coast— Smuggler Cove. To get there, turn left onto Brooks Road from the highway just beyond

Scuba divers at Coopers Green Regional Park

Halfmoon Bay. On the right near the end of Brooks Road is the **Smuggler Cove Provincial Marine Park** parking lot. It's a 40-minute (1.5-km) hike from the parking lot to Smuggler Cove, but the trail is very gentle and your effort will be rewarded. Hidden inside folds of rock and dotted with picturesque reefs and islets are the blue waters of Smuggler Cove. The daunting prospect of navigating the cove's narrow, rocky entrance has no doubt scared off some boaters, but this secluded spot is nevertheless one of the most popular anchorages on the coast.

Stories abound about how the cove got its name. In one, a smuggler named Larry Kelly used the cove as a hideaway for Chinese workers who came to Canada to build the Canadian Pacific Railway in the 1880s. When the CPR was completed, some of these men wanted to go to the United States to find jobs but they were denied legal entry, so Kelly charged a whopping $100 a head to smuggle them into the US by boat. In another story, moonshine made on Texada Island during American Prohibition was stashed at Smuggler Cove for pickup by American rumrunners. This delightful cove deserves all the stories that cling to it. It's an especially pretty little jigsaw piece of the coastline.

Secret Cove

For a satisfying meal or seaside accommodation with unforgettable views, turn left from Highway 101 onto Mercer Road and head for the **Jolly Roger** or **Lord Jim's** at Secret Cove. Then you can go back the way you came, or continue on Mercer Road, which joins Highway 101 again just a few minutes later.

Important Numbers

Emergency **911**
Hospital **604-885-2224**
Medical Clinic **604-885-2257**
Travel InfoCentre **604-885-0662**

The Pender Harbour Area

On up the highway about 12 km from Secret Cove is the yachters' and sport fishers' mecca—the "Venice of the West Coast." Pender Harbour comprises four separate communities, **Madeira Park**, **Irvines Landing**, **Kleindale** and **Garden Bay**. They are dotted around a body of water so puckered and notched and studded with islands and bays that boaters can spend days getting the gist of its geography. And that makes Pender Harbour a paradise for saltwater types.

Since the 1880s, when non-Native loggers and fishermen began coming to Pender Harbour, the locals have sought out their pleasures in boats. Some folks lived on the land where pockets of glacial soil made it possible to eke out a living from a mix of farming, logging and fishing. Others settled right on the water, living on float houses that could be towed from place to place according to the shifting fortunes of fishing or logging. When the people of Pender Harbour went to visit their kinfolk or gathered for community "dos," they almost always travelled by boat. "The old community hall at Irvines Landing didn't have one parking space, and what's more it didn't need one," recalls one Pender Harbour old-timer. "Local travel was largely a matter of taking a boat as far as you could and walking the rest of the way."

Pender Harbour

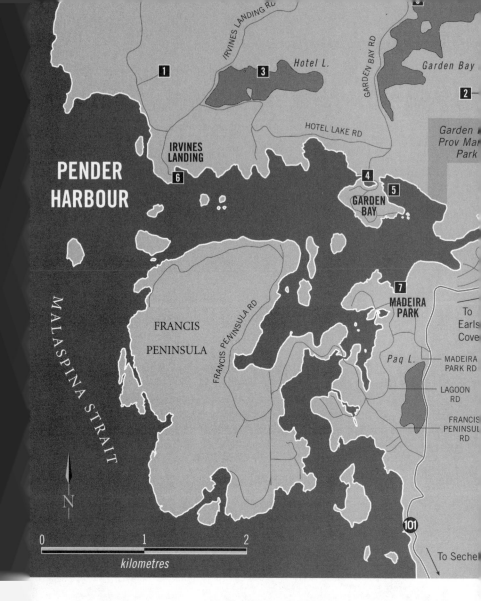

In the last forty years or so, roads have been tattooed on the arms of the harbour. Cars have replaced boats as the transport of choice among Pender Harbour residents, and Madeira Park has replaced Irvines Landing, former site of the Union Steamships wharf, as the commercial centre of Pender Harbour because it is closer to the highway. You have your pick of destinations if you want to explore Pender Harbour by car. The most picturesque side trip is by way of **Garden Bay Road** (left from Highway 101 at the gas station) to Garden Bay. This country road curves past placid Garden Bay Lake, a lovely place to stop for a picnic and a swim, or some fishing or canoeing. If you are beguiled by the combination of quiet countryside and picturesque seacoast, you may want to put down temporary roots in one of the nearby campsites or check into a room in Garden Bay or at a nearby B&B.

Postcard-pretty **Garden Bay**, with its yacht club, marinas, general store, restaurants and heritage inn, is a great place to view Pender Harbour's eclectic fleet of boats. You can arrange boat charters or cruises to Jervis Inlet and Princess Louisa Inlet (see p. 75) from either Garden Bay or Madeira Park. (For more information call the Pender Harbour InfoCentre, 1-604-883-2561, open July–August.) Enjoy a fine meal on the deck of the Garden Bay Hotel Restaurant, with its view of the yacht club, or visit the historic **Sundowner Inn** which overlooks Hospital Bay. The Sundowner was once St. Mary's Hospital, the first one on the lower Sunshine Coast and at one time accessible only by sea. Before it was built in 1930, loggers hurt in the woods or any other resident in a medical emergency had to be taken to Vancouver via a long journey by water. The Sundowner Inn has a restaurant with an unforgettable view, and hosts readings and other community events. It also sponsors the biannual (in odd-numbered years) Mission Boat Gathering to celebrate the coast's historic mission hospitals and ships.

Pender Harbour Hikes and Lakes

If you can fit in only one hike during your visit to this area, go to the top of **Mt. Daniel**, protected as part of the **Garden Bay Provincial Marine Park**. From the top you'll get sweeping views of the whole of Pender Harbour in all its complex beauty. Mt. Daniel was once a place of ritual for the Sechelts, and it is still considered sacred ground. Access is by way of a dirt road marked by a handmade sign on

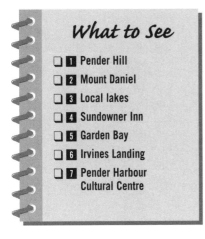

A decaying netshed illustrates the area's fishing history

Pender Harbour Recreation, Accommodations and Services

Recreation	**Campgrounds**
Bicycle rentals	RV Parks
Kayak/Canoe rentals	
Fishing charters	**Services**
Dive charters	Restaurants
Golf course	Pubs
Major hiking trails	Cafés
Parks	Bank (ATM)
	Grocery stores
Accommodations	Service station
Bed & Breakfasts	Marinas
Motels	Shopping centre
Hotels	Gift shops
Resorts	InfoCentre (seasonal)
Cottages	

Garden Bay Road 3.4 km from Highway 101.

For an easier, shorter hike and another commanding view of Pender Harbour, climb **Pender Hill**. Sechelt sentries were once posted here to watch for enemy raiders approaching by canoe from the north. To get there, turn left off Highway 101 onto Garden Bay Road, which turns right onto Irvines Landing Road, then right again onto Lee Road. Look for the Pender Hill sign about 1 km up Lee Road. Feel free to park along the roadside at any of the lakes you pass (Garden Bay, Mixal, Hotel) and dive in for a dip. On your way back to the highway, stop at **Roosendal farm** (open seasonally) just off Garden Bay Road for some fresh vegetables.

From Pender Harbour, Highway 101 winds northward past **Sakinaw Lake** and **Ruby Lake** where you can kayak, canoe, swim, or fish for trout. Both private and public boat launches are located on these lakes (look for the signs).

Skookumchuck

Next comes the turnoff to the little village of Egmont (pop. 120) about 6 km off the highway. Egmont straddles Sechelt Inlet just north of the famous Skookumchuck rapids. Apparently newcomers around the turn of the century couldn't decide which side of the inlet to settle on, so they bounced around from side to side. Water taxis still ferry folks across to North Egmont on the far side of the inlet. Egmont is small but picturesque enough to have been chosen as the backdrop for a TV series called *Ritter's Cove*, about the adventures of a float plane pilot.

The big attraction in Egmont is the Skookumchuck rapids—a highly recommended stop. Turn right from Highway 101 onto Egmont Road, then drive about 6 km to the **Skookumchuck Narrows Provincial Park** parking lot. The 4-km hike to the rapids is very easy and extremely pleasant. The wide, well-groomed trail, which winds through groves of sword fern beneath a green canopy of stately alders and mossy broad-leafed maples, is at least half the pleasure. It ends at viewpoints over Skookumchuck rapids where, if you get there at the right time, the sight and sound of the foaming whitewater tidal cataract in full fury—whirlpools and all—will make an unforgettable impression. In Chinook, the language used for trade among

Skookumchuck rapids

A wharf at Egmont, Jervis Inlet behind

Native groups and white traders across the Pacific Northwest for many decades, *skookum* is "strong" or "turbulent" and *chuck* is "water." These tidal rapids, among the largest on the west coast, deserve the name. Visit them when the tides are at their peak, for the most spectacular show. For information on tides, check the local newspapers, *Coast Independent* (604-886-4003), or call Bathgate's Store and Marina in Egmont (604-883-2222).

The waters near the rapids are a favourite haunt for experienced divers because of the exotic sea life, and "extreme" kayakers often tempt fate on its foaming lip. But caution is the by-word around these waters. In the old days, children playing near the "Skook" were tied to trees for their own safety, and more than a dozen people have drowned in the Skookumchuck. In fact, according to old Harry Roberts, "the gravest danger was to those of us who became so used to going through that familiarity bred, if not contempt, at least a certain disregard and one cannot disregard the sea, particularly at the Skookum Chuck." Harry had learned this lesson the hard way. He had once tried to push his boat *Chack Chack* through the rapids on a strong ebb tide, but the boat was caught in a whirlpool and thrown so high up onto a rocky islet that he couldn't get it back into the water until high tide the next day.

Egmont is also a popular departure point for cruises up Jervis Inlet, one of the most splendid trips you can take in British Columbia. About 50 km up the inlet from Egmont is **Princess Louisa Inlet** and the magnificent **Chatterbox Falls**, a spot so special and so beautiful it leaves most visitors at a loss for words. Not the mystery writer Erle Stanley Gardner, however. "Perhaps an atheist could view it and remain an atheist, but I doubt it," Gardner wrote. "One views the scenery with bared head and choking feeling of the throat. It is more than beautiful. It is sacred." Thanks to James F. "Mac" Macdonald, who gave this slice of paradise in trust to the public, there is now a provincial marine park in the inlet. For information about day cruises up the Princess Louisa Inlet contact the Egmont Marina (604-883-2222).

Important Numbers

Emergency 911
Health clinic 604-883-2764
InfoCentre 604-883-2561

THE UPPER COAST

Lund

Cranberry Lake

Highlights

Deep fjords and
rugged mountains

Prime kayaking and
diving spots

Myriad hiking trails

Pulp mill and forestry tours

Lake and
saltwater fishing

Mountain climbing

Great camping

E arls Cove, past Pender Harbour on Highway 101, is the jumping-off point for the upper Sunshine Coast. From here you cross Jervis Inlet on a 50-minute ferry voyage. Be sure to go out onto the ferry deck for a wide-angle view of Sunshine Coast fjord country, where rain clouds slam against the rugged Coast Mountains, and the green water is hundreds of fathoms deep in places. What you see is very little changed from what met Captain Vancouver's eyes as he travelled the trackless wilderness through wide **Agamemnon Channel** and then east up Jervis Inlet one damp morning in mid-June 1792. The channel's size once again raised Vancouver's hopes of discovering the Northwest Passage. "The width of this channel still continuing, again flattered us with discovering a breach in the eastern range of snowy mountains," he wrote in his journal, "notwithstanding the disappointment we had met with in Howe's Sound." But by the next afternoon they had reached the head of the inlet and, Vancouver noted sadly, "all our hopes vanished." Vancouver

What to See

- ☐ **1** To Chatterbox Falls
- ☐ **2** Lois Lake
- ☐ **3** Mermaid Cove Provincial Park
- ☐ **4** Lang Creek Hatchery
- ☐ **5** Willingdon Beach Park
- ☐ **6** Inland Lake and hikes

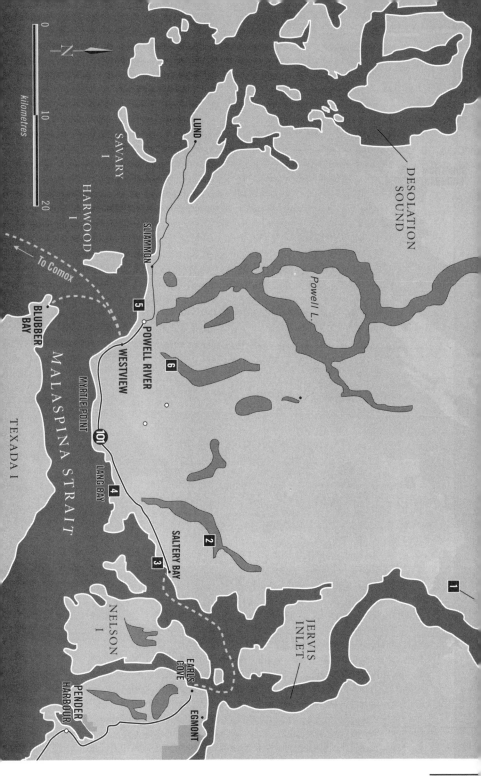

kilometres

0

10

20

N

DESOLATION
SOUND

LUND

SAVARY
I

HARWOOD
I

SLIAMMON

To Comox

BLUBBER
BAY

MALASPINA STRAIT

TEXADA I

MYRTLE POINT

WESTVIEW

POWELL RIVER

Powell L.

5

6

101

LANG BAY

4

SALTERY BAY

2

3

1

JERVIS
INLET

NELSON
I

EARLS
COVE

PENDER
HARBOUR

EGMONT

Under sail in Jervis Inlet

never again mentioned the quest for the Northwest Passage in his journal. Today many kayakers crisscross Vancouver's ghostly wake as they explore one of the west coast's prime kayaking territories. For more details and maps, see *Paddling the Sunshine Coast* (box p. 57). In fact, it's a favourite haunt for boaters of all kinds in the peak summer months. The area is justly famous for its awe-inspiring scenery.

The ferry docks at Saltery Bay, named for a Japanese salmon saltery that stood on stilts out in the bay early this century. The saltery is long gone, but the name has stuck. Many travellers on this route drive off the ferry and head straight for Powell River, the economic centre of the region. (In fact, Sechelt Peninsula-ites tend to call the whole upper Sunshine Coast "Powell River.") The drive to Powell River (you're on Highway 101 again) through second-growth forest with occasional glimpses of the ocean is quick and pleasant. But there are several intriguing turnoffs along the way.

About 2 km from the ferry terminal is **Saltery Bay Mermaid Cove Provincial Park**. This surprisingly uncrowded 45-site campground on a beautiful waterfront site is a great base for exploring the upper Sunshine Coast. (For information 604-898-3678. For reservations, phone Discovery Camping, 1-800-689-9025.) It has forested campsites, beaches, ocean views, a short hiking trail to Little Saltery Falls, a boat launch—and an unexpected extra. Eighteen metres underwater at Mermaid Cove is a buxom bronze mermaid with flowing tresses, upraised hand and delicate fish-scaled tail. This alluring 3-metre-tall statue known as the **Emerald Maiden** is a favourite with divers, and the beginner/intermediate dive site is wheelchair accessible. About 2 km farther up the road, look for signs for the Saltery Bay picnic site, where you will get to another beginner dive site called **Octopus City**. Here scuba divers can find great Pacific octopuses lurking among the rocks.

About 11 km up the road from Saltery Bay is the turnoff to the **Powell Forest Canoe Route** (opposite Louberts Road) where a logging road leads to **Lois Lake Forest Service Recreation Site** and the start of the route. Check with the Forest Service for a route map and information about local logging activity at 7077 Duncan St, Powell River (or phone 604-485-0700). The 80-km route, known for its magnificent scenery, winds through twelve lakes with about 10 km of portages between Lois Lake and Powell Lake. (You can also start at Powell Lake just outside Powell River and end at Lois Lake, but the portaging is much harder uphill.) Most paddlers plan on 5 to 7 days to enjoy great swimming, hiking and scenery along the way. A shorter route, which takes about 3 days, is another option.

Two other turnoffs may tempt you to stop before you reach Powell River. Turn down Lang Bay Road to **Palm Beach Regional Park** and relax on one of the coast's most beautiful white sand beaches. Just past Lang Bay is the turnoff to **Lang Creek Hatchery and Spawning Channel**. (Turn onto Duck Lake Rd, then right after the bridge and follow the signs to the hatchery.) A visit in September or October is a special treat. Hundreds of spawning salmon leap up the channel and eagles hover near the Lang Creek estuary waiting to swoop down on them. (For more information, 604-485-7612.)

The Powell River Area

Westview, once an independent community but now part of the city of Powell River, is just 31 km from Saltery Bay. This is the commercial and residential heart of present-day Powell River—the largest community on the Sunshine Coast with an estimated area population of 20,000 and the terminal for ferries to Texada Island and Vancouver Island.

Historically, Powell River was a one-industry town. The local pulp and paper mill has been the single biggest employer since the turn of the century, and it's still the dynamo of economic life. What made a thriving pulp and paper industry possible was the huge Powell Forest which stretched for miles along the coast and offered a steady supply of timber for decades. But all those trees—combined with mountains, lakes and ocean—are also a big part of Powell River's growing tourist trade. There are outdoor adventures galore, and Powell River is dedicated to helping visitors make the most of their stay. Local entrepreneurs have covered all the bases—biking, fishing, hiking, boat

Pacifica Pulp & Paper Mill

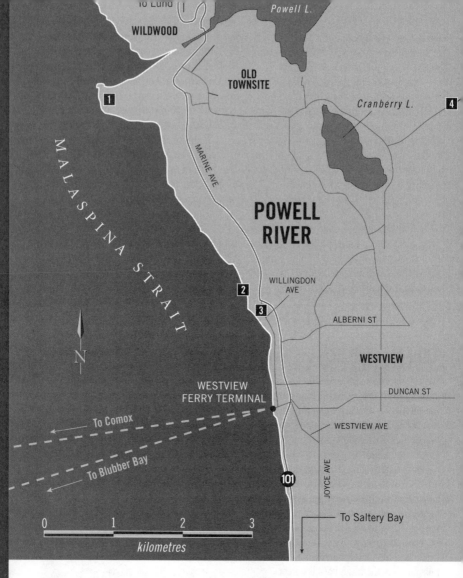

Powell L.

WILDWOOD

OLD
TOWNSITE

Cranberry L.

1

4

MALASPINA STRAIT

MARINE AVE

**POWELL
RIVER**

N

WILLINGDON
AVE

2

3

ALBERNI ST

WESTVIEW

WESTVIEW
FERRY TERMINAL

DUNCAN ST

To Comox

WESTVIEW AVE

To Blubber Bay

JOYCE AVE

101

0   1   2   3

To Saltery Bay

kilometres

charters, kayaking, camping, golfing, diving, and even houseboating on Powell Lake. Do-it-yourselfers can hire professional guides and get a full range of equipment. You can also arrange cruises through Desolation Sound and Princess Louisa Inlet. Ask the helpful people at the Powell River InfoCentre for what you need to enjoy the great out-of-doors (4690 Marine Dr, 604-485-4701).

What to See

- ☐ **1** Pacifica
  Pulp & Paper Mill
- ☐ **2** Willingdon Beach Park
- ☐ **3** Museum
- ☐ **4** To Inland Lake
  hiking trails

Powell River Hikes

Hiking is the number one inquiry at the InfoCentre, and new trails have been built and linked up to old ones to meet the growing demand.

Just north of **Willingdon Beach Park** on Powell River's waterfront is a wide, easy forested trail—once a railroad bed and later a secluded "lovers' lane"—that takes about 20 minutes to hike. Kids will have fun exploring obsolete logging equipment and looking at tree identification signs along the path. Combine the walk with a picnic and swim at the park and you've got a perfect family outing. (Willingdon Park also has 70 campsites for those who want to make it a longer

▶ **Upper Coast Annual Events**

July
Canada Day Celebrations
Kathaumixw Choral Festival (Biennial)
Texada Sandcastle Days
Texada Farmer's Markets (July to October)
Logger Sports (mid-July)

August
Blackberry Festival
Lund Family Daze

September
Sunshine Folk Fest

For more information, Powell River InfoCentre **604-485-4701**

adventure.) Another great family destination is the **Inland (Loon) Lake Trail**. The wide, mostly flat trail makes a 13-km sweep around beautiful Inland Lake. And it's wheelchair accessible, with wharves and a specially designed cabin for the physically challenged. From the highway, turn right at the traffic light at Alberni, then left on Manson Avenue to Cassiar Street, then right on Cassiar which becomes Yukon. Follow Yukon to Haslam Street, turn right on Haslam to the first junction and take the left fork, Inland Lake Road, to the marked turnoff to the recreation area.

Khartoum Lake. The Sunshine Coast offers dozens of Forest Service campsites.

From the Inland Lake Trail you can continue along the **Confederation Lake Trail** to Fiddlehead Farm. Fair warning: this is a strenuous day's trek. Think about phoning ahead to the farm to arrange a boat ride back down Powell Lake to Powell Lake Marina, just off the Highway 101 north of town.

Fiddlehead Farm, once a back-to-the-land 1970s commune, is now a hostel and a 32-ha working farm all rolled into one special wilderness experience. Most visitors arrive at Fiddlehead Farm by boat from Powell Lake Marina. Many plan to stay a week or so to take full advantage of the recreational possibilities in the area's beautiful lakes and mountains. And quite a few wind up staying even longer. They fall in love with the serene beauty of this unique homestead community and enjoy the generous hospitality of host Linda Schreiber and her family. Hostellers happily help out with milking, weeding the huge organic garden, slopping the pigs, milking the cows, collecting eggs, picking corn and zucchini, freezing blackberries, canning tomatoes, baking bread, cutting and stacking firewood—or they invent their own chores. After the work is done, they wander off to canoe, swim, fish or hike, or else they hang around with other folks from around the world in the farm's comfy kitchen, relax in the sauna, snooze on the verandah or spend a quiet moment in the "floating" meditation centre built by a visiting Japanese architect. The charge for room and board includes daily work on the farm. But you can pay a little bit extra to forgo the chores and simply enjoy the leisurely delights of the place. (Box 421, Powell River, BC V8A 5C2, phone 604-483-3018.)

Be sure to ask about the 180-km **Sunshine Coast Trail** (almost complete) that runs all the way from Desolation Sound to Saltery Bay. Twice as long as the West Coast Trail, this backpacker's trail is still a little-known gem. If you prefer daypacks to backpacks, you can access the trail at various points, including Fiddlehead Farm, for a day's outing. Plans are in the works for the "Tour de Powell River," a locally sponsored event that lets hikers choose how many days they want to hike the trail and provides home comforts (and the hiker's backpack) at each day's end. For information and maps, contact the Powell River InfoCentre (604-485-4701) or the Powell River Parks and Wilderness Society (PRPAWS) (P.O. Box 345, Powell River, BC V8A 5C2).

Log booms behind "The Hulks" floating breakwater

Upper Coast Recreation, Accommodations and Services

Recreation	Campgrounds
Bicycle rentals	RV parks
Kayak/Canoe rentals	**Services**
Fishing charters	InfoCentre
Dive charters	Restaurants
Golf courses	Cafés
Major hiking trails	Banks (ATMs)
Parks	Shopping malls
Accommodations	Gas/service stations
Bed & Breakfasts	Post office
Cottage/Cabin rentals	Hospital
Hotels	Medical clinic
Motels	

Powell River's Historic Townsite

North of Willingdon Beach Park is the Powell River Historic Townsite, the birthplace of Powell River and a fine example of a turn-of-the-century company town. The Powell River Company built the town in 1911 and ran it until 1955. The Townsite, as it's known locally, was the product of the British City Garden Movement—an extraordinary effort at town planning that combined gardening and green belts with social engineering and programmed company pride. Rows of workers' houses run out from the mill site in a tightly organized grid. Streets were laid out with power lines tucked into back alleys and swaths of trees down the street fronts. Workers and their families were encouraged to take pride in their gardens and compete in annual garden contests. Playing fields, banks, a school, a library, a hospital, an apartment block, a gymnasium, a movie theatre (said to be the longest-running cinema in BC), a grand community centre called Dwight Hall and, of course, the Company Store, all materialized according to plan. One street of substantial homes known as "Bosses' Row" tacitly declared the difference between managers and shift workers. The first commercial building in Powell River was a hotel and pub. It was built conveniently close to the mill gates to slake workers' post-shift thirst. Churches were constructed farther up the way to salvage their souls. On the **Lawn Bowling Green**, built in 1921, you can still see members out in their white garb enjoying friendly competition. Drop in at the **Powell River InfoCentre** to find out about guided or self-guided tours of the Townsite, or call the Townsite Heritage Society *at least a day in advance* (604-485-2222) to arrange a tour. You can also tour the **Pacifica Pulp and Paper Mill** in the summer. Tours are booked through the InfoCentre 250-485-4701. Once the world's biggest mill, it still churns out impressive quantities of forest products.

From the mill site you get a great view out across Malaspina Strait. Near to shore are the town's trademark **Hulks**—ten old ships (mostly concrete-hulled American freighters from World War II) that have been anchored, ballasted and chained together to make an extraordinary floating breakwater. Originally intended to protect the mill's harbour and log pond from waves kicked up by fierce southeasterly and northwesterly winds, the Hulks now do double duty as a favourite haulout spot for migratory **sea lions**.

The people of Powell River have always had clubs and activities galore. You'll find a first-rate **recreation centre**, and the **Powell River Historic Museum** (604-485-2222) complete with a mockup of the legendary hermit Billy Goat

Important Numbers

Ambulance **604-485-4211**

Fire **604-485-4321**

Police **604-485-6255**

Hospital **604-485-3211**

Medical Clinic **604-485-6261**

Marine Distress **1-800-567-5111**

Lund Water Taxi **604-483-9749**

Westview Ferry **604-485-2943**

Saltery Bay Ferry **604-487-9333**

InfoCentre **604-485-4701**

fax **604-485-2822**

e-mail **prvb@prcn.org**

The renowned Cranberry Pottery Shop

Smith's shack up on Powell Lake. (Smith apparently got his nickname from his shackmate goats. It was rumoured that this sharpshooting recluse had murdered an American architect and then hightailed it into the Canadian bush.) The Powell River community also puts on a full program of summer festivals (see Annual Events, p. 81), including the justly famous biannual **International Choral Kathaumixw** (pronounced Ka-thou-mew). *Kathaumixw* is a Salish word that means "a gathering of different peoples" and is it ever! As many as thirty choirs—a lively mix of children's, women's, men's, youth and adult choirs—come together from more than a dozen countries to share their love of music in Powell River. Kathaumixw was the brainchild of Boys Choir conductor Don James and his friend Dal Matterson. In true Powell River tradition, they turned a thought inspired by a hiking trip into a major international event. Kathaumixw enjoys the enthusiastic support of Powell Riverites who, every two years, happily open their doors to the world (604-485-9633).

T'eshusm

The Sliammon people, a Coast Salish group, have lived for more than 2,000 years at the village of T'eshusm, 3 km north of Powell River. The Sliammon are closely related to the Klahoose people of Toba Inlet and Cortes Island and to the Homathco people of Bute Inlet. They share the same language, *ey7a7juuthem*, a Coast Salish language whose name means "talk the language." (The 7s stand for a sound not found in English.) The Sliammon have always been a fishing people, and today they operate a fish hatchery on Sliammon Creek, the same river where their ancestors once caught salmon in stone weirs at the river mouth. The hatchery is open to the public (604-483-4111).

A restored building in Powell River's Heritage Townsite

Texada Island's unique "flower rocks"

Texada Island

Ten times every day a BC ferry makes the 35-minute crossing from Powell River (Westview terminal) to Texada Island. Known as "The Rock," this mountainous, mineral-rich island rises out of the water beyond Powell River like the humped back of a giant whale. Whaling was in fact an early industrial activity on Texada. **Blubber Bay**, where the ferry docks on Texada, was once a whaling station where bloody carcasses were processed. Now it is the site of a working limestone quarry, one of three quarries where many Texada Islanders earn a living. The quarry at Blubber Bay alone ships out 1.8 million tonnes of limestone a year.

Mining has been Texada's big industry since the 1880s, by which time the island's riches—iron ore, copper and gold—had all been discovered. Seven mines began churning out minerals and by 1910 Texada's **Van Anda** was a genuine boom town, the largest west coast city north of Seattle. It boasted an opera house, three hotels with saloons, stores, and even a newspaper, the *Coast Miner*. The town's streets—Aladdin, Midas and Copper Queen—suggest the fortunes made (and lost) in Texada's heyday. Little remains of those heady days, and Texada has eased back into quieter rhythms. One paved main road runs south from Blubber Bay to Van Anda and on to Gillies Bay. A gravel road runs back through the centre of the island to Van Anda. Texada offers biking, hiking, fishing, swimming, scuba diving, birdwatching and rock hounding (a greenish porphyrite called the "Texada flower rock" is a much-sought-after prize). You can camp at **Shelter Point Park**,

Texada Island Recreation, Accommodations and Services

Recreation	RV Park
Bicycle rentals	Campground
Kayak/Canoe rentals	**Services**
Fishing charters	Restaurant
Dive charters	Deli
Golf courses	Grocery stores
Major hiking trails	Markets
Parks	Credit union (no ATM)
Accommodations	Gas/Service station
Bed & Breakfasts	Galleries/Gift shops
Hotel	Medical clinic
Motel	(Gillies Bay)

Important Numbers

Ambulance **604-485-4211**

Fire **604-485-4321**

Police **604-486-7717**

Medical Emergency **604-483-6353**

Police non-emergency
604-486-7258

or find hotel, motel and B&B accommodations. If you go, take your vehicle or your bicycle rather than walking on the ferry. The island is big—about 86 km long and 8 km wide—and it's a fair distance from place to place. (For more information and a Texada map, check at the Powell River InfoCentre, 604-485-4701.)

Looking out from the boat basin at Lund

Lund, Savary Island and Desolation Sound

Lund

A trip to the upper Sunshine Coast wouldn't be complete without a drive to the little village of Lund. It sits at the end of Highway 101, also known as the Pan American Highway. This road starts in Chile and snakes its way north up the Americas for 24,000 km before it hits salt water at the government wharf at Lund. Of course, the people of Lund describe it as starting at the Lund government wharf and snaking its way south to Puerto Monte, Chile. Whichever way you care to see it, driving to the end/beginning of the road is a pleasure—and a well-recognized pleasure. Mark Vonnegut, the son of writer Kurt Vonnegut, once wrote of his 1970s sojourn in this area: "If I was going to find what I was looking for, the end of 101 seemed like where it would be." Vonnegut did go up Highway 101 past the Powell River Townsite, all right, and across the bridge. But then he took the fork to the right and landed up at Powell Lake instead of Lund. It was serendipity (and a good real estate agent) that led him 19 km up Powell Lake to found a commune with friends on the site of present-day Fiddlehead Farm (see p.82).

Lund was founded in 1889 by the two Swedish brothers, Fred and Charles Thulin, who—like Harry Roberts and Bert Whittaker of the lower Sunshine Coast—seem to have acted on the motto "If you build the wharf (and the store, post office, and hotel) they will come." And come they did. Steamers stopped at the Lund wharf to buy slab wood for fuel to make the run north. They also dropped off the mail. Loggers and fishermen rowed in from miles around to pick up their letters and stock up on provisions while they were at it. Because rowing back home again was hard work and life in the bush could be lonely, folks often stayed over in the Thulins' hotel to socialize and down a few "wet ones." Not long after, summer guests started arriving on the Union steamship SS *Cassiar* to holiday at Lund. By 1911, business had picked up so much the brothers opened a big new hotel. The imposing **Lund Hotel**, with two dining rooms, a lounge and a pub, stood amidst gardens where roses and honeysuckle perfumed the air.

The gardens are gone now, but you can still enjoy the pleasures of the historic old hotel. A venerable west coast landmark, it remains a favourite watering hole for locals and tourists. You can even rent rooms if you want to hang around longer (604-414-0700). The sea views from the pub and restaurant are well worth the price of a

Lund Area Recreation, Accommodations and Services

Recreation	Hotel
Bicycle rentals	Campground
Kayak/Canoe rentals	
Fishing charters	**Services**
Dive charters	Restaurant
Golf courses	Pub
Major hiking trails	Cafés
Parks	Gas/Service station
	Marina/Marine repair
Accommodations	Gift shops
Bed & Breakfasts	Grocery Store
Cottage/Cabin rentals	

Important Numbers

Ambulance **604-485-4211**

Fire **604-485-4321**

Police **604-485-6255**

InfoCentre (Powell River)
604-485-4701, fax **604-485-2822**,
e-mail **prvb@prcn.org**

Lund Water Taxi **604-483-9749**

The historic Lund Hotel

beer or a dinner. The hotel is also home to several shops and services, including a general store and liquor outlet, a really good ice cream shop, a kayaking outfitter, a laundromat and a marina. Near the dock is a bakery where the scent of fresh-baked cinnamon buns is irresistible.

The village, too, retains a pleasing aura of coastal pioneer life when settlers' homes were often huddled together, their lives linked by cedar boardwalks along the waterfront. You'll find some of the original **boardwalk** wrapped around the little bay by the hotel as well as a few of the original settlers' houses. Stroll out along the boardwalk and dip into the quaint **craft shop** or work your way past the **water wheel** and around to the **Carvers Coffeehouse**. This is another inviting place to put your feet up and watch the passing scene. Lund is a great little spot to enjoy the coast—it's picturesque, easygoing, slightly down-at-the-heels, and very down-home friendly.

Savary Island

If you notice a hubbub down at the Lund dock, it's probably time for the water taxi to Savary Island (604-483-9749). The only other ways to get to Savary are by private boat or by Harbour Air's seaplane (604-278-3478). Taking the water taxi must rate as the modern-day equivalent of Boat Day back in Union steamship times. Kids, dogs, old folks, year-round residents, Savary "summer people" and travelling daytrippers all mill around chatting and laughing and getting tangled up in the piles of stuff. Flats of beer, old bikes, a bed, boxes of groceries, variegated coolers, fishing gear, a child's stroller, a couple of dogs—somehow it all gets sorted out and onto the boat for the 10-minute crossing to Savary. At the last minute a passenger suddenly remembers that she forgot the bread! Everyone waits patiently as she rushes back up to the bakery for a warm baguette. The casual, good-natured, barefoot feel of the water taxi trip is just the right introduction to Savary Island. Even George Vancouver, despondent because he had not found the Northwest Passage, perked up when he got to Savary, and noted in his log that it had "a beauty such as we have seldom enjoyed." For centuries, the Sliammon had known this island as Ayhus (the two-headed serpent) for its narrow crescent shape, but on Vancouver's map it

The world's largest Arbutus

A peaceful anchorage in Desolation Sound

Vancouver's map it became "Savary's Isle" for an admiral in the French navy.

Fringed with white beaches and lapped by clear warm water, Savary Island quickly became a popular holiday destination. The white sand beach runs in both directions from the wharf and the water's warm, so grab your towel and sunscreen and go for it. Kids will love scouring the shore for shells and sand dollars. The island has no electricity and only a few cars, so relaxation and fun-in-the-sun are definitely the by-words here.

Savary has no campsites and no public facilities, except for a small restaurant and store. To find out about B&Bs or cottage rentals call Rosemarie Primrose (604-483-4789).

Desolation Sound

Lund is also the gateway to the 423-ha **Copeland Islands** (known locally as the Ragged Islands) **Provincial Marine Park** as well as 8,256-ha **Desolation Sound Provincial Marine Park**, the largest marine park in BC. Desolation Sound got its name from Captain Vancouver, who saw a dearth of significant geography and a lack of berries and fish to feed his men. "Not a fish at the bottom could be tempted to take the hook," he complained. But most visitors find Desolation Sound astonishingly beautiful. In the height of summer, as many as 300 boaters can be found cruising, paddling, kayaking or sailing its protected waters. The centrepiece of Desolation Sound is a delightful sprinkling of islands in a wide bay near the park's northeast boundary called **Prideaux Haven**. The warm waters here (26°C in summer) delight swimmers and scuba divers, and—Vancouver's experience notwithstanding—sea life abounds, including crabs, prawns, red snapper, mussels and tons of oysters. Be sure to follow fishing regulations for fish and shellfish, and respect commercial oyster leases. You can rent sailboats, powerboats, canoes or kayaks, arrange charters or book scheduled tours to explore the Ragged Islands and Desolation Sound. Contact the Powell River InfoCentre for details (604-485-4701).

SOUTHERN VANCOUVER ISLAND

DUNCAN

Cowichan L.

LAKE COWICHAN

PORT RENFREW

SALT SPRING ISLAND

SIDNEY

SAANICH

VICTORIA

SOOKE

JUAN DE FUCA STRAIT

CANADA
USA

LEGEND

Highway
Secondary Road
Logging Road
Park
Urban Area
Lake

CHAPTER 3
VICTORIA & AREA

Victoria's magnificent Parliament Buildings

Victoria is on an island—Vancouver Island—so you'll probably be getting there by plane, or helicopter, or by ferry from Port Angeles, Anacortes, Bellingham or Seattle in Washington state or from Vancouver on the British Columbia mainland. Most visitors arrive aboard a BC Ferry from Vancouver's Tsawwassen terminal, about a 45-minute drive south of Vancouver. Victoria-bound BC ferries sail through Active Pass and the beautiful Southern Gulf Islands, one of the most scenic passages in all of the BC Ferries extended coastal empire. En route you just might see orcas (killer whales) or dolphins just off the Tsawwassen terminal, and you're likely to spot seals and eagles in Active

Old Customs House, Bastion Square

Pass. If you're lucky, you'll sail aboard one of the two new S-class "Superferries." With their bright, clean, state-of-the-art facilities, these ferries are the pride of the British Columbia Ferry Corporation fleet.

From the ferry terminal at Swartz Bay, Hwy 17 (known locally as the Pat Bay Highway) takes you down the Saanich Peninsula toward Victoria, about a 30-minute drive to the south. The major attraction in this neck of the woods (or, more accurately, this pleasant patch of farmland) is the world-famous Butchart Gardens (see pp. 113–15). (Watch for signs along Hwy 17). Because tourism is big business, you'll find a full soup-to-nuts menu of visitor attractions right across the Greater Victoria area. But visitors typically start a holiday by heading straight through Victoria's sprawling suburbs and shopping malls to downtown Victoria on the Inner Harbour.

VICTORIA

Chinatown lic

Heritage in James Bay

Highlights

*Year-round
temperate climate*

*Beautiful parks
and gardens*

*Gorgeous ocean and
mountain views*

*Charming turn-of-the-
century architecture*

Whale watching

*Exploring unique
downtown shops*

I t's no wonder that readers of *Condé Nast Traveler* rated Victoria the number one city in the world for ambiance. Victoria is blessed with a drop-dead gorgeous physical setting. It's lapped by deep blue Pacific Ocean waters and backed by rolling hills where tree-shaded roads wind past stately homes in deep green gardens. And for a final touch, the steel blue mountains of Washington state's Olympic Peninsula decorate the horizon across the Juan de Fuca Strait. Warmer and drier than Vancouver, Victoria is also known for its year-round livability. Its weather station is the only one in Canada to have recorded a whole frost-free winter.

Victoria also delights visitors with its charming aura of Britishness and its remarkably fine collection of turn-of-the-century architecture. Victoria has preserved its downtown heritage buildings, and the city's Tudor Revival facades, whimsical Victorian homes, cricket pitches and rose gardens, antique

What to See
(outside of downtown)

- ☐ **1** BC Ferries to Vancouver & Gulf Islands
- ☐ **2** Butchart Gardens
- ☐ **3** Mt. Douglas
- ☐ **4** University of Victoria
- ☐ **5** Mt. Tolmie
- ☐ **6** Craigflower Farmhouse
- ☐ **7** Fort Rodd Hill National Historic Site

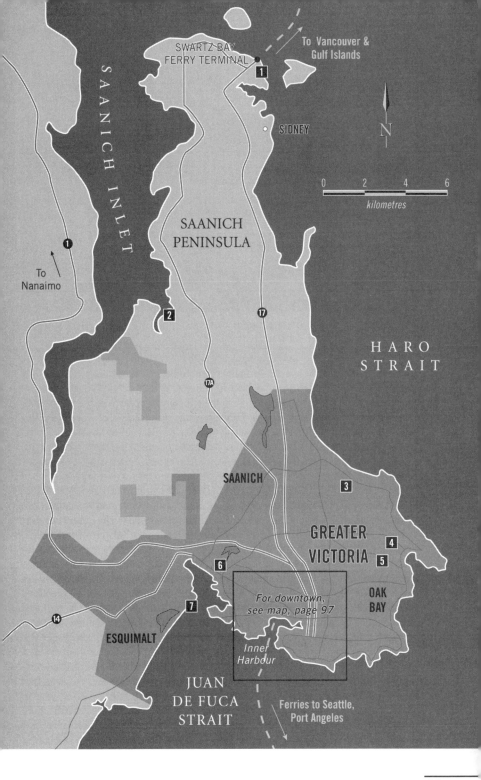

SWARTZ BAY
FERRY TERMINAL

To Vancouver &
Gulf Islands

1

SIDNEY

N

SAANICH
INLET

SAANICH
PENINSULA

0   2   4   6
kilometres

To
Nanaimo

1

2

17

HARO
STRAIT

17A

SAANICH

3

GREATER
VICTORIA

4

5

6

OAK
BAY

14

7

For downtown,
see map, page 97

ESQUIMALT

Inner
Harbour

JUAN
DE FUCA
STRAIT

Ferries to Seattle,
Port Angeles

The Empress Hotel at Victoria's Inner Harbour

shops and antiquarian bookstores are redolent with British Empire elegance. Victoria has also kept its new buildings in scale with their lovely older neighbours. As a result the city is still people-sized, and it has the quiet friendliness of a small city. Shopkeepers are happy to help a disoriented tourist set off in the right direction. Local residents point out their favourite restaurants or special little out-of-the-way places at the drop of a hat. Walkers out for their daily regimen of salt air and exercise greet out-of-town strollers with a briskly cheerful "Good morning!" Victorians may be quietly smug about their delightful city, but they are gracious enough to welcome newcomers to the pleasures of their little piece of paradise.

Downtown Victoria is so compact that you can just put on your walking shoes and head to nearby sights. A good first stop is the excellent **Visitor Information Centre**. Look for the jutting Art Deco monolith across from the **Empress Hotel** on the **Inner Harbour**. The centre is crammed with brochures on visitor attractions, festivals, music and theatre, restaurants, accommodations and more. Find out about a lantern-light tour with the **Old Cemeteries Society** of Victoria or a theme tour of the Empress Hotel. Discover where to find a full-sized replica of **Anne Hathaway's straw-roofed cottage** or the "flavour-of-the-month" music festival, from the **TerrifVic Jazz Party** (April) to the **Symphony Splash** (August). Get details on visiting Victoria's **specialty brew pubs** or **boat-building yards**, signing up for a drawing workshop in the gardens of **Government House** or taking a look at Canada's new warships in **Esquimalt Harbour**. And don't overlook the great outdoors. Victoria bills itself as the "Gateway to Outdoor Adventure" and serves up a hearty menu of adventurous fare, including **eco-touring, biking, kayaking, canoeing, camping, hiking, whitewater rafting and diving charters**. (Diving spots right around downtown Victoria are rated as world-class.) **Whale watching tours** are whale-sized in popularity. And if golf is your game, you're in the right place. Greater Victoria with its **nine golf courses**, fine year-round weather, great views and emerald-green landscaping, is a paradise for golfers. To bus it to attractions outside the downtown core, pick up the very helpful free BC Transit booklet Victoria by Bus (24-hour BusLine information 250-382-6161, website www.transitbc.com). Or rent a bike and cycle the city. (Most bike rental outfits offer up bike route maps along with lots of friendly advice. Be sure to ask about the 60-km Galloping Goose Trail, pp. 116–17.)

Victoria:
A Brief History

Victoria's temperate beauty has attracted visitors for more than a century. The city got its start as a fur trade outpost of the Hudson's Bay Company. When HBC officer James Douglas sailed into what is now Victoria's Inner Harbour in the early 1840s, he fell under the spell of the landscape's gentle beauty. Declaring it "a perfect Eden," Douglas chose the Inner Harbour as the place to locate HBC's new western headquarters. He oversaw the growth of the tiny settlement that sprang up around Fort Victoria and ultimately became governor of the two colonies of Vancouver Island and British Columbia. He built himself a fine Georgian colonial home near the harbour, and in December 1858 he penned a description of his winter garden to a faraway friend as a way of describing Victoria's gentle climate: "The weather is at present fine, and the opposite hills still retain their hue of green" he wrote; "a single Castle rose, somewhat faded, was picked yesterday, and the humble daisy, heart's ease, and wall-flower, growing exposed in my garden have not entirely lost their bloom. Those few facts will perhaps give a clearer idea of the climate than any description."

Getting to Victoria

From Vancouver (Tsawwassen) to Victoria (Swartz Bay) 1 hour & 35 minutes crossing time; 8 sailings daily year round.

Non-commercial vehicle reservations (additional charge).

BC Ferry Reservations:
In BC toll-free **1-888-724-5223**
Outside BC **604-444-2390**

BC Ferry 24-hour recorded schedule information: Victoria **250-386-3431**. Anywhere in BC: **1-888-BCFERRY (1-888-223-3779)**, or write: British Columbia Ferry Corporation, 1112 Fort Street, Victoria, BC V8V 4V2, Fax: 250-381-5452, website **www.bcferries.bc.ca**

Washington State Ferries to Victoria area:
Seattle to Victoria The Victoria Clipper *(Passengers only/Summer only)*

The Princess Marguerite III *(Vehicles and passengers/May–Sept only)*

For information: in Victoria **250-382-8100**, in Seattle **206-448-5000** or **1-800-888-2535**, website **www.victoriaclipper.com**

Bellingham to Victoria Victoria San Juan Cruises *(Passengers only/May–Sept only)*

For information: in Bellingham **360-738-8099** or **1-800-443-4552**.

Port Angeles to Victoria Black Ball Transport *(Vehicles and passengers)*

For information: in Victoria **250-386-2202**, in Port Angeles **360-457-4491**.

Victoria Express *(Passengers only/Seasonal)*

For information: in Victoria **250-361-9144** or **1-800-633-1589**

Anacortes to Sidney Washington State Ferries *(Vehicles and passengers)*

For information: in Victoria **250-381-1551** or **250-656-1531**, in Seattle **206-464-6400**.

When the British trading fort blossomed into the small capital city of the new province of British Columbia, its beauty continued to charm visitors. "To realize Victoria," wrote the globe-trotting British writer Rudyard Kipling, "you must take all that the eye admires in Bournemouth, Torquay, the Isle of Wight, the Happy Valley at Hong Kong, the Doon, Sorrento and Camp's Bay—add reminiscences of the Thousand Islands and arrange the whole around the Bay of Naples with some Himalayas for background." Soon, retired British military officers and civil servants—old China hands and ex-India colonials—discovered that in Victoria they could afford an ample lifestyle on their government pensions, complete with substantial houses, landscaped grounds and Chinese servants. They formed social alliances with local tycoons like the coal baron Robert Dunsmuir and nurtured the hothouse civility of a faux-British seacoast city even as the British Empire was crumbling in other far-flung corners of the world. Early entrepreneurs were quick to spot nostalgic attraction of all things British. By 1918 Canadian Pacific Railway publicists were describing Victoria as "a little piece of Old England" to entice well-heeled travellers to the new CPR Empress Hotel.

The opening of the grand Empress Hotel on Victoria's Inner Harbour in 1908 was the beginning of the city's booming tourism industry. Today four million tourists come to Victoria each year. Visitors delight in the city's consciously preserved Britishness along the Inner Harbour—the skirl of a bagpipe played by a kilted piper and bright red double-decker tour buses and horse-drawn carriages at the ready in front of the Empress Hotel. Nearby shops are full of British woollens, Irish linens, Scottish tartans, English bone china, handmade Victorian chocolates and antique British Empire bric-a-brac.

Until the mid-1960s Victoria was a retirement haven caught up in its own colonial British past, an unfailingly charming city but a tad Empire-fusty. But since 1960 the city's population has doubled, and many of the newcomers are a younger breed. The infusion of fresh blood has brought a new liveliness and sophistication to the city—and created a niche for good restaurants, a peppier night life and a slew of cultural events. Now Victoria is a more up-tempo place with plenty to offer sophisticated travellers. (Pick up freebie magazines *Monday*, *Boulevard* and *Pacific Island Gourmet* at downtown shops for the latest word on restaurants and happenings around town.) But Victoria is not a smaller Vancouver. Residents like this cohesive little city because they don't care for the rat-race pace of a bigger city. Even at the height of the summertime tourist bustle, unflappable residents always seem to have time to stop for a chat with neighbours or newcomers.

Downtown Victoria: the Major Attractions

In summer the **harbour causeway** a few steps below the information centre hums with activity. In the distance float planes zoom off the water trailing curtains of sparkling drops as they veer toward Vancouver. The pointed prow of the *Victoria Clipper* noses into the dock with its cargo of Seattle tourists while the huge red *Princess Marguerite III* heading back to Seattle looks almost too big to squeeze past the headlands. At the dock by the causeway a rusty fishing boat ties up next to an ultra-sleek powerboat where nautically clad nobs sip drinks on the upper deck. On the causeway camera-slinging tourists wander past a scattering of **buskers**—a bronzed bongo player here, a wailing guitar picker there, a quartet of Andean flute players up the

A whale watching tour leaving the Inner Harbour.

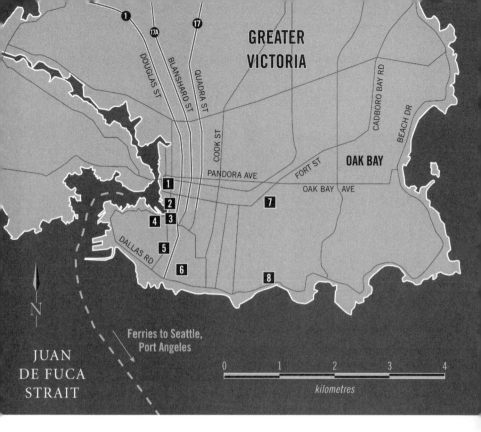

GREATER VICTORIA

DOUGLAS ST
BLANSHARD ST
QUADRA ST
COOK ST
CADBORO BAY RD
BEACH DR
FORT ST
PANDORA AVE
OAK BAY
OAK BAY AVE
DALLAS RD

1
2
4 **3**
5
6
7
8

N

Ferries to Seattle,
Port Angeles

JUAN
DE FUCA
STRAIT

0   1   2   3   4
kilometres

steps. **Artists** settled under bright umbrellas show off their wares. A knot of laughing spectators collects around a **street performer. Whale watchers** zip themselves into red flotation suits as they stride toward a waiting cruise boat at the dock. Busy little green and white **Victoria Harbour Ferries** (250-708-0201) scuttle in and out—and by the way, a harbour ferry ride is a great way to see Victoria from the water. Tour the harbour, pop over to **Fisherman's Wharf** for fish and chips at **Barb's Place** (locals say it's the best!), ride up the **Gorge Waterway** to the reversing falls where river currents battle it out with saltwater inflows. Stop off at **Point Ellice**

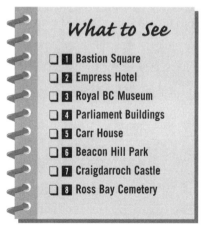

What to See

- ☐ **1** Bastion Square
- ☐ **2** Empress Hotel
- ☐ **3** Royal BC Museum
- ☐ **4** Parliament Buildings
- ☐ **5** Carr House
- ☐ **6** Beacon Hill Park
- ☐ **7** Craigdarroch Castle
- ☐ **8** Ross Bay Cemetery

House and tour the **O'Reilly family's restored Victoria villa and gardens** or take high tea on the old croquet lawn. (Open May–Sept. Reservations 250-380-6506.)

Overlooking the causeway is Victoria's famous landmark, the **Empress Hotel**. With its ivy-covered walls, liveried doormen and opulent Edwardian decor, the Empress is the first stop for many visitors. The hotel was given a $45-million facelift in 1987, which only enhances its status as one of the grandest of the grand old CPR hotels. For a taste of luxury from a bygone era, stroll through the hotel's many elegant shops, eat a curry in the imperial Bengal Room, eye the antique furnishings and portraits of royalty adorning the halls, or take afternoon tea in the ornately columned tea lobby. Don't miss the carved wood finishings in the former library bar, which also houses a fine Native arts gallery.

Victoria's Inner Harbour has been a sea dog's haven since the days of Captain Cook. Here wall plaques commemorate historic ships that have anchored in the harbour, and

Francis Rattenbury

Victoria plays host to events like the Victoria to Maui and **Swiftsure Lightship Classic** yacht races as well as the **Classic Boat Festival**.

The Gorge Waterway angling northwest from the Inner Harbour has two attractively landscaped parks. On the south side, **Kinsmen Gorge Park** with its **manicured gardens, tennis courts, beach, change rooms, food concession and waterside walkway** is a great family destination (off Tillicum Rd). On the north side Gorge Waterway Park, an invitingly landscaped green space that runs west to Craigflower School (2755 Admirals Rd) is perfect for a Sunday promenade.

Victoria's best-known architect, a flamboyant Brit named Francis Rattenbury, designed four of the major buildings on the Inner Harbour—the Empress Hotel, the Crystal Garden, the Parliament Buildings and the CPR Steamship Terminal (now the Royal London Wax Museum). Just behind the Empress on the other side of Douglas Street is the **Crystal Garden**. This glass-roofed conservatory was the largest winter "pleasure garden" in the British Empire in the 1920s, complete with tropical palm trees, trailing bougainvillea vines and canaries in ornate cages. Under its high dome well-dressed matrons sat chatting in the tea rooms, stylish swingers danced to the latest tunes on the dance floor and swimmers cavorted in the largest saltwater pool in Canada. But time was cruel to the building, and the Crystal Garden was an inch away from demolition when it

The picturesque Gorge Waterway

was saved as a heritage site. In its new incarnation the Crystal Garden still houses a **lush tropical garden** as a preserve for more than sixty endangered (and endearing) species. You'll find **fish, exotic birds, free-flying butterflies and the world's smallest monkeys** as well as a "marketplace" of shops and restaurants.

The **Parliament Buildings** at right angles to the Empress Hotel on the corner of Government and Belleville streets rivals the Empress as Victoria's most photographed landmark. Not long after Francis Rattenbury sailed into the Inner Harbour as a young man fresh from his uncle's architectural firm in England, he won the competition to design the Parliament Buildings over sixty-five rival submissions. The twenty-five-year-old Rattenbury's remarkable coup was achieved on what may have been inflated credentials, and on a plan that may have been "borrowed" from blueprints of a maharajah's pleasure palace. (Look twice and you can see shades of East Indian domes and arched pavilions.) Nevertheless, this building launched Rattenbury's prolific architectural career.

A small army of craftsmen set to work on the building as vast shiploads of materials arrived at the dock—including fine local products like slate from Jervis Inlet, granite from Nelson Island and iridescent grey andesite stone from Haddington Island, as well as Italian marble, English wrought iron, splendid stained glass and masses of mahogany, Kentucky white oak and other exotic woods. European-trained sculptors were commissioned for statuary, including an imperious Captain Vancouver on the cupola and a slightly bemused Queen Victoria surveying the Inner Harbour from the lawn. The Parliament Buildings cost nearly $1 million (nearly double the original estimate) but it was worth the price. Victoria nailed down its claim as capital city with this elaborate edifice. The Parliament Buildings' unmistakable silhouette—first illuminated in 1897 to celebrate Queen Victoria's Diamond Jubilee—is still outlined in lights as a tribute to its civic importance. (For information and tours, phone 250-387-3046.)

Just a block down Belleville on the Inner Harbour is the Rattenbury-designed CPR terminal building, once the ceremonial entryway for the rich and sometimes famous from the CPR's Asia-bound luxury ocean liners. With its colonnades and classic proportions, the building playfully mimics a Greek temple dedicated to the sea god Poseidon. Rattenbury was fond of this neo-classical Revival building, calling it "a handsome little building, as good as anything I have ever done." It now houses the **Royal London Wax Museum,** a popular family tourist attraction. The wax museum has more than 250 lifelike figures on display in galleries with titles like Royalty Row, Fantasyland and the Horror Chamber. Its newest addition is the $500,000 gallery Frozen in Time, featuring famous explorers (250-388-4461). Down the steps from the wax museum toward the harbour is

▶ **Victoria Annual Events**

March
Be a Tourist in Your Own Hometown

April
TerrifVic Jazz Party (late April)

May
Literary Arts Festival
Victoria Harbour Festival
Victoria Day Parade (May 24)

June
JazzFest International

July
Victoria Shakespeare Festival

August
Symphony Splash
West Shore Communities Summer Festival (Juan de Fuca Recreation Centre)

September
Vancouver Island Blues Bash
Classic Boat Festival

November
Santa Claus Parade

December
Christmas Lights Ceremony (Parliament Buildings)

For more information, Victoria Travel InfoCentre **250-953-2033**

A great mastodon at the Royal BC Museum

another family attraction, the **Pacific Undersea Gardens**. This is a good place to find out what rich life lurks just below the ocean surface and to view some of the myriad undersea creatures that thrive in BC's waters—the aquariums are right in the salt water of the harbour—and you can catch scheduled performances in which a diver displays some of the aquarium's most intriguing sea life, including a giant octopus named Armstrong.

Perhaps the finest museum in BC is the **Royal British Columbia Museum** at the corner of Government and Belleville between the Empress Hotel and the Parliament Buildings. The RBCM has very child-friendly walk-through displays where you can stroll along a turn-of-the-century street, descend into a coal mine, board Captain Vancouver's ship the Discovery, and take a submarine ride through the ocean depths. (Get your free tickets early for entry to the submarine display. It's popular, and only small groups can go at any one time.) Don't miss the museum's **First Peoples exhibit** which features a Big House from Alert Bay as well as fine displays of masks, totems and other First Nations artifacts. You won't find a better introduction to Native life in British Columbia. The museum is also known for its first-rate changing exhibits. (For information phone 250-387-3014 or 1-800-661-5411.) And for the foot-weary, the new IMAX National Geographic Theatre lets you be an armchair traveller to exotic worlds.

Just outside the museum is **Thunderbird Park** at the corner of Belleville and Douglas streets. Here you'll find replicas of **totem poles** and a **ceremonial longhouse** built by Mungo Martin. A commercial fisherman and chief of the Fort Rupert Kwakwaka'wakw (Kwakiutl), Martin came to the RBCM in 1952 as chief carver in the museum's totem pole restoration program. Martin's efforts were key to revitalizing Native arts and passing hereditary art forms on to a new generation. This longhouse—a half-sized reproduction of nineteenth century Kwakiutl Chief Naqapekim's house—was the site of the first potlatch publicly celebrated since the Canadian government banned potlatching, a gift-giving ceremonial, in 1884 (see p. 324). An ironic twist of fate: the ceremonial long house stands on the former site of James Douglas's estate. Governor Douglas, representing the Hudson's Bay Company and the Queen, was a key figure in negotiating Native title to lands under the terms of the "Douglas Treaty" signed by fourteen Vancouver Island First Nations in the 1850s. When Douglas retired, succeeding provincial governments argued that the

Douglas Treaty was not intended to recognize Native land title but simply an attempt to keep friendly relations with local bands. The dispute between First Nations people and the government over the meaning of the Douglas Treaty is still at issue.

Just a few paces beyond the longhouse is the home of Fort Victoria's first doctor, J. S. Helmcken, who later married Douglas's eldest daughter Cecilia. **Helmcken House** is the oldest home still standing on its original site in British Columbia. Today it is a museum where visitors are welcomed to step back into the days when Victoria was just a muddy little settlement on the outskirts of the British Empire (250-361-0021).

If you feel like leaving the tourist track for a while, walk into nearby **Beacon Hill Park** just down Douglas Street from Helmcken House. This sun-warmed 74-ha park with lovely Garry oaks meadows was once a favourite spot for local Coast Salish people, who tended their fields of camas bulbs here. The starchy bulb of the camas was a staple food, and in spring the meadows of Beacon Hill Park were carpeted with its beautiful blue flowers. In fact, Victoria's first name was Camosack or Camosun, a

Vancouver–Victoria–Nanaimo Triangle Tour

Seeing the Island Without Doubling Back

Many visitors combine a trip to Vancouver and Victoria with an easy 2-hour drive up the east coast of Vancouver Island to Nanaimo. Frequent BC Ferries sailings between Vancouver and Victoria and between Nanaimo and Vancouver make the Vancouver–Victoria–Nanaimo "Triangle Tour" a holiday winner. Visitors get a chance to see two of the world's finest (and very distinctive) cities, Vancouver and Victoria, and to enjoy the natural splendour of BC's beautiful coast. The ferry trips are comfortable for the whole family and take less than 2 hours each. And the sea routes—especially on the Vancouver–Victoria trip—are a scenic delight of islands and mountains layered above a grey-green sea. The drive from Victoria to Nanaimo, the third point in the triangle is breathtakingly beautiful. Rise up over the famous Malahat Drive on the outskirts of Victoria for a bird's-eye view of an island-studded sea and the pastoral Saanich Peninsula, dip into BC's First Nations cultures at Duncan, and discover the huge wall murals that revived a dying seaside mill town at Chemainus. Savour a sybaritic wine tasting tour along southern Vancouver Island's green country roads or go four-wheeling on the many old logging roads that crisscross the island's rugged mountain spine. From Nanaimo you can sail back to Vancouver aboard a BC Ferry.

Salish word meaning "the place for gathering camas." With admirable foresight James Douglas set the land aside for a park, and it continues to be a favourite retreat for Victoria's residents and visitors. Gardeners delight in the park's **hundred-year-old rhododendron plantings**, and little tikes have lots of fun in the children's **petting zoo** and the **playgrounds**.

Beacon Hill Park includes miles of fabulous waterfront walkways that wind around dramatic headlands. The mountain and water views are incomparable, and the salty tang in the air is the perfect antidote for lagging spirits. Watch fish boats and bright-coloured freighters heave through the waves between the bluffs and the snow-tipped mainland mountains of the Olympic Peninsula in the distance. Join Victoria's tee-shirted joggers and dog walkers with their muttly crews on the seaside. Intrepid kite flyers and model airplane enthusiasts favour the wide grassy knolls for catching updrafts, and binocular-bearing birders zoom in on small birds rising and dipping in the tall grass edging the bluffs. Occasional paths lead down to the shore where grey sand beaches are interlaced with glacier-scoured rock outcroppings. It's a wonderful natural escape just a few minutes away from downtown, and you can walk for miles. Near the western end of Dallas Road is

Ogden Point Breakwater, a favourite spot with anglers and joggers who truck out along the granite-slabbed seawall in pursuit of fish or fitness. The 800-metre-long breakwater was built to protect the harbour from fierce northeasterly winds. Behind the breakwater you can watch helicopters whisk business-suit types off to Vancouver from the heliport and see a freighter or Seattle-bound ferry swing in toward the Ogden Point docks. Or pop into the Ogden Point Dive Shop for the latest on area **scuba diving**. Just off Ogden Point is a federal marine sanctuary alive with sea creatures where beginners can explore underwater. And just a kilometre south is another favourite dive site at **Brotchie Ledge**, where the steamer *San Pedro* went aground in 1891.

James Bay, the old-time residential area named for James Douglas, lies behind Beacon Hill Park, between Ogden Point and downtown. For a change of scene wander through this area where cozy B&Bs and Victorian gingerbread houses with fanciful turrets and ornate eaves rub elbows with newer apartment buildings. Many stand in old-fashioned English gardens thick with snapdragons, lilacs, poppies, foxgloves and sweet-scented lavender.

Downtown Victoria: Shopping and Restaurants

In the mood for a shopping spree or a food fest? Then make your way back to the Empress Hotel and continue north on **Government Street**. This has been the heart of the business district since Victoria's mud-street days, and several of the stores here have plied their trade for decades. Murchie's Tea & Coffee is still run by descendants of the Scottish tea and coffee merchant who was a supplier to Queen Victoria. The Spode Shop is the oldest **china** shop in Victoria, W & J Wilson has sold **clothing** since 1862, and the Irish Linen Stores have been in the **linen and lace** trade since 1910. Be sure to step inside Rogers Chocolates, a splendid old-fashioned emporium at 913 Government Street, to admire its fine turn-of-the-century art glass, oak panelling and mosaic floor tiles. Only the strong-willed can walk out again without sampling one of the establishment's handmade Victorian cream **chocolates** prettily turned out in pink-and-white gingham wrappers. Even Queen Elizabeth sent a note in 1983 commending Rogers' "delicious-looking sweets." Then poke your nose into E.A. Morris Tobacconist Ltd. at 1116 Government for a whiff of earlier times when the after-dinner cigar was de rigueur. The shop still carries a

fine array of **cigars, pipes, tobacco**, lighters and other paraphernalia of the gentlemen's smoking room, displayed to perfection in gleaming mahogany cases designed by Thomas Hooper who also fitted out Rogers Chocolates. Munro's Books at 1108 Government is a two-thumbs-up for **book lovers**. Housed in the beautifully restored Royal Bank building with marble floors, an ornate oval dome and wonderful fabric wall hangings by Carole Sabiston, this is the perfect place to browse. Its delectable offerings include shelves full of Canadiana, contemporary literature and a first-rate children's section.

The landmark Munro's Books

The streets around Government are also fine for shopping. Tourism is Victoria's lifeblood and as a result the city has quite a range of small **specialty shops**. Collectors of **Native art** will find the whole spectrum from inexpensive tourist-market items to museum-quality pieces in places like the Alcheringa Gallery. Antique hounds should make their way up Fort Street to **Antique Row** (between Blanshard and Cook streets) for everything from silver, china and jewellery to fine furniture, antique books and maps, prints and engravings, stamps, coins, militaria—name it, and you're likely to find it on Antique Row.

Victoria's Old Town: A Brief History

Fort Victoria once stood just south of Bastion Square on Wharf Street. The tiny settlement huddled around the fort was a quiet place where, according to one nineteenth-century account, a gentleman could expect "no noise, no hustle, no gamblers, no speculators." But all that changed in 1858 with the influx of a huge rag tag population lured by the glitter of Cariboo gold. Twenty-five thousand prospectors, entertainers and adventurers descended on Victoria for supplies, diversions and transport to the gold fields. Dozens of rickety wooden structures were hastily thrown up, and saloons, hotels and outfitter shops were soon open for business. A visiting clergyman who sailed into Victoria harbour described the scene in 1858: "Innumerable tents covered the ground in and around Victoria far as the eye could reach. The sound of hammer and axe was heard every direction. Shops, stores and 'shanties' to the number of 225 arose in six weeks. Speculation in town lots attained a pitch of unparalleled extravagance. The land office was besieged, often before four o'clock in the morning, by the multitude eager to buy town property." Always a keen-eyed entrepreneur, James Douglas had the fort pulled down and sold off the land for a handsome profit. Today all that remains of the Hudson's Bay Company fort are iron rings for mooring company ships, set into the rock below the old Customs House on Wharf Street.

Victoria outgrew its rough-and-tumble gold rush days to become a thriving industrial city. The Inner Harbour was the centre of bustling shipping and shoreside industries—sawmills, canneries, a naval depot at Esquimalt, a shipbuilding industry, breweries, rice

A paddlewheeler in front of of Fort Victoria, circa 1890

and flour mills, granite and brickyards, clothing and boot manufacturers, a soapworks, and more. Wholesale merchants and shipping companies built substantial warehouses on Wharf Street which was conveniently situated between the docks of the Inner Harbour and the banks and shops along Government Street. You can still see the names of those long-departed firms stencilled across the second storeys of some of Wharf Street's historic buildings.

The boom times lasted until Victoria lost out in the competition for the cross-country railway terminus. The railway line had been expected to run north of Vancouver and then island-hop to Vancouver Island and down to Victoria. But the track was finally laid closer to the US border with a terminus in Vancouver, and trade shifted to Vancouver while the engines of Victoria's economic life began to falter. The warehouses and factories shut down one by one, and economically the area was quiet until an imaginative restoration program began in the 1960s. Now Victoria is up and running again with new shops and restaurants settling comfortably into the carefully preserved heritage buildings. Ask at the InfoCentre about guided walking tours of Old Town or look for self-guided tour books in local bookstores.

Bastion Square and Wharf Street

Bastion Square, a pedestrian square bordered on three sides by heritage buildings, anchors one end of the area known as Old Town. Here you'll find classic Georgian architecture, good **restaurants** and attractive little **specialty shops**, including one catering to **gardeners** and another to **airplane buffs**, as well as the **Maritime Museum** housed in the former Victoria law courts. The Maritime Museum is a reminder of Victoria's seafaring past and a must for anyone who loves the sea and ships. All sorts of salty objects are on view, from displays about famous ships to tales of lighthouses and their keepers to intricate ship models, including the famous Canadian Pacific liners that sailed from the Rattenbury-designed CPR Steamship Terminal across the harbour. The small gift shop offers intriguing items and a fine collection of books on nautical themes.

From Bastion Square you can walk up **Wharf Street** to admire its fine old buildings and new shops, or stroll along any of the side streets to admire more intriguing architecture and a range of tempting specialty shops. This is a good place for a serendipitous lunch or dinner. One favourite is **Swans Hotel and Brew Pub** at Pandora Street, a traditional

meeting place for Victorians with a thirst to quench. It has accommodations, a pub, and a restaurant and a good microbrewery.

Market Square, Chinatown, and Westsong Way

Don't pass up a visit to Market Square a block-square shopping complex developed from eight heritage buildings on Wharf Street between Johnson and Pandora. It offers an eclectic mix of forty-odd shops and **eateries**, including a **toy bear store**, **quilt shop**, **stringed instrument shop**, **fudge factory** and more. Walk through the impressive iron-work gateway half a block up on Johnson Street and enjoy Market Square's huge inner courtyard enclosed by two-tier inner galleries

Maritime Museum of BC

lined with shops. The courtyard is hung with colourful banners and fitted out with benches and tables, and in summer street performers add to the fun. If you're lucky you might hit the annual **three-day jazz festival** featuring local talent and big-name international musicians. Here and there along the galleries are wall displays giving interesting snippets of the history of the area which was the flip side of genteel Victoria. Here miners, loggers and sailors found their noisy pleasures in local saloons and brothels. Call the Victoria Travel InfoCentre (250-953-2033) for dates and information.

Just a block beyond Market Square on Fisgard Street is Canada's oldest Chinatown. It was also BC's largest until 1910 when Vancouver's Chinatown overtook it. In the mid-1880s this was a thriving community of 15,000 people—nearly half of Victoria's population. It covered half a dozen blocks and had stores, schools, temples, benevolent societies, two theatres and a hospital. This area was home to most Victorians of Chinese descent, mostly men who had come to prospect for gold or work on the railways and who stayed on in Canada. Some became wealthy merchants and manufacturers but most worked as cooks, laundrymen, gardeners or household servants for Victoria's well-to-do white residents. Because of Canada's infamous $500 "head tax" on Chinese immigrants, only the richest men could afford to bring their wives and children to Canada. The rest lived out their lives as bachelors in crowded Chinatown tenement rooms.

Behind Chinatown's everyday facade lay another, more mysterious place—a honeycomb of intricate alleyways, underground tunnels, secluded courtyards, gambling dens and secret opium rooms—that gave the area its other name, the Forbidden

Fan Tan Alley, Chinatown

City. The manufacture and sale of opium was legal in Canada until 1908—licensing fees were a handy source of government revenues—and raw opium was shipped from China for processing in Victoria's fourteen opium factories. One local old-timer recalled that when opium "was being made from crude opium into salable opium, or smoking opium, you could smell it all over Victoria—the odour was very much like boiling potatoes."

One way into Chinatown from Market Square is by way of **Fan Tan Alley**, a narrow lane on the far side of Pandora Street named for a popular Chinese gambling game. (Fan means to turn over and tan means to spread out.) The narrow alley was the site of two opium factories. Now it is lined with **quirky boutiques**, **galleries** and a **Chinese gift shop**. Fan Tan Alley leads out to Fisgard Street, the heart of today's revitalized Chinatown. It's a lively place of historic building fronts, neon-studded **Chinese restaurants**, lampposts painted red and yellow, and sidewalk stands bright with **fruits and vegetables**. The elaborately painted **Gate of Harmonious Interest** which arches over Fisgard Street at Government Street is a visual feast for the eyes. Its two handsome hand-carved lions were a gift from the people of Suzhou, China, to their sister city of Victoria in 1981. The gate is a proud symbol of harmonious relations between Victoria's Chinese community and the rest of its residents.

Another quiet escape from the city awaits you not far from Market Square. Cross over the blue **Johnson Street bridge** and walk to your left to **Westsong Way**, along the new **pedestrian walkway**, which runs 2 km to the **West Bay Marina**. The stroll, with its great views across the busy Inner Harbour, couldn't be more pleasant. At various points you'll pass rocky headlands where, if you look closely, you can see ragged white scars left by the last ice age. The walk is also brightened by outcroppings of arbutus trees—known as madrona from Washington to California—with their twisted red-barked trunks and long shiny green leaves. According to Coast Salish legend, a handful of survivors of the Great Flood saved themselves by tying their canoe to an arbutus on top of Mount Newton. It is said that to this day some members of the nearby Saanich band will not burn arbutus for firewood out of respect for the tree. If you get tired, you can catch an **Inner Harbour ferry** back downtown from a choice of pickup points. If you're hungry or thirsty, stop at **Spinnakers Brew Pub**, Canada's oldest brew pub just above the walkway at Catherine St. Or stop in at the **Ocean Pointe Resort**, Victoria's elegant new hotel beside the Johnson Street bridge. You'll get a bonus served up with your drink: the huge lobby window frames a splendid view of the Parliament Buildings across the harbour.

Scenic Marine Drive and Nearby Parks

One last treat awaits you on your way back to the Swartz Bay ferry terminal. Leave downtown Victoria a good hour or so before you want to arrive at the terminal and drive along Victoria's marine drive, which starts on Dallas Road. Follow the scenic drive signs east and north along the coast till you meet Hwy 17 where Cordova Bay Road turns inland and becomes Sayward Road just north of big **Elk Lake**. The route switches streets (and directions) several times as it loops and curves around Oak Bay, Cadboro Bay and along Cordova Bay, so keep an eye out for signs en route.

You'll find yourself looking all directions at once to take in headlands and beaches, the undulating green ribbon of the **Royal Victoria Golf Club**, and street after street of *House Beautiful* homes (many with touches of Tudor) set in rhododendron-thick gardens. Three of Victoria's best public parks are located just off this scenic drive. Take the signed turnoff from Beach Drive onto the **Cattle Point** loop. It runs between the ocean and the finest **Garry oak meadow** in the whole city and then back to Beach Drive. Now a boat launch and a scenic **beach** overlook, Cattle Point was once a herding area where cattle destined for a nearby slaughterhouse were driven off barges and onto the shore. A large map in the parking lot shows the criss cross of **trails** through the adjacent 31-ha **Uplands Park**. It was originally part of the posh turn-of-the-century Uplands Estates, but the parkland was given to the municipality of Oak Bay in the 1940s. A walk in Uplands Park can be glorious in late spring when wildflowers—blue-eyed Mary, sea blush, shooting stars and more—light up the meadows.

For a delightful duo of Garry oak meadows and sweeping vistas of Victoria and its coastline, head for 18-hectare **Mount Tolmie Park** near the **University of Victoria** campus. From the entrance off Cedar Hill Road just east of Shelbourne St, a winding road leads up to the summit. Go for the splendid views or stretch your legs on one of the well-built **trails** threading the mountainside. Not far away is **Mount Douglas Park** near the corner of Ash Road and Cordova Bay Rd. It's the **biggest wilderness park** in greater Victoria (184 ha) and boasts the **highest local mountain** peak (227 m). At its foot is a gravel and rock beach where **beachcombers** can discover lots of treasures and picnickers can eat up the ocean views. (Look for the parking lot on Cordova Bay Rd.) Lower down on "Mount Doug" the thick covering of native and imported trees gone wild is riddled with trails and bushwhacked paths. Hike up or take the well-signed road to the summit.

Garry Oaks in Uplands Park

At the top you'll see the city spread like a pastel patchwork before you. On a clear day you can see way across Haro Strait to the San Juan Islands and the Olympic Peninsula in Washington state. It's a fine spot to say farewell to Victoria.

Revisiting Victoria's Past: Historic Highlights

Craigflower Farmhouse and Schoolhouse

In 1852 Scottish and English colonists—some twenty-five families in all—set sail for far-away Fort Victoria. Recruited by Hudson's Bay Company bailiff Kenneth Mackenzie, the men had promised to work for the HBC for five years in return for homesteads on Vancouver Island. After a perilous six-month journey around Cape Horn, their ship was nearly smashed on the reefs within eyesight of Esquimalt Harbour. But the colonists landed safely and set to work. Two years later they had hacked out a clearing along the Gorge Waters and built Craigflower Farm, a cluster of twenty-one buildings including barns, a brick kiln, a blacksmith shop, a bakery, a sawmill, a farmhouse and a schoolhouse.

The farmhouse and schoolhouse are still standing today. Craigflower farmhouse, the Mackenzies' fine **Georgian Revival manor**, has been restored to the look of its former days as a gathering place for Victoria's social elite. In summer you can follow **costumed guides** through the door and back into the 1850s. You'll see a replica of the Mackenzies' pride and joy—a cast-iron kitchen range displayed at the Great Exhibition of 1851 in London's Crystal Palace—and you may get to sample a fresh-baked scone from the kitchen. Wander through the small **heritage orchards** and past the **barnyard** with its kid-pleasing chickens and sheep. Watch for occasional craft displays and farm demonstrations, costume exhibits and special Sunday events.

Then cross the bridge over Gorge Inlet to Craigflower School for a peek into an 1855

Craigflower School House Museum

classroom. The thirty children of Craigflower Farm were day students here, and teachers and boarders from the other three HBC farms lived in the second storey. The tall white clapboard school stands on the grounds of a 2,500-year-old Kosapsom village of the Esquimalt people. An interpretive sign describes fascinating findings from an archaelogical dig on the site.

The two museums, located near the intersection of Craigflower Rd (Hwy 1A) and Admirals Rd, are just a ten-minute drive from downtown Victoria. Tours run between 12:00 and 4:00 p.m. daily from July to early September, Thursday to Monday from late May to July and mid-September to early October. The grounds are open all year round (250-387-4697 or 250-387-3067).

Ross Bay Cemetery

Victoria's old Ross Bay Cemetery is on lovely southwest sloping land running between Fairfield and Dallas roads. It was named for Charles Ross, who had the doubtful honour of being the first European to die at Fort Victoria. He was buried close to the fort's palisades, but his bones were later moved to the burying ground beside Christ Church Cathedral on Quadra Street. By the early 1970s the church burying ground had filled up, and Ross's old farm above Ross Bay became the new cemetery. It was far enough from the settlement to assuage fears of diseases seeping from the graves, and its gentle contours and delightful prospect over Juan de Fuca Strait made it a perfect final resting place. With its winding carriage paths, sudden artful prospects and picturesque plantings of yew and boxwood, hawthorn and laurel, Ross Bay Cemetery was designed as a tranquil mortuary garden where Victorians could meditate on God and mortality.

Victoria's upper crust raised proud monuments to their deceased on Ross Bay Cemetery's higher, drier slopes. Every denomination—Anglican, Roman Catholic, Methodist, Presbyterian—had its own plots safe from religious contamination by other sects. The muddier plots down by the sea were reserved for Chinese and Native people.

Storm-driven waves often clawed off chunks of the foreshore. A seawall was finally built in 1911 to put a stop to the spectacle of bones and splintered coffins scattered on the beach.

The tombstones are a fascinating record of BC's colourful history. The first governor, Sir James Douglas, lies in state beneath an ornate Celtic cross. A mile-long procession of sixty carriages attended his body to the grave. Here, too, lie the bones of Douglas's mortal enemy Amor De Cosmos ("lover of the universe") who changed his name from William Smith and founded the Victoria newspaper the *British Colonist*. A zealous reformer, he never tired of attacking Douglas and the all-powerful Hudson's Bay Company. De Cosmos became BC's premier in 1872 but died in obscurity in 1897. Ten more premiers are buried here, as is Douglas's good friend, the famous "hanging judge" Sir Matthew Baillie Begbie, and other famous Victorians like Robert Dunsmuir and Emily Carr.

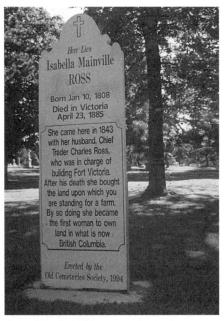

Ross Bay Cemetery

Ross Bay Cemetery is a popular spot for the quick as well as the dead. Joggers and history buffs, sightseers and strolling lovers share the sun-dappled peace in this seaside cemetery garden. For a self-guided tour, pick up John Adams' "Historic Guide to Ross Bay Cemetery" in a local bookstore. For special events and guided tours with titles like "Gossip in the Graveyard," "Echoes of Distant Wars" and "Murder Most Foul," contact the Old Cemeteries Society (250-598-8870, website www.oldcem.bc.ca) or inquire at the Victoria Travel InfoCentre (250-953-2033).

When Charles Ross died, his wife Isabella inherited the farm at Ross Bay and became the first woman to own land in British Columbia. Isabella Ross died in 1885 and was buried in an unmarked grave in Ross Bay Cemetery. The Old Cemeteries Society has erected a cairn in her memory.

Emily Carr House

Emily Carr (1871–1941), one of Canada's best-known artists and writers, was the last of nine children born to Richard Carr, a British-born Victoria merchant. He had prospered in the dry goods trade in the California gold rush, and in 1863 he settled his large family in James Bay at the outskirts of tiny Victoria. Their comfortable Italianate villa was surrounded with fields and pastures, ponds and tall stands of fir trees. Carr's mother deplored the "lonesomeness of going to live in the forest," but Emily was enchanted by James Bay's half-tamed wilderness where wild roses grew along the muddy roads and daisies and lilies brightened the grass along the seaside bluff. Both parents died by the time Carr was sixteen. She headed to San Francisco to study painting in 1890 but money

Carr House

Emily Carr

problems forced her back to Victoria. Aside from stints in England, France and Vancouver, she stayed on Vancouver Island for the rest of her life.

Carr, who was in her own words "contrary from the start," cut an eccentric figure in staid Victoria as she strode Beacon Hill Park in a loose old dress, a hairnet pulled down on her forehead, cigarette between her fingers, pushing a Capuchin monkey in a battered old baby carriage with a dog or cat or two at her heels. Over the years Carr made painting trips to the remote BC and Alaska coast to sketch Native villages. Her consummate renderings of the mystery and power of the wild Northwest coast brought her belated recognition but little money. A heart attack in her late sixties made painting difficult. So Carr set out on her writing career. "One approach is cut off, I'll try the other," she wrote. "I'll 'word' these things which during my life have touched me deeply." Her first book *Klee Wyck* (1941) recounted stories from her coastal travels. It won the Governor General's Award for literature and enthusiastic readers flooded her with flowers and letters. She also wrote *The Book of Small* (1942) about her Victoria childhood and *The House of All Sorts* (1949) about her years as a landlady in the boarding house she built near Beacon Hill Park. Today Emily Carr is recognized as one of Canada's finest artists.

Her family home was saved from demolition in the 1960s and restored as a National Historic Site. Emily Carr House is just four blocks from the Parliament Buildings at 207 Government Street. Open daily from mid-May to mid-October with special events at other times. Carr's books are for sale in the gift shop (250-383-5843).

"The house was large and well-built, of California redwood, the garden prim and carefully tended. Everything about it was extremely English." —from *The Book of Small* by Emily Carr.

Craigdarroch Castle

Craigdarroch Castle is Robert Dunsmuir's final tribute to his own triumphal rise to fame. Born in modest circumstances in Ayrshire, Scotland, Robert Dunsmuir died the wealthiest man in nineteenth-century British Columbia. While working for the Hudson's Bay Company, Dunsmuir found coal under the roots of a fallen tree at Wellington near Nanaimo in 1869 and made his first fortune from Vancouver Island "black gold." He reaped a second windfall from building the Esquimalt & Nanaimo Railway. The venture was subsidized by the Canadian government to the tune of $750,000 for construction costs, tax concessions, and a gift of 770,000 hectares of land—nearly a quarter of Vancouver Island—including all coal and timber rights.

In 1887 Dunsmuir bought land on the highest hill in Rockland, Victoria's poshest neighbourhood, and hired an American architect to build a home to rival the Scottish baronial castles of his childhood. Named Craigdarroch (Gaelic for "rocky place") for its

Craigdarroch Castle

commanding site overlooking the city, Dunsmuir's thirty-nine-room "castle" was filled with the best that money could buy. Fine sandstone sheathed the exterior. Interior walls and stairways gleamed with ornately carved mahogany, walnut and cedar. Richly coloured Art Nouveau stained glass refracted the light from landings and bay windows. Eighteen fireplaces warmed the house. The rooms were filled with Oriental carpets and brocades, lustrous wood furnishings, and fine china and silver. But Robert Dunsmuir died in 1869 before he could enjoy the greatest symbol of his success. His wife Joan lived in Craigdarroch until her death in 1908 when the children sold the property. Too ostentatious for most tastes, the monument was given away in a lottery for buyers of lots when the estate was subdivided. Craigdarroch changed hands several more times between 1919 and 1979, doing service as a military hospital, a college, a school board office and a music conservatory.

James K. Nesbitt, a Victoria historian and newspaper man, spearheaded the restoration of the rapidly fading Craigdarroch Castle in the 1960s. It became a historic house museum in 1989, and today some 150,000 visitors tour the house at 1050 Joan Crescent every year. Helpful docents are on hand to answer questions and serve up fascinating tidbits about the Dunsmuir family. Open daily (250-592-5323).

Fort Rodd Hill/Fisgard Lighthouse National Historic Sites

In the tense times during the Russian war scare, the British installed a string of artillery guns on the brow of Rodd Hill to protect against a surprise attack. That was in 1878. A couple of decades later the aging wooden batteries were pulled down and concrete installations went up. The First World War brought renewed tensions to the BC coast, and the garrison went on the alert. But the only wartime encounter occurred when Fort Rodd

gunners mistook the newly bought Canadian submarines sliding into Esquimalt Harbour for German attackers and nearly blew them out of the water. During the Second World War, the threat of a Japanese invasion seemed very real after the bombing of Pearl Harbor. A fortress plotting room deep underground was built to make calculations for counter-bombardment weapons at Mary Hill and Albert Head, but the Japanese never appeared. During the Cold War, the plotting room was refitted for anti-aircraft observations but modern radar systems made the Fort Rodd installation obsolete. It was closed for good as a military site in 1956.

In 1962 Fort Rodd Hill became a National Historic Site. The 42-ha site has a wide lawn

Fisgard Lighthouse National Historic Site

rolling down to the sea, rocky knolls dotted with Garry oak, shady forests, a scallop of beaches and sweeping views from the ships of Esquimalt Harbour right around to Esquimalt Lagoon. It's a great destination for a half-day **family outing**. Explore the old installations from guardhouses and emplacement guns to underground artillery magazines and the old plotting room. Relax with a **picnic** on the sunny lawn, pick a **hike** from a selection of short trails, poke into **tidal pools** on the beach, and then head for the striking white lighthouse with its bright red lightkeeper's residence across the short causeway.

The causeway was built in 1951 to give the lightkeeper and his family a safe overland route. When storms came up, high wind, fog and pounding surf made the short boat trip from lighthouse to shore impossible for days at a time. Fisgard lighthouse, the **first permanent light station** on Canada's west coast, was built to guide vessels past the ticklish entrance to Esquimalt Harbour. The base of the lighthouse is a .6-m thick slab of granite, and its walls are of 1.2-m thick brick. Inside visitors can climb the spiralling iron staircase up to displays of antique lighthouse lenses and accounts of shipwrecks and deaths along Vancouver Island's west coast—the infamous "graveyard of the Pacific" (see pp. 238–39).

Fort Rodd Hill/Fisgard Lighthouse National Historic Sites at 603 Fort Rodd Hill Rd are a 15-minute drive from downtown Victoria. Follow Hwy 1 north and take the turnoff to Sooke (Hwy 1A/Hwy 14). Turn left onto Ocean Blvd just past Juan de Fuca Recreation Centre and follow signs to the park. Open daily March–October. Limited services mid-October–April (250-478-5849, email fort_rodd@pch.gc.ca, website www.harbour.com/parkscan/frh).

Butchart Gardens

Victoria is nicknamed the City of Gardens, and residents are justly proud of their super-green city. There is even a one-day February Flower Count when Victorians circle their gardens tallying up their blossoms—sometimes the grand total is more than 4 billion flowers—while many other Canadians are still shivering in deep winter snow. The Butchart Gardens is the jewel in Victoria's emerald crown. Millions of visitors have flocked to the estate where Jenny Butchart (1868-1950) worked her green magic on a barren quarry. Jenny's husband Robert Pim Butchart, founder of the Vancouver Portland Cement Company, had mined the limestone just beyond their estate for his nearby cement plant. With his blessing, the help of English landscape designer William Henry Westby and a small army of Chinese quarry workers, the energetic Mrs. Butchart transformed an environmental eyesore into the magical Sunken Garden. Under her guiding hand a flagstone walkway descended into the quarry to wind past ornamental trees and curving borders brimming with blooms. A statue was tucked away here, a quiet pool there, and waterfalls at the far end. The quarry walls were curtained with ivy and pockets of flowers. Mrs. Butchart herself swung from a bos'un's chair to plant trailing vines in the rock face. Her flower-tapestried **Sunken Garden** evokes comments like "stunning," "dazzling," and "breathtaking" in the visitors' book.

The "Private Garden" at Butchart Gardens

The "Sunken Garden" was once a limestone quarry

The Butcharts' passion for gardens was boundless, and they travelled the world, bringing back exotic plant species and finely crafted lawn ornaments for their Saanich Peninsula estate. Over the years they built four gardens. The very first—built even before the Sunken Garden—was the impeccable **Japanese Garden** above Tod Inlet. With its artfully pruned trees, stone lanterns, teahouse, reflecting pool and arched wooden bridge, the Japanese Garden is a Zen-like place of serenity. The formal **Italian Garden** on the estate's old tennis court is centred around a luxuriant water lily pond in the shape of a Florentine cross rimmed with begonias and heliotrope. The richly scented **Rose Garden** in the Butcharts' former vegetable patch is abloom each summer with over 280 varieties from floribunda to climbing roses.

Jenny Butchart vowed to share the pleasures of her garden with those less privileged. The Butcharts delighted in welcoming hundreds of visitors to their 20-ha garden estate and often invited them to tea. Much against their wishes, the Butcharts were forced by financial crisis to charge admission in 1941. Since then the Butchart Gardens has become a thriving enterprise. Today fifty gardeners help keep as many as 300,000 plants in bloom at a time in the immaculate gardens. The Butcharts' warmly elegant residence, named Benvenuto ("welcome" in Italian), is now home to the **Dining Room Restaurant** and the **Plant Identification Centre**. (Mrs. Butchart wanted visitors to share her delight in her private garden and felt that plant identification tags would turn the experience into a "scientific" botanical exercise. Except for the Rose Garden, the plant species are not labelled, in accordance with her wishes.) The 1930 conservatory with its delightful profusion of tropical plants is now the **Blue Poppy Restaurant**. There's also an information centre, coffee bar, show greenhouse, and the **Benvenuto Seed & Gift Store**. The Butcharts set up the Benvenuto Seed Company in 1920 to help finance the upkeep of the gardens—and to discourage enthusiastic visitors from snipping cuttings for their own gardens! Visitors can also enjoy summer evening light displays and concerts, Saturday night fireworks in July and August, and festive lights and carolling during the Christmas holiday.

The Butchart Gardens is 21 km from downtown Victoria and 20 km south of the Swartz Bay ferry terminal. Take Hwy 17 and follow the signs to the gardens. Benvenuto Ave, Brentwood Bay (recorded information 250-652-5256, dining reservations 250-652-4422, website www.butchartgardens.com).

Other Favourite Public Gardens:

Beacon Hill Park: waterfront wildflower meadows, hundred-year-old hybrid rhododendrons (Fountain Lake), formal flower beds planted with 30,000 annuals, Garry oaks, rock and alpine gardens, ornamental ponds and a medieval-looking stone bridge are all part of the 74-ha park overlooking Juan de Fuca Strait. Corner of Douglas and Dallas roads.

Government House: Formal gardens on the grounds of Lieutenant Governor's residence include a lily pond, rose garden, perennial beds and rock garden. Stroll down rock-walled Lotbiniere Ave to the right of the main gate for a taste of early Victoria's native landscape. 1401 Rockland Ave (250-387-2080).

University of Victoria Gardens: One of the finest rhododendron collections in the Pacific Northwest; also wildflowers, annuals and perennials. University of Victoria campus (250-721-7014).

Horticulture Centre of the Pacific: A teaching garden with a fuchsia and begonia arbour, Japanese-style garden, rhododendrons, perennials, flowering bulbs, as well as vegetable beds and fruit trees covering 44.5 ha. Blooming plants every month. 505 Quayle Rd, at the intersection of Beaver Lake Rd (250-479-6162).

Saxe Point Park: A secret even to longtime Victorians, combining ornamental gardens, native plant life and forest walks with great ocean views across the Juan de Fuca Strait to the Olympic Peninsula. Cross the Johnson Street Bridge at the foot of Pandora St and continue along Esquimalt Rd. Turn left onto Fraser St, about 3 km and follow it to the park.

The Government House Gardens are another favourite

The West Shore: Day Tripping from Victoria

Thinking of a day trip from Victoria? Try the West Coast Road (Hwy 14). It winds 34 km through the semi-rural Western Communities (Colwood, Langford, Metchosin, Highlands and View Royal) to Sooke. The 34-km drive from downtown Victoria to Sooke takes a leisurely 50 minutes, but you'll be tempted by lots of fascinating stops along the way. Who knows? You might get sidetracked and decide to put down temporary roots. Sooke has campgrounds and a surprisingly good selection of B&Bs, including the world-famous Sooke Harbour House. For information contact the Sooke Travel InfoCentre 250-642-6351.

Ready for outdoor adventure? Follow Hwy 14 past Sooke into the heart of the west coast wilderness. The road kinks northwest for 70 km (1 1/2 hours) along the spectacular west coast to Jordan River and Port Renfrew. Pacific breakers roll up against this ruggedly beautiful coast where you can surfboard or sailboard, go tidal pooling or beachcombing, or sunbathe on a sandy beach. The newest attraction is the Juan de Fuca Marine Trail where you can backpack along 47 km of coastline or dayhike shorter sections of the trail.

Galloping Goose Trail Regional Park

Don't overlook Victoria's best-kept secret, this **60-km trail** that runs on old railway beds from downtown Victoria past Sooke to the abandoned gold-mining town of Leechtown. The Galloping Goose was the gas railcar that ferried passengers between Victoria and Sooke from 1911 until the mid-1940s, and freight until 1979. The trail winds through all kinds of terrain from city to countryside, seaside to rain forest, over trestle bridges and through local regional parks. Its easy grades and many access points in the Sooke area make it ideal for **biking**, **hiking**, **horseback riding** and even **rollerblading** on the paved sections. Two popular day trips for **cycle-and-swim** fun start at **Roche Cove Regional Park** (Gillespie Rd, East Sooke). One leads west and north to two historic trestle bridges on the **Sooke River** with a **swimming** break at **Sooke Potholes Provincial Park** (below). The other heads east through rural Metchosin with a swimming break at

Sooke Potholes Provincial Park

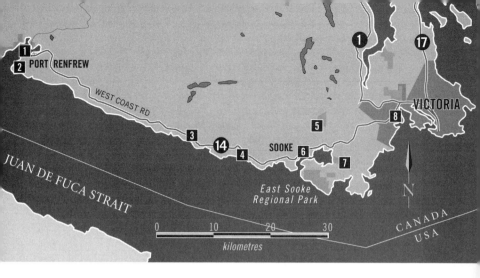

PORT RENFREW

WEST COAST RD

JUAN DE FUCA STRAIT

VICTORIA

SOOKE

East Sooke
Regional Park

N

0   10   20   30

kilometres

CANADA
USA

Matheson Lake Regional Park. Other trail access points include Six Mile Road (behind Six Mile House), Luxton Fair Grounds, Happy Valley Rd, and Sooke River Rd (near Sooke Potholes Provincial Park). Trail maps available from Capital Regional District Parks, 490 Atkins Ave, Victoria, BC V9B 2Z8 (250-478-3344, fax 250-478-5416), the Sooke Visitor InfoCentre (below), and most cycle shops, email crdpark@pinc.com

Hatley Park

James Dunsmuir's elegant Tudor-style Hatley Castle was built in 1908. The eldest son of coal baron Robert Dunsmuir, James took over his father's business and later became BC's premier (1900–1902). Hatley Castle, with its huge ballroom, twenty-two

What to See

- [ ] **1** Port Renfrew
- [ ] **2** Botanical Beach Park
- [ ] **3** China Beach Provincial Park
- [ ] **4** Jordan River
- [ ] **5** Sooke Potholes Provincial Park
- [ ] **6** Sooke Museum
- [ ] **7** Matheson Lake Park/ Galloping Goose Trail
- [ ] **7** Hatley Park

bedrooms, nine bathrooms and exquisite detailing from an Art Nouveau bell-push to monogrammed drainpipes, outshone even his father's ostentatious Craigdarroch Castle (pp. 111–12). The Hatley Park estate once had 9 km of road, 320 hectares of land including a hunting park, and even a village for Dunsmuir's 120 estate workers. Hatley Castle is now home to Royal Roads University, but the splendid Hatley Park gardens overlooking Esquimalt Lagoon are open to the public daily until dusk. Take a self-guided tour of Dunsmuir's renowned Italian, Japanese and Rose Gardens and stroll the 324 ha of parkland where deer and peacocks still roam. Maps in castle foyer. Tours by Friends of Hatley Park, 2000 Sooke Rd, Colwood (250-391-2511).

East Sooke Regional Park

This huge 1,422-ha coastal park on the Sooke Peninsula is the regional park par excellence in the Victoria area. Tuck up on a secluded beach, watch the surf shatter against rocky ledges, or **hike** the rugged 10-km Coast Trail through towering forests of spruce, fir

East Sooke Regional Park offers something for everyone

and hemlock and out over windswept bluffs where you can see all the way to the Olympic Peninsula. Scan the sea for killer whales and harbor seals, and the shoreline for river otters. Or search in **tidepools** for periwinkles, sea anemones, starfish and mussels. Wander through the old apple orchard at Aylard Farm, look for **petroglyphs** near Alldridge Point, hike to the old fisherman's trap shack at Cabin Point, find wild onions and orchids on the Creyke Point headland, or **climb** to the top of Mt. Maguire or Babbington Hill for a bird's-eye view of Juan de Fuca Strait. Be sure to pick up a trail map since the park and trailheads can be tricky to find. Available from Capital Regional District Parks, 490 Atkins Ave, Victoria, BC V9B 2Z8 (250-478-3344, fax 250-478-5416) or the Sooke Visitor InfoCentre (below). The park is about a 60-minute drive from Victoria. Follow Hwy 1A to Sooke Rd. Turn left onto Happy Valley Rd and then right onto Rocky Point Rd (which becomes East Sooke Road). Park entrances are at Aylard Farm, Anderson Cove, and Pike Rd.

Sooke Regional Museum & Travel InfoCentre

First a Native settlement where Coast Salish people (the T'Sou-kes) caught salmon in weirs, briefly a gold rush town, and now a logging and fishing community, Sooke has had a fascinating history. See it all at the little Sooke Regional Museum. Visit reconstructions of a **blacksmith shop** and the Sheringham Point light as well as the restored **Moss Cottage** (1870) where "Aunt Tilly" tells you all about raising children in pioneer days. In the museum you'll find exhibits, memorabilia, film shows, a gift shop with a great collection of regional books, and one of the best travel information centres in BC. This is the place to find out about nearby B&Bs, craft studio tours, regional parks and hiking trails, whale watching, boat rentals and fishing charters and local festivities like the annual logging sports. Located just off Highway 14 beyond Sooke River Bridge at the corner of Sooke and Phillips roads (250-642-6351, fax 250-642-7089).

Sooke Potholes Provincial Park

The all-time great **swimming hole** on the Sooke River. A riverbed of water-smoothed stones, natural pools ("potholes") and crystal-clear water draws big crowds in high summer. Salmon leap up the river in autumn. Follow signs from Hwy 14. The park is 5 km up Sooke River Rd.

The West Coast Road: Sooke to Port Renfrew

This stretch of road is packed with **beaches** and **hiking trails** where you can soak up the world of BC's raincoast. See the **Sheringham Point lighthouse** and Juan de Fuca Strait from Gordon's Beach. **Picnic** or **camp** at **French Beach Provincial Park** where huge Pacific breakers crash onto the beach, gray whales feed during their spring migration, and kids play on the **adventure playground**. Stop at the little logging community of **Jordan River** where wet-suited **surfers** catch the waves when the surf's up. Climb down the short (20-minute) but steep gravel trail through tall Sitka spruce to the long sweep of sandy **China Beach**. This is a real favourite with beachcombers (but please don't remove the shells).

China Beach is also a trailhead for the new **Juan de Fuca Marine Trail.** (Three more trailheads are located at Parkinson Creek, Sombrio Beach and Botanical Beach.) This **wilderness hiking trail** runs up the coast from China Beach to Botanical Beach near Port Renfrew. It's meant for strenuous day hiking or multi-day hiking and is still not fully developed, but stretches of the trail range from easy to difficult. For information, BC Parks (250-391-2300, fax 250-478-9211, website www.bcparks.gov.bc.ca).

From China Beach Hwy 14 narrows as it winds toward its terminus at little **Port Renfrew**. Once a coastal logging town, Port Renfrew is also an exit and entry point for the famous **West Coast Trail** (see p. 242) The old Port Renfrew Hotel and Pub is the watering hole for local loggers and fishermen and dirty, thirsty backpackers stumbling off the West Coast Trail. **Botanical Beach Provincial Park** is down a rough gravel road about 8 km past Port Renfrew. Researchers have been studying the wealth of marine life at world-famous Botanical Beach since the turn of the century. Over 230 plant species and about 101 invertebrates have been identified. Go at low tide to see sculpted sandstone tidepools swarming with tiny critters like sea palms, purple sea urchins, black chitons and giant green anemones. Watch for seals, whales, dolphins and porpoises in the water and for birds and the occasional bear feeding along the shore. The setting is west coast with pounding surf, tall sea stacks and rocky headlands, but beware of "rogue waves" that can sweep the unwary walker right off the beach.

Tidepools at Botanical Beach Provincial Park

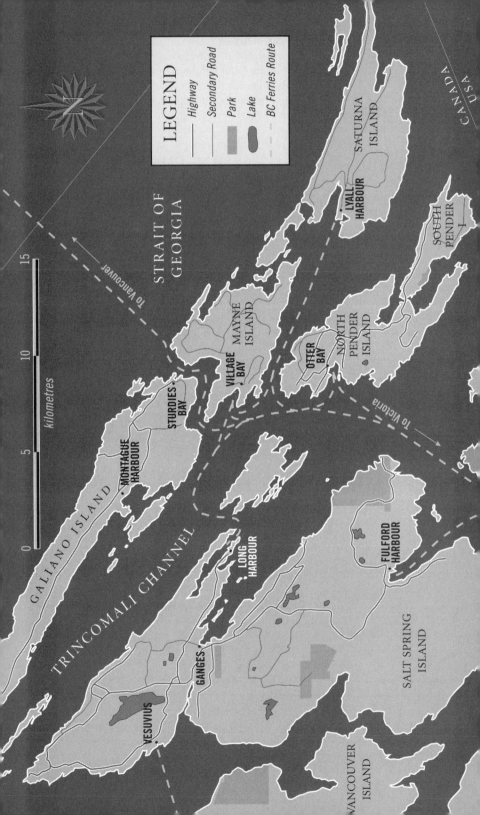

LEGEND

Highway
Secondary Road
Park
Lake
BC Ferries Route

CANADA
USA

SATURNA ISLAND

LYALL HARBOUR

SOUTH PENDER

STRAIT OF GEORGIA

To Vancouver

MAYNE ISLAND

VILLAGE BAY

OTTER BAY

NORTH PENDER ISLAND

STURDIES BAY

MONTAGUE HARBOUR

To Victoria

GALIANO ISLAND

15

10

kilometres

5

0

TRINCOMALI CHANNEL

LONG HARBOUR

FULFORD HARBOUR

GANGES

VESUVIUS

SALT SPRING ISLAND

VANCOUVER ISLAND

CHAPTER 4
THE SOUTHERN GULF ISLANDS

A quiet cove on Salt Spring Island

"I love islands—who doesn't?" commented the American novelist John Updike. Another writer, James Michener, even made up a word for the love of islands—"nesomania," from the Greek *neso* (island) and *mania* (extreme enthusiasm). Nesomaniacs abound in the southern Gulf Islands. The five major ones—Salt Spring, Mayne, Saturna, Pender and Galiano—lie at the south end of a raggedly beautiful archipelago of 225 islands between Vancouver Island and the BC mainland. Sheltered from rough Pacific storms by the mountains of Vancouver Island, these islands are blessed with an enviable climate, even by west coast standards. Winters are mild and summers are warm and dry—so dry that fresh water is a precious resource hereabouts. The southern Gulf Islands are more often called simply "the Gulf Islands," although there are several northern Gulf Islands as well.

The Active Pass light station on Mayne Island.

These evergreen islands are quietly beautiful, close-to-home sorts of places, pastoral retreats that are in some magical way deeply familiar. They are a real home to real people, many of whom have given up the fast-paced urban life to put down roots in their own tranquil corner. The locals take their time to savour the natural pleasures of their surroundings. Woolly homemade caps, sturdy walking sticks and cozy woodstoves are part of the scenery here, and local kids hitchhike into town without a second thought. The counterculture spirit of the '60s wafts gently over the landscape. The islands are home to a delightful mélange of people—artists and writers, farmers, poets and filmmakers, electricians, carpenters, fisherfolk and retired executives; the rich and the poor, the famous and the famously eccentric. The community halls are still the centres of island life where residents gather for club meetings, holiday festivities, local music and theatre productions, Halloween fun, fall fairs and craft fairs.

The Gulf Islands' spectacular scenery, benign climate, and abundance of animal,

Getting to the Gulf Islands

From Vancouver Drive aboard the BC Ferry from the Tsawwassen terminal. Crossing times and number of sailings per day vary depending on your destination and time of year. The Gulf Island ferry to and from Tsawwassen is often full to capacity at peak times—weekends (especially holiday weekends) and most days during the summer. Friday evening and Saturday morning sailings must be reserved. All reservations must be paid in advance and a service fee is charged for any cancellation or change within five days of the travel date. Reservations must be claimed 40 minutes prior to the scheduled sailing time.

During holiday weekends the ferry schedule varies to accommodate the increase in traffic (refer to BC Ferries Southern Gulf Islands schedule or telephone to check changes). If at all possible avoid travelling on holiday weekends or expect sailing waits.

From Victoria Drive aboard the BC Ferry from the Swartz Bay terminal to reach any of the southern Gulf Islands, or stay aboard for the four-island day trip. Crossing times and number of sailings per day vary, depending on your destination. Reservations are not available.

From Tsawwassen via Swartz Bay As there is often less traffic to the Gulf Islands from the Vancouver Island side than from Vancouver, BC Ferries offers a Throughfare Ticket. This ticket allows passage from Tsawwassen terminal to the Swartz Bay terminal, thence connections to the Gulf Islands. Note, however, that a Throughfare Ticket does not guarantee connecting ferry service.

From Crofton (Vancouver Island) Drive aboard the BC Ferry from the Crofton terminal to reach Salt Spring Island. Reservations are not available.

Walking Aboard the Ferry If you are taking a day trip to the islands, exploring one or more islands by bicycle or being met by a friend or recreation guide, you may want to board the BC ferry as a foot a passenger. Your vehicle can be parked at any of the ferry terminals for a small fee. Note: **Get to the terminal early** if you are walking aboard the ferry to or from Tsawwassen terminal. Private operators also offer pay parking just outside the Tsawwassen terminal.

Travel to Saturna Island Depending on your terminal of departure, travel to or from Saturna Island might include a transfer to another ferry at Mayne Island, Galiano Island or Pender Island. Check the BC Ferries Southern Gulf Islands schedule or consult with a BC Ferries passenger service agent.

Travel Between Islands Inter-Gulf Islands BC Ferries connections are available year round. Reservations are not available for travel between the southern Gulf Islands.

Ferry Information For passenger service agents, reservations (7 a.m. to 10 p.m. daily) or recorded information (24 hours), telephone **1-888-BCFERRY (1-888-223-3779)**. From Victoria **250-386-3431**. Fax **250-381-5452**. Website **www.bcferries.bc.ca**.

marine and plant life have drawn superlatives from travel writers—"Magical Islands," "Canada's Hawaii," "Islands of Delight," and "Fragments of Paradise," among others. Like any beautiful place, the Gulf Islands attracts developers, and residents know how easily the balance can be disrupted. They are intent on protecting the islands' fragile beauty: visitors are welcome but they are asked to treat these islands with respect.

All five islands have regular vehicle and foot passenger ferry service from Vancouver (Tsawwassen terminal) and/or Vancouver Island (Swartz Bay terminal). Most days you can take a one-day getaway to any of the islands, or stay aboard for an inexpensive round-trip voyage from Swartz Bay. Once in a while so many foot passengers show up that not everyone gets on board. Some Gulf Island entrepreneurs will pick you up at the island dock for kayaking or biking excursions or for sea cruises. To enjoy the relaxing charm of these beautiful islands to the fullest, book a B&B or motel (well in advance in summer) and settle into island time.

Important Numbers

*Tourism Association of Vancouver Island,
#203 - 335 Wesley Street, Nanaimo, BC,
V9R 2T5 Phone: **250-754-3500**
Fax: **250-754-3599**
website: www.islands.bc.ca*

*Canadian Gulf Islands Bed & Breakfast
Reservation Service **250-539-5390**. Free
booking for accommodations, tour packages and rentals for all the Gulf Islands.*

*Super, Natural British Columbia
Accommodation BC **1-800-663-6000**.
Provides free of charge BC
Accommodations Guide and BC Bed &
Breakfast Directory.*

*Discover Camping Reservations
1-800-689-9025*

Information for the Gulf Islands Visitor

All of the southern Gulf Islands have year-round residents, so they are all equipped with essential services. Salt Spring is the largest and most populated of the southern Gulf Islands and therefore has the most services and facilities. For example, the only two bank machines on the southern Gulf Islands are both located on Salt Spring. Banks are not available at all on Mayne, Saturna or Galiano. Salt Spring is also home to the only hospital on the southern Gulf Islands although Galiano, Mayne, Pender and Saturna are all equipped with health care centres for non-emergencies. During the off-season, many businesses shorten their hours considerably, and some close altogether for the winter. Each of the southern Gulf Islands has a variety of tourist accommodations including inns, motels and campgrounds. Saturna is the only one with no overnight camping, either public or private. By far the most popular and rapidly growing style of accommodation is the bed-and-breakfast. B&Bs are an ideal place to stay on the Gulf Islands. They provide all the comforts of home while allowing you to get a good "feel" for the island you are visiting. Be sure to make reservations, particularly in the summer.

Swartz Bay Ferry Terminal

SALT SPRING ISLAND

Great blue he[ron]

Farmhouse at Ruckle Park

Highlights

Old style farms and orchards

Great spots for
wildlife viewing

Wide variety of
hiking trails

A slower pace of life

Fishing/boating

Great camping

Swimming

The biggest of the southern Gulf Islands and the most populated—with 9,500 year-round residents—is Salt Spring Island. That number nearly doubles in July and August when all the "weekenders" arrive. Ganges, the island's main village, is home to more than 1,100 people. The island is about 185 sq. km in area with 650 km of road, eleven lakes, two golf courses, a small movie theatre, a shopping mall, lots of places to eat, and even a scattering of (hotly debated) condo developments.

According to Captain John T. Walbran, author of the 1909 *British Columbia Coast Names: Their Origin and History*, the island was given its name "by officers of the Hudson's Bay Company, because a number of springs of brine (3,446 grains of salt to the imperial gallon) exist on the island." Despite official dictum from Ottawa that the island's name is to be spelled Saltspring, residents have resolutely stuck to its traditional spelling. About those salty springs (fourteen of them): they are all on private property and reputedly not much to look at. But Salty Springs Sea Spa at 1460

What to See

☐ **1** Ruckle Provincial Park
☐ **2** Ganges
☐ **3** Mahon Hall
☐ **4** Lake Stowell
☐ **5** Mt. Maxwell
☐ **6** Vesuvius Bay
☐ **7** Akerman Museum
☐ **8** St. Mary Lake

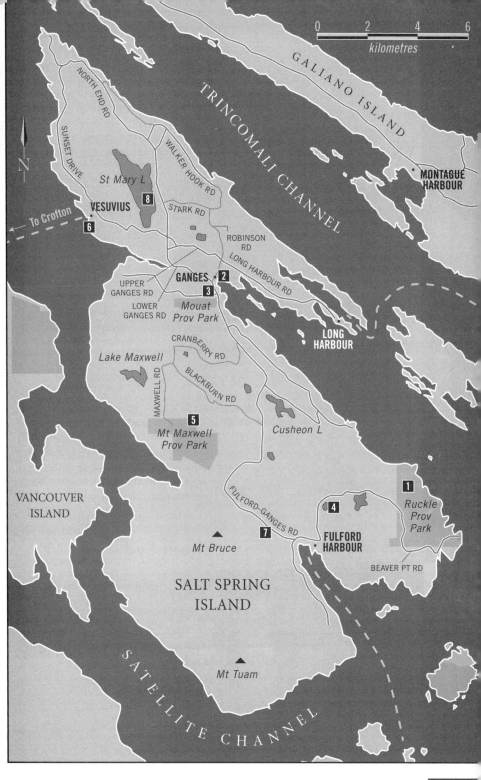

0   2   4   6
kilometres

GALIANO ISLAND

TRINCOMALI CHANNEL

MONTAGUE HARBOUR

NORTH END RD

WALKER HOOK RD

SUNSET DRIVE

St Mary L

VESUVIUS

8

STARK RD

To Crofton

6

ROBINSON RD

LONG HARBOUR RD

GANGES **2**

3

UPPER GANGES RD

LOWER GANGES RD

Mouat Prov Park

LONG HARBOUR

CRANBERRY RD

Lake Maxwell

BLACKBURN RD

MAXWELL RD

Cusheon L

5

Mt Maxwell Prov Park

1

Ruckle Prov Park

VANCOUVER ISLAND

FULFORD-GANGES RD

4

7

FULFORD HARBOUR

Mt Bruce

BEAVER PT RD

SALT SPRING ISLAND

Mt Tuam

SATELLITE CHANNEL

N

Government wharves are available for public use

North Beach Road (250-537-4111) offers therapeutic saltwater baths and accommodations in modern but "woodsy" cabins.

From the early days of white settlement in the 1850s, Salt Spring has been a farming community, known for its fine products including apples, peaches, dairy products and especially for its delicious lamb. Many of the island's old farms and apple orchards are still standing, and the famous Salt Spring sheep graze contentedly in green pastures. The island even hosts fun-for-all-comers sheepdog trials in September. Not all of the dogs know exactly what they're supposed to be doing, but everyone—dogs, dog owners and spectators—have a great time. At this and the many other community events on Salt Spring, a spirit of playfulness prevails.

Fulford Harbour Ferry Terminal

South End

Fulford Harbour

Fulford Harbour is a welcoming gateway to the island. This little community, nestled in the arms of the main harbour, is as friendly as it is picturesque. The south end of the island has a higher ratio of sheep to people than the north end, and it tends to attract people who like lots of breathing room. You'll sense the magical easy-going ambiance of the south end as soon as you hit dry land. Stop and explore the delightful old-time clapboard buildings that house a

Getting to Salt Spring Island

From Vancouver Drive aboard the BC Ferry from Tsawwassen terminal. 1 hour and 10 minutes to 2 hours and 45 minutes crossing time to Long Harbour; 4 sailings daily, year round. The Gulf Island ferry to and from Tsawwassen is often full to capacity at peak times—weekends (especially holiday weekends) and most days during summer. Reservations are recommended at peak times and required Friday nights and Saturday mornings.

From Victoria Drive aboard the BC Ferry from Swartz Bay terminal. 35 minutes crossing time to Fulford Harbour; 10 sailings daily year round. Reservations are not available.

From Crofton (Vancouver Island) Drive aboard the BC Ferry from the Crofton terminal. 20 minutes crossing time to Vesuvius Bay; 13–15 sailings daily year round.

From Other Gulf Islands Access is available from other southern Gulf Islands serviced by BC Ferries. Routes and times vary depending on the day, point of departure and time of year. Contact BC Ferries for schedule information. Reservations not available.

Ferry Information For passenger service agents, reservations (7 a.m. to 10 p.m. daily) or recorded information (24 hours), telephone 1-888-BCFERRY (1-888-223-3779). From Victoria 250-386-3431. Fax 250-381-5452. Website www.bcferries.bc.ca.

general store/gas station, laid-back little gift shops, bike and kayak rentals and Rodrigo's cafe, a great local favourite. Turn right as soon as you exit the terminal and park on the narrow country road that heads off into Fulford. If you're a sea-going soul, stop at the marina not far from the ferry dock. You can park there (for a small fee) and walk back along the road to explore the shops.

Ruckle Provincial Park

Straight up the road, a few hundred metres from the Fulford dock is the well-marked right-hand turnoff to Ruckle Provincial Park (call 250-391-2300, or for group reservations, 250-539-2115). As you drive 10 km down the winding Beaver Point Road, you'll pass little Beaver Point School (1885–1951), the second-oldest school still standing in BC and now part of a provincial park. You can park here and follow the trail behind the school for a long hike into the beautiful forest and oceanside trails of Ruckle Park. Or continue along the road 2 km to the park gate.

Ruckle Provincial Park is not only a park, but the oldest working farm still operating on Salt Spring. Descendants of the Ruckle pioneers gave land to the BC government for a provincial park in 1974 but stayed on to work the farm and to live in the delightful Victorian farmhouse built in 1876, near the park gate. Another farmhouse nearby serves as the park headquarters, and outbuildings scattered across the pretty sweep of pastureland are part of the working farm. From time to time in the summer Gwen Ruckle treats park visitors to an unscheduled slide show in the barn about changing times on the Ruckle farm. A family story of disappointment in love is a local legend. William Ruckle intended to live with his bride-to-be in a house built on the property in 1938. But the relationship soured, the wedding was called off, and the house stood unoccupied for years. Eventually it was used to store potatoes, and it is still known as "the potato house."

The rolling pastures of Ruckle Provincial Park are delightful, but the special beauty of the park lies just beyond. Follow the road to the parking lot and then walk out along the spectacular wind and water-carved sandstone headlands overlooking Swanson Channel. The walk-in campsites are some of the most beautiful in BC, and wildlife abounds here. You may see whales, seals, sea lions, porpoises, raccoons, river otters, black-tailed deer, ospreys, great blue herons and a multitude of waterbirds, but mercifully no bears and hardly ever a cougar. (Cougars were once a serious threat to livestock and children, but

Sheep grazing at pastoral Ruckle Park

sharp-shooting farmers and bounty hunters drastically reduced their numbers. Occasionally a cougar swims over from Vancouver Island, but it is quickly tracked and relocated.) Check the park bulletin board for more information on wildlife. You may even find you've pitched your tent underneath a tree that's an eagle's favourite fishing perch. If you're day tripping, take advantage of the park's picnic tables and barbecues for an al fresco family feast.

On your return from the park, look for roadside **"honesty stands"** where you can put your money in the box and walk away with honey, flowers, veggies, jams, eggs and whatever else local folk have for sale. You'll also pass **Lake Stowell** where you can stop for a refreshing swim before heading up the island.

If you follow Beaver Point Road back to Fulford you can swing right onto the main road leading to Ganges, the commercial and communal heart of Salt Spring Island. Just before the road curves to the right around the very prominent Fulford Inn, look for the little red-roofed **St. Paul's Church** tucked into a grassy slope above a scattering of tombstones. This is Salt Spring's oldest church, founded by a Roman Catholic missionary in 1878. It was built in part by immigrants from Hawaii who came to the west coast aboard Hudson's Bay Company trading ships to work as labourers in HBC outposts. Several Hawaiians chose to settle on the south end of Salt Spring to log, fish and farm. Many built their cabins near the shore, and some of the men married Native women. They cultivated enviable gardens and occasionally held communal luaus (feasts) that lasted days or weeks. Their anglicized names are etched into the headstones of St. Paul's churchyard. Descendants of several families still live on Salt Spring and have maintained their distinctive culture. In 1994 more than 300 people of Hawaiian ancestry gathered at a small Salt Spring beach for a traditional luau, feasting on succulent mussels, clams and oysters steamed in seaweed inside a traditional Hawaiian imu (covered firepit) and enjoying the chance to find relations they never knew existed.

The Fulford–Ganges Road runs through the fertile Fulford Valley. Here you sense the island's history in the two small churches—Anglican **St. Mary's Church** (1894) and the old Union Church (now the **Burgoyne Bay United Church**) (1887)—and in the few remaining pioneer farmhouses in apple orchards planted in the days when Salt Spring farmers shipped their produce all over Canada. The **Fulford Hall** across from St. Mary's Church has been the centre of community get-togethers for Fulford Harbour and Burgoyne Bay residents for half a century.

Look for the **Akerman museum** about half a kilometre north of Fulford Harbour at 2501 Fulford–Ganges Road. (The museum is open if the sign is out, or call ahead at 250-653-4228.) This private collection includes many local Native artifacts. Salt Spring was long the site of summer fishing and shellfish harvesting expeditions by nearby Wsanec bands, and there may have been a permanent First Nations village on the south end of Salt Spring near the Tsawout Band reserve. Many local families have grandparents or great-grandparents of Native heritage, including the museum's curator himself, Bob Akerman. His maternal grandmother, Granny Gyves, was the daughter of a Cowichan chief. According to

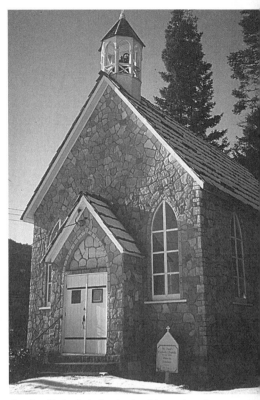

St. Paul's is Salt Spring's oldest church

a local historian, Granny Gyves could use a gun but chose to shoo animals away with an old broom handle. Her husband once joked that the cougars were more afraid of her stick than of his gun.

▶ Salt Spring's Famous Lamb

Sheep have graced the pastures of Salt Spring Island for generations. Salt Spring lamb is a highly rated delicacy. So are the sheep's milk cheese and yogurt made by ex-Torontonian David Wood. His famous David Wood Food Shop in Toronto was a favourite haunt of the well-to-do, including the Eaton family and former Loblaw's president Dave Nichol. Tired of the Toronto fast track, Wood escaped to the greener pastures of Salt Spring and began raising sheep and goats. Many other Islanders have struck a happy bal-

ance between cosmopolitan tastes and the charms of rural life.

Mountain Hikes and Views

Another reminder of Salt Spring's first peoples is the evergreen-covered hump of **Mt. Tuam** at the southwest tip of the island. According to ancient legend, it was the home of the sun god, and the mountain is still considered a sacred place by nearby Native groups.

For hikers, Salt Spring Island is the number one destination in the southern Gulf Islands because it is so big and mountainous, with so many peaks and ridges to explore. Mt. Tuam is just one of the mountains on the rugged south end. You can see **Mt. Bruce** off to your left as you drive through Fulford Valley. This is Salt Spring's highest peak (698 m) where hang-gliders sometimes tempt fate by soaring off the summit. The imposing forehead of **Mt. Maxwell** rises up at the head of this lovely pastoral valley. A 1.3-km trail leads up to its summit from the end of Seymour

Panoramic view from Mt. Maxwell

Heights Road (accessed from Dukes Road and the Fulford Ganges Road). But many visitors just drive to the parking lot at the top of the mountain. To drive to Mt. Maxwell Provincial Park, take the sharp right turn from the Fulford–Ganges Road onto Cranberry Road, before you reach Ganges. After about 4 km, the well-paved Cranberry Road becomes the gravel-surfaced Mount Maxwell Road, and it becomes narrow and rough enough that RVs are discouraged from trying to negotiate this last 3 km to the park. But the drive is worth the effort. The views from the summit of Mt. Maxwell—known as Baynes Peak—are exhilarating. You look down almost 600 metres to see the whole Fulford Valley spread out below your feet, with Burgoyne Bay and Vancouver Island in the distance. Camping isn't permitted in the park, but picnic tables placed at strategic intervals let you linger for a picnic before heading to town.

▶ **Salt Spring Island Annual Events**

March Erotic Festival	**August** Fulford Days
April Saturday Markets (April–Oct)	**September** Fall Fair Sheepdog Trials
June Sea Capers Festival	**November** Guild's Christmas Craft Fair
July Canada Day Celebration Festival of the Arts	For more information, Salt Spring Island Chamber of Commerce **250-537-4223**

Ganges

Just north of the turnoff to Mt Maxwell, the Fulford–Ganges Road curves and dips down into Ganges. This charming seaside village is a mix of historic buildings like the Embe Bakery building (once the site of a thriving commercial dairy) and bright new commercial structures. The mix of old and new seems quite successful so far, but the struggle to achieve the right balance between preservation and development is a hot topic on all the Gulf Islands. Salt Spring is close enough to Victoria to be a home for commuters, large and developed enough to attract new residents who like the quiet but don't want to "rough it," and beautiful enough to send casual visitors scurrying to real estate offices in search of their own piece of paradise. The sheer number of realtors in Ganges is a gauge of Salt Spring Island's love-at-first-sight attractiveness.

The bustling Saturday market in Ganges

Like many other islands all over the world, Salt Spring is a place where the visitor can become aware of the "drawbridge mentality"—the last one inside pulls up the bridge to keep outsiders away. The famous wildlife artist and Salt Spring resident Robert Bateman wryly admitted to the urge to pull up a drawbridge to keep Salt Spring from being destroyed by development. The BC government established the Islands Trust to "preserve and protect" the area's irreplaceable natural beauty, and the Trust's activities are as hotly debated as the issue of preservation. On Salt Spring and all the southern Gulf Islands, visitors are in the company of people who care passionately about their part of the world.

Ganges is a village full of colour and activity. You can feel immediately that this is the heart of the community. Park your car (be patient if it's a summer weekend) and walk around town and along the waterfront. Ganges and its harbour were named for the British man-of-war HMS *Ganges* captained by John Fulford and described in a London newspaper in 1847 as "the handsomest and swiftest ship in the British navy."

You'll find establishments to meet all your needs in or near Ganges: banks, shops, supermarkets, laundromats, service stations, public showers, pharmacies, a liquor store, marinas and a hospital—as well as a wide array of good restaurants, pubs and delis. Ask the friendly people at the **Visitor Information Centre** for updated maps and insider's advice on where to shop, eat and sleep. Leave time for a visit to Mouat's Trading Company and Mall, built in 1912 by Jane Mouat and her son Gilbert after Jane's husband died and left her with eleven children to raise. They operated it under the name of G. J. Mouat & Company, apparently because women were not supposed to be store owners in those days. Mouat's still sells the dry goods, hardware, fishing gear and household items that have been its stock in trade for decades. Even though it has all kinds of modern goods, Mouat's

Food Plants of the First Peoples

The Coast Salish were the most numerous of all the Northwest Coast First Nations peoples. They were hunters and gatherers who lived in a rich forest "garden" of edible plants. The land abounded with animals, the surrounding sea was full of fish, the shore was encrusted with succulent shellfish. Seasonal food-gathering work patterned the people's lives. From spring to fall they travelled by canoe to summer camps where they harvested berries and other plants, shucked and dried clams, oysters and mussels, collected birds and birds' eggs, hunted deer and other mammals, and caught salmon and other fish. In winter they returned to the big cedar longhouses where they engaged in potlatching and other winter ceremonials. Look closely at some of the most common plants of the coastal forests, and you will see the outdoor pantries of the Coast Salish.

Thanks to ethnobotonists like Nancy Turner, whose work is a major source of the following descriptions, we know much more about how BC's First Nations people used coastal food sources.

Oregon Grape (*Mahonia* species) Two species of this low-growing shrub, tall Oregon grape and dull Oregon grape occur locally. They have stiff, holly-like leaves and light yellow-grey bark. Oregon grape has bright yellow flower clusters and dark blue berry clusters. The very sour berries were eaten raw or else mashed or boiled with sweeter berries and then dried. Today the berries are used for wine or jelly.

still has the air of an old-fashioned general store. Downstairs, in Mouat's Mall you can browse in several eye-catching stores and boutiques.

If you happen to be in Ganges on a Saturday between May and October, the **Farmer's Market** in Centennial Park is a must-see. This is a place to watch islanders and visitors, dogs and children, craftspeople and souvenir shoppers, food vendors, market gardeners, jugglers and musicians, all milling around the downtown Ganges park in glorious disarray. Everything for sale must be handmade or home-grown, and Salt Spring has an extraordinary number of talented artists and craftspeople. You'll find everything from perennial plants to toys and puppets, from jams and relishes to muffins and Mexican food, from clothing and jewellery to pottery and wood crafts. It's a feast for the eyes—and you can happily fill your stomach, too.

Salal (*Gaultheria shallon*) This member of the heather family is one of the most common shrubs of coastal forests. It grows from 30 cm to 2 m tall. The tough evergreen leaves are oval with fine-toothed edges, the stems are hairy and branching, and the bark is reddish or greyish. It has white or pinkish bell-shaped flowers growing in one-sided clusters and fleshy reddish blue to dark purple berries, also in one-sided clusters. These juicy and very plentiful (but mealy-textured) berries were the most important fruits among coastal peoples. They were eaten fresh or dried into cakes. At feast times these much-prized cakes were soaked in water, mixed with eulachon grease, and served.

Kinnikinnick (*Arctostaphylos uva-ursi*) This member of the heather family, another common shrub on the coast, is an evergreen with small, oblong or spoon-shaped green leaves and reddish bark. Its long trailing branches form thick mats 5–15 cm high. It has clustered pink bell-shaped flowers and bright red berries. These very dry berries were sometimes eaten fresh but more often they were first soaked in water, melted grease or seal oil (partly to prevent constipation). The dried leaves were also smoked like tobacco by many coastal groups.

Fireweed (*Epilobium angustifolium*) This member of the evening primrose family is sometimes called willow herb. Often found growing in disturbed or burned-out areas, it is a tall perennial plant that is abloom all summer with red-purple flowers along its stem. Several Coast Salish groups ate the sweet inner part of the young plant stems as a raw green vegetable. The Saanich picked the leaves of young plants to make tea that was rich in vitamin C.

Further Reading:

Food Plants of Coastal First Peoples by Nancy J. Turner (UBC Press, 1995)
Plants of Coastal British Columbia, including Washington, Oregon & Alaska by Jim Pojar and Andy MacKinnon (Lone Pine Publishing, 1994)
Indians of the Northwest Coast by Peter Drucker (Natural History Press, 1955)

For another superb sampling of quality Salt Spring arts and crafts, make your way to **Artcraft** at **Mahon Hall**, the old agricultural hall at the intersection of Lower Ganges Road and Rainbow Road. In the summer months more than 200 artisans display their works in there, and you won't find better work anywhere on the coast.

Approximate Distances

From Ganges to Fulford Harbour 14 km

From Ganges to Long Harbour 6 km

From Ganges to Vesuvius 7.5 km

From Ganges to Beaver Point 23.5 km

From Vesuvius to Long Harbour 11 km

Just across the street, above the Ganges Marina, is **The Fishery**. Here you can buy fresh-caught salmon, cod and crab as well as smoked fish. If you want your fish and chips fried by other hands, you can find it at several local pubs and restaurants on Upper Ganges Road, with great views over Ganges Harbour.

A discreetly signed lane on Upper Ganges Road indicates the right turnoff to the formidable **Hastings House**. Set in a magnificent garden overlooking the harbour, this Tudor-style manor house was built by Barbara Wedgewood, a British pottery heiress who was known to tootle around Salt Spring's dusty country roads in a Rolls Royce. This fine B&B offers luxurious accommodation at prices to match and the Hastings House restaurant, which has been featured in *Gourmet* magazine, is known internationally for its impeccable cuisine. As well as dinner, the restaurant offers lavish and moderately priced Sunday brunch. Reserve well in advance as registered guests have priority. (250-537-2362 or 1-800-661-9255).

North End

Be sure to leave plenty of time for a leisurely tour of the north end of Salt Spring by car or by bike. You can take a looping route from Ganges along the Upper Ganges Road, Robinson Road, Walker Hook Road, North Beach Road, North End Road and then back

south down Sunset Drive to Salt Spring's third village, sleepy little Vesuvius Bay. The route might sound complicated, but it's actually easy to follow. You'll go past pasturelands enclosed in blackberry-tangled split-rail fences and tucked-away homes, past stands of cedar, fir, and alder trees, and then edge along Trincomali Channel where you get delightful peek-a-boo views of swatches of blue water dotted with water birds. This picturesque route is a fine choice for bicycling, but it's narrow so be careful of cars. If you want to stop and make your way down to the beach, watch for public entry points. Access is limited but the beach below the high tide mark is public property.

A pleasing Salt Spring Island touch is the occasional beautifully carved and painted signs along the roads, made by a

A rustic barn and a dusting of snow

local sign-maker. Some of these direct you to **artists' studios**. You can combine your north end loop tour with serendipitous studio-hopping on Sunday afternoons from May through October and visit by appointment at other times of the year. Pick up studio tour maps at the information centre or in galleries, B&Bs and other establishments around the island. If the "blue sheep" studio tour sign is posted by the road, the studio is open to visitors.

Vesuvius Bay

Sunset Road, which takes you into Vesuvius Bay, got its name from the wonderful displays of light and colour on the western edge of the island. If you're near Vesuvius at sunset, slide down to the beach or sit back with a cold beer on the deck of the Vesuvius Inn, just past the BC ferry dock, and have your fill of sunset splendour. The neighbourhood pub is a replica of the original 1873 inn built by a wandering Portuguese sailor and gold miner named Estalon Jose Bittancourt. Next to the ferry dock is a little Catholic chapel, known as **The Ark,** that Bittancourt built for his family and neighbours. It was deconsecrated in 1940 and is now an intriguing home/gallery.

Vesuvius Bay was also home to several of Salt Spring's black pioneers, who were among the first settlers on the north end of the island. Many were former slaves from California. One of the black settlers was Sylvia Estes Stark. According to Ethel Wallace Claibourne, Stark's ninety-seven-year-old granddaughter and a lifelong Salt Spring Islander, her grandmother was in Placerville, California, working in the cotton fields when the word came that California might bring in slavery. At the same time, Sir James Douglas, afraid that the US might make a land grab for territory north of the 49th parallel if it wasn't colonized quickly, invited blacks to settle north of the border and promised them freedom.

A happy customer in front of the Vesuvius Store

At the age of twenty-one, Sylvia Stark clambered down the side of a ship on a rope and into a canoe that took her ashore near Vesuvius Bay. She lived to the ripe old age of 105, and Stark Road is a reminder of her family's presence on the island.

The village of Vesuvius Bay is full of charming old seaside cottages knitted together by winding lanes. The Vesuvius Store, with its homey, old-fashioned ambiance, offers back-garden organic produce in wicker baskets and healthy take-out foods, as well as the usual corner-store items. Several B&Bs and a motel make Vesuvius a pleasant place for a night's rest.

If this is the end of your stay on Salt Spring, you can take a ferry from the Vesuvius terminal to Crofton on Vancouver Island. The ferry crossing is just 20 minutes long, and from Crofton you can drive to Nanaimo or to Victoria to catch a ferry back to the lower mainland (see Getting to Victoria, p. 95).

Central Salt Spring

If you're leaving Salt Spring from Long Harbour, Ganges or Fulford, you can take the Vesuvius Bay Road back to the area known as "central." You'll pass **St. Mary Lake**, a major island resort area and the biggest freshwater lake in the Gulf Islands. You'll also see the island's major recreation area with its soccer and baseball fields, outdoor swimming pool and tennis courts. Public washrooms are available here. Just beyond, at the intersection of Vesuvius Bay Road and North End Road, is **Central Hall**. This was once an agricultural hall, but now it is a church on Sundays and the island's only **movie theatre** in the evenings. Joining the local crowd for a show is a splendid way to have fun the island way. It's a warm, family-oriented community event.

Fishing for bass on St Mary Lake

From here you can drive straight ahead onto Upper Ganges Road, then jog right onto Long Harbour Road which leads to the **Long Harbour ferry terminal**. For a picturesque last view of Ganges Harbour, swing right onto Old Scott Road (just opposite Quebec Drive). From Long Harbour Road this pretty little lane wanders along the northern shore of Ganges Harbour before it angles back to the Long Harbour ferry terminal. A small park and picnic tables at the terminal will make your wait for the ferry most enjoyable on a nice day.

Alternatively, from Central Hall you can turn right onto Lower Ganges Road and curve past the inviting green fairways of the golf course back to Ganges and on to Fulford Harbour.

Chances are good that whichever exit you take from the island, you'll want to come back. Salt Spring has lots of secrets to discover.

Salt Spring Island Recreation, Accommodations and Services

Recreation
Bicycle rentals
Kayak/canoe rentals
Fishing charters
Dive charters
Golf courses
Tennis courts
Major hiking trails
Parks
Horseback riding ranch

Accommodations
Bed & Breakfasts
Hotels/Motels/ Resorts
Cabins/Cottages

Campgrounds/RV parks
Hostel

Services
InfoCentre
Restaurants
Pubs
Take-out
Banks
ATM's
Post offices
Grocery stores
Service stations
Car/Truck rentals
Taxi service
Studios/Galleries

Police/Fire/Ambulance emergency **911**

RCMP non-emergency **250-537-5555**

Hospital (Ganges) **250-538-4800**

Salt Spring Island Tourist Infocentre, P.O. Box 111 Ganges, BC V0N 2J0. Phone **250-537-5252** Fax **250-537-4276**

Tourism Association of Vancouver Island, #203 - 335 Wesley Street, Nanaimo, BC, V9R 2T5 Phone: **250-754-3500** Fax: **250-754-3599** website: www.islands.bc.ca

Canadian Gulf Islands Bed & Breakfast Reservation Service, **250-539-5390**. Free booking for accommodations, tour packages and rentals for all the Gulf Islands.

Super, Natural British Columbia, **1-800-663-6000**. Provides free of charge BC Accommodations Guide and BC Bed & Breakfast Directory.

Deer are plentiful throughout the Gulf Islands

MAYNE ISLAND

Miners Bay

Mayne Island Museum

Highlights

A slower pace of life

Hiking

Biking

Fishing

Mountain and ocean vistas

Rolling farmland

Quiet spots for swimming and other water sports

Worldwide gold fever struck in 1858, when rumours began circulating about gold finds up the Fraser River in British Columbia. Thousands of prospectors and speculators poured into BC, many of them having turned their backs on the California gold fields, and converged on Victoria from all directions. From there gold-seekers with ready cash boarded steamboats and headed for the mouth of the Fraser River near Vancouver. But hundreds of others set out in small sailboats, sail-rigged rowboats and dugout canoes to brave the dangerous tides of Active Pass on their way to the mainland. This deep, narrow channel was named not for its fast-running currents, but for the first steamboat to navigate it in 1885, the small wooden paddlewheeler USS *Active*.

Mayne Island, an irregular-shaped 21-sq.-km island, is on Active Pass almost exactly midway between Victoria and Vancouver. A well-protected cove on the northwest shore of the island was soon dubbed **Miners Bay**. It offered gold seekers a welcome respite from the treacherous waters of "The Pass." They camped on the broad gravel beach, drank from nearby streams and rested up for the long haul across open water to Vancouver. Legend has it that they also planted the first apple trees to grow on the island. Several miners who found nothing but disappointment in the gold fields returned to Mayne Island to try their luck at homesteading. This was the beginning of the Mayne Island community centred on Miners Bay.

After a wharf was built at Miners Bay in 1885, Mayne Island became one of the earliest tourist destinations on the west coast. Well-

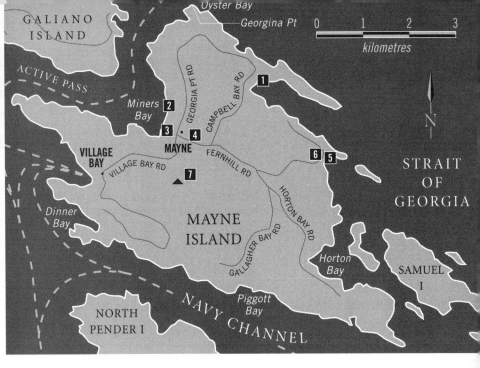

heeled families from Vancouver and Victoria began arriving aboard steamships to summer on the island. They lodged in genteel hotels and boarding houses, enjoyed afternoon tea, polite games of croquet and tennis on the lawn, and the pleasures of walking, fishing and ocean bathing.

Today the same attractions still draw visitors to Mayne Island. It is a tranquil getaway with mountain and ocean vistas, quiet roads and rolling farmlands, good swimming beaches and sport fishing spots. Sports like kayaking and bicycling are also bringing the active crowd to explore the island.

What to See

- ☐ **1** Campbell Bay Beach
- ☐ **2** St. Mary Magdalene Anglican Church
- ☐ **3** Springwater Lodge
- ☐ **4** Mayne Island Museum
- ☐ **5** Bennett Bay Beach
- ☐ **6** Mayne Inn
- ☐ **7** Mt. Parke

Mayne Island is a fine destination for a day trip, a leisurely sojourn or a home base for day-tripping to other Gulf Islands serviced by BC Ferries. Several sailings connect to other islands through Mayne Island's Village Bay terminal (see Getting to Mayne Island, p. 141). You'll find accommodations ranging from the posh Oceanwood Country Inn (250-539-5074) to small welcoming B&Bs. Fernhill Lodge offers theme rooms, an eclectic library, a delightful herb garden and "historical dinners" featuring meticulously researched meals from far-distant times and places (250-539-2544). Operators of many B&Bs will pick you up at the ferry terminal and even equip you with bicycles—a good way to tour the island if the occasional hilly stretch of road doesn't sound too daunting.

Travelling to Mayne Island aboard a BC ferry from either Vancouver or Victoria, you will find the trip spectacular. Dramatic evergreen islands and islets rise up on all sides.

A sheep farm on Mayne Island

Seals slide past the rocky foreshores, and eagles soar and dip on the updrafts high overhead. In the distance you can see the layered mountains of the mainland and the blue spine of Vancouver Island. Earlier this century, when the globe-trotting Edward VIII threaded through Active Pass and the beautiful southern Gulf Islands on his way from Vancouver to Victoria, he declared it "the most beautiful trip of the kind in the world."

Village Bay

The ferry terminal on Mayne Island is at Village Bay, on the west side of the island. It was named by a British Royal Navy surveyor, Captain George Henry Richards, on a map-making expedition in 1858. When he sighted the cedar longhouses of a Native settlement enfolded gently in this bay, he penned "Village Bay" onto his map. Today the traditional cedar houses of the Natives have been replaced by more contemporary homes, but there is still a Native presence on the island. Much of the land to your left as you drive off the ferry is part of the 129-hectare Helen Point Indian Reserve, a beautiful piece of land which sweeps along the southern boundary of Active Pass. It was established in 1877 and still belongs to the Tsartlip Band.

Kayaking is a great way to see the Gulf Islands

Start your island exploration by taking a left at the top of the ferry terminal and then a right at the stop sign onto Village Bay Road. If you glance off in the opposite

Getting to Mayne Island

From Vancouver Drive aboard the BC Ferry from Tsawwassen terminal. 1 hour to 1 hour and 30 minutes crossing time; 3–5 sailings daily year round.

The Gulf Island ferry to and from Tsawwassen is often full to capacity at peak times—weekends (especially holiday weekends) and most days during summer. Reservations are recommended at peak times and required Friday nights and Saturday mornings.

From Victoria Drive aboard the BC Ferry from Swartz Bay terminal. 50 minutes to 2 hours and 10 minutes crossing time; 4 sailings daily year round. Reservations not available.

From other Gulf Islands Access is available from other southern Gulf Islands serviced by BC Ferries. Routes and times vary depending on the day, point of departure and time of year. Contact BC Ferries for schedule information. Reservations not available.

Ferry Information For passenger service agents, reservations (7 a.m. to 10 p.m. daily) or recorded information (24 hours), telephone *1-888-BCFERRY (1-888-223-3779)*. From Victoria *250-386-3431*. Fax *250-381-5452*. Website *www.bcferries.bc.ca*.

direction, you'll see pastureland that was orginally homesteaded by the Portuguese sailor John Silva, who reportedly jumped ship in Victoria in 1852. He married a Cowichan woman, Louisa, and they cleared a homestead here and raised their family. Like most island youngsters, the Silvas' ten children were free to roam the local waters in small rowboats almost as soon as they could lift the oars. But the Silvas lost a boy and a girl to the fast-running waters of Active Pass in 1880, and Louisa was so broken-hearted that the family sold up and moved away to Gabriola Island. John and Margaret Deacon took over the homestead, and not long after they built the landmark Deacon barn. Look for the old green-roofed barn in the valley just below the ridge of Mt. Parke and for Margaret's favourite yellow roses along Dalton Drive which runs to the right from Village Bay Road. Descendants of the Deacons still live on Mayne Island, and for a long time Wilbur Deacon was the best-known well-witcher on the Gulf Islands. He cut fresh willow sticks from a tree that still stands just at the crest of the hill on the road to Miners Bay.

Miners Bay

Miners Bay, about 2.5 km down Village Bay Road, is still the centre of island life and services. Here you can stock up on gas, food, liquor and baked goodies or enjoy a pub meal or a deli snack. Stop at the new Mayne Street Mall on Village Bay Road to admire the locally created mural, and drop in at the bakery cafe for a cappuccino or fresh soup and sandwich. The Tru Value store next door is impressively well supplied, and the Trading Post at the T-junction of Village Bay Road and Fernhill Road stands where a general store has operated since the First World War. It is still a general store as well as the BC government liquor outlet.

You won't want to miss the historic **Springwater Lodge** just to the left on Fernhill Road at the head of the wharf. It has great pub food—its burgers are famous—and the view of Active Pass from its flower-brightened verandah is one of the best spectator spots in the islands. You can sometimes see three ferries at once threading through the pass. The recently renovated Springwater has been a local favourite since the mid-1890s, when Mayne Island was the social hub of the area by virtue of having the only pubs in the southern Gulf Islands. It may be the oldest inn in continuous operation in BC.

According to one old-time Mayne Islander, everyone from Salt Spring and the other islands used to come over and spend the weekends. Thirsty Gulf Islanders were known to row to Mayne Island from miles away, sometimes risking thick fog and strong currents to wet their whistles. It was an unwritten rule that dances never ended till dawn when it was

Bald eagles can be seen throughout the Gulf Islands

safe for revellers to clamber back into their boats for the trip home. The pubs of Mayne earned the island the nickname "Little Hell" from disapproving neighbours on "dry" islands.

Back up Fernhill Road a block and a half is the **Mayne Island Museum** where you can find out more about the island's history for a few hours a week in summer (250-539-5286). This little 4.5 by 7 metre building was once the Plumper Pass Lockup, constructed in 1896 with two small cells. According to local legend, the first prisoner to be locked up here simply pried up the wooden floorboards and escaped the very same night. The jail housed only ten prisoners over its eleven-year history, and the local constable, Arthur Drummond, had to get around the islands in a sixteen-foot rowboat equipped with a sail—not the most efficient way to track down smugglers, boat thieves and livestock rustlers!

Across the street from the Mayne Museum is the old **Agricultural Hall** where the **Mayne Island Fall Fair** is still held on the third Saturday in August. This colourful, friendly community affair began way back in 1925 and it still has the flavour of the good old days. You can watch the parade, second-guess the judges at the exhibits of local produce, baked goods and crafts inside the hall, or enjoy the log-sawing and other fun-for-all contests just outside.

Mt. Parke

On up Fernhill Road about 2 km is **Fernhill Centre**, on the right, where you'll find a small grocery store, a restaurant and the turnoff to the only public hiking trail at **Mt. Parke Regional Park**. To get to this new 50-hectare park, turn right from Fernhill Road onto Montrose Road and drive about .5 km to the parking lot. The trail is a fairly easy 30- to 40-minute hike up to the top of Mt. Parke. You will be rewarded with wonderful views over the Gulf Islands as far as Vancouver Island and the chance to relax on a superb bluff covered with arbutus and Garry oak trees. This is the quintessential Gulf Islands experience, but you may have to share your experience with others—Mt. Parke is a popular hike.

Beaches

If you'd rather just stretch out on the beach and enjoy the panorama from sea level, then head for **Bennett Bay Beach**. Continue on Fernhill Road, which becomes Bennett Bay Road. On the way, you'll pass the picturesque **Hardscrabble Farm**, where John and Margaret Deacon worked their 120-hectare farm in the 1880s. At the end of Bennett Bay Road you'll see Wilkes Road on your left, which leads to the beach access to Bennett Bay. This driftwood-backed rock-and-sand beach is a local favourite for its warm waters and delightful prospect across Georgeson Island to the blue volcanic peak of Mt. Baker in Washington state. The **Mayne Inn** stands on a low promontory overlooking Bennett Bay. Originally built as a workers' boarding house for a failed brickworks project at Bennett

Bay, the Mayne Inn has been renovated and reopened as a pub, restaurant and hotel. The deck behind the Mayne Inn is another fine place to have a meal and savour vistas of deep blue water and bright evergreen islands.

Campbell Bay is another favourite swimming beach. From Miners Bay, take Fernhill Road to Campbell Bay Road, turn left and watch for parked cars near the beach access. The eye-catching wind- and water-sculpted rocks at Campbell Bay are so dramatic that they served as the model for the artificial rocks around the killer whale pool in the Vancouver Aquarium.

Approximate Distances

From Village Bay to Miners Bay 2.5 km
From Village Bay to Gallagher Bay 3 km
From Miners Bay to Oyster Bay 3 km
From Miners Bay to Bennett Bay 4 km
From Bennett Bay to Gallagher Bay 4 km
From Bennett Bay to Horton Bay 6.5 km

Dinner Bay beach is a small and perfect spot to watch the sunset. To get there, from Miners Bay, go back along Village Bay Road, continue past the ferry terminal, then take Dalton Drive to the T-junction at Mariner's Way, take a right, then an immediate left onto Dinner Bay Road and follow it to the park. It's called Dinner Bay, according to one story, because it was once teeming with fish and shellfish. "When the tide goes out," the old prospectors' slogan goes, "the table is laid for breakfast." Now shellfish gathering is subject to regulation and there is sometimes danger of contamination—including paralytic shellfish poisoning (red tide), so inquire before harvesting any seafood in the Gulf Islands. Just above Dinner Bay beach is the island's pretty community park with its wide grassy areas, picnic tables, covered barbecue pit, fenced play area, volleyball court and softball field. **Dinner Bay Community Park** (which includes the beach) has the only public water and toilet facilities outside the ferry terminal. It is a 20- to 25-minute walk from the ferry terminal and a great place for a laze on the beach, and a picnic lunch. (Bring your own supplies since there are no nearby stores.)

Two other beaches, **Oyster Bay** and **Piggott Bay**, are also accessible to the public (see map, p. 139).

The beach at Dinner Bay

Georgina Point

For history buffs, the trip along **Georgina Point Road** from the Springwater Lodge in Miners Bay to the **Georgina Point Lighthouse** is a natural—and it's one of the most picturesque routes on the island. Just up Georgina Point Road from the Springwater is the **St. Mary Magdalene Anglican Church** (1898). It stands high on a hill amidst a beautiful grove of red arbutus trees overlooking Active Pass. The steeple has been a landmark for sailors for a century, and the headstones in the mossy graveyard beside the church are a silent testament to Gulf Islands family history. The church was built by the "fire-and-brimstone" Canon William Francis Locke Paddon, who is buried in the little cemetery. He personally saw to it that a 180-kg curved sandstone slab from a Saturna Island beach was hefted into a rowboat and then hauled up to the church. It took four men, including Canon Paddon, eighteen hours to accomplish the task, but to this day the church has an unusual and beautiful sandstone baptismal font. Paddon was also inordinately fond of the golden-flowered broom plant. He carried broom seeds in his pocket wherever he travelled around the islands and cast them out at the side of the road. Today some islanders view broom as a merciless destroyer of native plant varieties and brigades of "broom-killers" on Mayne, Salt Spring and other islands roam around pulling the Canon's beloved plants out by their roots.

From the church you can follow Georgina Point Road to the **Georgina Point lighthouse**, where the newly-created Georgina Point Heritage Park is open to the public between 9 a.m. and 9 p.m. daily. Officially known as Active Pass Light Station, the lighthouse was recently "decommissioned"—that is, automated—as a federal government cost-cutting measure. It is a perfect spot to watch all of the boat traffic in Active Pass. You'll also get fine views of the Strait of Georgia and Sturdies Bay on Galiano Island. One visitor, a guest at the beautiful thirty-five-room Tudor-style Point Comfort Hotel about 180 metres from the lighthouse, described, in the mid-1900s, how tennis players dressed in sedate white togs could see the ocean and snow-capped mountains from the court. To many of Point Comfort's globe-trotting visitors, the Gulf Islands on a beautiful day were unparalleled for scenic splendour. The hotel was torn down in 1958, but the view is just as stunning.

St Mary Magdalene Anglican Church
was built in 1898

The first lighthouse on the point was built in 1885, when steamship traffic through Active Pass increased and spelled potential disaster at sea. The sandstone-laden *Zephyr* had already struck the treacherous shoals off Georgina Point and sunk in 1872. Once the new light and fog bell were in place, Active Pass became the major shipping channel between Victoria and Vancouver. Henry "Scotty" Georgeson was the first lighthouse keeper at Georgina Point, and four years later his brother James became the keeper at the East Point lighthouse at Saturna Island. Over the next sixty years, several of Scotty and James's children became lightkeepers in their turn. Scotty Georgeson retired at the age of eighty-five and went to live nearby in a scaled-down version of his beloved lighthouse.

On the afternoon of October 13, 1918, the foghorn was sounding when Georgeson's grandson Archie looked at his watch and realized the steamer *Princess Adelaide* was overdue. He sent a visiting friend out to listen for the ship. Just as his friend rounded the corner of the building, the ship's whistle sounded. Then he saw the *Princess Adelaide* right next to the beach. He shouted at Archie who looked out the window just in time to see the ship pile up on the rocks. The impact ripped up its propeller and snapped its rudder, but otherwise the ship was not badly damaged. The next day when the weather cleared, Archie saw the ship looming over the lighthouse looking like "a great big city." It was three days before a trio of tugboats managed to pull the big ship off the rocks. That was mercifully the biggest excitement at the Active Pass Light Station.

From the lighthouse you can return to Miners Bay the way you came, or take a circle route: turn left onto Waugh Road and follow its circuitous path (it eventually becomes Campbell Bay Road) to the T-junction with Fernhill Road. Turn right on Fernhill and return to Miners Bay.

Or check the map and plot a route to another unexplored nook or cranny. Horton Bay, Piggott Bay and nearby Oyster Bay are worth visiting, and the fun of discovery will be all yours.

Mayne Island Recreation, Accommodations and Services

Recreation
Bicycle rental
Kayak/Canoe rental
Fishing charters
Dive charters
Tennis court
Hiking trails
Parks

Accommodations
Bed & Breakfasts
Hotel
Inns/Resorts
Private campgrounds
Hostel

Services
Restaurants
Pubs
Inns
Grocery stores
Post office
(Miner's Bay)
Gas/Service stations
Taxi service
Studios/Galleries
Health centre

Important Numbers

Police/Fire/Ambulance emergency **911**
RCMP non-emergency **250-539-2155**
Mayne Island Chamber of Commerce, Mayne Island, BC V0N 2J0
Tourism Association of Vancouver Island,
#203 - 335 Wesley Street, Nanaimo, BC, V9R 2T5
Phone: **250-754-3500** Fax: **250-754-3599**
website: www.islands.bc.ca
Canadian Gulf Islands Bed & Breakfast Reservation Service,
250-539-5390. Free booking for accommodations, tour packages and rentals for all the Gulf Islands.
Tourism BC, **1-800-663-6000**. Provides free of charge BC Accommodations Guide and BC Bed & Breakfast Directory.
BC Provincial Parks Reservations: **1-800-689-9025**.

ISLAND PUB-HOPPING

Since the turn of the century when southern Gulf Islanders rowed over to enjoy the hurly-burly taverns on Mayne Island, pubs have been a centre of community life. Locals gather to relax, share gossip and swap tall tales. Island visitors drop in for a cold one after a day's exploring or cycling along island back roads. Beer flows, glasses clink in friendly toasts, and the click-click of billiard balls

Salt Spring Island's Vesuvius Inn

in the background is a stacatto counterpoint to lively table banter. But southern Gulf Island pubs offer much more—ocean views from some of these pubs are nothing short of glorious. Look for the outside decks where you can enjoy the pleasures of salt air and sunshine. And sample the local food, which rates from very good to excellent. You're just as likely to find a really good Thai curry as a super-tasty basket of fish and chips. A few of our favourites:

Salt Spring Island

Vesuvius Inn (Vesuvius Bay) 250-537-2312
Delightful near-replica of historic Victorian inn that burned down in 1974. Overlooks Crofton/Vesuvius ferry terminal. A boaters' landmark for three decades. Great views across Stuart Channel to Vancouver Island from seaside verandah. Cozy British pub atmosphere, including darts. Fifteen kinds of wine by the glass and Merridale (Vancouver Island) cider. Home-cooked meals.

Moby's Marine Pub (Ganges Harbour) 250-537-5559
Contemporary marine pub opened in 1990. Above Saltspring Marina at Harbour's End. Great harbour views from cathedral-sized windows. Big beams and multi-levelled wood floors make for a relaxed and comfy touch. Extensive menu from great burgers (including delectable fresh salmon or veggie burgers) to ethnic appetizers and savoury entrees like Caribbean fish pot and Louisiana lamb curry. A local favourite for dinner. Ten beers on tap. Showers, laundry and sundries for boaters.

Mayne Island

Springwater Lodge (Miners Bay) 250-539-5521

The Mayne Mast is another popular watering hole

BC's oldest continuously operating inn (1892). Tastefully renovated, low-key old-time inn. Incredible views of Active Pass and BC ferries from the outdoor deck. Legendary hamburgers and inventive additions to lunch and dinner menus. Locals and visitors keep on coming back. Restaurant area and games room. Summer salmon derby an annual hit. Our sentimental favourite.

Mayne Inn (Bennett Bay) 250-539-3122
The other historic inn with a view. Once a bunkhouse for a brickmaking project (1912). Renovated and reopened in 1992. Inn property so spectacular that a huge marina/condominium complex was once planned for the site. Yet another outside deck with a view worth raving about. Pool table and darts.

Pender Island

Bedwell Harbour Marine Bar & Bistro (Bedwell Harbour, South Pender) 250-629-3212 or 1-800-663-2899 (Open seasonally)
Above marina and US Customs dock in upscale Bedwell Harbour Island Resort complex. Outdoor deck and welcoming atmosphere. Unbeatable view of dockside activity at Bedwell Harbour where there's moorage for 180 boats. A favourite with American yachters. Very busy in July and August. Outdoor pool and kids' play area. Restaurant, showers, groceries and marine supplies. Bicycle, sea-doo and boat rentals. Definitely the place (the only place) on South Pender.

Port Browning Marina (Port Browning, North Pender) 250-629-3493
Above Port Browning beach (east on Hamilton Road just south of the Driftwood Centre). Inviting stone and rock "watering hole" with Native decor, including totem. Can we say it again? Great views of hills and harbour of Port Browning. Cheerfully downscale from Bedwell Harbour Resort. Definite local favourite for good food and relaxed fun.

Galiano Island

Hummingbird Inn Pub 250-539-5472
Classic west coast cedar-and-beam architecture with lots of wood and stained glass detailing. No water view—it's in the middle of the island—but a great deck in a lush garden setting. Non-licensed second deck and lawn area for families. Hearty fare at reasonable prices. Big choice of burgers, salads and English pub favourites. Billiard tables and darts. Take-out food. A local institution. Pub shuttle bus to provincial park campground.

SATURNA ISLAND

Killer whale

Winter Cove Marine Park

Highlights

Rural seclusion

Parks for
picnicking

Beautiful beaches

Hiking trails

Annual
lamb barbecue

In many minds, Saturna Island and barbecued lamb are almost synonymous.
Saturna's **Canada Day Lamb Barbecue**
on July 1 is legendary. It began quietly
enough in 1950 when a fellow named Jim
Cruickshank, who had learned the "Argentine
style" of barbecuing meat while in Patagonia,
organized a school picnic featuring lamb.
There were lots of sheep—Saturna was too
mountainous and too thin-soiled to raise
much else—and Saturna Islanders have
always enjoyed impromptu celebrations.
(One islander describes community events
as being organized by "self-actuated ad
hockery.") The lamb barbecue was such a hit
that it became an annual Gulf Islands event.
Hundreds of yachters, boaters, walk-on and
drive-on ferry passengers, locals and off-
islanders alike, gather at the Winter Cove
Provincial Marine Park every Canada Day.
(For information, call the Salt Spring Tourist
Information Centre, 250-537-5252.)

It's an irony that the biggest public event in
the whole Gulf Islands is hosted by the island
that guards its solitary splendour with the
most passion. Saturna Islanders—there are
just 300 residents on this 31-sq.-km island—
like the peace, quiet and solitude. There are a
couple of stores and galleries, one pub/restau-
rant at the ferry terminal, one public park and
another in the works. There is no hospital,
doctor or dentist. Overnight camping is not
permitted, but other very satisfying accommodations are available. Make sure to reserve.
(Call the Canadian Gulf Islands B&B
Reservation Service, 250-539-2930.) Saturna
Islanders are a friendly lot, and their island is
a rural gem. Naturalists will discover a super-
abundance of marine and bird life, and

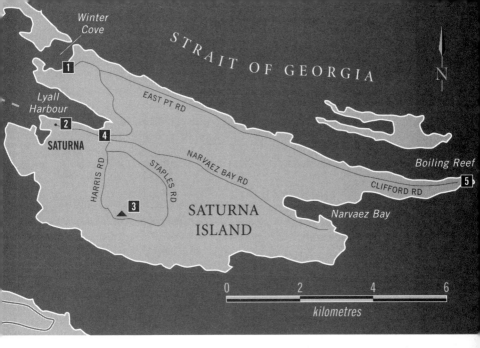

cyclists, kayakers, boaters and hikers can explore this relatively undeveloped island to their hearts' content.

Saturna makes a good day trip, but it sometimes takes two ferry rides to get to the island. You'll need to check the BC Ferries Southern Gulf Islands schedule carefully to make sure you can come and go in one day (see Getting to Saturna Island, p. 151).

What to See

- ☐ **1** Winter Cove Provincial Marine Park
- ☐ **2** Community Hall
- ☐ **3** Mt. Warburton Pike
- ☐ **4** Narvaez Bay Trading Post
- ☐ **4** East Point

Lyall Harbour

The ferry's approach to Saturna down Navy Channel sets just the right tone. The softly rounded hills of nearby islands and the sparkling blue sea exude an almost magical tranquillity that typifies life on Saturna. The ferry docks at the Lyall Harbour terminal on Saturna Point. This is a good launching spot for kayakers and canoeists who want to paddle the bays around Boot Cove and Winter Cove. Just up from the dock is the **Lighthouse Pub** and **Saturna Point Store** where you can stock up on necessities or just put your feet

Approximate Distances

From Lyall Harbour Ferry Terminal to East Point 15 km

From Lyall Harbour Ferry Terminal to Winter Cove 5.5 km

From Lyall Harbour Ferry Terminal to Narvaez Bay 8 km

up and enjoy the view from the outdoor deck. East Point Road winds away from the pub through a pleasing cluster of older buildings. The **Community Hall** on the left is the nucleus of island life and the site of a Saturday Market in the summertime. Not far beyond on the right is **St. Christopher's Church**, a tiny chapel converted from an old Japanese boathouse. About 1.5 km farther,

East Point is a naturalist's delight

the East Point Road hooks to the left and Narvaez Bay Road veers off to the right. At the **Narvaez Bay Trading Post** near the junction, you'll find a post office and liquor store as well as groceries, hardware, gifts and fast food items.

Mt. Warburton Pike

One destination is a 4.5-km drive or hike up **Mt. Warburton Pike** to the summit at Brown's Ridge, the highest point on Saturna Island. It was named for the legendary English "gentleman adventurer" Warburton Pike, the biggest property owner on Saturna at the turn of the century. A member of the British gentry and an Oxford graduate, Pike was temperamentally better suited to adventure in the great outdoors. Even after he built a pretty, well-furnished little bungalow on Saturna he preferred to sleep under a large maple tree in the yard. A courteous but reticent man, Pike was by turns a big-game hunter, a Wyoming cowboy, an Arctic and Icelandic explorer, a businessman and community benefactor, a mining and railroad promoter, a Yukon gold prospector, sheep rancher, and the author of two books on the North. Among many stories about this elusive adventurer is the one tale about how Pike used the ocean as his washtub. He just tied his clothes to a long rope and trailed them behind his sailboat *Fleetwing* while he stretched out at his ease on the gunwale.

To get to Mt. Warburton Pike, start up Narvaez Bay Road but take an immediate right turn at Harris Road and then a left turn onto Staples Road. This gravel road winds up to the summit through a 131-hectare forest ecological reserve. It is narrow, bumpy and sometimes slippery in wet weather, but the beautiful Douglas fir forest more than makes up for the occasional rough patch of road. At the top, turn your back on the unlovely sprawl of TV towers and enjoy fantastic bird's-eye views of the Gulf Islands and the American San Juan Islands. The word "panoramic" fails to do justice to the sweep of scenery at your feet. You may spot paths along the edge of the bluff made by feral goats, wild descendants of domestic goats imported in the early 1900s, and you may just catch sight of these shy creatures.

Winter Cove

Ninety-one-hectare **Winter Cove Provincial Marine Park** is both a nature lover's delight and a great place for kids. A gentle loop trail takes you along pretty beaches, across marshes, over outcroppings of tree-dappled rock and through beautiful forest lands. The wildlife, especially the birdlife near the marshes, is as varied as the terrain. What more can you ask?

To get there, follow East Point Road, about 5.5 km from the ferry terminal. It's also a pleasant day's outing to hike or bike to there, despite a dip down into a fertile valley and a long rise up the other side.

Winter Cove is for day use only. It has fine picnic tables, toilets, drinking water, a boat launch, a softball field, walking trails and lovely sea views.

Winter Cove was the first place on Saturna to be settled by Europeans—two sheep-farming brothers named William and Theo Elford who arrived in 1872. Saturna developed more slowly than its neighbours because its lack of fertile farmland discouraged settlers. This relatively big, mountainous island slumbered while other Gulf Islands felt the axe-bite of white settlement. According to one local historian, it was considered so remote that up until 1895, Royal Navy ships practised firing off their cannons at the bluffs on Saturna's eastern shores.

The Island Spirit

Settlers who did come cherished the island's remoteness, and a little community of free-thinking, nature-loving, neighbour-helping individualists flourished. The same spirit pervades Saturna Island today. Residents tend to fit their work around their lives, not their lives around their work. Take the owners of the **Haggis Farm Bakery**, whose organic breads and baked goods are sold all over the Gulf Islands and in Vancouver. "We want to belong to a place and a life that values integration of family, friends, work, community and the land," wrote Priscilla Yubank in the *Gulf Island's Guardian* about the business she built from scratch with her husband Jon Guy. "We chose to have the bakery within shouting distance of the house because we wanted a business that keeps us close as a family and provides economic experience and opportunity for our three daughters. The land affords us the ability to share the spaciousness and beauty we so value. It also supports the chicken flock, my gardening, Jon's orchard, a big swamp full of frogs, eagles, dragonflies and other wild creatures. Every Saturday, friends and family come for a sauna and potluck dinner. Invariably, we break bread together." Many other local residents are likewise Saturna Islanders first and foremost.

East Point

From Winter Cove the tree-lined road runs close to the water another 10 km out to **East Point**. Black-tailed deer are a common sight on Saturna, especially browsers along the edge of the road. In some places you will get glimpses of the ocean through a fringe of cedar and fir trees. In others the view opens up and you can see clear to the horizon. At low tide you can walk out onto the shelving rock-and-sand beaches for some beachcombing. Seals and sea lions visit these shores, and pods of killer

▶ **Saturna Annual Events**

June–August
Saturday Market

July
Lamb Barbecue (Canada Day)
Winter Cove

November
Christmas Craft Fair

whales (orcas) are often spotted between May and November, rounding East Point near the lighthouse where they come to feed on salmon. An early Saturna settler, Geraldine Hulbert, remembered one day years ago when she and her mother went fishing off East Point. They had just put out in a little dinghy when a huge pod of killer whales suddenly surfaced all around the boat, some just feet away, before they went steaming away toward the Gulf. Her mother, who had never learned to swim and was terrified of the water, turned dead white with fear. "Row me to the shore, dear," she instructed her daughter, and stayed perched stiffly on a rock at the water's edge for the rest of the day.

We saw a pod of killer whales in nearby Active Pass, and they thoughtfully slowed to breach (leap out of the water), spy-hop (spin upright in the water to see what's around them), and fin (slap their fins on the surface to make a loud clapping sound) before accelerating away down the channel.

Whether or not you spot a killer whale, East Point is a naturalist's delight. To get there, park at the end of the road and take the trail leading to the left along the fence enclosing the lighthouse and then out onto the point. From the spectacularly sculptured sandstone headlands you get magnificent ocean views in all directions. The rocks have been carved and honeycombed by wind and waves. Tidal pools created by the weathering of the rock are filled with starfish, anemones, limpets, mussels, spider crabs, hermit crabs, little bull-heads and more. The waving kelp beds just off the point are a haven for small fish.

Honeycombed rocks at East Point

Predatory birds like cormorants, oystercatchers, gulls and eagles swoop and dive over the kelp on fishing expeditions. Behind the headlands is a grassy slope that invites picnicking or a short snooze.

You can also take the trail down to the lighthouse to another intriguingly sculpted sandstone outcropping above the surging waters of **Boiling Reef**. From this vantage point you can watch the big ships navigating their way between the East Point light and its partner light on American Patos Island. East Point is the southernmost point of the Gulf Islands, and it marks the entrance to the Strait of Georgia from Boundary Passage and Haro Strait. In the late 1800s this was a major route for deep-sea vessels bound for Vancouver, and the jagged rocks of Boiling Reef caught their share of mariners off-guard. "Lighthouses often went up over the hulks of wrecks," commented Donald Graham, a BC lightkeeper and historian, "just as the East Point light on Saturna Island marked the final destination of the *John Rosenfeld*." The *Rosenfeld* was filled with the largest shipment of coal ever to float out of Nanaimo Harbour when it veered into these rocks and stuck fast in 1886. As one Saturna pioneer recalled, the ship stayed on the rocks of East Point for a year before it finally broke up and disappeared beneath the waves. In the meantime, hunters shot ducks from the ship's deck, a scavenger built a cabin on the shore with salvaged timber, and many an islander enjoyed bright winter fires stoked with *John Rosenfeld* coal. The wreck of the *Rosenfeld* demonstrated the need for a light on the Canadian side opposite the light just being built on Patos Island. The East Point lighthouse was built in 1888 and manned by James Georgeson in 1889. James was brother to Scotty Georgeson, the lightkeeper on Mayne Island. James's son Peter succeeded his father at the East Point light, and at his retirement thiry years later he pointed with pride to the Georgeson family's service: his father, uncle, brother, son, nephew and two grand-nephews all served on west coast lights. Much to the dismay of many lightkeepers, sailors and islanders, the federal government has destaffed a number of west coast light stations, including East Point. By the time the Coast Guard staff had left East Point in June 1996, Saturna Islanders had formed a commission dedicated to turning the property into parkland. So far they have been given an occupation permit, and hopes are high that East Point will become a park.

KILLER WHALES (ORCAS)

Killer whales or orcas (*Orcinus orca*) are the largest member of the dolphin family and the top predator in the sea. BC has one of the biggest populations of killer whales in the world. Watching these spectacularly fluid black-and-white-patched creatures coursing through the water is an unforgettable sight. Yet we knew little about killer whales until the mid-1970s when the late Michael Biggs, Graeme Ellis and other BC biologists developed a technique for using photographs to identify individual killer whales. To ordinary eyes, killer whales look more or less alike. But to trained whale researchers, differences in the shape of a killer whale's dorsal fin and distinctive patterns of nicks, scars and back colouration are as revealing as a human fingerprint. Being able to identify individual whales has given researchers an important tool in understanding these awesome creatures of the deep.

In the last century, killer whales were known only as savage predators bent on destruction or as threats to fishermen or whalers competing for the same prey. It is true that killer whales attack and devour other mammals, including seals, sea lions, and dolphins. In fact, their name was originally "whale killers"

Killer whale pod

since they are known to attack other, larger whales. They have been called "sea wolves" because of their penchant for hunting in packs and for attacking their prey with a terrifying ferocity. Recently, two killer whales—a mother and son duo—were observed killing a great white shark near San Francisco. But attacks on humans by killer whales in the wild are extremely rare, and no deaths from a killer whale attack have ever been recorded. Only in captivity do killer whales sometimes turn on human beings. The most tragic incident was in 1991 at Victoria's Sealand of the Pacific, when a young trainer fell into the pool by accident and was drowned by three killer whales.

Recent scientific research has given us a whole different perspective on the killer whale's nature. According to veteran whale researcher Paul Spong, the killer whale is capable, self-controlled, well aware of its environment, blessed with a sense of humour, and possessed of a surprising fondness for human beings. Whales are also highly social animals with a complex structure of social interactions. They typically live in "pods," lifelong family groupings ranging in size from five to thirty members and headed by the oldest female. And they are keenly intelligent. Killer whales

Whale breaching

even have a "language" of patterned whistles, squeals and clicks that not only helps them navigate murky waters and detect prey using a kind of whale sonar, but also lets them communicate with one another as they travel. Researchers have discovered that individual "pods" have their own distinctive vocal dialect. Recordings of a pod's repertoire of calls—usually about a dozen well-defined sounds and phrases—help identify particular pods in the wild.

Researchers have also found that some killer whales are "resident" and some are "transient." Residents do not travel outside certain boundaries. The territory of three pods known collectively as the southern residents—about 96 whales in total—takes in the Strait of Georgia, Juan de Fuca Strait, Puget Sound and Vancouver Island's southwest coast. The territory of sixteen other pods known as the northern residents—some 210 whales in all—encom-

▶

Killer whale in kelp

passes the waters north of Campbell River up to southeast Alaska and off the west coast of Vancouver Island. The southern and northern resident killer whale communities apparently respect each other's territory and have never been seen to mingle. However, two or more pods within a community will join together in a "superpod" for a time, perhaps to feed or to breed. Summer is the best time to see resident killer whales. They arrive with the salmon in the spring and then disappear in the fall once the salmon have migrated upriver. Where they go in the winter months is an unsolved mystery.

Transient killer whales are nomadic. They appear and disappear erratically along the west coast all the way from California to Alaska, and they never stay in one place for long. Unlike residents who travel in stable family pods, transients swim alone or band together in small packs or "gangs" of changing size and membership. About 100 transient whales in approximately 45 gangs have been identified in the waters off southeast Alaska and along the outer coasts of BC and Washington. The transient whales also seem to rate the epithet "sea wolves." Unlike residents which feed primarily on salmon, herring, halibut and other fish, transients hunt warm-blooded prey including seals, sea lions, dolphins, porpoises, and other sea-going mammals. Seals are a favourite target, and researchers have recorded many incidents of whales battering a seal for an hour or more before eating it. Transients also have a different shape to their dorsal fins, and they seem to "speak" a different language. They may even be a separate species.

Now scientists are excited about the possibility of a third type of killer whale—the "offshore." In September 1992, 60 or 70 "mystery" killer whales were sighted in Juan de Fuca Strait, and a few more sightings followed. Whale researchers think they may come from far out at sea. Are scientists looking at a whole new species? Or are the "offshores" a combination of residents and transients? Do they travel in pods or in gangs? Do they eat primarily fish or do they hunt mammals? It may be a decade or more before scientists have enough "close encounters" to piece together an understanding of these mysterious new killer whales.

Whales at play

Further Reading
Whales of the West Coast by David A.E. Spalding (Harbour, 1999)
Guardians of the Whales by Bruce Obee and Graeme Ellis
(Whitecap Books, 1992)
Killer Whales by John Ford, Graeme Ellis, and Kenneth Balcomb
(UBC Press/University of Washington Press, 1994)
Orca: The Whale Called Killer by Erich Hoyt (Camden House Publishing, 1990)
Whales, Dolphins and Porpoises: The Visual Guide to All the World's Cetaceans
by Mark Cardwardine (Stoddart, 19950)

PENDER ISLAND

Otter Bay

The Galloping Moon Gallery

Highlights

Hidden coves and beaches

Parks for camping
and picnicking

Historic sites

Boating/fishing

Hiking trails

A slower pace of life

Bike touring

P ender is the second most populated of the five major southern Gulf Islands (with approximately 2,000 residents) and the second most popular visitor destination, but you wouldn't guess it from a swing down Pender Island roads—and that's its special charm.

Originally Coast Salish peoples made summer camps on the island while they fished and harvested shellfish. By the late 1800s, this 34-sq.-km island was quilted with farms and cottages. Picturesque clusters of homes sprang up around general stores at Port Washington and Hope Bay at the top end of the island. Many of the old cottages and orchards can still be found tucked into pleasant green valleys.

Pender Island is dotted with a dozen or so artisans' home galleries where visitors are welcome to drop in and browse for stained glass, pottery, carvings, jewellery, masks, drums, calligraphy and more. Pender is also known as the island of hidden coves and beaches. Its pocketed coastline is full of peaceful spots to enjoy the ever-changing beauty of the sea. Pender Island also has several parks, some with picnic areas and overnight camping. Boating, kayaking, hiking and biking are popular ways to explore the generous bounties of nature at a pace in keeping with "Pender Island time." The challenging 9-hole golf course and the disc (Frisbee) golf park are also popular destinations.

The people of Pender are known for their friendliness. So far, the island's population is small enough, according to one longtime resident, that the sight of another human being still conjures up a smile. A growing population could compromise Pender Island's amiable

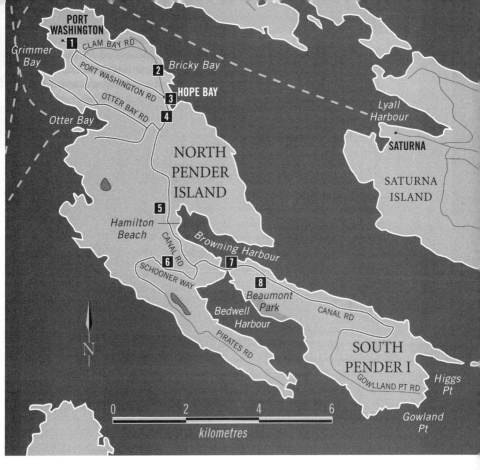

tranquillity. In fact, it was the development of a maze of roads and 1,200 suburban lots at Magic Lake Estates in 1963 that launched the Islands Trust, an elected government body created to curb development on the Gulf Islands. But, although the population has more than doubled since 1963, the rural ambience is still alive and well on Pender Island.

Pender Island was once an hourglass-shaped island whose centre was a narrow isthmus of land between Port Browning and Bedwell Harbour. For centuries, Coast Salish people set up seasonal camps here and portaged between the harbours. (Two archaeologically important shell middens dating from 4500 BC were excavated in this area in 1984–86.) Later, when settlers from the north end wanted to visit friends on the

What to See

- [ ] **1** Port Washington
- [ ] **2** Bricky Bay
- [ ] **3** Hope Bay
- [ ] **4** United Community Church
- [ ] **5** Driftwood Centre
- [ ] **6** Prior Centennial Provincial Park
- [ ] **7** Mortimer Spit Park
- [ ] **8** Mt. Norman Regional Park

south end, they'd row down to Port Browning, drag their boats across the isthmus and

The bridge joining the two Penders

then row down Bedwell Harbour so as to avoid rough water around the south end. But in 1903 a seventy-foot wide canal was dredged out to make boat travel easier, and the singular "Pender Island" became plural—"the Penders."

North Pender and South Pender were reunited by a one-lane bridge over the canal in 1956. By that time, according to one account, the two Penders had become rivals. Folks on North Pender looked at southerners as country hicks while South Penderites looked down their noses at northerners as parvenu subdivision squatters. Whether or not this account is accurate, you can't help noticing that North Pender is significantly larger (2,685 hectares), and it also has the lion's share of the population, the subdivision at Magic Lake and almost all the commercial services. South Pender is smaller (810 hectares) and still sparsely populated. However, its southern tip is within shouting distance of the US border. Lots of American boaters check in at the Canada Customs office at Bedwell Harbour before heading into Canadian waters. The large new marina and resort complex there—strategically located on the well-travelled Boundary Pass—is a colourful kaleidoscope of people and pleasure boats in the summer months. (Closed off-season.) You can easily drive from the BC ferry terminal at Otter Bay (North Pender) to Bedwell Harbour (South Pender) in an hour. But if you're day tripping, you may want to limit yourself to a leisurely circuit of North Pender Island. Then you can really explore the island's back roads and isolated coves and beaches.

The view from Mt. Norman regional park.

Getting to Pender Island

From Vancouver Drive aboard the BC Ferry from Tsawwassen terminal. 1 hour to 2 hours and 15 minutes crossing time; 2–3 sailings daily year round.

The Gulf Island ferry to and from Tsawwassen is often full to capacity at peak times—weekends (especially holiday weekends) and most days during summer. Reservations are recommended at peak times and required Friday nights and Saturday mornings.

From Victoria Drive aboard the BC Ferry from Swartz Bay terminal. 40 minutes to 2 hours and 20 minutes crossing time; 4 sailings daily year round. Reservations not available.

From Other Gulf Islands Access is available from other southern Gulf Islands serviced by BC Ferries. Routes and times vary depending on the day, point of departure and time of year. Contact BC Ferries for schedule information. Reservations not available.

Ferry Information For passenger service agents, reservations (7 a.m. to 10 p.m. daily) or recorded information (24 hours), telephone **1-888-BCFERRY (1-888-223-3779)**. From Victoria **250-386-3431**. Fax **250-381-5452**. Website **www.bcferries.bc.ca**.

North Pender

Taking a circle tour of the historic **Port Washington–Hope Bay** area is a perfect introduction to North Pender. From the Otter Bay ferry terminal it's just 3 km to Port Washington. If you want to rent a bicycle for the circle tour, turn right at the top of the terminal and dip down to Otter Bay Marina (250-629-3579; closed off-season). You'll find bicycle and boat rentals, kayak rentals and tours, moorage and groceries, an outdoor swimming pool, and even a snack bar complete with cappuccino. This picturesque marina, with its tidy green and white buildings, wide lawns and willow trees arching over the water, is a delightful spot to start a journey. Another good place to start—or to finish—is "The Stand" at the ferry terminal. The owners of this Winnebago-cum-latticed-arbour serve snack foods, tasty burgers and the whimsically titled "Winnebagel" —Winnipeg cream cheese on a bagel.

Port Washington

Less than a kilometre from the ferry terminal, take the (signed) left turn onto Otter Bay Road and you're off to Port Washington. The road goes right through the **Pender Island Golf and Country Club** (250-629-6659). The rolling greens and surrounding hills and pastures make this a very relaxing scene. The course, clubhouse and coffee shop are open to the public. From the outside patio you can enjoy a snack and a fine prospect of this peaceful valley. As you continue up Otter Bay Road, you will see Grimmer Valley off to your left. At the intersection with Port Washington Road, take a left and make a .5-km detour down to **Port Washington**. Grimmer Valley and Port Washington were both named after Washington Grimmer, an early white settler. Described by his eldest son as "a quick, wiry little man with a quick temper which, like a storm in a teapot, was over in minutes," Washington Grimmer was a prominent local farmer and an active member of the early community. Old-timers remember with pleasure his warm hospitality and the delicious venison and fresh-caught salmon that graced the Grimmer table. Like many other Gulf Islands pioneers, Grimmer lived a long and healthy life.

Port Washington has so many charming old cottages and orchards tucked around pretty little Grimmer Bay that it is reminiscent of a turn-of-the-century coastal village. The old general store (1910) still stands at the head of the once-busy wharf. It housed Pender's first post office, and Washington Grimmer was the island's first postmaster. The building is now home to an art gallery. Next door is a quaint waterfront place, now a private residence, with the words "Rosebay Coasting Company, Est. 1941, Proprietor R. Hunt"

Grimmer Bay and historic Port Washington

still legible on its side. The wharf just below was once a hub of island life as mail, goods and people arrived and departed on sturdy little coastal steamers.

As you leave town on Port Washington Road, look on your left for **Old Orchard Farm**.

The Gulf Islands are a sailor's paradise

This lovingly restored Victorian house was built by Washington Grimmer in 1882. He sold the property in 1903 and moved to Grimmer Valley where he raised championship dairy cattle. In summer you'll find apples, pears, plums and flowers, from the fine heritage orchard, for sale at the stand near the gate. Look for other **honesty stands** along Pender's roads, offering potatoes, zucchini, walnuts, eggs, jams, relishes and other delicacies. You'll also see **St. Peter's Anglican Church** (1915) on the left along Port Washington Road just past the junction with Otter Bay Road. Washington Grimmer was a devout Anglican and a moving force behind the building of the church. A ship's bell and a bench outside are memorials to Grimmer's oldest son Neptune ("Nep") and Dorothy Grimmer. Nep got his name from the circumstances of his birth in April 1889. When Nep's mother went into labour, her brother hustled her into a boat and began rowing her across Navy Channel to the Gulf Islands' only midwife on Mayne Island. But it was too late. The baby was born mid-channel and christened Neptune in memory of his birth at sea. Everyone thought his full name was Neptune Navy Grimmer, but Nep later discovered to his delight that there was no middle name on the official registry of his birth. "I never did like 'Navy' tacked in the middle of it," he said.

Approximate Distances

From Otter Bay to Hope Bay 3 km
From Driftwood Centre to Otter Bay 4 km
From Driftwood Centre to Wallace Point 6.5 km
From Driftwood Centre to Gowlland Point 9 km

Hope Bay

Hope Bay is the other historic settlement on North Pender. The **Hope Bay Store** (1912) is still standing and its name remains, but it is now part of the expanded **Galloping Moon gallery** next door. The original owner, R.S.W. Corbett, surveyed the island women for their favourite grocery brands before ordering his first shipment of supplies—and he had a ready-made clientele when the door first opened. The store did so well that two more generations of Corbetts made their living as merchants at Hope Bay. A partial list of items from the 1909 stocktaking book is a window into Pender Island life a century ago: "20 sacks rice bran; 25 sacks coconut oil cake; 15 yards red sateen; 9 bathing-suits; 19 pairs ladies' high button boots; 7 lbs. gun-powder; 15 lbs. shot; 1 keg cooking molasses; 3 doz. hat-pins; 1 caddy plug tobacco; 2 school slates; 1/4 gross slate pencils." The historic buildings at Hope Bay are picturesque, and the whole place feels friendly and habitable. Hope Bay has remained a popular island meeting place, and locals often rub shoulders with visitors on the boardwalk in front of the store. You can also browse through a small assortment of nearby craft galleries and enjoy beautiful ocean views from the wharf. Kids will have fun looking for anemones and purple starfish clinging to the pilings, or searching for marine life on rock outcroppings. All in all, Hope Bay has the easy feeling of a long-established small waterfront community.

Pender Island has a number of smaller roads, and wandering off in whatever direction seems to beckon is a pleasant way to enjoy the island. For a sampler of backroad wandering, try a side trip to **Bricky Bay** just up the hill from Hope Bay. Take a right onto Clam Bay Road and about 1 km along turn right onto Coast Shale Road. Stop near the T-junction with Armadale Road. Then walk down Armadale Road to the trail onto the beach. If your idea of heaven is a pretty little cove with a magnificent view of volcanic Mt. Baker on the mainland, then Bricky Bay is your place. You can still find shards of red brick from a turn-of-the-century brickworks scattered amongst the stones on the beach. Other special favourites on "the Penders" are **Hamilton Beach** (swimming and boat launch), **Mortimer Spit** (swimming and shell beach), and **Gowlland Point** (tidal pools and seals) (see map, p. 159).

Bedwell Harbour Road is the main road out of Hope Bay. The charming little **United Community Church** (1906) is nestled into a hillside just above the point where Bedwell Harbour Road swings sharply to the left. You'll wander through farm country and then descend Einar's Hill to the Driftwood Centre.

▶ Pender Island Annual Events

May
International Disc Golf Tournament

June
Summer Solstice Festival

July
Garden Party
Home and Garden Tour
Art Show

August
Fall Fair
Annual Pender Yacht Race

November
Christmas Craft Fair

December
Santa's Christmas Ship

Sculptured sandstone along the Pender Island shoreline

There is no real village in the traditional sense on Pender, but the modern **Driftwood Centre**, a mini-mall just above the large bay known as Port Browning, does duty as the nucleus of island life. You'll find a grocery store, bank, bakery, pharmacy, hair salon, laundromat, post office, liquor store, insurance and real estate offices, and service station. Here, you can pick up a bite to eat and eavesdrop on local gossip at the picnic tables thoughtfully provided for patrons. But the grey-sided mall was built to blend in quietly with the rural surroundings. Across the road is a pretty tree-bordered pasture dotted with cows. A small sign on the fence advertises the bull, "Mr. Chips," at stud. The **Saturday Market** at the Driftwood Centre (May to October) is a fine place for sampling island-grown produce, homemade baked goods and local craft items, and for mingling with low-key, friendly Pender Islanders. If you plan to do any touring of the Magic Lake subdivision (see p. 159), you may want to pick up a detailed map at the realty office.

Parks and Beaches

Bedwell Harbour Road changes to Canal Road as it heads for the canal linking North and South Pender. A sign marks the right-hand turn to the 17 forested campsites of **Prior Centennial Provincial Park** (250-391-2300). Not far beyond is the right-hand turnoff at

Aldridge Road which leads to Medicine Beach and Magic Lake. If you're fascinated by native plants or looking for good birding, make a side excursion to **Medicine Beach**. Turn left onto a small unmarked road from Aldridge Road where it begins to rise up a hill. The marshland just behind the beach at the north end of Bedwell Harbour is now protected, thanks to the efforts of the Pender Island Conservancy Association. Nine plant communities thrive here, of which many species were used by Native peoples for food and medicines. An information sign gives some information about the marshland. (A fine guidebook is *Food Plants of Coastal First Peoples* by Nancy J. Turner (UBC Press).) The marsh is home to herons, ospreys, blackbirds and the elusive Virginia rail among other birds.

If you're a Frisbee—excuse us, "disc"—fanatic, then don't miss the free **disc golf course** in **Magic Lake Estates**. Follow the subdivision's main road, Schooner Way, to Privateers Road. Follow Privateers Road and then take a right onto Galleon Way. The disc park is on Galleon Way—but it's easy to miss! Watch for a small circular sign saying "Golf Island Disc Park" hanging on an arbutus tree. The disc park itself is back in the trees on a stony ridge of arbutus and evergreen. Look for a fire hydrant, a gravelled pullout and a "Walk" sign indicating a hiking path just where Galleon Way curves up to the left. The disc park is right there. And it is lots of fun once you've found it. The "tees" are metal poles tucked here and there in the forest, and it's a real trick to keep your Frisbee from ricocheting off nearby trees on its flight to the target. On the last weekend in May, dedicated disc golfers come from all over the Pacific Northwest to play in the Pender Island Invitational Disc Tournament. The park also has picnic tables, a water fountain and a pit toilet. By the way, those "Walk" signs lead you to a series of short hiking trails threading through Magic Lake Estates.

South Pender

To get to South Pender, return to Canal Road and head south over the bridge. The only services on South Pender are at **Bedwell Harbour** (in season). However, there are several beaches for sunseekers as well as Mt. Norman Regional Park for hikers and Beaumont Provincial Marine Park for boaters. The trailhead for **Mt. Norman Regional Park** is just beyond the bridge. Turn right onto Ainslie Point Road and look for a small signed parking area on the left. A fairly uninteresting gravel access road leads to the summit of Mt. Norman where you'll get spectacular views over Bedwell Harbour and over to Salt Spring Island and the mountains of Vancouver Island. The 1-km hike takes about 25 minutes, and the panoramic views are a fine payoff for the effort.

Bedwell Harbour Marina

You can also get to **Beaumont Provincial Marine Park**, about 250 m below Mt. Norman on Bedwell Harbour, on a new trail. It branches off from the trail up Mt. Norman not far past the parking area, and is about a 40-minute hike to one of the Gulf Islands' prettiest and most popular marine parks (250-391-2300). Alternatively you can row or paddle to the park from Bedwell Harbour. (Canoes and kayaks can be rented from Bedwell Harbour Resort, 1-800-663-2899 or 250-629-3212.) Or you can drive or cycle the peaceful winding roads of South Pender.

This remote part of the island has always attracted independent, hard-working, fun-loving spirits who didn't mind the isolation. Higgs Road was named for Leonard Higgs, a well-to-do young British eccentric who built boats and wrote for the tonier English papers such as the *Spectator*. Visitors reported finding pet seagulls, a cow in the house, and even a tame seal stretched out on the rug in front of the fireplace. Spalding Road was named for Higgs's relative, Arthur Spalding, whose family were in the publishing business. A voracious reader and a Sunday painter, Spalding was well respected for his upright and courteous character. Yet he too was an eccentric figure in his youth, roaming the

Beaumont Provincial Marine Park on South Pender

Pender Island Recreation, Accommodations and Services

Recreation
Bicycle rentals
Kayak/Canoe rentals
Fishing charters
Dive charter
Golf course
Tennis court
Hiking trails
Parks
Horseback riding ranch
Disc Golf (Frisbee) course

Accommodations
Bed & Breakfasts
Inns/Resorts
Campgrounds

Services
Restaurants
Pubs
Grocery stores
Bank
Post office (Driftwood Centre)
Gas/Service stations
Car/Truck rental
Taxi service
Studios/Galleries
Health centre

Pender Island golf course

Important Numbers

Police/Fire/Ambulance emergency **911**
RCMP non-emergency **250-629-6171**
Pender Island InfoCentre, 2332 Otter Bay Rd., Box 75, Pender Island, BC, V0N 2M0
Tourism Association of Vancouver Island, #203 - 335 Wesley Street, Nanaimo, BC, V9R 2T5
Phone: **250-754-3500** Fax: **250-754-3599**
website: www.islands.bc.ca
Canadian Gulf Islands Bed & Breakfast Reservation Service, **250-539-5390**, fax **250-539-2930**. Free booking for accommodations, tour packages and rentals for all the Gulf Islands.
Super Natural British Columbia BC, **1-800-663-6000**. Provides free of charge BC Accommodations Guide and BC Bed & Breakfast Directory.

countryside dressed in red football shorts and followed closely by two huge dogs.

Perhaps the oddest character of all was the tiny little American smuggler from nearby San Juan Island, known only as Old Burke. Smuggling wool, of all things, from Canada into the United States was a lucrative business. And South Pender was an ideal spot for wool smuggling. It had plenty of sheep, half a dozen little coves and bays, few people and no constable, and it was a stone's throw from San Juan Island. A South Pender pioneer recalled with fondness Old Burke's yearly visits to pick up wool bales and row them back to San Juan Island and how he always brought little candies for the children. According to another South Pender pioneer, the police got suspicious about Old Burke's wool crop—one of the biggest in Washington State—since his little island wasn't much more than a rock. Burke was eventually caught red-handed. But Leonard Higgs, who was fond of the old man, testified that because of the tides that day, Burke couldn't have been where the authorities said he was—and the old smuggler was set free. The illicit wool trade is just a footnote in history, but the attractions of this very rural retreat are still yours on South Pender.

GALIANO ISLAND

Looking out from Galiano

Highlights

Beaches

Abundant
marine wildlife

Hiking trails

Bike touring

Historic sites

Crafts gallery

Camping

On the mid-week ferry run from Galiano to Vancouver you can see half a dozen business types hunched over computers, getting ready for a day's work in the city. Galiano is the Gulf Island closest to the mainland, and commuting is challenging but possible. But these folks are atypical of Galiano's 950-odd residents. In fact, the chances are that if you followed them home, you'd see them slip into old jeans and head out to watch the sun dip into the ocean in a crescendo of colour. Galiano is above all a place where people come to enjoy a life in communion with the island's natural beauty. As you become attuned to Galiano's rhythms, you'll begin to notice the lapping of water on pebbled beaches and the eerie fluting sound of eagles overhead. You'll step outside at night to marvel at the starry sky or walk down to the shore of a rocky bay to see a heron silhouetted against midnight blue water. Galiano's varied topography and many species of plant and animal life are a magnet for outdoor enthusiasts, and its tranquillity attracts hundreds of visitors every year. But this very dry island has particularly fragile ecosystems, so please tread with care. (For details, pick up the free pamphlet "Galiano Island: A Sensitive Environment" at the Galiano InfoCentre near the ferry terminal.)

This long, skinny island is about 26 km from top to bottom and no more than 2 km across at most places. Its peculiar geography has shaped its development. In the 1870s, the only significant settlement was at Sturdies Bay at the southeast end on Active Pass. "The Pass" was the main sea route between Vancouver and Victoria and the artery of commerce among the Gulf Islands. A smaller settlement

sprang up in north Galiano near Retreat Cove, but the two communities were connected only by a very rough trail. People from Sturdies Bay sent messages up-island by pinning them to a stump with an axe blade for delivery by anyone who might be walking or riding horseback north. Once Porlier Pass Road was built, more people built tucked-away houses in the long centre stretch of the island. Until the early 1960s, Galiano Islanders were mostly people born on the island and a few who came

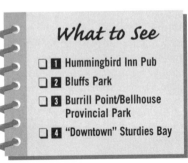

What to See

- ☐ **1** Hummingbird Inn Pub
- ☐ **2** Bluffs Park
- ☐ **3** Burrill Point/Bellhouse Provincial Park
- ☐ **4** "Downtown" Sturdies Bay

from "off-island" to find work in forestry and fishing. Then the new government-run BC Ferry Corporation began service to the Gulf Islands, and '60s-style back-to-the-landers and retirees began to move to Galiano to find a simpler, quieter way of life. Since then a new wave of weekenders and a generous helping of artists and writers have arrived, and now there are more than 900 year-round residents, most of whom still live close to Sturdies Bay. Like all the other Gulf Islands, Galiano is trying hard to achieve the right balance between development and natural splendour.

As the BC ferry sails into the encircling arms of Sturdies Bay, look in the trees on either side for bald eagles. It's an unusual day when you don't see at least one of the awesome

The magnificent view from Bluffs Park

raptors. If you're looking for outdoor fun, the choices range from golfing and sailing to kayaking, cycling, hiking and swimming. Local Galiano entrepreneurs also offer diving services, fishing charters and catamaran cruises. (For information, Galiano Island InfoCentre, Box 73, Galiano Island, BC, V0N 1P0, 250-539-2233.)

Sturdies Bay

Sturdies Bay is Galiano's "downtown" and well worth a stop. In fact, on a short visit you can find plenty to do right in Sturdies Bay with a couple side excursions. Here, you'll find a gas station, grocery store, liquor store, craft shops and a real estate office. The Galiano Lodge has rooms and a good restaurant overlooking the bay and ferry terminal. The

Dandelion Gallery, the local artists' co-op, is known around the islands for the quality of the works for sale. And the Trincomali Bakery and Deli just along Sturdies Bay Road is great for a midmorning coffee or lunchtime snack.

An important landmark at Sturdies Bay is the island's first store, which islanders still call the **"Old Burrill store"** (1903). The bachelor Burrill brothers, Joseph and Fred, bought 32 hectares on Galiano in 1896. They were careful and provident, so neighbours fell into the habit of borrowing or buying items from them. (The only alternative at the time was to row across to Mayne Island to shop at the Miners Bay store.) The Burrills decided that it was better to sell goods than lend them and built a store on their property. Galiano historian Elizabeth Steward recalls in her delightful self-published *Galiano: Houses and People Looking Back to 1930*, "This turned out to be an ideal partnership as Fred became chief cook and gardener while Joe played the piano and ran the store. Fred's cooking was a little hard to take actually—very weighty mince pies (little ones), very strong tea, thick dark beer, but it was always a pleasure to sit in their kitchen with them." Like his brother, Joe was a kindly man and always gave children treats at the store—a bag of candy or all-day sucker for little folks and a box of chocolates for young ladies. Fred rarely left home but Joe, who had a fine tenor voice and played the violin, banjo and guitar, as well as the piano, was in great demand at parties. They both lived well into old age, and when they retired in 1947, Joe remarked that they just wished they could do it all over again.

The rocky point of land south of Sturdies Bay is known as **Burrill Point**. It is now the site of the 2-hectare, day-use-only **Bellhouse Provincial Park** and one of the prettiest spots on the whole island. The peninsula is resplendent with wide shelves of mossy rock, sculpted sandstone formations rimming the point, and a magnificent grove of coppery-red arbutus trees. Sun-warmed benches and picnic tables are invitingly arranged for visitors to take in views of Sturdies Bay and Active Pass. This is an ideal spot to have a picnic, spin-cast for salmon, or watch wildlife, especially in the spring. Seals, sea lions, porpoises and killer whales travel through **Active Pass**, and gulls, cormorants, loons, ducks and other seabirds can be sighted at different times of year. So don't forget your binoculars.

Active Pass is also the busiest marine passageway in the area, where huge blue-and-white BC Superferries, pleasure craft, fishing boats, tugboats, barges, and the occasional freighter or naval ship are part of the daily view. Active Pass has been busy since the turn of the century.

J.W. Bellhouse, for whom the park was named was a local farmer who

Getting to Galiano Island

From Vancouver Drive aboard the BC Ferry from Tsawwassen terminal. 1 hour to 1 hour and 30 minutes crossing time; 2–4 sailings daily year round.

The Gulf Island ferry to and from Tsawwassen is often full to capacity at peak times—weekends (especially holiday weekends) and most days during summer. Reservations are recommended at peak times and required Friday nights and Saturday mornings.

From Victoria Drive aboard the BC Ferry from Swartz Bay terminal. 1 hour to 2 hours and 10 minutes crossing time; 4 sailings daily year round.

From Other Gulf Islands Access is available from other southern Gulf Islands serviced by BC Ferries. Routes and times vary depending on the day, point of departure and time of year. Contact BC Ferries for schedule information. Reservations not available.

Ferry Information For passenger service agents, reservations (7 a.m. to 10 p.m. daily) or recorded information (24 hours), telephone **1-888-BCFERRY** (1-888-223-3779). From Victoria **250-386-3431**. Fax **250-381-5452**. Website **www.bcferries.bc.ca**.

▶ Beer recipe

This is a recipe for hops beer from the diary kept from 1881–1887 by Galiano pioneer Charles Groth:

"Mix 14 pounds of molasses and eleven gallons of water well together and boil them for two hours with six ounces of hops. When quite cool, add a cupful of yeast and stir in well. Let it ferment for 16 hours in a tub covered with a sack, then put it in a nine gallon cask and keep it filled up. Bung it down in two days."

worked hard, played hard and had a penchant for naming his dairy cows after characters in Charles Dickens novels. His daughter, Winifred Bellhouse Spalding, remembers that even in the early years of the century there always seemed to be boats passing through Active Pass—tugs and barges, gleaming white Empress ships bound for the Orient, the *Princess Victoria* on its daily run to Victoria, and the ill-fated *Iroquois* that sank on its shuttle around the Gulf Islands in 1911, taking many of its passengers down with it.

To get to the park from the ferry terminal, follow Sturdies Bay Road for about .5 km and turn left onto Burrill Road. Just past the church, turn left again onto Jack Drive and park at the end of the road.

If you're feeling energetic, head for nearby **Bluffs Park** where you'll get a whole different ent perspective on Active Pass. The views from these 120-m bluffs deserve rave reviews. Take your binoculars for wildlife sightings, especially eagles catching the updrafts. And look for wildflowers in season—wild honeysuckle, deep-pink rabbit ears, lavender-blue blue-eyed Marys and dark purple early camas all grace this beautiful ridge. The park opened in 1948, thanks to the efforts of the Galiano Island Development Association and the generosity of Marion and Max Enke, who sold 38 hectares of land for $1,000 and then threw in another 92 hectares for free. The land was turned over to the Galiano Club, a local residents association which still administers and maintains the park.

To get to Bluffs Park from the ferry terminal, follow Sturdies Bay Road about .5 km and turn left onto Burrill Road. Burrill Road winds past farmland and older cottages and then becomes Bluff Road where it begins to climb up toward the bluffs. About 1 km along, the road narrows and the surface changes from pavement to gravel. (Be careful! This

A BC Ferry about to enter Active Pass

stretch of road has serious potholes.) Look for a sign indicating the park entrance. Not far from the entrance is a well-marked side road on the left that leads to the parking lot. Park and walk up the trail to the ridge. You can walk in either direction along the bluff for wonderful views of both Mayne Island, straight across Active Pass, and North Pender Island just to the right of Mayne on the far side of Navy Channel.

Montague Harbour

The Galiano Island community has saved several beautiful sites for public enjoyment, including the 89-hectare **Montague Harbour Provincial Marine Park**, on the southwest side of Galiano, where you can swim and

Montague Harbour Park.

beachcomb to your heart's content along gorgeous shell and gravel beaches. There is also a boat ramp and fine protected anchorage, including 23 mooring buoys, and a marina and store. The park has picnic tables set amid trees on a bluff overlooking the wide bay as well as 15 walk-in campsites, 25 drive-in sites, drinking water, toilets and a nature house. (Look for a schedule of free interpretive talks on Galiano's plants, animals, history and natural history in July and August.) The park's hiking trails include an easy 3-km forest-and-beach walk around Gray Peninsula.

Montague Harbour has been occupied for millennia. Six shell middens in the park have been identified by archaeologists as ancient Coast Salish settlements dating back as far as 3,000 years. To this day you can see where ancient peoples shucked clams, oysters and abalone and tossed away the shells along a white broken-shell beach at the north end of the park. Montague Harbour is bustling in summer when whole families descend to enjoy fun in the sun. Kids have a great time swimming, fishing for shiners off the dock, paddling the protected bay, exploring the trails and collecting driftwood and shells. But when the park empties out in autumn and the broad-leafed maples burst into colour, it is hard to imagine a place more beautifully serene.

> ## ▶ Galiano Island Annual Events
>
> **May**
> *Artists' Guild Invitational Show*
>
> **July**
> *North Galiano Jamboree
> (Canada Day)
> Wine Festival
> Lions Fiesta*
>
> **October**
> *Blackberry Festival
> Oktoberfest*
>
> **November**
> *Christmas Craft Fair*

To get to the park from the ferry terminal, follow Sturdies Bay Road about one kilometre past the log booming ground at Whaler Bay and on to **Hummingbird Inn Pub** on your right at 47 Sturdies Bay Road (250-539-5472). This friendly eatery-and-drinkery is a local favourite, and the outdoor deck in a pleasantly cool, well-treed garden is an oasis on hot days. (From Montague Harbour you can catch the pub's shuttle bus back in the evening. It runs hourly 6:00 p.m. to 11:00 p.m. from May to October.) Just beyond the pub, turn left from Sturdies Bay Road onto Georgeson

Hummingbird Inn Pub

Bay Road. The brightly painted Daystar Market on your right, is another local favourite and well worth a stop just to get a feel for Galiano life. Here, you can buy organic produce and fresh bakery items, pop next door to the Candlelite Cafe for lunch or dinner, and explore the handful of nearby shops. About 1 km farther, turn right onto Montague Road. The well-signed park entrance is about 4 km up the road. (For camping reservations, call Discover Camping campground reservation service at 1-800-689-9025.)

North Galiano has a wilder, more remote feel than South Galiano. To tour the north end of the island, follow Sturdies Bay Road from the ferry terminal to the Hummingbird Pub and turn right onto Porlier Pass Road just beyond the pub. Or, from Montague Harbour Provincial Park, drive back along Montague Road and then take a left onto Clanton Road. Turn right onto Porlier Pass Road, and you're on your way up-island.

This stretch of the road is dense with cedar and fir trees on both sides, interspersed with maple and alder stands. Pockets of housing and the occasional B&B or craft studio are tucked away here and there in the forest, often at the bottom of lanes marked with hand-carved wood signs. For an interesting side trip, watch for the left-hand turnoff to Retreat Cove Road and make your way to **Retreat Cove**. This little bight was the site of a Japanese fish saltery built just before World War II. A number of Japanese families lived aboard their fishing boats and seined the waters around Porlier Pass for cod and herring. The fish were soaked in brine at salteries on North Galiano and then shipped off to China. But the saltery at Retreat Cove never did open for business. After the bombing of Pearl Harbor, every person of Japanese ancestry, old and young, was taken to internment camps away from the coast. The saltery was eventually torn down.

Retreat Cove has a natural aquarium right off the dock. Look down by the pilings to see myriad sea life, including purple, mottled and sunflower starfish, and the beautiful orange and white plumed anemones ("sea flowers"). Or make your way through the gate to **Brammall Point** where you'll find a miniature undersea garden in the wonderfully sculpted rocks just below the water. (This is private land generously kept open for public use, so please treat it with respect.) Fleets of gently pulsing moon jellyfish propel themselves through the water right under your nose, and hermit crabs and minnows flit in and out of the rocky crevices. The air is full of bird calls—ravens, kingfishers, herons and seagulls all contribute their music to the chorus. River otters and harbor seals are also likely to bob up along the water's edge, and eagles often fish from perches in nearby trees. The views over Trincomali Channel are a delight.

Farther up the island beyond Cook Road are more homes, especially around pleasing little Spanish Hills General Store (open seasonally) and the government wharf. The road runs close to Trincomali Channel and you get delicious sea views. Once we were in the general store when we heard a shout from the wharf. The storekeeper wheeled around, looked out the window, then took off for the wharf, leaving the cash drawer wide open and the store full of customers. We followed him down to the dock to see what all the ruckus was about—and then we looked out to the water. A pod of thirty killer whales was slicing down Trincomali Channel. The sight of those majestic animals surging through the water was an indescribable thrill.

Side trips to **Bodega Ridge** and **Mt. Galiano** are two great wind-up activities for your stay on Galiano. Both areas are public parks acquired by Galiano conservationists from MacMillan Bloedel, a large forest products company that once owned 3,156 hectares of forest land on Galiano—more than half the island. Through creative fundraising strategies such as sales of Canned Land ("a special blend of the finest organic Galiano soils") and Loonies for the Mountain (fishing for loonies at the Sturdies Bay ferry terminal) the community successfully negotiated the purchase of Mt. Galiano for a park, and not long after they secured Bodega Ridge as a park, too.

The moderate 3-km Mount Galiano trail climbs up Galiano's highest peak (311 m) to a beautiful clearing dotted with Garry oaks where you get huge views of the Gulf Islands. The easy 3-km Bodega Ridge trail is a fine ridge walk with nonstop views of Trincomali Channel and Salt Spring Island as a backdrop. The trail begins at a gate at the end of Cottage Way Road, which intersects Porlier Pass Road from the east not far north of Retreat Cove.

At the northern end of Galiano is beautiful **Dionisio Point Provincial Park**. It too was acquired from MacMillan Bloedel and declared a park in 1993. Because of subsequent disputes, however, land access to Dionisio Point via MacMillan Bloedel property is not allowed. The park can only be reached by water. (For up-to-date information about access and trails for Mt. Galiano, Bodega Ridge and Dionisio Point Provincial Park, contact the Galiano Chamber of Commerce, 250-539-2233.)

Galiano Island Recreation, Accommodations and Services

Recreation
Bicycle rentals
Kayak/Canoe rentals
Fishing charters
Dive charter
Golf course
Hiking trails
Parks
Horseback riding ranch
Catamaran cruise

Accommodations
Bed & Breakfasts
Inns/Resorts
Cottages/Cabins
Campgrounds

Services
Travel InfoCentre
(Sturdies Bay; not staffed)
Restaurants
Pubs
Fast food
Grocery stores
Post office (Sturdies Bay)
Gas station (Sturdies Bay)
Repair stations
Studios/Galleries
Health care centre

Important Numbers

Police/Fire/Ambulance emergency **911**

RCMP non-emergency **250-539-2309**

Galiano Island Visitor's Association, P.O. Box 73, Galiano Island, BC V0N 1P0. Phone **250-539-2233**

Tourist InfoCentre/Chamber of Commerce, **250-539-2233**, **www.galianoisland.com**, *email* **info@galianoisland.com**

Tourism Association of Vancouver Island, #203 - 335 Wesley Street, Nanaimo, BC, V9R 2T5 Phone: **250-754-3500** *Fax:* **250-754-3599** *website: www.islands.bc.ca*

Canadian Gulf Islands Bed & Breakfast Reservation Service, **250-539-5390**, *fax* **250-539-2930**. *Free booking for accommodations, tour packages and rentals for all the Gulf Islands.*

Super, Natural British Columbia BC, **1-800-663-6000**. *Provides free of charge* BC Accommodations Guide *and* BC Bed & Breakfast Directory.

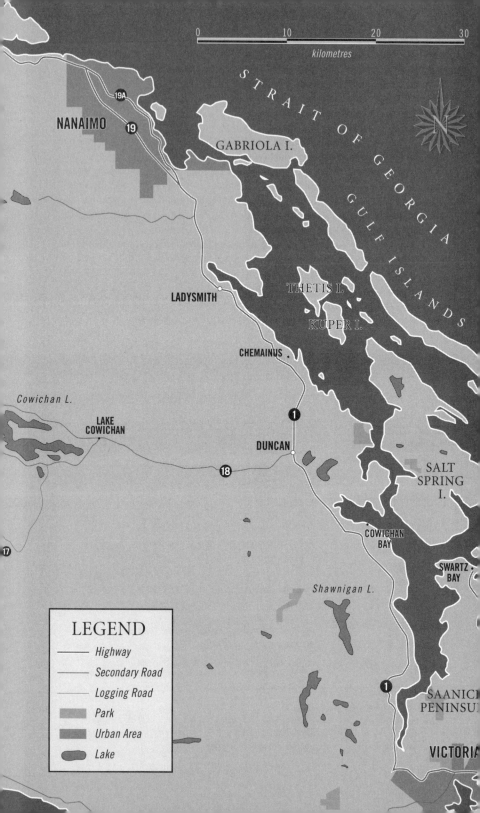

STRAIT OF GEORGIA

GULF ISLANDS

NANAIMO

19A

19

GABRIOLA I.

THETIS I.

KUPER I.

LADYSMITH

CHEMAINUS

Cowichan L.

LAKE COWICHAN

1

18

DUNCAN

SALT SPRING I.

COWICHAN BAY

17

SWARTZ BAY

Shawnigan L.

1

SAANICH PENINSUL

VICTORIA

0   10   20   30

kilometres

LEGEND
— Highway
— Secondary Road
— Logging Road
▨ Park
▨ Urban Area
▨ Lake

CHAPTER 5

VANCOUVER ISLAND SOUTH

There are hundreds of beaches to explore

In Chemainus, an artist touches up a mural

T he drive between Victoria and Nanaimo along the southern part of Vancouver Island is full of wonderful surprises—everything from rural tranquility to outdoor adventure abounds along this scenic stretch of highway. It takes about 1 1/2 to 2 hours to drive to from Victoria to Nanaimo on Hwy 1 (better know as the "Island Highway"). This road is Vancouver Island's only north-south artery so at any given time a sizable chunk of the island's traffic will be somewhere along this route. In summertime the "up-island crawl" can be unnerving. However, the BC government has launched the huge Vancouver Island Highway Project to ease the island's traffic problems by creating a four-lane highway. Some sections, including the Nanaimo Parkway which skirts the city of Nanaimo, are already open, while other sections are still in the works. For cyclists, a bicycle-safe shoulder from downtown Victoria to Campbell River is also part of the highway construction plans. (For information, 250-953-4949.)

Getting to Victoria

See page 95

Getting to Victoria

See page 95

Approximate Distances

From Victoria to Duncan 64 km
From Lake Cowichan to Duncan 25 km
From Duncan to Nanaimo 45 km
From Chemainus to Nanaimo 35 km
From Ladysmith to Nanaimo 20 km

VICTORIA TO NANAIMO

Newcastle Is.

The BC Forest Museum

Highlights

Breathtaking side-of-the-highway views

Rural landscapes

Hiking and camping in ancient forests

Rich First Nations culture and history

Prime freshwater and saltwater fishing

Historical sites

Island hopping

Goldstream Park/Malahat Drive

Just 18 km north of Victoria on Hwy 1 is the turnoff to Goldstream Provincial Park (250-391-2300). To experience the BC coast at its natural best, don't pass up this park. Goldstream has 159 **reservable campsites** for overnight stays (toll free in North America, 1-800-689-9025, Vancouver or overseas, 604-689-9025) and it has **great loop day hikes** for exploring a whole range of ecosystems from the **deep forests** of Douglas fir, western red cedar and bigleaf maple up to the higher and drier **upland ridges** with arbutus and Garry oak, or down to a **salt marsh estuary** at the head of Saanich Inlet. A new trail even lets campers day hike from the park to Butchart Gardens. (Park maps are available at the **Freeman King Visitor Centre**.) The estuary is a habitat for **birds** and also an important **salmon spawning** run. Long ago the Salish peoples gathered at the estuary here in the fall to harvest the returning salmon and collect potatoes and fruit from nearby plantings.

Goldstream Provincial Park is near the start of the section of Hwy 1 known as the Malahat Drive. This ribbon of highway climbs 180 metres up the rugged mountainside through deep green forests and out along cliff faces on its way to the Cowichan Valley. From roadside pullouts you get **spectacular views** over the Saanich Inlet and across the Gulf Islands to the imposing white volcanic peak of Mt. Baker in Washington state.

If the prospect of negotiating the steep Malahat Drive is daunting, you can bypass it by taking Hwy 17 up the Saanich Peninsula from Victoria and then hopping aboard the BC ferry that runs across the Saanich Inlet from Brentwood Bay to Mill Bay. This ferry route is

popular in summer, so get to the ferry terminal early. You can explore the little village at the head of the ferry dock or grab a bite in the cute dockside eatery. The 25-minute trip across Saanich Inlet is a scenic pleasure trip, and picture-snapping passengers are generally in a feel-good holiday mood. From Mill Bay it's a short drive to rejoin Hwy 1 beyond the Malahat and head north through the Cowichan Valley.

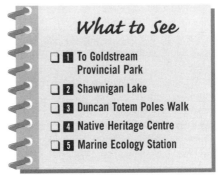

What to See

- [ ] **1** To Goldstream Provincial Park
- [ ] **2** Shawnigan Lake
- [ ] **3** Duncan Totem Poles Walk
- [ ] **4** Native Heritage Centre
- [ ] **5** Marine Ecology Station

Shawnigan Lake

Another route to the Cowichan Valley is to follow Hwy 1 up the Malahat Drive to the (left) turnoff to East Shawnigan Lake Road. Instead of going over the top of the Malahat, you'll

The Mill Bay ferry (far left) offers an alternate route up island

drive along Shawnigan Lake. You can then take the Shawnigan Lake–Mill Bay Road back to Hwy 1 near Mill Bay. This road winds through **tree-covered hills, marshland and hobby farms** to Shawnigan Lake. The lakeside communities are small but the lake itself is big—almost 8 km long. You'll find several boat launches at the north end of the lake. Favourite water sports here include **swimming, boating, windsurfing and water-skiing**. Several B&Bs tucked here and there near the lake offer the chance to stop and enjoy a rural breather before heading north.

Shawnigan Lake is the spot where Prime Minister Sir John A. Macdonald drove the last spike on the Esquimalt & Nanaimo Railway in 1886. In the days before good roads were built and air travel became more popular, vacationers flocked to take the E&N train up the Malahat to the resort community at Shawnigan Lake or travel on to commodious lodges farther along the route built by the E&N. Via Rail still runs a daily passenger train, the Malahat, along the former E&N line between Victoria and Courtenay. Passengers have unlimited stopover privileges at its nineteen stops along the way, including Shawnigan, Duncan, Chemainus and Nanaimo. Although the view out the window tends to be of trees and more trees, the excursion train does make a spectacular run over the Malahat and across enough creeks and trestle bridges to gladden any railroader's heart (for schedules and fares, 250-383-4324 or 1-800-561-8630).

Lying in the sun on the far side of the Malahat is the wide, gentle Cowichan Valley. It has been a farming and lumbering region for more than a hundred years. Recently, gas stations, motels, used car lots and fast food outlets have popped up, and the scenery along Hwy 1 is an uneasy mix of delightfully wooded hills, farms and fields dappled with cloud-shadows, and not-so-scenic mini-strip malls. The Cowichan Valley's real charm is hidden along the side roads and back ways. If you have the time, pick a motel or a B&B—the Cowichan Valley has a selection of accommodations from good to superlative—and go exploring off the highway. (Valley maps and B&B listings are available at local Visitor InfoCentres. Or phone the Duncan–Cowichan InfoCentre at 250-746-4636.) Wine lovers can mix the pleasure of relaxed back road driving with leisurely stops for wine tasting at **local vineyards**. "Cowichan" means "the sun-warmed land," and the Cowichan Valley with its almost Mediterranean climate is a fine place for growing wine grapes. Cherry Point Vineyards combines wine tasting evenings with a bed and breakfast (250-743-1272). Venturi Schulze winery hosts special wine-making dinners and has two guest rooms in a 100-year-old farmhouse (250-743-5630). Vignetta Zanatta farm winery offers a menu emphasizing west coast and rustic Italian cuisines complemented by their own Italian-style wines (250-748-2338). Blue Grouse Vineyards specializes in German wines (250-743-3834). For a little change of pace, don't overlook Merridale Cider just off the Shawnigan–Mill Bay Rd (250-743-4293).

▶ **Shawnigan Lake, Cobble Hill, Mill Bay and Cowichan Bay Annual Events**

April/May
Vancouver Island Indoor Rodeo (Mill Bay)

May
Cowichan Goes Country (Mill Bay)

June
Mill Bay Country Music Festival (Mill Bay)

July
Shawnigan Lake Writers' Village

August
Shawnigan Lake Craft Fair
Cobble Hill Fair & Exhibition

October
Oktoberfest (Cobble Hill)

December
Shawnigan Lake Country Craft Fair

For more information, South Cowichan Chamber of Commerce 250-743-3566

Cowichan Bay

Taking the turnoff to the small fishing village of Cowichan Bay is another pleasant side trip. This bay where the Cowichan River meets salt water was home to the Cowichan tribes, who had established thirteen villages along the Cowichan River between Cowichan Bay and Kaatza at Cowichan Lake. James Douglas's arrival with the first group of settlers in 1862 marked the beginning of white settlement. The poet Robert Service also lived at Cowichan Bay and worked in the post office in the days before the siren call of Klondike gold lured him north. (Some locals claim that Service wrote his very first poem in Cowichan Bay.) Later British royalty came to fish in the Cowichan River, which was famous worldwide for its rainbow and steelhead trout and its rich salmon runs.

Today Cowichan Bay is a pleasantly weathered collection of buildings built on stilts out over the water. You'll find marinas, hotels, a pub, craft galleries, restaurants, fishing charters and the **Marine Ecology Station** on Pier 66 with exhibits of marine habitats and microscopes for up-close views of undersea life (250-748-4522). Buy **fresh fish** straight off the dock or tuck into a tasty meal at the Masthead Restaurant in the historic Columbia Hotel building (c. 1868), and enjoy the great views of Cowichan Bay's resident fishing fleet, huge log booms from a nearby mill, and the mountains of Salt Spring Island scalloping the horizon. For a short stroll you can take the **shoreline footpath** from the village through 1.5-ha Hecate Regional Park and Theik Reserve Footpath. It crosses a Cowichan Tribe reserve and lets you enjoy shorebird watching and views of Mt. Tzouhalem.

Shawnigan Lake, Cobble Hill, Mill Bay and Cowichan Bay Recreation, Accommodations and Services

Recreation
Golf courses
Recreation centre
Boat charters
Fishing charters
Vineyards/Cidery
Hiking/Biking trails
Parks

Accommodations
Bed & Breakfast
Hotels/Motels
Campgrounds/RV Parks

Services
Places to eat (including pubs, restaurants, cafés.)
Banks (ATMS)
Grocery stores/Markets
Service stations
Shopping Centres
Medical centre

Important Numbers

Police **911**
Fire **911**
Ambulance **911**
Medical Clinic (Mill Bay) **250-743-3211**
South Cowichan Chamber of Commerce **250-743-3566**

Duncan

Cowichan Bay is just a hop and a skip from Duncan, the largest centre in the Cowichan Valley and a good place for tourist services. Duncan also calls itself the **City of Totems**. Beginning in 1985 the city's mayor began promoting Native carving and today forty-one totem poles are located throughout the city. (You can get a map of the totems from the helpful folk at the Duncan InfoCentre.) On the bank of the Cowichan River at the south end of Duncan is the **Native Heritage Centre** (250-746-8119). To get to the centre turn left immediately after you cross the bridge heading north over the river. Here you can watch a multimedia film presentation about Cowichan life and culture

Duncan's Native Heritage Centre

▶ Duncan Annual Events

May
Regional Heritage Days

June
Gathering in the Valley
(Native Heritage Centre)

July
Island Folk Festival (Providence Farm)
Duncan–Cowichan Summer Festival

September
Cowichan Exhibition
Cowichan Fringe Festival
Labour Day Celebrations
(BC Forest Museum)

November
Native Heritage Centre Annual Art Show
and Sale

For more information, Duncan–Cowichan
Chamber of Commerce **250-746-4636**

St. Ann's church

called *Great Deeds*, enjoy **storytelling, dancing and traditional feasting**, have a snack at the restaurant, venture into the impressive cedar-plank Big House where Cowichan weddings and other important community functions are held, and watch totem pole carving and hand knitting. The Cowichans were traditionally known for their skill as weavers, and the famous Cowichan sweaters (available in the gift shop) are a contemporary version of ancient woven goat-hair blankets. Cedar bark and the hair from a special breed of little white woolly-haired dogs were sometimes woven into the blankets. They were coloured with dyes made from cedar bark mud, stinging nettles and wild onions. When Scottish sheep farmers came to the valley in the 1860s, Cowichan women quickly learned how to knit with lamb's wool and adapted traditional patterns of whales, eagles and thunderbirds to knitted sweaters. You can see a small but excellent display of valuable old Cowichan sweaters here. The real treasures at the cultural centre, however, are the Native artists and elders who are there to pass on to the next generation the culture of their ancestors.

Important Numbers

Police **911**
Fire **911**
Ambulance **911**
Hospital **250-746-4141**
Police (non-emergency)
250-748-5522

Duncan Recreation, Accommodations and Services

Recreation
Bicycle rental
Golf courses
Recreation centre
Hiking trails

Accommodations
Bed & Breakfasts
Inns/Motels
Campgrounds/RV Parks

Services
InfoCentre
Places to eat (including restaurants, pubs, fast food)
Banks (ATMs)
Service stations
Grocery stores
Galleries/Gift shops
Hospital

A side trip to Cowichan Lake and the Carmanah Valley

Cowichan Lake and the Carmanah Valley offer more off-the-beaten-track adventures. This large lake is 31 km west of Duncan on Hwy 18. The 43-km-long lake is a favourite with **boaters, campers, fishers, water skiers and swimmers**. There is also **golfing and hiking** nearby. In summer you can stop at the Lake Cowichan InfoCentre for maps and information (250-749-3244). You may also want to slip into the **Kaatza Station Museum** in the old E&N railway station. For decades the Lake Cowichan area has been home to miners and loggers. This museum does itself proud with limited but lively displays on pioneer life and on local mining and logging activities. From the village of Lake Cowichan the road splits to run around the lake on the north and south shores. The pavement ends partway along so plan for slow travel on gravel if you want to make the full circuit.

Where the two roads meet, a rough-surfaced and active logging road takes off toward the saltwater inlet on the island's west coast, called **Nitinat Lake** located 70 km west of Lake Cowichan Village. Nitinat Lake is the home of the Dididaht First Nation where you'll find the only services in the entire area—a motel, café, grocery store and gas bar as well as the **Dididaht Nation Visitor Centre**. (For more information, 250-745-3848.) It is also the takeoff point for excellent **windsurfing** on Nitinat Lake and for **canoeing and kayaking** (for experienced backcountry trekkers only) on the chain of lakes known as the Nitinat Triangle. And it's a trailhead for the famous West Coast Trail (see pp. 242–245). (Most hikers don't realize it, but you can day-hike the West Coast Trail without a trail pass.) Last but not least, it's the start of the 45-km climb up a rough switchbacked logging road to the **ancient rain forests of Carmanah Walbran Provincial Park**. Saved from clearcut logging by the efforts of hundreds of concerned citizens, led by the Western Canada Wilderness Committee, this magnificent old-growth forest is now protected as a provincial park. The park is known for its **groves of huge Sitka spruce**. The Carmanah Giant—a staggering 95 metres tall—is thought to be the largest Sitka spruce in the world. When Randy Stoltmann, who first discovered these ancient trees, died unexpectedly in a

The ancient rain forests of Carmanah Valley

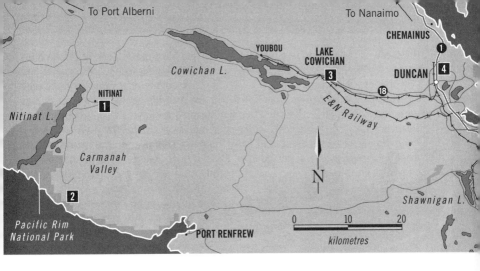

mountaineering accident in 1994, a grove of Sitka spruce was named in his honour. This is a true wilderness park, very remote, with only primitive camping facilities and extremely variable weather, flash floods, changing creek levels, and very slippery road and trail conditions. Plan carefully before venturing in. (For further information, 250-728-3234.)

The Carmanah–Walbran watershed has been saved from the saw, but lumbering has long been a major industry on Vancouver Island. To find out more about its history, stop at the **BC Forest Museum** just north of Duncan on Hwy 1. This 40-ha museum complex features indoor displays, but you'll probably be quickly lured outside by the wailing of the steam engine whistle. Board the train for a swing past the outdoor displays, including a water wheel, blacksmith shop, working sawmill, logging camp, turn-of-the-century farmyard and collection of old-time logging equipment. Visitors are free to wander the grounds and enjoy watching activities like log sawing, shake splitting and paper making.

What to See

- ☐ **1** Dididaht Nation Visitor Centre
- ☐ **2** Carmanah Walbran Provincial Park
- ☐ **3** Kaatza Station Museum
- ☐ **4** BC Forest Museum

Cowichan Lake Recreation, Accommodations and Services

Recreation
Excellent fishing at Cowichan Lake & surrounding lakes ("fly fishing capital of Canada")
Golf course
Several hiking trails

Accommodations
Bed & Breakfast
Cabin/Cottage resorts

Motels
Campgrounds/RV Parks

Services
InfoCentre
Places to eat (including pub, restaurants, café)
Bank/Credit Union (ATM)
Grocery stores
Gas/Service stations
Gift shops
Gallery

Important Numbers

Emergency **911**
Hospital **250-746-4141**
Ambulance **911**
Fire **911**
Police (non-emergency) **250-748-5522**

Chemainus

If you choose one place to stop between Victoria and Nanaimo, make it the coastal community of Chemainus, the "Little Town That Did." In 1983, when the local lumber mill shut its gates after more than 120 years, Chemainus might have rolled over and died except for the inspired madness of Karl Schutz and the willing suspension of disbelief of the people of Chemainus. Schutz, a German-born cabinetmaker envisioned the town as an open-air gallery with bigger-than-life-sized **murals of rich local history** on its walls. Residents embraced his dream and today thirty-three murals attest to their combined determination. The town really did it—and did it right. Even though the mill was modernized and reopened in 1985, Chemainus's real focus is on tourism: 300,000 visitors stop to see the murals every year.

> ### Chemainus Annual Events
>
> **July**
> *Chemainus Fun Daze*
> *Chemainus Market Day*
> *Chemainus Ceilidh*
> *Festival of Murals*
> *Teddy Bears Picnic*
>
> **September**
> *Fall Market Day*
>
> **December**
> *Christmas Light-Up*
>
> *For more information, Chemainus and District Chamber of Commerce*
> **250-246-3944**

The mural project works because the murals are selected in a juried competition among professional artists, and because the people of Chemainus have taken the project to heart. The art work tells their own history, and their pride and sheer pleasure are still evident more than a decade later. A couple of the contributing artists were so taken with the spirit of the community that they picked up and moved to Chemainus. The murals have even shaped the town's history. In the summer of 1991 the town celebrated two new murals—*The Winning Float* (#29) by Joyce H. Kamikura and *The Lone Scout* (#30) by Stanley Hiromichi Taniwa—to recognize the three hundred

Chemainus mural

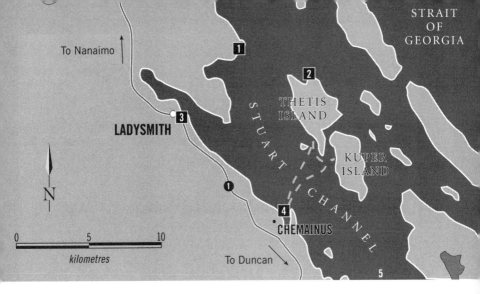

To Nanaimo

1

2

THETIS ISLAND

STUART

LADYSMITH

3

KUPER ISLAND

N

CHANNEL

1

4

CHEMAINUS

0   5   10

kilometres

To Duncan

5

Japanese Canadians who settled in the area before the 1940s and were forced to leave their homes for internment camps during World War II. The reunion between the Japanese families of Chemainus and their old friends and neighbours was a memorably joyous (and tearful) event in the town's life.

You can follow the big yellow footprints from mural to mural (walking tour maps are available at a nominal price at the InfoCentre and the Mural Information kiosk in the heart of Chemainus) or climb aboard a horse-drawn carriage to clop through the streets and listen to a colourful live commentary. The town also has lots of attractive little boutiques and gift shops and a couple of very good restaurants. There are several good B&B's in Chemainus, and the new **Chemainus Theatre** draws an enthusiastic audience year-round with the combined offering of a buffet dinner and popular theatre classics (reservations: 250-246-9820 or 1-800-565-7738). Everywhere you go, you'll find townsfolk who are genuinely friendly. "These welcoming people still dish out island hospitality, along with ice cream and afternoon tea and scones just as they always have," wrote one Chemainus PR type, and it's true.

What to See

- ☐ **1** Yellow Point
- ☐ **2** Thetis Island
- ☐ **3** Ladysmith Historic Downtown
- ☐ **4** The Chemainus Murals

Chemainus Theatre

A converted tug explores local waters

Chemainus Recreation, Accommodations and Services

Recreation
Bicycle rentals
Canoe/Kayak rentals
Fishing/Boat charters
Golf course
Tennis courts
Parks
Hiking trails

Accommodations
Bed & Breakfasts
Inns/Resorts
Motel
Campgrounds/RV Parks
Hostel

Services
InfoCentre (seasonal)
Places to eat (including restaurants, cafés, fast food)
Credit Union (ATMs)
Antique malls
Gas/Service stations
Hospital

Thetis Island

At the foot of Maple Street in Chemainus is the BC Ferries terminal where ferries make the 30- to 45-minute sailing to Thetis Island about ten times daily. The trip to Thetis is a wonderfully scenic—and cheap (if you go as a foot passenger)—ocean cruise. The little passenger-and-car ferry **MV *Klitsa*** sails past small evergreen-covered islands, sometimes close enough for you to see the textured granite rocks shaded by the leafy umbrellas of arbutus trees. You'll get **stunning views** of the Coast Range on the BC mainland as well as the mountains of Vancouver Island. The ferry usually makes a stop at **Kuper Island**. This is the reserve of the Penelakut First Nation and permission from the band is needed to visit. Then it's on to little Thetis Island (pop. 271), which was joined to Kuper Island near **Telegraph Harbour** until the federal government dredged out a canal in 1905. You can either take the ferry back to Chemainus or stop to explore.

Life on this very rural island proceeds at a quiet, unhurried pace, and Thetis Islanders like it that way. Local zoning has allowed only three commercial developments

Important Numbers

*Emergency **911***
*Chemainus Hospital **250-246-3291***
*Arts & Business Council **250-246-4701**/Fax **250-246-3251***

on the island, and there are no public amenities like campgrounds or toilets. A few B&Bs are popping up and the island has a local taxi company (250-246-5055), but tourism is definitely a minor key here. Head left as you leave the terminal, and you'll come to a fork where the island's two major roads—Pilkey Point Road and North Cove Road—diverge to run up opposite sides of the island. Pilkey Point Road (to the right) is the prettier choice, and **Pilkey Point**, 6 km from the ferry dock, is a small but beautiful rocky point lapped by clear blue water with fine island and mountain views. But hikers and cyclists, beware! Pilkey Point Road climbs up a major hill about 4 km from the terminal and then descends to Pilkey Point. You'll have to negotiate this beast both coming and going. North Cove Road (to the left) is less challenging but also less scenic.

Pilkey Point on Thetis Island

If you just want a stroll and some pleasant diversion, that's easy. Scattered along Pilkey Point Road are **several artisans' studios**, including the popular Spinning Wheel Studio and Alpaca Ranch overlooking Telegraph Harbour. The farthest afield is the Pot of Gold Coffee Roasting Company tucked away in a charming little log house about 3 km from the ferry dock. Just walk or drive along the road and look for the signs to the studios. On your way back you can stop for a drink or a bite to eat at either the Telegraph Harbour Marina or the Thetis Island Marina and Pub. The Telegraph Harbour Marina on Marine Drive off Pilkey Point Road has a friendly family-style café (no alcoholic drinks) and what one islander described as "super-sized" ice cream cones from a fifties-style soda fountain, as well as groceries, gifts, and fishing supplies. The Thetis Island Marina on Telegraph Harbour is a short walk from the ferry

Getting to Thetis Island by Ferry

Drive aboard a BC Ferry at Chemainus. 30–45 minutes crossing time; 8 sailings daily year round, additional sailings on Fridays. Vehicle reservations not available.

For more information about travel aboard BC Ferries, see p.8.

The rustic Coffee Roasting Company on Thetis Island

terminal. (Turn right onto Foster Point Road and then take the first left onto Harbour Road.) The food and views are great, the proprietor is friendly, and the thirty or so eagles perched in the trees across the harbour are a sight to see. In summer they come to fish for bullheads, and you can watch them swooping down to snatch their prey. (Bring your binoculars for closer viewing.) The two marinas are alive with powerboats and yachts in the summer, and a few **kayakers** have twigged to the fact that the protected waters of Thetis and the nearby islands are a great place to paddle. If your Thetis Island sampler makes you yearn for a longer stay, check the community bulletin board just above the BC Ferries terminal for accommodations or call the Chemainus InfoCentre (250-246-3944 or 250-246-4701).

Ladysmith

When you leave Chemainus, you can return to Hwy 1 or take the pleasantly rural Chemainus Road. It runs along the coast with peek-a-boo views of the water, then intersects Hwy 1 just before the town of Ladysmith. James Dunsmuir, son and heir to coal baron Robert Dunsmuir, founded this town at the turn of the century to house miners well away from the Extension coal mine pithead a few miles north. In its heyday tons of Extension's bituminous coal were shipped all over the world from the port at Ladysmith. The mine at Extension had

▶ Ladysmith Annual Events

June
Ladysmith Celebration Days

September
Fall Ladysmith Fair

November
Ladysmith Festival of Lights

For more information, Ladysmith InfoCentre 250-245-2112

Ladysmith's downtown has recently been revitalized

Ladysmith Recreation, Accommodations and Services

Recreation
Bicycle rental
Kayak/Canoe rental
Community parks
Several hiking trails
Fishing/Boat charters
Tennis courts
Golf course

Accommodations
Bed & Breakfasts
Inns/Resorts
Campgrounds/RV parks

Services
InfoCentre
Several places to eat (including restaurants, pubs, fast food)
Grocery stores
Banks (ATMs)
Post Office
Gas/Service stations
Galleries
Hospital

a dramatic history of disasters and labour strife. A deadly explosion in 1909 killed thirty-two miners, and a long and bloody strike lasted from 1912 until the outbreak of World War I. By the early 1930s the mine was played out, but Ladysmith was saved from economic ruin when the Comox Logging Company based its headquarters here in 1935. By the 1980s the lumber industry was slowing down and the townsfolk of Ladysmith turned to tourism. History buffs should take the left-hand turnoff to Ladysmith from Hwy 1 and cruise down **First Avenue** where many of the town's original buildings still stand. A recent downtown revitalization program won a national Main Street Canada award. Ladysmith's **heritage buildings** are now spiffied up and decked out with historic markers, and walking tour maps are available at the local InfoCentre. When you've had your history hit, swing back onto Hwy 1 at the north end of Ladysmith.

Important Numbers

Ambulance **911**	Fire **911**
Hospital **250-245-2221**	Chamber of Commerce
Police **911**	**250-245-2112**
	Fax **250-245-2124**

Backroad scene near Yellow Point

Yellow Point

Just before Nanaimo is your last chance for a backroad excursion on the Cedar Loop. Take the (right-hand) turnoff to the Yellow Point (Cedar Road) exit and make your way around the 23 km loop formed by Cedar Road and Yellow Point Road. This is a great drive and a terrific **bicycle tour**. You travel along quiet sun-dappled back roads, over gentle hills and along **sheep pastures** edged with a tangle of blackberry bushes, and out onto a **sandstone beach** with sweeping vistas at **Roberts Memorial Provincial Park**. Here and there you'll find **farm stands** with vegetables or honey, a gift shop, a stained glass studio, a pottery studio, and an herb farm selling fresh herbs, dried flowers and special skin creams. To end your day, try the fine traditional pub food at the Crow and Gate—but go early or make a reservation because this very English pub, set amidst grassy lawns and flower gardens just off the north end of Cedar Road, is a local favourite (250-722-3731).

If you're not ready to return to the real world, check into the Yellow Point Lodge (250-245-7422). Opened in 1939, this special place has a number of regular guests—they call themselves "Yellow Pointers"—who come back year after year for the lodge's special blend of natural beauty and open hospitality. It has 72 hectares of fern-splashed forests and more than a mile of stunning waterfront. Add a huge seaside saltwater swimming pool, tennis, volleyball, bikes, badminton, canoes, kayaks and lots of wildlife, and you can see why folks just keep coming back for more.

Its first proprietor, Gerry Hill, was known for his kindliness, genial humour and deep concern for the fragile landscape. One of the stories he used to tell was about trying to get cabins built in time for the summer season. When a couple of guests arrived, he asked them to go with him down to the rocks in front of the lodge. Then he pointed to a cabin on a float raft, just coming into view around the point. "That's your cabin," he told them. "As soon as we get it in to shore, I'll take your bags." Luckily, his guests had a fine-honed sense of humour, too.

The old lodge burned down in 1985. When the new one was built on the same foundation and with the same massive wooden rafters, cedar planking, sprung dance floor and gigantic maw of a fieldstone fireplace, staunch Yellow Pointers breathed a collective

Yellow Point Lodge has been in business since 1939

sigh of relief. Some of the very rustic old cabins (no running water!) still hug the shoreline while newer cottages, with modern conveniences, are scattered about in just-so spots in the meadows or overlooking the water. Volunteer work parties of the Friends of Yellow Point Society pitch in to build cabins and bridges, plant trees, restore the meadows and generally help the next generation of Hills keep the spirit of Yellow Point alive.

The popular Crow & Gate pub

NANAIMO

The Bastion

Miss Nanaimo contestants

Highlights

Beautiful
harbourfront walks

Historic downtown
architecture

Stunning ocean views

Nearby
secluded islands

Swimming, boating
and kayaking

Big city amenities

Ferries to Vancouver

N anaimo is the largest centre on Vancouver Island outside Victoria. You'll find all the expected amenities including banks, motels, restaurants and shopping malls. This is a good place to stock up before heading north or west on Vancouver Island.

Nanaimo calls itself **The Harbour City**. The port, with its deep-sea docks and ferry terminal, has always been a large export centre and still ships out more than a million tonnes of cargo every year. Recently the city has beautified its harbourfront with **seafront gardens, walkways, lawns and beaches** as part of a major downtown revitalization program. Nanaimo's downtown waterfront is now the place to head on a blue-sky day. You can see lots of action on the water, including tugs, ferries, pleasure craft, and fishing boats. At the south end of the water front is the **boat basin**, a lovely little marina with funky fish boats, docks decorated with flowers and a popular fish-and-chips stand. This is where you can catch the passenger ferry to **Protection Island**. The restaurant/pub there is a great place to enjoy heaping portions of fish and chips and views of the Nanaimo Harbour.

What to See

- ☐ **1** Harbourside Walkway
- ☐ **2** Maffeo-Sutton Park
- ☐ **3** The Bastion
- ☐ **4** Historic Downtown
- ☐ **5** Harbour Park
- ☐ **6** Petroglyph Provincial Park

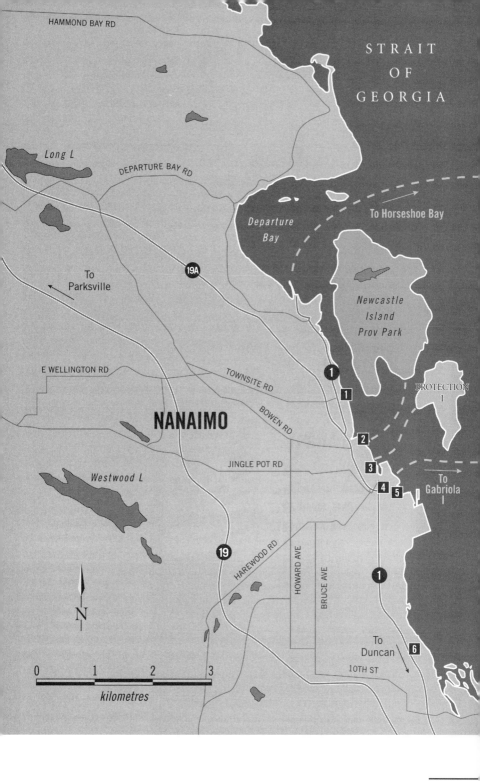

HAMMOND BAY RD

STRAIT
OF
GEORGIA

Long L

DEPARTURE BAY RD

Departure
Bay

To Horseshoe Bay

19A

To
Parksville

Newcastle
Island
Prov Park

E WELLINGTON RD

TOWNSITE RD

PROTECTION
I

NANAIMO

BOWEN RD

1

1

Westwood L

JINGLE POT RD

2

3

4 5

To
Gabriola

HAREWOOD RD

19

HOWARD AVE

BRUCE AVE

1

N

To
Duncan

6

10TH ST

0   1   2   3

kilometres

You can often buy fresh seafood right off the boat at Nanaimo Harbour

The Nanaimo Harbour was once the territory of the Coast Salish group known as the Sne ney mux (Nanaimo) peoples, and their cedar lodges once stood at present-day Departure Bay ferry terminal and the **Harbour Park** shopping mall. Across the street just beside the Harbour Park mall in Piper Park is the **Nanaimo District Museum** (250-753-1821) with displays on Sne ney mux culture and legends, band elders and land claims. Kids will enjoy the hands-on feel of this fine little museum, where they can poke through display drawers of Native artifacts and walk through replicas of a turn-of-the-century main street, an old-time Chinatown and a Nanaimo coal pit.

The white settlement at Nanaimo grew up around coal. As the story goes, a Sne ney mux man carried a lump of coal from the Nanaimo Harbour to Hudson's Bay Company Chief Factor James Douglas at Fort Victoria. Douglas immediately ordered an HBC officer to return with him to Nanaimo to see just how big those coal deposits were. The HBC officer was reportedly so delighted by the outcroppings of bituminous rock above the beach that he "started dancing on top of the coal." Douglas was equally delighted. "This discovery has afforded me more satisfaction than I can express," he wrote. A week later the Hudson's Bay Company laid claim to the Nanaimo coal deposits.

In 1854 twenty-seven English and Scottish mining families arrived by boat to work the Hudson's Bay Company mines. They settled near a defensive bastion built in 1853 by the HBC to protect them from raids by northerly tribes. By the 1890s the Nanaimo Harbour was riddled with coal mines—some tunnels snaked right under the harbour to coal-rich Newcastle Island—and yearly production was in the hundreds of thousands of tonnes. But the Nanaimo bituminous coal deposits were highly volatile, and explosive methane gas sometimes seeped out into mine shafts from cracks in the coal. Just before 6:00 p.m. on May 3, 1887, two explosions shattered the evening calm. Black smoke belched out of both shafts at the Number 1 mine on Esplanade Street. The smoke signalled the worst disaster to hit the Pacific Coast. In all, 148 men lost their lives that terrible May evening. Only seven miners made it out of the pit alive.

One of the stops along Nanaimo Heritage Walk

The Nanaimo District Museum offers Native artifacts and early Nanaimo replicas

Newcastle Island Provincial Marine Park

Imagine yourself on an island with no cars and 306 hectares of parkland. Welcome to Newcastle Island Provincial Marine Park! A 10-minute private foot passenger ferry ride from **Maffeo-Sutton Park** just off Front Street in downtown Nanaimo takes you to the city's "offshore playground." This gentle island has wide beaches where kids can splash in the shallow water, a wharf where they can fish for shiners, open grassy meadows for lazing in the sun, and views, views, views in every direction. Behind the beaches are **forests**

▶ Nanaimo Annual Events

January
Sea Lion Festival

May
Festival of Banners
Farmer's Market
Empire Days Celebration

July
Nanaimo Marine Festival and
International Bathtub Race

August
Vancouver Island Exhibition

For more information, Tourism
*Nanaimo **1-800-663-7337***

of Douglas fir, arbutus and Garry oak trees. Hikers can explore the park's sandstone cliffs and gravel beaches from trails circling the island and enjoy ever-changing vistas of ocean, islands and distant mountains.

Newcastle Island is also steeped in history. Coast Salish middens along the shore are testament to its days as the site of ancient First Nations fishing villages. In the nineteenth century it became an industrial island, and was home to a coal mine, a sandstone quarry, a pulpstone quarry, a Japanese herring saltery and a shipyard. You can still see evidence of commercial activity at well-marked interpretive stops, including giant pulpstones in the abandoned quarry site. But the island's natural beauty wasn't lost on visitors, and in 1931 the Canadian Pacific Steamship Company built a popular resort on the island with a dance pavilion, hundreds of picnic tables, a soccer field and a teahouse. Shiploads of vacationers arrived by steamer from Vancouver to savour balmy summer days and dance away the nights. The historic dance pavilion is now the park's restaurant/snack bar.

For more information, Newcastle Island Ferry 250-753-5141; Newcastle Island Provincial Park 250-754-7893.

The distinctive octagonal Hudson's Bay Company bastion, made from hand-hewn Douglas fir logs, still stands above the harbour at the corner of Bastion and Front streets. Now a museum of militaria and historical documents (250-756-2554), it is the oldest surviving blockhouse in the west. In summer the "Bastion Guards" fire off the Bastion's cannon every day at noon.

Newcastle Island makes a great day outing from Nanaimo

Nanaimo Recreation, Accommodations and Services

Recreation
Bike rentals
Canoe/Kayak rentals
Several Fishing/Boating charters
Dive charters
Golf courses within 1 hour of Nanaimo
Adventure tour companies
Horseback riding
Tennis courts
Several hiking trails
Eagle Point Archery (largest indoor archery range in western Canada)
Bungy Zone Bridge & Park (only legal bridge jump site in North America)

Accommodations
Bed & Breakfasts
Hotels/Motels
Campgrounds/RV Parks
Hostel

Services
InfoCentre
Places to eat (including pubs, restaurants, fast food)
Banks (ATMs)
Shopping centers
Galleries
Post office
Hospital

Important Numbers

Emergency **911**
Nanaimo Hospital **250-754-2141**
RCMP **250-754-2345**
Tourism Nanaimo
250-754-0106/ Fax **250-756-0075**
1-800-663-7337 (in North America)
website
www.iNTERspace.com/tourism/nanaimo
email
info@tourism.nanaimo.bc.ca

Nanaimo's newly completed 4-km **Harbourside Walkway** runs below the bastion along the waterfront all the way up to BC Ferries Departure Bay ferry terminal. You can amble through a new harbourside development with gift shops, a cappuccino bar and a waterfront pub and restaurant. Just beside the pub, float planes zoom off from a new seaplane dock over beautiful Protection Island and Newcastle Island in the Nanaimo Harbour. Off in the distance are the mainland mountains with billowy white clouds piled high against their peaks.

Follow the Harbourside Walkway north through the wide green lawns of several interlinked parks where a **man-made swimming lagoon, changing rooms, picnic tables, an adventure playground, tennis courts** and hot dog and ice cream vendors offer lots of family fun. You'll also find the dock for the little red-and-white **paddlewheeler** that shuttles between the park and Newcastle Island Provincial Marine Park. If your harbour visit falls on the fourth Sunday in July, you can enjoy the zany **International Bathtub Race**, in which participants dash from Nanaimo Harbour to the finish line at Departure Bay in an outrageous fleet of floating bathtubs. It's the highlight of the three-day Nanaimo Marine Festival.

Downtown Nanaimo has an eye-catching array of historic buildings, and several have been smartly refitted with great little shops and restaurants. Pick up a walking tour map at the InfoCentre and take a walk through Nanaimo's early history. Among the best spots are the **1889 Palace Hotel**, the **1896 courthouse**, and the turn-of-the-century Central Drugs pharmacy in the **1911 Dakin Building**. Somewhere on your travels you may get the chance to tuck into that famously gooey chocolatey confection, the Nanaimo bar. According to local lore, turn-of-the-century Nanaimo miners used to get packets of these sticky delights from their relatives way across the Atlantic Ocean. Anything worth sending that far has got to be good. (Ask at the Nanaimo InfoCentre for a recipe.)

GABRIOLA ISLAND

Fogo art

St. Mary's Church

Highlights

Rolling hills
and meadows

Accessible beaches

Abundant parks
and forest hikes

Orchards and farms

Unique folk art

great cycling

Amazing natural
rock formations

G abriola Island is less than 5 km from Nanaimo Harbour, and the ferry crossing is under half an hour. Gabriola's name is undoubtedly a legacy of the Spanish explorers who sailed these waters in 1792 when Spain vied with England and Russia to claim sovereignty over this strategic and resource-rich corner of the globe. On June 15, 1792 the Spaniards anchored in the bay where the BC Ferry now docks on Gabriola, and asked the local Coast Salish people where to find fresh water. They named the little bay Cala del Descanso—"small bay of rest"—and it still carries the name Descanso Bay.

The Spanish expedition's official artist, José Cardero, made a pen-and-wash sketch of the local Native chief at Descanso Bay. Cardero's sketch shows a man with a moustache and small goatee, wrapped in a fine cedar bark blanket and wearing an ornate cedar headdress ornamented with feathers and shells. The chief was probably a member of the nearby Sne ney mux (Nanaimo) band. The Sne ney mux people traditionally left their winter village near Nanaimo in April for a summer encampment on Gabriola Island. There they gathered clams and camas bulbs and fished for cod before crossing the Strait of Georgia to the mainland in August for the huge salmon run up the Fraser River. Petroglyphs (rock carvings) on the island testify to the presence of aboriginal peoples on Gabriola for as long as 5,000 years.

The first white inhabitants settled on Gabriola after coal was discovered at Nanaimo in the early 1850s. Gabriola loggers cut lumber for the new buildings springing up at Nanaimo, and Gabriola farmers shipped out

supplies of island-grown produce for Nanaimo coal mining families. In 1887 a sandstone quarry was opened at Descanso Bay and hewn sandstone blocks were shipped to Victoria and Vancouver. A decade later a brickyard opened at Bricky Bay. (Shards of bricks still redden the shoreline at Brickyard Beach.) And in the early 1930s the ear-splitting sound of drum saws cutting massive cylindrical pulpstones out of Gabriola sandstone rocked the island. These massive pulpstones, which were used to grind wood fiber into pulp, were shipped to paper mills far up the coast.

The site of the original sandstone quarry is now the parking lot of the **White Hart Pub** just above the ferry terminal. The pub is also the site of the eye-catching cyclist named Mary Ann pedalling like fury on her recycled bike. Mary Ann, a life-sized polychrome folk art carving, is the brainchild (or brain lady—she's definitely seen some years) of Fogo Folk artists Bob and Dee Lauder, whose tongue-in-cheek wood creations turn up all over Gabriola and in homes across Canada and abroad (250-247-8082).

Mary Ann's madcap gaiety captures the open spirit of contemporary Gabriola Island. It's a

What to See

- ☐ **1** Malaspina Galleries
- ☐ **2** Gabriola Sands Provincial Park
- ☐ **3** Berry Point
- ☐ **4** Orlebar Point
- ☐ **5** Sandwell Provincial Park
- ☐ **6** Gabriola Museum & Historical Society
- ☐ **7** Silva Bay
- ☐ **8** Drumbeg Provincial Park

Getting to Gabriola Island by Ferry

From Vancouver Island (Nanaimo) to Gabriola Island:
Crossing time 20 minutes; 15 or 16 sailings daily year round. Vehicle reservations not available.

For more information about travel aboard BC Ferries, see p.8.

Berry Point Lookout is a great picnic spot

welcoming, caring community where kids often feel as if they've been raised by the whole "village." For us that friendly feeling started back at the Nanaimo ferry terminal where the ticket taker went out of her way to say hello, hand us an island map and give us tips about what to see and do. Since we had arrived early, she even asked us if we wanted a coffee! The next thing we knew, we were deep in conversation with another passenger headed for her Gabriola home. She told us all about the women writers on the island. (Gabriola has a full quota of writers, playwrights, journalists and songwriters of both sexes, and good bookshops at the Folklife Village and Pages Marina.) Then she invited us to stop by for a visit. And so it went as we made our way around the island.

Gabriola Islanders' friendliness and home-island pride runs deep. So does their commitment to keeping their beautiful island community safe from development. "Keep it rural" is the Gabriola slogan—not an easy goal when the island is just a short ferry commute from the urban sprawl of Nanaimo.

Gabriola's permanent population is about 2,500, but the number rises to about 4,000 in summer when cottagers come to enjoy its rolling hills, meadows, forests and distinctive fretworked sandstone foreshores. This island has an **abundance of accessible beaches** by comparison to its neighbour islands. (Most beach access points are marked by yellow cairns.) It also has **three provincial parks** and **half a dozen local parks**. The quiet road that loops the island makes Gabriola a perfect place for a day trip by car or by cab (Gabriola Cabs, 250-247-0049). You'll find pubs, marinas, beaches and parks dotting the circuit along at satisfying intervals. Or take your cue from madcap Mary Ann. Bring your bike (or rent a bike in Nanaimo or on Gabriola) and cycle the island at your own pace. But beware: you might fall in love and want to stay for a while. If you're staying over in summer, be sure to make accommodation arrangements ahead of time. Pressed for time? Just hop on the ferry as a foot passenger at Nanaimo, enjoy the great ocean views on the way to Gabriola, relax on the deck of the White Hart Pub with a cold one, and catch the next ferry back to town.

If you have a half-day or less to spend on Gabriola, take a short tour of the northern end of the island. You can explore the famous sandstone formation called the Malaspina

Galleries, laze on the twin sandy beaches of **Gabriola Sands Provincial Park**, picnic at beautiful **Berry Point Lookout**, and hit the island's **two commercial/craft centres** before heading back to Descanso Bay. To get to the Malaspina Galleries, turn left onto Taylor Bay Road just beyond the terminal. (You'll know you're on the right road if you spot wonderfully woolly little long-horned cattle. People who live on islands seem particularly partial to raising outlandish animals. Ostriches, llamas, peacocks, Vietnamese potbellied pigs live happily on one island or another all over the west coast.) It's about 3 km to Malaspina Drive, where you turn left and park at the end of the road. A well-marked path leads you out onto a lovely sandstone outcropping covered with dry grass and twisting arbutus trees. The rocky point is creased with **tidal pools** that are chock full of tiny marine life, including crabs, fish and sea anemones. Kids can spend hours peering into these worlds-in-miniature. And for bigger folks the scenery in every direction is stunning. Bring a lunch and enjoy watching the big BC ferries sailing into Nanaimo under the blue peaks on Vancouver Island, or turn your head to see the clouds wreathing the mountains of the mainland.

Best of all: hidden away under the south edge of the bluff are the famous **Malaspina Galleries**. This sandstone sea cave is a wide ledge with what looks like a petrified wave cresting high overhead. This impressive honeycombed sandstone formation measures approximately 100 metres long, 3 metres high, and between five and six metres wide. It's big enough for a dozen people to move around it very comfortably. You may find scuba divers getting ready to explore the sea-life-rich surrounding waters, and you're almost sure to find ardent photographers trying to capture just the right image of this amazing natural formation. The Spaniards felt the same need to reproduce the **Malaspina Galleries** for the pleasure of other people two hundred years ago. The crew's artist, José Cardero, made a sketch of the galleries. Then engravings made from Cardero's sketch were

published in accounts of the Spanish expedition, larger engravings were framed and hung for public viewing, and the remote Malaspina Galleries became a well-known natural phenomenon in nineteenth-century Europe.

You can get to **Gabriola Sands (or Twin Beaches) Provincial Park** by beachwalking north along the shore from the Malaspina Galleries to Taylor Bay or by driving up Taylor Bay Road and swinging right onto Berry Point Road. At Twin Beaches Shopping Centre you will find a grocery store, restaurant, liquor store and the **Gabriola Artisans cooperative**, among other services. Turn left down Ricardo Road just across from the shopping centre, and you'll end up at the unmistakable twin beaches of Pilot Bay and Taylor Bay. This park is a great place for families. It has **picnic tables, washrooms, a grassy playing field**, and lots of sand and water for beach play.

The Malaspina Galleries are an amazing natural formation

If you'd rather get great views of mountains, islands and huge white ferries with the photogenic **Entrance Island Lighthouse** in the foreground, then stay on Berry Point Road till you come to the **Orlebar Point lookout**. This is the favourite spot on the island for watching the sunset, but it's a delight any time of the day. Settle down at a picnic table and have lunch with a view. Across the road you'll also find the prettiest **"honesty stand"** anywhere in the islands. This vine-covered hut surrounded by flowers offers fresh bouquets and carefully selected little gifts for sale. Just put your money in the box, take what you want, and enjoy being in a place where honest dealings are still the norm. You can carry on around the corner to the right and make your way to a picturesque **organic farm and orchard** where you can sometimes buy fresh fruit and vegetables, free-range eggs or honey.

When you've had your fill, retrace your steps to the ferry terminal or head for the island's other commercial centre just minutes away at the **Folklife Village Centre** on North Road. To get to the Folklife Village from the junction of Taylor Bay Road and South Road, turn left onto South Road and then left again onto North Road. The Village is not "folky," but quite a swish new shopping mall housed in the recycled **Folklife Pavilion** from Expo 86. The Village features a very well-stocked grocery store, several eye-catching gift boutiques and chic dress shops, a small but good bookstore-cum-cappuccino-bar, a restaurant, washrooms, and a first-rate Visitor Information Centre (250-247-9332). It's an impressive addition to island life. Don't miss **Huxley Park** next door if you like **tennis, basketball or skateboarding**.

If you have a day or more on Gabriola, you'll want to take a left from the Folklife Village and loop down the island on South Road, which becomes North Road near Silva Bay. You can follow North Road through a deep, quiet stretch of woodland back to the village centre, and you'll find a delightfully mixed bag of attractions along the way. The **Gabriola Museum & Historical Society**, near the RCMP station (check at the Visitor Information Centre for hours, or phone 250-247-9987), is a fine little museum with changing exhibits on topics like Gabriola family history, a commemoration of the 200th anniversary of the arrival of Malaspina, and pioneer schooling on the island. You can also make rubbings from casts of the **famous Gabriola Island petroglyph**s located behind the museum. (The original petroglyphs are too weather-worn to stand up to abrasion.) Not far beyond is the very pretty 9-hole **Gabriola Golf and Country Club**. Visitors are welcome to play the course or to drop by the log clubhouse, which includes a pro shop, snack bar and lounge, to enjoy the rolling valley views. Gardeners will delight in the Wheelbarrow Nursery on the right just past the community hall. Their motto is "Come shop in a garden"—which describes it in a nutshell. Petroglyph seekers should keep a sharp eye out for the United Church on the left, approximately 10 km south of the ferry terminal. With over fifty images carved into stone, the provincial heritage site in a field behind the United Church parking lot is the best place to

▶ **Gabriola Annual Events**

January
Sea Lion Festival

May
Silva Bay Fishing Derby

July
Summer Festival of the Arts

August
Salmon barbecue
Celebrity Pro-Am Golf Tourney &
Concert (mid Aug)

September
Gabriola Islander Days

October
Thanksgiving Gallery Tour

December
First Night (New Year's Eve)

For more information, Gabriola Island
Visitor InfoCentre 250-247-9332

see petroglyphs. You'll find a trail map of the heritage site in the parking lot as well as information about these mysterious images, which may date back 5,000 years. These petroglyphs were discovered by Mary and Ted Bentley in the 1970s. Together they wrote a book, *Gabriola: Petroglyph Island* (Sono Nis Press), which includes intriguing photographs, rubbings, and drawings of the petroglyphs, descriptions of their locations and forms, and details about dating techniques and possible meanings.

Sea-and-sun enthusiasts have several choices for getting down to the waterside. **Drumbeg Provincial Park** at the southeast tip of Gabriola is a perfect destination for swimming, picnicking and shorewalking along smooth sandstone outcroppings. Follow South Road past the sign for Drumbeg Provincial Park and take a right on the unmarked road just beyond the sign. Turn right on Coast

The view from Gabriola Sands Provincial Park

Gabriola Island's Pioneer Cemetery

Sunset over Gabriola

Road, right again on Stalker Road and watch for the sign directing you down the gravel path to the parking lot. This very fine day-use-only park is known for lovely natural sandstone sculpture, and for its delightful stands of rare Garry oak and for the almost 360-degree views of snow-capped mountains and islands from the path circling to the left from the swimming beach. It's well worth the detour.

Another Fogo folk art sculpture

Two other seaside destinations—**Silva Bay** and **Sandwell Provincial Park**—also deserve their popularity. Once you leave Drumbeg, follow Coast Road down to Page's Resort and Marina on the southern side of Silva Bay. You'll find more chuckle-making Fogo folk, including wooden caricatures of the marina's owners, Ted and Phyllis Reeve, and you'll also find marine supplies, campsites, scuba equipment, groceries and a fine small bookstore. Or follow South Road to Silva Bay Road and turn right to the marina. This picturesque bay is a charmer and boaters flock in all summer long. Plans are in the works to rebuild the historic boat yard as a school teaching the art of building wooden dinghies and kayaks. And speaking of kayaks, there's **great paddling** in the nearby Flat Top Islands. Don't miss the Chapel of Our Lady of Victory and Saint Martin's Church at the turnoff to Silva Bay Road. This pioneer **log church** has a painting over the entryway depicting Mary holding a protective cloak over Gabriola Island. It perfectly sums up the islanders' feeling about their piece of coastal paradise.

To get to Sandwell Provincial Park, follow North Road through the "tunnel" of second-growth trees arching over the road back toward the north end of the island. Sandwell Provincial Park is on the northwest shore at Lock Bay, and the footpath to the park is well signed from North Road. If you're travelling with small children or older companions, be aware that the trail to the beach is a kilometre long and fairly steep.

Entrance Island Lighthouse from Orlebar Point lookout

If you can get there, you'll find a long, secluded crescent beach backed with driftwood—a great place to settle into a sandy pocket and luxuriate in views of the mainland mountains and big white BC ferries plying the waters between Horseshoe Bay and Nanaimo. On your return down North Road toward the ferry terminal, you'll pass another scattering of shops and services before you hit the T-junction with South Road. The circuit ends here, but you may be tempted to stay on for more of Gabriola's tranquil beauty.

Gabriola Island Recreation, Accommodations and Services

Recreation
Bicycle rentals
Kayak/Canoe rental
Dive shop/charter
Fishing/Boat charters
Golf course
Tennis courts
Major hiking trails
Community parks (day-use only)

Accommodations
Bed & Breakfasts
Resorts
Campgrounds/RV Parks

Services
InfoCentre
Places to eat (including restaurants, pubs, cafés)
Grocery stores
Bank (ATM)
Post office
Service station
Taxi service (Gabriola Island tours available)
Galleries/Studios
Medical clinic

Important Numbers

Police **911**
Fire **911**
Ambulance **911**
Medical clinic **250-247-9922**
Nanaimo Hospital **250-754-2141**
RCMP **250-247-8333**
InfoCentre **250-247-9332**

STRAIT OF GEORGIA

GULF ISLANDS

VANCOUVER

ISLAND

PACIFIC

OCEAN

JUAN DE FUCA STRAIT

CANADA
USA

VICTORIA

17

1

CHEMAINUS

DUCAN

18

LAKE
COWICHAN

Cowichan L.

PORT RENFREW

14

LADYSMITH

NANAIMO

19A

19

PARKSVILLE

QUALICUM BEACH

19

191

4A

4

PORT
ALBERNI

Great Central L.

Sproat L.

BAMFIELD

BARKLEY SOUND

BROKEN
GROUP
ISLANDS

WEST COAST
TRAIL UNIT

UCLUELET

Kennedy L.

TOFINO

4

LONG
BEACH
UNIT

PACIFIC
RIM
NATIONAL
PARK

CLAYOQUOT SOUND

0   10   20   30   40   50

LEGEND

——— Highway
——— Secondary Road
——— Logging Road
     Park
     Urban Area

CHAPTER 6

VANCOUVER ISLAND: FROM NANAIMO TO THE WEST COAST

Spectacular Long Beach is one of BC's great destinations

European adventurers exploring the west coast of Vancouver Island called it the "back of the world." Its scattered inhabitants—isolated by the treacherous power of the Pacific Ocean to the west and the sharp spine of Vancouver Island's mountains to the east—lived until recently in near-solitary splendour. Now a paved highway links this once-remote destination to the outside world.

Steller sea lions at rest

The west coast of Vancouver Island is very different from the gentle farmlands and protected waterways of its inner coast. At the turn of the century, one young English bride accompanied her husband to the remote western edge of Vancouver Island. "There were no fields, no grass, no people, no anything!" she described to oral historian Derek Reimer. "There was a great rock out there and the sea was surging up against it ... This was a loneliness unknown and unheard of. There was nothing there, just the long beach and the wild sea." But she soon came to love the west coast's blue waters embroidered with islands, wave-combed beaches, and deep forests of cedar and fir.

Every year, thousands of visitors make their way to the west coast of Vancouver Island

Getting to Nanaimo

From Tsawwassen drive aboard BC Ferry from Tsawwassen terminal (just south of Vancouver). Ferry runs to Duke Point terminal, just south of Nanaimo. 2 hours crossing time; 8 sailings daily year round.

From Horseshoe Bay drive aboard BC Ferry from Horseshoe Bay terminal (just north of Vancouver). Ferry runs to the Departure Bay terminal at Nanaimo: 1 hour 35 minutes crossing time; 8 sailings daily year round.

From Victoria drive up Highway 1 to Nanaimo (see chapter 3). The 113-km drive takes about 1 1/2 to 2 hours.

(For more information about travel aboard BC Ferries, see p. 8)

Intricate coves and sandy beaches typical of the west coast of Vancouver Island.

in search of the wild beauty that captured a young bride's heart nearly a century ago. Anticipating the surge of international interest in the area, British Columbia passed the West Coast National Park Act in 1969. Now the Pacific Rim National Park Reserve stretches along the southwest coast of Vancouver Island. Although the park is not yet a legal entity—negotiations with the forest industry over timber rights and with First Nations groups over land claims are still in process—it has been in operation for more than two decades. Tourist facilities have sprung up around the park in the nearby towns of Tofino, Ucluelet and Port Alberni, catering to everyone who enjoys the out-of-doors—from adventuresome backcountry trekkers to urban escapees seeking a special weekend getaway.

Pacific Rim National Park Reserve

The Pacific Rim National Park Reserve was created to protect a portion of the wild and beautiful west coast of British Columbia. The park runs 125 km down the Island's west coast from just below Tofino to Port Renfrew and encloses almost 500 square km. Over a third of that area is made up of ocean waters and offshore islands. Within its boundaries is the spectacular 9.6-km white sweep of Long Beach, more than a hundred islands and islets, miles of waterways and reefs rich with undersea life, and some of the finest stands of temperate old-growth rain forest in the world. Anyone who enjoys the outdoors will find a perfect activity somewhere in the park, from riding the surf at Long Beach to taking a quiet walk in the filtered green light of an ancient rain forest.

Pacific Rim National Park Reserve is actually three parks in one. Each of the three park units—the West Coast Trail, the Broken Group Islands and Long Beach—is distinctive, and each offers a special experience "on the edge" of the Pacific.

The 75-km West Coast Trail lies between Bamfield and Port Renfrew along the harrowing stretch of coast known as the "Graveyard of the Pacific" (see pp. 238–39). It was carved out of the remains of an old lifesaving trail for shipwrecked mariners. This wilderness trail is known for its stunning coastal scenery—and for its extremely challenging terrain. It takes preparation, skill and stamina to hike the trail in safety. (For more information see p. 244)

The Broken Group Islands is a marine park that encloses a hundred-odd islands scattered in the waters of Barkley Sound between Bamfield and Ucluelet. The unspoiled islands of the Broken Group—

Approximate Distances

From Nanaimo to Port Alberni 84 km
From Nanaimo to Tofino 206 km
From Nanaimo to Ucluelet 180 km

looking much as they did when Captain Barkley first sailed among them in the late 1700s—and the protected waters that surround them are fast becoming a haven for boaters, kayakers and canoeists. This too is a wilderness destination where park visitors are expected to be self-sufficient and prepared for emergencies. (For more information see pp. 246–49)

Long Beach, between Barkley Sound to the south and Clayoquot Sound to the north, is the most popular and accessible part of the park. For thousands of visitors of all ages and inclinations this is the "must-see" destination. Its spectacular white sand beaches and the annual migration of gray whales along its shores are its best-known attractions. Seals, sea lions, porpoises, half a dozen species of whales and many other types of marine life live in its waters. The park also contains magnificent stands of old-growth rain forest where deer, black bears, the occasional cougar and many smaller animals make their home. Because the park's ecosystem is so diverse, it is a first-rate destination for camping, fishing, boating, kayaking, surfing or windsurfing, beachwalking and nature watching. (For more information see p. 221–24)

Just outside the park are the towns of Ucluelet and Tofino. Both towns provide full services, including the ever-popular whale watching expeditions and a range of accommo-

Wickaninnish Centre at the south end of Combers Beach

dations from homey B&Bs to luxurious oceanfront resorts. And just beyond are two magnificent watery adventurelands—Barkley Sound at Ucluelet and Clayoquot Sound at Tofino. This is a something-for-everyone sort of place. It is no wonder 450,000 people a year come from all over the world to experience the Long Beach area.

PARKSVILLE TO PORT ALBERNI

Eagles: Wildl
Recovery Cen

Historic McLean Mill

Highlights

Beautiful waterfalls

Gentle hiking trails

Up-close wildlife viewing

*Magnificent
old-growth trees*

*Swimming and other water
sports*

Freshwater fishing

Camping in the forest

From Nanaimo, drive north on Highway 19. Just south of Parksville, take the well-marked exit to Port Alberni and Highway 99. This route becomes Highway 4 which you'll follow all the way to the west coast of the Island. You'll find several tourist attractions in and near the small village of **Coombs**, including the **North Island Wildlife Recovery Centre and Museum of Nature** (250-248-8534), **Vancouver Island Butterfly World** (250-248-7026) and **Coombs Country Market** where goats nibble at the grass on its sodded roof. The highway also winds along several lakes and rivers on its way to the Pacific Rim. You may want to pack a lunch and have a bathing suit or fishing gear handy for a picnic and some roadside relaxation.

Provincial Parks Between Parksville and Port Alberni

The area between Parksville and Port Alberni is an emerald patchwork of provincial parks, a ruggedly beautiful region that has been a favourite destination for in-the-know outdoor adventurers for upwards of a century. You may want to plan a rest stop or a longer stay to enjoy the many outdoor activities in the parks (see map p. 213).

Each park has something special to offer. **Englishman River Falls Provincial Park** and **Little Qualicum Falls Provincial Park** are known for their river gorges with tumbling waterfalls, easy view point trails, picturesque natural pools for swimming, and well-developed picnic areas. For more information on these parks, p. 256. And don't let all the cars parked along the highway at **MacMillan Provincial Park (Cathedral Grove)** discourage you. This park is well worth the stop. Short

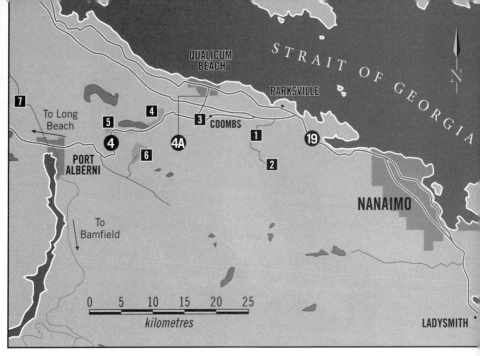

interpretive trails lead through stands of huge Douglas fir trees arching more than 60 metres above the fern-covered forest floor. Even with tour buses and campers parked nearby this quiet sanctuary of ancient trees is—no other word for it—awe-inspiring. **Stamp Falls Provincial Park** (Reservations 1-800-689-9025) has steelhead and cutthroat trout fishing, and in late summer and fall visitors can watch salmon leap up fish ladders to their spawning grounds in Great Central Lake.

Port Alberni

West of MacMillan Provincial Park the highway climbs past the turnoff to scenic **Mount Arrowsmith Regional Park**, a popular destination for hiking and skiing, and then descends toward the wide, mountain-circled **Alberni Valley**. Port Alberni, a town of 20,000 wrapped around the tip of Alberni Inlet, serves as the major commercial centre for communities of the west coast. In summer, stop at the tourist information centre at the entrance to Port Alberni for maps and guides to the area (2533 Redford St, 250-724-6535). There are no tourist services and no gas stations between Sproat Lake, just west of Port Alberni, and Ucluelet/Tofino. So check to see if you need to

What to See

- ☐ **1** North Island Wildlife Recovery Centre and Museum of Nature
- ☐ **2** Englishman River Falls Provincial Park
- ☐ **3** Vancouver Island Butterfly World
- ☐ **4** Little Qualicum Falls Provincial Park
- ☐ **5** MacMillan Provincial Park (Cathedral Grove)
- ☐ **6** Mount Arrowsmith Regional Park
- ☐ **7** Stamp Falls Provincial Park

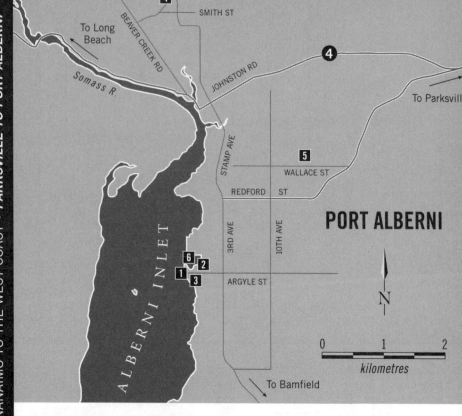

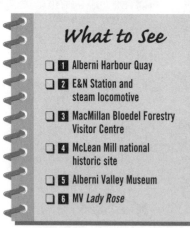

What to See

- ☐ **1** Alberni Harbour Quay
- ☐ **2** E&N Station and steam locomotive
- ☐ **3** MacMillan Bloedel Forestry Visitor Centre
- ☐ **4** McLean Mill national historic site
- ☐ **5** Alberni Valley Museum
- ☐ **6** MV *Lady Rose*

stock up, fuel up and maybe rest up before heading for Long Beach.

Like so many other places on this resource-rich island, the Alberni Valley with its lure of natural treasures has attracted hopeful newcomers for more than a century. The town's fortunes rose and fell as its resource-based industries—lumbering, fishing and mining—cycled through booms and busts.

Port Alberni began its life as a sawmill town in 1860 at the site of the **Alberni Harbour Quay**. When the English shipmaster **Captain Edward Stamp** cruised the west coast in 1855, he was struck by the magnificent Douglas fir trees of British Columbia. He dreamed of the money to be made from cutting down these coastal giants for lumber and spars. Once back in Britain, Stamp persuaded wealthy English merchants to back his scheme for a sawmill at the tip of Alberni Inlet. Armed with a letter from Governor Douglas of the Crown Colony of Vancouver Island granting him land and timber rights, Stamp sailed up the inlet with men and materials for the sawmill in September 1860.

The site Stamp had chosen for his mill was an encampment of the Tseshaht, the Nuu-

> ### Port Alberni & Coombs Annual Events

June
Harbour Days

July
Folkfest Celebration
Robbie Shick Charity Golf Tournament
Sockeye Salmon Derby
Coombs Old Time Fiddlers Event
Coombs Rodeo

August
Coombs Country & Bluegrass Festival

September
Salmon Festival & Derby

For more information,
Alberni Valley Chamber of Commerce
250-724-6535

chah-nulth people who had lived around the tip of the Alberni Inlet for hundreds of years. They armed themselves and formed a human barricade to keep the newcomers from landing. But under threat of cannonfire from the ships, they yielded and moved their village. From their new site nearby, one of Stamp's companions recounts, the Tseshaht watched as "buildings, wharves, steam engines, ploughs, oxen, horses, sheep, and pigs, which they had never seen before," appeared before them.

By the following spring a raw little settlement had sprung up around the sawmill. The trees were stripped from surrounding hills and dragged down skidroads to the inlet where they were milled and loaded onto ships for transport abroad. The timber of the Alberni Valley was so fine that one 76-metre spar was sent to London to be erected as a flagpole in Kew Gardens. Even though 9 metres snapped off the spar as it was unloaded on the Thames River, the sawmill's investors saw to it that the pole was raised as advertising for the wondrous properties of the little-known Douglas fir. A scant five years later, all the usable trees had been reduced to stumps and slash. The mill shut down and its 200 workers left for other parts. In 1869 the derelict mill burnt to the ground. But Port Alberni revived at the turn of the century with the arrival of the railroads, and it is now the centre of a multi-billion-dollar forest industry.

Port Alberni grew up as a pulp-and-paper town, but with the increasing popularity of the Pacific Rim National Park Reserve, it is becoming a tourist destination as well. More visitors are using Port Alberni as a base for day tripping to nearby recreation areas, including all three units of the Pacific Rim National Park Reserve. Port Alberni also bills itself as the "Salmon Capital of the World." Each year large runs of chinook and coho

salmon gather in Barkley Sound to swim up the Alberni Inlet to spawning grounds in nearby lakes and rivers and hundreds of fishing enthusiasts come to catch the "big ones." The town hosts an annual **Salmon Festival** on Labour Day weekend with more than $65,000 in prizes. Freshwater anglers also come to the Alberni Valley to flycast for trout in high mountain lakes or fish for steelhead in the **Stamp River**. Fishing guides, boat charters and heli-fishing excursions can all be arranged at Port Alberni.

If you plan to stop in town, head downtown to the newly redeveloped **Alberni Harbour Quay** at the foot of Argyle Street for restaurants, gift and souvenir shops, or

Port Alberni's Harbour Quay

just to sit and people-watch. The Quay offers everything from cappuccino bars to a water park for the kids. For views of the beautiful Alberni Inlet, climb up to the observation decks on the clock tower or stroll out onto the docks of the deep-sea harbour. Keep an eye out for the coloured sails of windsurfers catching the dependable afternoon winds of the inlet. You can also visit **MacMillan Bloedel's Forestry Visitor Centre** and sign up for a tour of a local mill or an active logging site, or pick up a logging road map if you'd like to venture into the backcountry.

It was the building of several logging railways on Vancouver Island during the 1890s, including the **Esquimalt and Nanaimo (E&N) Railway**, that sparked Port Alberni's growth as a centre for forest industry. On summer weekends you can board the old "Number 7" steam locomotive at the E&N Station at the entrance to the Harbour Quay for a ride along the waterfront. Soon the train will run to **McLean Mill**—on Smith Road north of town just off Beaver Creek Road—the heritage steam-powered sawmill and village now being restored as a National Historic Site. (Presently the site is open restricted hours. For more information phone the Alberni Valley Museum, 250-723-2181.) For more Alberni Valley history, be sure to stop at the **Alberni Valley Museum** in the Echo Centre near the intersection of 10th and Wallace. Its displays on local First Nations and pioneer history are engaging and eclectic.

MV *Lady Rose*

Harbour Quay is also the departure point for day cruises down the spectacular Alberni Inlet to Barkley Sound aboard the historic MV *Lady Rose*, the last remaining ship of the famous Union Steamship Company fleet that served communities of coastal British Columbia for more than fifty years. Launched in 1937, the *Lady Rose* steamed around the islands between Vancouver and Vancouver Island before shifting to run in Barkley Sound in 1969. She was restored to her original appearance as a Union Steamship by her present owners, the Alberni Marine Transportation Company, in 1990. The stout little ship with her black hull, white topsides and bright red funnel is a nostalgic favourite with passengers and crew alike.

The *Lady Rose* is still a working ship, subsidized by the British Columbia Ferry Corporation. Passengers can observe firsthand life aboard a coastal freighter as it delivers mail, passengers and all manner of cargo—from newspapers and groceries for general stores, to equipment for logging camps, to laundry for a fishing resort—to the scattered residents of this coast. Like the coastal freighters of yesteryear, the *Lady Rose* calls in at isolated houses and tiny settlements whenever there is a need. It's all in a day's work

MV Lady Rose *on her way down Alberni Inlet*

to drop off a refrigerator, take a special order to an oyster farm, or stop for a motorboat delivering an outbound passenger or a package to be mailed.

Kayakers and canoeists headed for the **Broken Group Islands** can take the *Lady Rose* to the drop-off point at the site of the old **Sechart whaling station.** (The owners of the *Lady Rose* also rent kayaks and canoes, and they have built a lodge at Sechart for visitors who want to sample the wilderness without having to "rough it.") Hikers bound for the **West Coast Trail** can catch a ride to **Bamfield**, the picturesque little fishing village a few kilometres north of the trailhead. And round-trip passengers have a chance to wander along the famous **wooden boardwalks** of Bamfield, take a walk to secluded **Brady's Beach,** or even stay over for some fishing, diving or hiking out of Bamfield before returning up the Alberni Inlet on the *Lady Rose.* Summer round-trippers can take a day trip through the Broken Group Islands to Ucluelet and back.

These cruises have become so popular that the owners of the *Lady Rose* recently added the vessel MV *Frances Barkley* for the busy summer runs. It was named in honour of the eighteen-year-old bride of British Captain Charles Barkley, a trader in otter skins for China. The Captain brought his young wife to North America aboard his ship the *Imperial Eagle* in 1787. She was the first European woman to set eyes upon this far-off coast. The newlyweds took to naming the places they visited together—including Barkley Sound for the Captain and Frances Island for Mrs. Barkley. (For further information, Alberni Marine Transportation Company, 250-723-8313, or toll free April to September, 1-800-663-7192.)

MV Frances Barkley *takes on cargo*

PORT ALBERNI TO THE PACIFIC

Killer whales

The back of beyond

Highlights

Surfing and beachwalking

18,000 gray whales

75 km West Coast Trail

The breathtaking
Broken Group Islands

Nuu-chah-nulth
First Nations heritage

Old-growth rainforest

Winter storm-watching

MV Lady Rose

To many old-time British Columbians, Long Beach is still remembered as the "back of beyond"—a genuinely remote destination. In the mid-1950s a precarious dirt logging road was cut from Port Alberni to the coast, but Long Beach remained a destination only for hardy adventurers. Two years after the park was created, however, a paved highway was built to the west coast. It opened in 1972, and what was once remote wilderness is now a rugged coastline for all to explore. Long Beach is less than a 3-hour drive from Parksville, but this mostly two-lane road is heavily travelled in the summer, and RVs and campers can slow traffic, so relax, allow plenty of travel time and enjoy the trip. You'll find lots to see and do along the way.

Highway 4 west of Port Alberni is often called the Pacific Rim Highway. From Port Alberni it winds through mountains and river valleys to **Kennedy Lake** where the road twists up through switchback curves on a cliff above the water and then descends toward the coast. A visit to **Sproat Lake Provincial Park** (Reservations 1-800-689-9025) just outside Port Alberni makes for a pleasant side trip. The warm waters of Sproat Lake are ideal for swimming, boating and fishing. An added bonus is the chance to see the **Martin Mars** flying tankers—the world's largest water bombers used to fight forest fires—at their anchorage in Sproat Lake.

When the Pacific Rim Highway splits at a T-junction, you have arrived "at the edge." The south (left-hand) fork leads to Ucluelet, the jumping-off point for Barkley Sound. The north (right-hand) fork leads to Tofino, the gateway to magnificent Clayoquot Sound. Between Ucluelet and Tofino is the Long

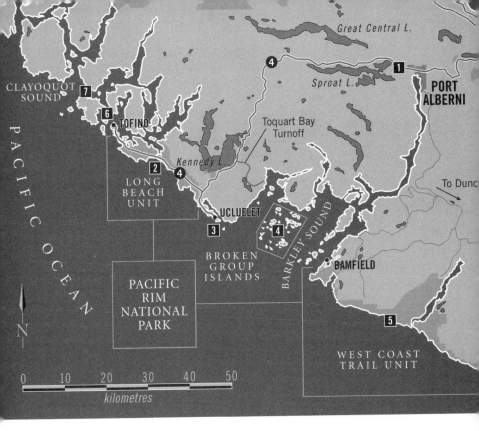

Beach Unit of the Pacific Rim National Park Reserve. Just beyond the trees is the Pacific Rim and the unparalleled beauty of its long sweeping beaches and dramatic headlands backed by dense rain forests.

Pacific Rim National Park Reserve: Long Beach

The Long Beach Unit of Pacific Rim National Park Reserve offers something for everyone, from simple pleasures like kite flying or surf-casting to high energy sports like sailboarding or surfing the green-

What to See

- [ ] **1** Sproat Lake Provincial Park
- [ ] **2** Long Beach
- [ ] **3** Ucluelet
- [ ] **4** Broken Group Islands/ Barkley Sound
- [ ] **5** West Coast Trail
- [ ] **6** Tofino
- [ ] **7** Clayoquot Sound

walled breakers of Long Beach. Tofino and Ucluelet are geared up to supply equipment and instruction for all popular local sports. Stop at the **seasonal info centre** at the Tofino–Ucluelet T-junction for the very useful free area map and other information. Then head for the **Park Information Centre**, a 4-km drive to the right from the T-junction, to get all the information you need to custom-design your own adventures in the Pacific

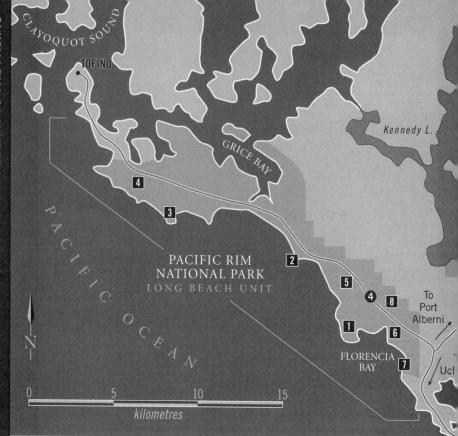

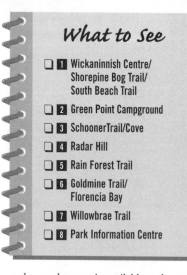

What to See

- ☐ **1** Wickaninnish Centre/
  Shorepine Bog Trail/
  South Beach Trail
- ☐ **2** Green Point Campground
- ☐ **3** SchoonerTrail/Cove
- ☐ **4** Radar Hill
- ☐ **5** Rain Forest Trail
- ☐ **6** Goldmine Trail/
  Florencia Bay
- ☐ **7** Willowbrae Trail
- ☐ **8** Park Information Centre

Rim National Park Reserve. (Open May to mid-October, 250-726-4212. Year-round information: telephone 250-726-7721, on the web http://fas.sfu.ca/parkscan/pacrim.) You'll find maps, guidebooks, brochures, displays and friendly park staff to fill you in on everything from park campgrounds and park events, to the cultural and natural history of the Pacific Rim. You may also want to buy the park's handy guidebook, *Official Guide to Pacific Rim National Park Reserve*, published by Blackbird Naturgraphics Inc.

Park-use fees are in effect in the Long Beach Unit of the park from mid-March to mid-October. All vehicles require a park pass for access to park trails, beaches, picnic areas, washrooms and the Wickaninnish Centre. Information about the hourly, daily and annual passes is available at the park Information Centre.

A short jaunt past the Information Centre heading north on Highway 4 is the turnoff to the **Wickaninnish Centre**. The commanding grey cedar building sits astride a rocky promontory at the south end of Long Beach. Formerly a popular private resort, the building was acquired and renovated to become the park's interpretive centre in 1984. One wing houses north Pacific Ocean exhibits, including a two-storey mural on sea creatures of the open ocean, a display on traditional whaling practices of the Nuu-chah-nulth peoples, and an imaginary underwater journey aboard the submersible *Explorer 10*. You can also purchase tickets for guided walks and evening programs such as Bear Necessities, Weather It's Good or Bad, Exploring the Seashore, Fabulous Forest, Island of Whales and Spell of the Broken Group. The other wing is a vaulted cedar-and-glass restaurant offering spectacular views of the coastline. Decks and walkways wrapped around the centre look out over the foam-laced Pacific breakers and the dramatic expanse of Long Beach which sweeps northward to another rocky headland in the far distance. This is an ideal spot to stop and enjoy your first encounter with this magnificent coastline.

Exploring Long Beach
The breaker-lined waters of Long Beach still bear the name of the Tla-o-qui-aht's mighty chief—Wickaninnish. Many park maps show three beaches bordering Wickaninnish Bay: Wickaninnish Beach, Combers Beach and Long Beach. This trio of beaches is collectively known as Long Beach, the centrepiece of the Pacific Rim National Park Reserve.

Near the midpoint of Long Beach is **Green Point Campground**. The campground has 94 drive-in sites (by reservation only) and 35 walk-in beach or forest sites (first come, first served). This is the only camping facility in the park. If you are planning to camp in the park between April and October, be sure to make reservations early (up to three months in advance). (Phone 1-800-689-9025.) Each evening at **Green Point Theatre**, located in the campground, visitors can enjoy lively and informal lectures, movies, concerts, audio-visual presentations and evening walks. These programs run from June to September.

Many people come to Pacific Rim National Park to kick back and unwind. They are content just strolling the surf-packed sands of Long Beach or settling against a driftwood log and drowsing in the sun, lulled by the sibilant wash of Pacific breakers. There is always something to catch the eye. Fingers of fog appear, shift and withdraw. Sun lights up a high

Long Beach

bank of cumulus clouds from behind and then breaks free to pour down sunshine on sea-glazed sand. Waves break into foaming rivulets high on rocky headlands. Wet-suited surfers bob in the water far off the shore, waiting to catch the perfect wave. Closer in, a kayaker deftly hovers, turns and dives through cresting breakers. On the beach a child tugs on a kite rising and plunging with the play of updrafts. For many, it is enough to simply sit and look and look again, taking in the pleasures of this long and beautiful beach.

Sea Life at Long Beach: The beach is an exciting and beautiful place to explore. At low tide, the diminutive world of tidal pools is an absorbing spectacle. You can expect to see crabs, sculpin, and red and green anemones. Snails, limpets and barnacles find safe anchorage on sea-washed ledges. Starfish, beds of blue mussels and clusters of goose bar-

Common Trees of the West Coast Rain Forest

Sitka spruce (*Picea sitchensis*): A large, hardy conifer that often grows up to 70 m high. It is found along the coastline between sea level and 700 m, primarily on the fringes of beaches or near stream flood plains. Its sharp, stiff needles are light green or bluish-green and arranged in spirals around the twig. Its greyish bark is thin and tends to be scaly. The Nuu-chah-nulth people sometimes tied Sitka spruce boughs on wooden fences anchored in the ocean to catch herring spawn. When enough spawn had collected, the boughs were pulled out of the water and dried, and the spawn was then scraped off. Spruce roots served as ropes, thread and fishing lines, and the fresh inner bark was apparently an effective laxative.

Douglas fir (*Pseudotsuga menziesii*): This very large tree can grow as high as 85 m in locations near the coast. It is found right across Vancouver Island except at the northern tip. Each flat, yellowish-green needle has a groove down the centre and a sharply pointed tip. The needles stand out in all directions around the twig. The tree's grey-brown bark is thick and deeply grooved with darkish brown ridges. Some of the Douglas firs on the west coast are known to be more than 1,000 years old. Native peoples sometimes covered the floors of their lodges and sweat lodges with fir boughs. In the eighteenth century Europeans discovered that this hard, durable wood was ideal for heavy construction, and soon after, wide-scale logging began on the coast.

nacles cling to exposed rocks. The basalt outcrop near Green Point Campground is a good place to start your search for intertidal sealife. Another prime spot is **Lismer Beach** just south of the Wickaninnish Centre (see pp. 220–21).

Vancouver Island's west coast is also home to thousands of seals and sea lions, including harbour seals, northern fur seals, California sea lions, and even the occasional elephant seal. Using binoculars from **Combers Beach** or **Green Point**, you can spot hundreds of ruddy blond Steller's sea lions on their favourite year-round haulout on Sea Lion Rock. Sometimes you can pick out a huge bull sea lion by its sheer bulk—a big male weighs a tonne or more—and its thick blubber-swathed neck. It will likely be keeping a close eye on the harem of females sprawled nearby to protect them from the attentions of rival bulls. If you hike to the south end of **Florencia Bay** (see pp. 226–27), you can sometimes see the

Western red cedar (*Thuja plicata*): The official tree of British Columbia, this evergreen can grow 60 m tall. It is found in moist areas at mid-elevations all along the BC coast. It has drooping branches with leaves arranged in flat, fanning sprays. Its stringy grey bark sometimes tears off in long strips. This was the "Tree of Life" for Native peoples of the west coast and was put to a myriad of uses both secular and spiritual. Fishing implements, utensils and storage boxes, clothing and blankets, dugout canoes and plank lodges, ceremonial masks and totem poles were just some of the items made of cedar.

Western hemlock (*Tsuga heterophylla*): This big shade-tolerant tree typically attains heights in the 30–50 m range. It prefers humid climes and is found between sea level and mid-elevations along the entire BC coast. Its flat, blunt needles are yellow to dark green on top and whitish underneath. Its thick bark is dark brown to reddish-brown and deeply furrowed. The tree has swooping branches of soft, feathery sprays, and it is topped with a drooping crown (leader). Several Native groups along the BC coast made the slimy cambium tissue of the Western hemlock into thick cakes. These cakes were sometimes used as food offerings to supernatural beings during ceremonial feasts. In winter some of the more northerly groups whipped the cambium cakes up with snow and eulachon (fish) grease for a much-favoured treat.

Red alder (*Alnus rubra*): This deciduous tree grows to a height of 24 m. It is found all over the BC coast, particularly in disturbed areas or along roadsides where it has more access to sunlight. Its bright green leaves are oval-shaped with roughly toothed edges. Its bark is greenish or white-green, depending on the age of the tree. Alder bark was used by Native peoples to produce dyes ranging in colour from orange-brown to black. Alder wood was used to make utensils and ceremonial objects and to build fires for smoking salmon.

smaller, darker California sea lions at a haulout on an islet off **Wya Point**, especially during their winter migration. And if a shiny round head with bright eyes pops up in the waves off Long Beach, it's probably a harbor seal following herring into the shallows of Wickaninnish Bay. Sea otters are extremely rare near Long Beach. (They were hunted nearly to extinction in the early 1800s and were reintroduced on Vancouver Island's west coast in the late 1960s.) But you may see families of playful river otters rolling and diving in the surf.

Whales are the biggest drawing card at Pacific Rim National Park. Up to 18,000 gray whales migrate past Long Beach between March and May. Visitors from every corner of the world gather here to scan the horizon for a glimpse of the whales' trailing vapour spouts. Some grays come in close to shore during their migration, usually just beyond the breaking surf. With luck and a good pair of binoculars, you may get what locals call a "real show" when the bottom-feeding whales slow to rest and roll on their sides to feed on tiny critters of the sea floor before powering away up the coast. Typically 40-odd gray whales remain behind their companions to summer in the waters near Pacific Rim National Park Reserve. Orcas (killer whales) also pay irregular visits along the coast. Gangs of transient orcas, known to feed on seals and sea lions, have been sighted prowling the waters around **Sea Lion Rock** waiting to make a kill. Other species, like finback, humpback and minke whales also put in occasional appearances off Long Beach. If you want a closer look at these magnificent mammals, you can take a whale watching tour from Tofino or Ucluelet (see p. 233).

Exploring Other Beaches and Trails

Long Beach may be the jewel of Pacific Rim National Park Reserve, but it isn't the only treasure. The park is full of beaches, trails and lookout points, and all of the turnoffs from Highway 4 are well signed. Well-developed boardwalk trails provide access to large numbers of visitors with minimum disturbance to the park's delicate ecosystem.

Between Tofino and Long Beach are several intriguing destinations, including Grice Bay, Radar Hill and Schooner Cove. Each one offers some special bit of magic.

Grice Bay

For birdwatchers Grice Bay is a wonderful destination. If you're heading north, take the signed turnoff right from Highway 4 just south of Tofino and follow the signs through a canopy of alders to Grice Bay on Tofino Inlet. When the tide is out, waterfowl descend on the exposed mud flats to feed, and great blue herons high-step through the shallow water in search of fish. In fall and winter the flats are alive with migrating birds, including Canada geese, trumpeter swans and a dozen kinds of ducks—mallards, goldeneyes, pintails, widgeons and more. An additional temptation in the springtime is the chance to whale watch. Gray whales have been sighted feeding in Grice Bay recently, and studies of food sources in the bay are under way.

Radar Hill

For stunning elevated views of Long Beach and Clayoquot Sound, make your way to the view points at Radar Hill at the well-marked turnoff not far north of Grice Bay. And don't forget your camera. If you have always wanted to take the ultimate photograph of sunset over the ocean, this just may be the place to get your shot.

Schooner Cove

Just north of Long Beach is another beautiful white sand crescent punctuated with rocky headlands called Schooner Cove. Schooner Cove is a tranquil place to take a picnic and enjoy views of small islets just offshore and stands of spectacular old-growth Sitka spruce in the forest behind the beach. You can get to Schooner Cove by taking a boardwalk trail from a well-signed parking lot south of Radar Hill on Highway 4. The 1-km walk itself is half the pleasure. It winds through fern-splashed rain forest to make an ever-so-gentle drop down to the beach. From the end of the trail, you can walk south along Long Beach or around the headlands to the north and into Schooner Cove proper. A walk to Schooner Cove is best attempted at low tide. During high tide, the only route is a very rough trail through the underbrush. This route is not maintained by parks staff and should be used at your own risk.

Rain Forest Trail

Besides offering spectacular beaches, Pacific Rim National Park also protects some of the finest examples of old-growth rain forest on the west coast. Two boardwalk loops of the Rain Forest Trail are located on either side of Highway 4 between Green Point Campground and Wickaninnish Centre. We suggest the 1.2-km B loop from the far end of the Rain Forest Trail parking lot. It is an enchanting descent through towering stands of red cedar, hemlock and fir. Dappled sunlight brightens a rich undergrowth of salal thickets, dwarf dogwood and deer fern. Hanging gardens of moss, lichens and licorice ferns reach for the light through the upper branches of the trees. New tree seedlings spring from the nutrient-rich trunks of fallen "nurse logs." Blueberry and huckleberry bushes dangle their summer offerings of fruit. Coho salmon fry dart through the shallows of Sandhill Creek. Helpful park signs explain the life cycles of the many plants, animals and insects that live in the diverse communities between the forest floor and the arching canopy of branches high overhead. The experience of exploring a temperate jungle and the rich forest life of its mammoth trees make this a place the whole family will enjoy.

Shorepine Bog Trail

The Shorepine Bog Trail leads you into the bizarre Lilliputian world of the bog rain forest. It's anything but "boggy"—this very easy .8-km boardwalk located halfway down the turnoff to the Wickaninnish Centre is a fascinating place to visit, especially on a foggy day. The sight of stunted gray shorepine twisting up into mist-shrouded air is delightfully eerie. Some are 300 years old but—dwarfed and deformed by the bog's acidic soil— stand only metres high. The floor of the bog is a spongy carpet of sphagnum moss at least a metre thick. You can pick up a free guide along the trail and use it to identify bog plants with intriguing names like sundew, skunk cabbage, sweet gale, bog cranberry and bog dandelion.

Shorepine Bog Trail

Willowbrae Trail, once the main route between Tofino and Ucluelet

South Beach Trail

If you like your solitude with the sting of salt spray, continue down the turnoff to the Wickaninnish Centre and the trailhead to South Beach Trail. The sound of water pounding into surge channels has given South Beach its evocative nickname, the "Edge of Silver Thunder." This is a fine place to enjoy the spectacle of huge Pacific breakers crashing against the rocks and exploding out of crevices. The trail, which begins behind the Wickaninnish Centre, is a 1.5-km round trip through the forest above the shore.

Gold Mine Trail and Florencia Bay

Along the 3-km return-length Gold Mine Trail, you can walk in the footsteps of turn-of-the-century gold rush fortune-hunters. The gentle trail starts in a signed parking lot off Highway 4 between the Wickaninnish Centre and the Information Centre. It winds along Lost Shoe Creek, where interpretive signs describe historic placer mining operations, and then descends to beautiful Florencia Bay. Prospectors flocked here in the late 1890s, attracted by tales of gold for the taking in the sands of Florencia Beach. Some arrived by boat while others made their way to Port Alberni and then hiked the rough telegraph trail that twisted up over the Mackenzie Range to the Pacific Rim. No one knows how much alluvial gold was found by solitary goldseekers armed with pans, picks and shovels, but one placer operation equipped with heavy machinery took out some $23,000 in gold in three years. Now one of the few remaining relics of gold fever is a rusting dredge on the beach. Florencia Beach was originally called Wreck Beach for the Peruvian ship *Florencia* which broke up on a small island nearby in 1861.

Florencia Bay once again lured dreamers and seekers to its shore in the late 1960s and early 1970s. This time it was "hippies," "back-to-the-landers" and other footloose travellers who drove rattling VW vans or hitchhiked over the rough dirt road from Port Alberni lured by the romance of the frontier and by tales of free land. All traces of the 1960s squatters whose driftwood settlement once flourished on Florencia Beach have been swept away. But their influence lingers on in many communities along the BC coast, including Tofino.

Willowbrae Trail

You can also get to Florencia Beach from Willowbrae Trail. If the struggles and triumphs of the west coast's pioneers fires your imagination, Willowbrae Trail is the route for you. This remote stretch of coast was slow to be settled by Europeans. Captain James Cook arrived in 1778 and spent several months here in search of the fabled Northwest Passage. In his wake came other explorers as Britain and Spain jockeyed for supremacy in the New World. European and American traders of all stripes arrived soon after to trade with First Nations people for the sea otter pelts so prized in China. Once the sea otters had been hunted to extinction, European visitations dropped off, except for the occasional whaling station, white fur sealers who hired Nuu-chah-nulth hunters to capture fur seals, and a scattering of traders and missionaries who settled here and there along the west coast. Then, near the turn of the century, opportunities in commercial fishing, logging and mining drew another wave of newcomers to this remote coast. With government encouragement, these new arrivals took up homesteads on what were traditional Nuu-chah-nulth lands. Some turned their hands to farming in the belief that the dense vegetation of the rain forest promised lush green farm crops. But the soil proved too acidic and nutrient-poor to grow vegetables, and many would-be farmers were defeated by the harsh conditions of the coast. Some moved to Tofino and Ucluelet and worked at odd jobs in fishing, lumbering and other industries. Others left the coast for good.

Willowbrae Trail is a link to this pioneer past. In the early days, there was only one overland route between Tofino and Ucluelet, a rough "corduroy road" made of cedar slabs laid side by side. The road was once wide enough for a wagon to pass, but the forest has reclaimed its own. Only traces remain of the corduroy road along what is now Willowbrae Trail.

The trailhead can be hard to find. Two kilometres south of the Tofino–Ucluelet junction, just on the outskirts of Ucluelet, look for a street sign for Willowbrae Road on your left as you head toward Ucluelet and turn right on a gravel road on the opposite side. The parking lot and trailhead are past a sign marked "private road." The 2.8-km trail splits at the far end to drop down to **Half Moon Bay** on the left and to Florencia Bay just a little farther down the trail on the right. Both descents are by way of steep boardwalks that skirt delightful fern-covered ravines. If you crave solitude, try Half Moon Bay, a small crescent beach off the regular tourist track. If you prefer the drama of long wave-swept beaches, try 6.4-km Florencia Beach.

THE NATIVE HERITAGE

The island-spattered western shore of Vancouver Island has been home to the Nuu-chah-nulth (Nootka) peoples for centuries. Today their descendants still live in the region, including the Tla-o-qui-aht (Clayoquot), Toquaht, Ucluelet, Hesquiaht, and Ahousaht First Nations. The word Nuu-chah-nulth, meaning "mountains-in-a-row," describes how the west coast looks when it is approached from the sea. It designates the traditional coastal territory of the Nuu-chah-nulth peoples which lay between the long mountainous spine of Vancouver Island to the east and the open Pacific Ocean to the west.

Historically the Nuu-chah-nulth were a maritime people. Because the steep, heavily forested mountains at their backs were difficult to traverse, the open ocean and the intricate waterways of Barkley and Clayoquot Sounds served as highways. The Nuu-chah-nulth depended on this fragmented coastline for fish and shellfish, they hunted its waters for seals and whales, and they made their homes on protected inlets along its shores. Every reef and bay and beachhead was named, every stream and island was known. Every place along the coast belonged to one particular village or group—that is, the rights to resources from a particular clam beach or salmonberry patch, halibut bank or salmon stream were the hereditary entitlements of the village chief. War sometimes broke out along the coast over control of a particular territory and its natural riches.

When the first European explorers arrived on the west coast of Vancouver Island in the late 1700s, many of the Nuu-chah-nulth peoples were ruled by two powerful chiefs whose names still echo along the coast—Maquinna and Wickaninnish. Maquinna was chief of the substantial Nuu-chah-nulth village at Yuquot on Nootka Sound when Captain Cook sailed this coast with his ships *Discovery* and *Resolution* in 1778. Cook was the first European to set foot on these shores when he disembarked at Nootka Sound and was greeted by Chief Maquinna with gifts of precious otter pelts. The Nuu-chah-nulth elder Winnifred David recounts the story of Cook's arrival and how the Nuu-chah-nulth people were mistakenly named the Nootkas as she heard it from her elders. When the ship sailed toward the village, the people were fearful that it would run aground on the rocks. They began signalling the ship to go to a better anchorage around the harbour by shouting "Nu-tka-icim," meaning "go around." Captain Cook thought they were calling out the name of the place—Nootka—as he heard it. So he mistakenly dubbed the place and the people

"Nootka." Winnifred David also recounts that the pale-faced foreigners were given the name "Muh-mul-ni" because they sailed in tall strange ships that looked like "Muh-mul-ni," or "houses on the water." This encounter was the beginning of an active trade between Europeans and Native people in which food, clothing items and furs—especially the highly prized sea otter pelts—were exchanged for mostly metal trade goods. Maquinna was an adroit trader and a powerful chief, and he kept a tight hold over the rights to trade for the "Muh-mul-ni" wealth in the region around Nootka Sound.

Wickaninnish was chief of the Tla-o-qui-aht people. In winter most of the Tla-o-qui-aht made their homes in the village of Opitsaht on Meares Island across the water from Tofino (see pp. 240–41). In summer they moved to Long Beach, territory they had wrested away from the fierce inhabitants of a village called Hisaawista ("clubbed to death"). Under Wickaninnish's leadership the Tla-o-qui-aht subdued ten or more neighbouring groups. Always mindful of possible attack, the Tla-o-qui-aht had established lookout points and earthenwork defensive sites along Long Beach. One such site, located among the sand dunes just north of the Wickaninnish Centre, was covered in thick mats of the low evergreen shrub known as bearberry or kinnikinnick. The Tla-o-qui-aht used to gather the dry red berries of kinnikinnick and mix them with fermented salmon eggs to make "Indian cheese." Today Hisaawista (Esowista)—the only First Nations village in Canada within the boundaries of a national park—is still home to 130 people of the Tla-o-qui-aht Nation. The Tla-o-qui-aht of Hisaawista as well as other Nuu-chah-nulth communities on the west coast are now active in tourism, and run operations ranging from arts and crafts stores to whale watching cruises, fishing charters, water taxis and lodging.

Mighty Chief Maquinna

> ## Winter Storm Watching: A New West Coast Favourite

Most tourists visit in July and August when the weather is likely to be fine. (Of course, west coast weather can be fickle, so packing a warm sweater, waterproof jacket, pants and shoes is a good idea whatever the time of year.) But a new breed of visitors is beginning to visit the west coast in the winter months to experience dramatic storms that lash its shores. The pleasure of looming skies

Storm off the coast near Wickaninnish Inn

and turbulent seas enjoyed in solitude or shared with special companions has a magic all its own. The area's newest luxury inn, the Wickaninnish Inn, has even "miked" the lodge so that guests enjoying the comfort of its cosily handsome restaurant can thrill to the sound of pounding breakers. If you want to witness the awesome power of a wild Pacific storm, the Long Beach area is the place to go. Many tourist facilities close in the off-season, so you won't find a full range of services, but you will find lots of peace and quiet. And quite a few lodges do remain open year round.

But wave-watching visitors do need to be vigilant. People have died by getting too close to the action. If the waves are high, approach the shoreline with extreme caution. Large sets of waves hit without warning and can sweep unwary beachwalkers straight out to sea.

Ucluelet and Barkley Sound

Ucluelet (pronounced you-CLUE-let) lies along a peninsula between the protected waters of Ucluelet Inlet and the Pacific Ocean. It is an open, comfortable, friendly place, slightly larger than Tofino and a touch more sedate. Its modest population of just under 2,000 doubles in July and August when visitors arrive to take advantage of Ucluelet's tourist facilities, including markets, restaurants and delis, motels and B&Bs, gift shops, and even a historic steamer, the *Canadian Princess*, now a floating hotel and centerpiece of the harbour.

Ucluelet Harbour is a major hub of the west coast fishery—townsfolk are quick to point out that the commercial catch here is the third largest in BC—and it's pleasant to stroll the docks when the fishing boats come in or watch the activity from a restaurant window overlooking the inlet. Ucluelet Harbour is at the doorstep of Barkley Sound and the Broken Group Islands (see pp. 246–49). The extended sport fishing season in Barkley Sound, from April to October, is consistently good, and its abundance of salmon, giant halibut, rockfish and ling cod attract anglers from early to late in the season. You can also book nature cruises and fishing charters at Ucluelet.

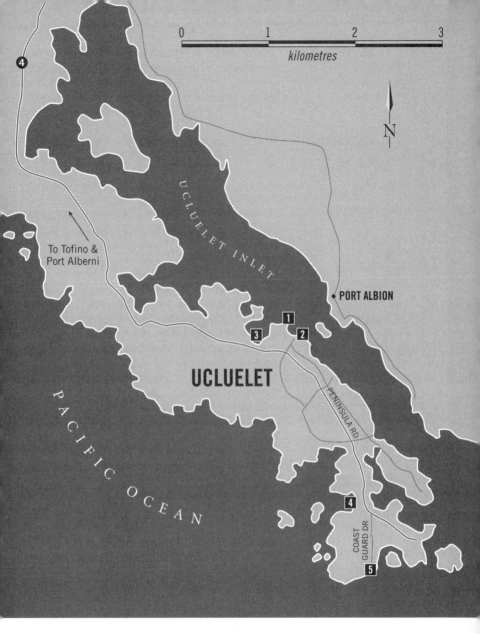

0   1   2   3
kilometres

N

To Tofino &
Port Alberni

UCLUELET INLET

• PORT ALBION

1

3   2

UCLUELET

PACIFIC OCEAN

PENINSULA RD

4

COAST GUARD DR

5

What to See

- ☐ **1** Ucluelet Harbour
- ☐ **2** Government Wharf
- ☐ **3** *Canadian Princess*
- ☐ **4** He-Tin-Kis Park
- ☐ **5** Amphitrite Lighthouse

Ucluelet area Recreation, Accommodations and Services

Recreation
Bicycle rental
Kayak rentals
Surf shop
Helicopter tour
Fishing charters
Whale watching charters
Diving charters
Hiking trails

Accommodations
Bed & Breakfasts
Hotels
Motels
Campgrounds
RV parks

Services
InfoCentre
Restaurants/Pubs/Cafés
Banks
ATM
Grocery stores
Gas/Service stations
Galleries/Gift shops

Important Numbers

Police **911**
Police non-emergency
250-726-7773
Fire **911**
Ambulance **911**
Hospital (Tofino)
250-725-3212
Doctor **250-726-4443**
Ucluelet Chamber
of Commerce
250-726-4641
or **250-726-7289**
Fax **250-726-4611**

Amphitrite Point

The **Amphitrite Point lighthouse**, located on Coast Guard Drive at the southernmost tip of the Ucluelet peninsula, is a favourite spot for watching wild winter storms. You can climb down toward the point for a dramatic reminder of nature's power, but do exercise caution and obey warning signs.

Toothy black rocks whitened with sea foam frame the wind-whipped channel where, in the words of an early west coast historian, "it often requires more than a stout heart and a good engine to bring the little fishing boats safely home." It was on Christmas Day 1905 that the steel-hulled four-master *Pass of Melfort* was driven aground by high winds just off Amphitrite Point. Every soul aboard perished. The disaster triggered the building of the first lighthouse the following year. The frail wooden structure was swept away by a tidal wave not long after, and the present sturdy red and white light station was built in 1914. But the comforting presence of the light has not guaranteed safe passage for all. At least seventeen more ships have foundered off Amphitrite Point since the sinking of the *Pass of Melfort*.

Ironically, yesterday's maritime disasters have become today's ecological successes. These broken hulls have proved a congenial habitat for an astonishing assortment of marine creatures, and they are now brightly garlanded with undersea life. In winter when the water clears, the wrecked ships of Barkley Sound are some of the best diving spots in Canada. Diving charters can be booked in Ucluelet.

The historic West Coast steamship Canadian Princess *(1932) is now a floating hotel in Ucluelet Harbour.*

Whale watchers heading out for adventure

Whale Watching

The Amphitrite Lighthouse is a reminder of Ucluelet's early days as an isolated village when a steamship out of Victoria was the only transportation link to the outside world. It took the threat of war along the Pacific Coast during World War II to force the completion of a long-delayed road between Ucluelet and Tofino. Now it is an easy jaunt between the two towns, and they have become partners in tourism. Each year Ucluelet and Tofino join with the staff of the Pacific Rim National Park Reserve in putting on the **Pacific Rim Whale Festival** from mid-March to mid-April. The whale festival celebrates the yearly migration of 18,000 gray whales from their calving lagoon in Baja California to their summer feeding grounds in the Arctic. These gentle giants often pause to feed on plankton in the shallow waters close to the coast where they share the waters with orcas (killer whales). Whale watching has become so popular that now Ucluelet's official mascot is "Ukee the Gray Whale" and Tofino's is "Orkie the Killer Whale."

Whale watching and nature cruises with reputable operators like Tofino's Seaside Adventures (1-888-332-4252 or 250-725-2292, website www.seaside-adventures.com) are a great way to discover the coast from the "wet" side. You aren't guaranteed whale sightings but the quest is still exciting, especially the roller-coaster ride across the waves in a rubber Zodiac. If killer whales are sighted, you may meet a killer whale researcher

PACIFIC GRAY WHALES

First a geyser of mist erupts from the ocean surface. Then a massive mottled grey hump surges up out of the depths and rolls forward in a movement at once stunningly smooth and awesomely powerful. A three-metre span of barnacle-encrusted tail fluke lifts out of the water and then disappears as the huge creature knifes down toward the ocean floor. You have just had a close encounter with a gray whale.

These gentle behemoths have been known by many names—Pacific gray, California gray, devilfish, scrag, and musseldigger. The gray whale is a medium-sized baleen (or toothless) whale that grows to a length of 13.5 metres. Unlike other baleen whales, the gray whale lives mostly in shallow water and feeds on tiny creatures in the water column and on the ocean bottom. When bottom feeding, it eats by rolling on its side, laying its head against the ocean floor and then sluicing the muddy sea sediment through the fine mesh of baleen plate hanging from the roof of its mouth. Small bristles on the baleen plate comb out minute invertebrates like opossum shrimp, tubeworms and amphipods (near kin to "beach hoppers"). The whale then gulps down the sieved-out invertebrate stew.

A gray whale pokes its head up for a look around

Gray fluke. Whale sightings and photo-identification are used to study gray whale behaviour in the wild

For centuries gray whales coasted along Vancouver Island's western shore on their 9,600-km migration between winter breeding lagoons in Baja, Mexico, and summer feeding grounds between Alaska and Russia. And for centuries Nuu-chah-nulth people hunted them from large sea-going cedar canoes. Whales were much valued for their meat, oil and bones, and whale hunting was attended by great ceremony and rituals of purification. In the mid-1800s European whalers discovered the gray whale breeding lagoons in Baja and unceremoniously slaughtered them by the hundreds. Gray whales earned the name "devilfish" for the fierceness of the female grays fighting to save their newborn calves from the whalers' harpoons. The gray whales were hunted to the edge of extinction before the remaining few animals were left to reestablish their traditional patterns of feeding and breeding. Their numbers grew steadily until once again the slaughter began in the 1920s. Gray whales were given worldwide protection under the International Whaling Commission in 1947, and now the gray whale population is estimated to be 18,000. Gray whales are under study in an attempt to learn more about their numbers and habits. Researchers can identify individuals from photographs, by the distinctive patterns of skin pigmentation along their backs and sides. Whale sightings and photo-identifications are used to track gray whale population, distribution, reproduction rates and patterns of behaviour.

Unlike killer whales (orcas), gray whales do not travel in pods (lifelong family groupings). Instead they swim alone or in loose groups of up to fifteen individuals. Adult males, juveniles and pregnant females begin the migration to the northern feeding grounds in mid-February. They are followed by cows and their new calves in early April. Gray whales travel between 60 and 80 km a day, staying within 3 km of the shore. Upwards of 40 gray whales stay around Vancouver Island's west coast all summer, and a few remain all year. Good view points for spotting gray whales in the Long Beach area are at headlands near Schooner Cove, Quisitis Point and Wya Point, and from Radar Hill, Green Point and the Wickaninnish Centre.

from Tofino-based Strawberry Isle Research Society. Whale watching tour operators donate $1 per passenger to the society for their research into killer whale behaviour. Tour operators also help Strawberry Isle researchers make extended observations of the whales by handing them from one tour boat to another when the researcher's host boat has to peel off for the return to Tofino.

The whale watching tour will also give you stunning views of the coast and offshore islands. Your guide may take you around **Seal Rock** where you'll encounter several hundred large and exceedingly curious Steller sea lions rubbernecking at your boat or spilling into the surf for a closer look. Other popular tour boat stops are large seabird colonies on nearby islands, where you may be lucky enough to see bright-billed little tufted puffins—and Deadman's Island, a Nuu-chah-nulth burial ground where bodies of important personages were suspended in the treetops, and now home to a pair of nesting eagles and their offspring.

Tofino and Clayoquot Sound

As you drive north from Ucluelet past Pacific Rim National Park Reserve toward Tofino, you will see Chesterman Beach Road and MacKenzie Beach Road on your left. Many of the Long Beach area's lodgings are located along these roads. They lead to two more beautiful sandy beaches which are outside the park boundary but still open to the public. In the peak summer season, check out **Chesterman Beach** and **MacKenzie Beach**, two attractive alternatives to busy Long Beach.

When you reach the outskirts of Tofino, look for a sign on the right for Tofino's **crab dock** at Olsen Road. This is a good place to buy an ocean-fresh crab if the crab boats are in. Fresh-cooked crabs are served at restaurants and take-outs in Tofino. The crab dock is also a good place to get your first soul-satisfying glimpse of Clayoquot (pronounced KLAK- what) Sound with the wide volcanic peak of Lone Cone on Meares Island rising in the middle distance.

Tofino began its modern life as a little settlement supplying the needs of scattered families of loggers and fishermen around Clayoquot Sound. In the 1970s, counterculture

Tofino's crab dock is a perfect place to pick up some fresh Dungeness crab

FLORES
ISLAND

AHOUSAT •

6

CLAYOQUOT
SOUND

P
A
C
I
F
I
C

O
C
E
A
N

VARGAS
I.

5

OPITSAT

MEARES
ISLAND

3

2

1 TOFINO

4

N

0   5   10   15   20   25

kilometres

folk heading for the end of the road
landed up in Tofino. Seduced by the
wild beauty of Clayoquot and the
town's laid-back lifestyle, many stayed
and put down roots. Once the road was
paved, tourists began coming to Tofino
for much the same reasons, and
tourism is now a prime source of
income for many local people.

Tofino has made the leap into
tourism without losing much of its picturesque charm, but the tempo of life
definitely shifts up several notches in
July and August. On summer weekends
the place is jumping by midmorning.
Some visitors start off at a leisurely pace

What to See

☐ **1** McKenzie Beach/
  Chesterman Beach

☐ **2** Crab Dock

☐ **3** Government Wharf

☐ **4** Hot Springs Cove
  (Maquinna Provincial Park)

☐ **5** Big Cedar Trail/Hanging Garden
  Tree (Meares Island)

☐ **6** Wild Side Heritage Trail
  (Flores Island)

with cappuccino and cinnamon buns at the Common Loaf Bake Shop, a laid-back Tofino

THE "GRAVEYARD OF THE PACIFIC"

In summer the rugged southwest coast between Barkley Sound and Port Renfrew is seductively beautiful—so beautiful that a turn-of-the-century Victoria real estate company, promising a northern beach paradise, sold more than a hundred lots at fabulous prices. Not one of the hopeful buyers could stick it out. In the depths of winter this wild coastline is plagued by raging storms, fierce onshore winds and pounding surf. Known as the "Graveyard of the Pacific," the southwest coast of Vancouver Island has been in evil repute with mariners ever since the first vessels foundered on its treacherous shores. As more and more ships sailed for Victoria, Vancouver and Seattle in the late nineteenth and early twentieth centuries, the grim tally of death rose. Each winter the southwest shore was littered with smashed masts, the ribs of broken hulls, drifting cargo and human corpses. No one knows for certain how many perished in these frigid waters or died of exposure in the tangle of rain forest above the shore. But by the early 1900s it was estimated that 700 lives had been lost on the island's southwest coast.

The Valencia

The "Graveyard of the Pacific" captured the world's attention in 1906 when the American steamer Valencia went down before the eyes of helpless would-be rescuers near Pachena Point. Of 164 passengers aboard the Valencia, 117 were lost. Not one woman or child aboard the stricken ship lived through the two-day nightmare. The Valencia had steamed out of San Francisco in fair weather on Saturday, January 20, 1906, bound for Victoria. But by Monday a thick fog had wrapped itself tight against the ship, and the captain ordered the whistle to be kept sounding through the night. Then the wind picked up and the Valencia was soon in the midst of a howling storm.

In the years before modern navigational aids, a weather-blinded ship could easily miss the entrance to Juan de Fuca Strait and be flung ashore. This is exactly what happened to Captain Johnson as he struggled to find his position with only his charts, depth soundings and intuition to guide him. Just after midnight on January 22 the ship was inching ahead as seamen heaving out the sounding lines called out the marks—"60 fathoms," then "56 fathoms" and then "30 fathoms." Suddenly there was the gut-wrenching sound of steel grinding on rock. The ship swung wide, struck another rock full force, and shuddered to a standstill.

The *Valencia* had foundered on a hidden reef near Pachena Point. The ship was just 27 metres from land, but a sheer cliff rose 24 metres straight up from the boiling surf. Frank Lehm, a freight clerk who survived the disaster, later described the ghastly spectacle on deck just minutes after the ship ran onto the reef:

> Screams of men, women and children mingled in awful chorus with the shriek of the wind, the dash of the rain, and the roar of the breakers. As the passengers rushed on deck, they were carried away in bunches by the huge waves that seemed as high as the ship's mastheads. The ship began to break up almost at once and the women and children were lashed to the rigging above the reach of the sea. It was a pitiful sight to see frail women, wearing only night dresses, with bare feet on the frozen ratlines, trying to shield children in their arms from the icy wind and rain.

The captain ordered passengers into the lifeboats, women and children first. Just as the first boat swung away, a towering breaker swept its terrified human cargo into the foaming waves. The next lifeboat was loaded and ready to launch when another huge breaker crushed it against the *Valencia*'s steel hull. A third boat was quickly lowered away when it suddenly tilted stern downward, spilling women and children shrieking into the foaming waves. A fourth boat was launched and had nearly escaped when it was caught by the wind, hurled against the ship and capsized. The *Valencia*'s searchlight played across the surging water, revealing terrified white faces locked in the storm-black sea and lifeless bodies tumbling towards the jagged rocks on shore. Then the ship's lights died, plunging the horrified watchers into darkness.

When dawn broke the captain ordered the last two lifeboats launched. One was lost among the waves. The other reached the shore where a handful of survivors managed to scale the cliff and stagger to a telegraph linesmen's cabin where they rang through to the lighthouse at Cape Beale. From Cape Beale the news of the disaster was telegraphed to Victoria and around the world.

Rescue ships made their way to the site of the disaster but they could only get within half a mile of the *Valencia*. An officer from the salvage tug *Salvor* later recalled: "It was terrible to stand off there and watch the wreck break up and see all the people who were in the rigging drop off into the boiling sea."

The terrors recounted by the survivors of the *Valencia* prompted the building of the West Coast Lifesaving Trail—sometimes called the Shipwrecked Mariner's Trail—with shelter shacks every 10 km, a lighthouse at Pachena Point and a lifesaving station at Bamfield. The trail later fell into disrepair and was finally abandoned by the Canadian government in the 1950s. It became part of Pacific Rim National Park Reserve in 1970. Rebuilt as a hiking trail and renamed the West Coast Trail, it is now one of the most popular backpacking destinations in North America.

Tofino area Recreation, Accommodations and Services

Recreation
Kayak rentals
Canoe rental
Bicycle rental
Golf course
Surf shop
Boat/Fishing charters
Whale watching
Ecotour charters
Hiking trails
Float plane charter for
scenic cruising and
wilderness camping

Accommodations
Bed & breakfasts
Inns
Resorts
Campgrounds

Services
InfoCentre
Restaurants/Pubs/Cafés
Grocery stores
Banks
ATMs
Galleries
Post office
Gas/Service stations
Hospital

Important Numbers

Police **911**
Police non-emergency
250-726-7773
Ambulance **911**
Hospital **250-725-3212**
Fire **911**
Marine/Aircraft Distress
1-800-567-5111

bakery where young '60s-style hippies rub elbows with loggers, camera-toting tourists and the occasional big friendly dog on the outdoor terrace. Other visitors are busy shopping in Tofino's galleries and gift shops or zipping into padded floatsuits for a heart-stopping Zodiac ride in search of whales.

The bright red **government wharf** is the centre of activity in Tofino, and the gateway to adventures in the island-studded waters of Clayoquot Sound. The goal of sustainable development—protecting the natural beauty of Clayoquot while allowing economic development—has made "ecotourism" a watchword in this area.

Exploring Clayoquot Sound
Although whale watching naturally tops the ecotourism agenda at Tofino, the natural wonders of Clayoquot Sound—a vast area comprising hundreds of nautical miles and a maze of offshore islands—are just now being discovered. Float planes taking off from just beside the wharf offer their passengers spectacular aerial views of Clayoquot Sound. Small flotillas of colourful sea kayaks head for outdoor adventure on nearby **Meares**, **Flores** and **Vargas** islands. You can rent a kayak and explore at your leisure. Or you can join guided kayak wilderness tours that typically include lessons, rainforest and beach walks, and sometimes lodging thrown in the bargain. If you are attracted by the beauty of Long Beach but seek something more remote, you can arrange for water taxi drop-offs on the fine sand beaches of Flores and Vargas islands.

Hot Springs Cove
One of the most popular destinations for water taxis, nature cruises, kayakers and float planes is **Hot Springs Cove** in **Maquinna Provincial Park** 40 km north of Tofino. From the public wharf in Hot Springs Cove, you can take a 2-km boardwalk trail through lush rain forest to the hot springs. Here you will find a series of enticing natural rock pools fed by steaming water that pours from a rocky outcropping. But the word is definitely out on this place so, in summer at least, expect to share the pools with other folks. There is even a nearby lodge operated by the Hesquiaht First Nations if you want a more leisurely visit.

Meares Island
If you enjoy visiting First Nations sites, you can take a water taxi to the **Tla-o-qui-aht First Nations village of Opitsaht** on **Meares Island** just across the inlet from the government wharf, where visitors are welcome to share the magic of Meares Island's old-growth rain forests. Even though it is

within sight of Tofino, Meares Island seems a world away. This still-pristine wilderness is wrapped in a mantle of ancient spruce, cedar and hemlock. A temperate climate and lush rains have nurtured this spectacular old-growth rain forest. The **world's largest living cedar** with a diameter of 4.2 metres was recently discovered on Meares Island and dubbed **Hanging Garden Tree** for the many plants growing along its trunk.

The deep shell midden in front of the village of Opitsaht is silent testimony to 5,000 years of continuous habitation of Meares Island. Ancestral home of both the Tla-o-qui-aht and Ahousaht First Nations, Meares Island has had a long and unsettling history. It was a centre for the lucrative fur trade in the late 1700s—a trade that was controlled by powerful Nuu-chah-nulth chiefs Maquinna and Wickaninnish. The fur trade led to rivalries among different Native groups and also to skirmishes between European and Nuu-chah-nulth traders.

In the winter of 1791-92 the American fur trader Captain John Gray anchored his ship the *Columbia* in a little cove on Meares Island and set his men to building a small sloop for use in shallow waters. Chief Wickaninnish led a Tla-o-qui-aht raid in an attempt to capture the *Columbia*. The effort failed, but in retaliation the fiery-tempered Gray ordered his men to burn Opitsaht to the ground. Sixteen-year-old Lieutenant John Boit confessed in his diary that he felt "grieved to think Capt. Gray shou'd let his passions go so far." Nevertheless, the young officer was a reluctant participant in the destruction of Opitsaht: "This village was half a mile in Diameter, and contained upwards of 200 Houses, generally well built for Indians. Ev'ry door that you enter'd was in resemblance to an human and Beasts head, the passage being through the mouth, besides which there was much more rude carved work about the dwellings some of which was by no means inelegant. This fine village, the work of ages, was in a short time totally destroy'd."

Recently, a different battle was being fought on Meares Island. This time the adversaries were the lumber giant MacMillan Bloedel, environmental activists and First Nations groups. The struggle began in the early 1980s when local Native people and anti-logging activists tried to stop MacMillan Bloedel from clearcutting on the island. Since then the battle has expanded to include all of Clayoquot Sound, home to what some call the largest intact temperate lowland rain forest in the world. The campaign made international headlines in the early 1990s when 10,000 protesters came to support blockades against clearcutting in Clayoquot Sound, and more than 900 protesters were arrested and tried in 1993. A government-brokered compromise was reached, and a new spirit of co-operation based on the principle of sustainable development has emerged. In 1998 MacMillan-Bloedel announced a halt to all clearcutting in the area.

The Tla-o-qui-aht have built **Big Cedar Trail**, a two-hour boardwalk loop trail on Meares through some of the biggest trees in Clayoquot Sound. A rainforest boat shuttle leaves at passengers' convenience from the government wharf in Tofino.

Flores Island

You can also book guided cultural tours of Flores Island, home of the Ahousaht First Nations. A seabus provides twice-daily service from Tofino. Seaside Adventures (see p. 233) has also developed a gentle walking trail on Flores Island called the Wild Side Heritage Trail with the approval of First Nations bands and the Nuu-chah-nulth Tribal Council. The trail gives families a chance to enjoy the flavour of the West Coast Trail experience without the hardships. If you are an adventurous and experienced backpacker, you can also custom design your own hiking or fishing trip to one of dozens of deep wilderness destinations and make transportation arrangements in Tofino. West coast folk are generally a friendly lot and willing to help you make the very most of your time on the west coast.

Pacific Rim National Park Reserve: The West Coast Trail

When backpackers stagger out of the West Coast Trail tired, muddy and in serious need of a hot bath, they use words like "challenging," "rugged" and "hazardous" to describe the trail. In fact, Parks Canada bills it as "one of the most gruelling treks in North America." So what continues to attract thousands of people from all over the world year after year? The answer—some of the most spectacular coastal scenery British Columbia has to offer and a once-in-a-lifetime wilderness adventure.

Access to the 75-km West Coast Trail is restricted to three trailheads: Bamfield (Pachena Bay) at the north end, Nitinat Lake at the midway point, and Port Renfrew (Gordon River) at the south end. You can hike the trail from end to end in about 6 days. Or you can start in the middle of the trail at Nitinat Lake and choose a shorter, yet equally impressive 3- or 4-day trip either south to Port Renfrew or north to Bamfield. It's a good idea to allow extra time for unexpected stops due to bad weather, injuries or poor trail conditions. Hikers two days ahead of our party encountered a rare and surprising delay—a black bear and her cub just happened to be taking a nap on the trail, and no one was about to disturb them! Experienced West Coast Trail aficionados strongly recommend allowing a couple of extra days simply for the pleasure of shedding heavy backpacks and savouring life at the edge.

The West Coast Trail alternately threads along the beach and rises to the cliffs behind the shore when steep slopes and headlands prevent passage at sea level. Its highest point of elevation is only about 200 metres. Nevertheless, its reputation for many hazards is well deserved, especially toward Port Renfrew. The combination of west coast rains and heavy use can make for very muddy trail conditions, and rain-soaked boardwalks and bridges

A cable-car crossing and steep trail ladders on the West Coast Trail

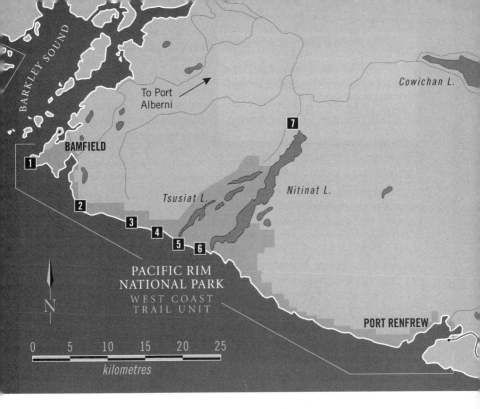

are extremely slippery. Exposed tree roots can trip up a tired backpacker and beach rocks can tip without warning under a hiker's boot. Stories about severe bruises, twisted ankles and broken bones are all too common. But the challenges of this demanding trail are also a big part of the adventure. Backpackers find themselves wading thigh-deep across rivers, doing tricky tightrope acts on logs laid across creeks, and leaping over foam-lashed surge channels. Suspension bridges and hand-propelled cable cars looped over rivers and dizzyingly vertical ladders running between shoreline and cliffs make the West Coast Trail the quintessential adult adventure playground.

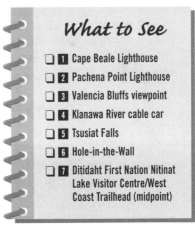

What to See

- ☐ **1** Cape Beale Lighthouse
- ☐ **2** Pachena Point Lighthouse
- ☐ **3** Valencia Bluffs viewpoint
- ☐ **4** Klanawa River cable car
- ☐ **5** Tsusiat Falls
- ☐ **6** Hole-in-the-Wall
- ☐ **7** Ditidaht First Nation Nitinat Lake Visitor Centre/West Coast Trailhead (midpoint)

The most rewarding parts of the trail are its spectacular natural wonders. One day you can be strolling through a rain forest of giant Sitka spruce, western hemlock and red cedar, and the next day you can be on the beach marvelling at sandstone outcroppings jewelled with starfish and sea anemones or on a high bluff taking in breathtaking vistas of the wave-tossed ocean. On any given day you are sure to spot some of the abundant wildlife that inhabits this area, including sea lions, bald eagles, blue herons and orcas.

Certain places are perennial favourites with hikers of the West Coast Trail. It's well worth braving the steep ladders down to the beach to view Tsusiat Falls, a dramatic cascade of water that drops four storeys over a shelving rock face to the sea. This waterfall, with its soft mists and fragmented rainbows, is a refreshingly natural bathing spa for the

▶ Planning Your West Coast Trail Adventure

You must buy a Trail Use Permit before you are allowed onto the trail. It is open April 15 to September 30, and Parks Canada allows only 60 hikers per day (26 each at Bamfield and Port Renfrew, and 8 at Nitinat Lake) on the trail. Although not required, reservations for Trail Use Permits are strongly recommended. The booking service begins taking reservations on March 1 and requires a non-refundable reservation fee. You can book up to three months in advance of your planned departure date. Trail quotas fill up very quickly, so book as early as possible. Your only other option is to place your name on a waiting list in person at the entry point office where you want to start hiking the trail. This method is risky—only a few Trail Use Permits are available each day for hikers who show up at the trailhead and demand is high.

Once you have made a reservation, Parks Canada will send you a West Coast Trail information package complete with a Hiker Preparation Guide, an excellent map, and updated information on the itinerary and logistics of your trip, including information on transportation. Before starting the trail you must attend an orientation session where you will pay for your Trail Use Permit and be given the most recent information on trail conditions, including bear and cougar sightings. At this session you can also buy ferry passes which are required to cross Nitinat Narrows, Thrasher Cove and Gordon River Trailhead. The West Coast Trail crosses Indian reserve land. Access across these lands is possible only with permission from First Nations. Parks Canada does not control, or guarantee access. Parks Canada is endeavouring to reach agreement with First Nations for access to the West Coast Trail. For updated information on access, call the Pachena Bay or Gordon River information/registration centre.

To make a reservation

Super, National British Columbia Reservation and Information Service:
Greater Vancouver **604-663-6000**
Canada/USA **1-800-663-6000**
Outside Canada **604-387-1642**

For more Information:
Pacific Rim National Park Reserve
Box 280 Ucluelet, BC V0R 3A0
250-726-7721

Pachena Bay WCT Hiker Information/Registration
(North End near Bamfield)
Open daily Apr 15–Oct 5
Phone/Fax **250-728-3234**

Gordon River WCT Hiker Information/Registration
(South End near Port Renfrew)
Phone/Fax **250-647-5434**

Alberni Marine Transport
(Lady Rose and Frances Barkley)
250-723-8313 or
toll-free Apr–Sept **1-800-663-7192**

Further Reading: **West Coast Trail**

Timeless Shore: Canada's West Coast Trail *(Allen, George, Bayeux Publishing, 1994).*

Hiking on the Edge:West Coast Trail, Juan de Fuca Trail *(Gill, Ian and David Nunuk, Raincoast Books, 1998).*

The West Coast Trail & Nitinat Lake: A Trail Guide by the Sierra Club of Western Canada *(Leaden, Tim, Douglas & McIntyre, 1992).*

Official Guide to Pacific Rim National Park Reserve *(MacFarlane, J.M. et al., Blackbird Naturgraphics Inc., 1996).*

Bamfield area Recreation, Accommodations and Services

Recreation
West Coast Trail
Fishing charters
Dive charters
Ecotour charters
Kayak rentals
Whale watching charters

Accommodations
Bed & Breakfasts
Lodges
Inns
Resorts
Campgrounds

Services
Restaurants
Pubs
Grocery stores
ATM
Gas stations
Marinas
Galleries/gift shops
Hospital

weary adventurer. About 2 km along the beach south of Tsusiat Falls is Hole-in-the-Wall, an aptly named, naturally sculpted opening in a thick outcropping of rock. Roomy enough to dwarf hikers posing under its ragged archway, Hole-in-the-Wall is easily accessible at low tide. These and many other delights await backpackers on the wild West Coast Trail. Come well prepared and allow enough time to enjoy yourself. You will be rewarded with a memorable outdoor adventure.

Important Numbers

Emergency **911**
Hospital **250-728-3312**
Coast Guard
1-800-567-5111
Bamfield Chamber
of Commerce
250-728-3006

Tsusiat Falls on the West Coast Trail

Pacific Rim National Park Reserve: The Broken Group Islands

The Broken Group Islands of Pacific Rim National Park Reserve are scattered through the centre of Barkley Sound. These islands are bounded on the inside by Vancouver Island and on the outside by the Pacific Ocean. To the west is Loudoun Channel and Imperial Eagle Channel lays to the east.

Imperial Eagle Channel was named for Captain Barkley's ship, and Loudoun Channel for the original name of the *Imperial Eagle*. Its British owners apparently changed the ship's name from the *Loudoun* to the *Imperial Eagle* and sailed it under an Austrian flag to avoid paying the East India Company—which had been granted exclusive rights to fur trading in North America—for a licence to trade along the northwest coast.

Park wardens strongly discourage paddlers from attempting to get to the Broken Group Islands by crossing either Imperial Eagle Channel from Bamfield or Loudoun Channel from Ucluelet. These crossings are long, and the channels are unprotected and subject to strong winds and swells. It is much safer to take the passenger ferries *Lady Rose* or the *Frances Barkley* from Port Alberni, which will drop you and your kayak/canoe at Sechart, a launching spot 1 km north of the Broken Group Islands. When you go this way, you can enjoy a spectacular 3-hour cruise and a piping hot breakfast in the ship's coffee shop in the bargain. Reservations for the *Lady Rose/Frances Barkley* are strongly recommended. Call Alberni Marine Transport Ltd. at 250-723-8313, or toll free from April to September 1-800-663-7192. Paddlers can also arrange drop-offs and pick-ups from Ucluelet.

The other recommended entry point is from Toquart Bay. This is also the safest launch for small pleasure boats. To get there follow Highway 4 west from Port Alberni for about 85 km. When you reach Kennedy Lake, turn left at the gravel logging road and follow it for 16 km to Toquart Bay. There is a car park, boat launch and BC Forest Service campsite here. In summer this area is extremely busy, so be prepared for crowds. The crossing from Toquart Bay to the Broken Group Islands is an 8-km paddle through mostly protected waters.

The exposed outer islands of the Broken Group, including Wouwer, Howell and Cree islands, bear the full brunt of the Pacific Ocean. These islands are known for heavy winds and strong tidal currents in the surrounding waters. Storms can blow up without warning. Paddlers or boaters in these areas must be knowledgeable about navigation and weather, experienced in handling their craft, and equipped with appropriate tide tables and wilderness survival gear.

Behind the wind-battered outer islands are the more sheltered islands so popular with outdoor enthusiasts. This is a fine place for families or relative novices to paddle. But even in these calmer waters it is important to have enough experience and survival equipment to be self-sufficient. Paddlers should know about wind patterns, tides and tidal currents, and get regular updates on the weather. Paddlers must also be able to perform self-rescue and group-rescue techniques and know how to treat hypothermia, which can set in in a matter of minutes.

Summer days are mostly sunny and dry—average summer rainfall is just 46 cm—but fog is common, especially in August, and rain can descend, sometimes for days. It is important to be well supplied with food, warm and dry clothes, and the camping gear sufficient to wait out bad weather if necessary. This is a wilderness destination, and preparation can make the difference between safety and disaster. For detailed information and checklists, see *Sea Kayaking Canada's West Coast*. If in doubt, taking an excursion with

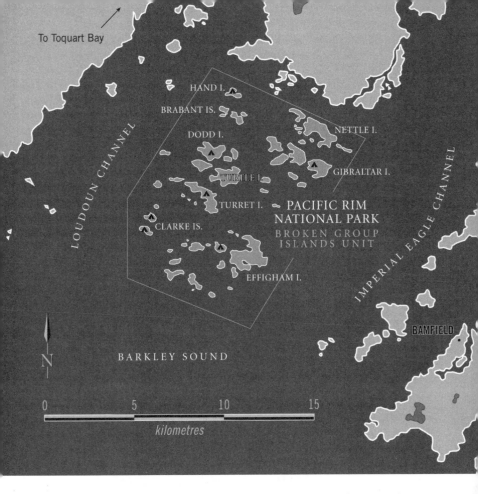

To Toquart Bay

HAND I.

BRABANT IS.

NETTLE I.

DODD I.

GIBRALTAR I.

TURTLE I.

TURRET I.

PACIFIC RIM
NATIONAL PARK

CLARKE IS.

BROKEN GROUP
ISLANDS UNIT

EFFIGHAM I.

LOUDOUN CHANNEL

IMPERIAL EAGLE CHANNEL

BAMFIELD

BARKLEY SOUND

N

0   5   10   15

kilometres

certified guides is a good way to get acquainted with these captivating islands. Kayaking excursions can be booked in Port Alberni and Ucluelet.

There is so much to explore in this area. Natural forces have carved out rocky caves and surge channels, and in some places large wind-and-water-sculpted stone arches span the foreshore. The islands are covered with stands of spruce, hemlock and cedar. Many are

Further Reading: **Broken Group Islands**

Sea Kayaking Canada's West Coast (Allen, Gelnce, John and Heidi Köttner, Raxas Books, 1982).

Official Guide to Pacific Rim National Park Reserve (McFarlane, J.M. et al.,Blackbird Naturographics Inc., 1996).

Barkley Sound: A History of the Pacific Rim National Park reserve Area (Scott, R. Bruce,Victoria, 1972).

Small Craft Guidebook: British Columbia, Vancouver Island, vol. 1. Canadian Hydrographic Society, 1989.

Island Paddling: A Paddler's Guide to the Gulf Islands and Barkley Sound (Snowden, Mary-Ann, Orca Books, 1990).

Cruising Guide to the West Coast of Vancouver Island (Watmough, Don, Evergreen Pacific Publishing, 1993).

The Broken Group Islands are an increasingly popular destination

Kayaking is one of the best ways to explore the west coast

▶ Camping on the Broken Group Islands

Camping on the Broken Group Islands is permitted only in the designated camping areas. 4 days is the maximum length of stay at any site and 14 days is the maximum length of stay in the area. Parks Canada may implement a reservation and quota system much like the one for the West Coast Trail, in order to protect the Broken Group Islands from the impact of the increasing number of visitors. Contact the park administration at 250-726-7721 for more information.

rimmed with inviting shell or gravel beaches, secluded coves and reefs colourful with sea life. These islands are prime seabird habitats and provide one of the largest nesting grounds for bald eagles in North America. Seals and orcas sometimes cruise the channels in pursuit of salmon, and gray whales appear from time to time. Marine life abounds with fish, crabs, clams and mussels, however, Parks Canada discourages harvesting in the park reserve. Also, shellfish may be contaminated due to Paralytic Shellfish Poisoning ("red tide"). Eating contaminated shellfish can be deadly.

For more information:

Pacific Rim National Park Reserve
Box 280, Ucluelet, BC V0R 3A0
250-726-7721

Canadian Coast Guard
Office of Boating Safety
Suite 330, 800 Burrard Street
Vancouver, BC V6Z 2J8
604-666-0146

One of the pleasures of exploring these islands is discovering signs of the early habitation of the Nuu-chah-nulth people who occupied the Broken Group Islands for centuries. There are ancient "canoe runs" (cleared paths from the beach down to the tide line), stone fish traps for catching herring and anchovies, the sites of earthen defence structures, fragments of stone and bone tools, and nearly two-hundred middens. You may even see a "culturally modified" tree—a living cedar with long strips of bark removed. The Nuu-chah-nulth used the cedar bark for making all kinds of household items from hats and blankets to ropes and baskets. All archaelogical sites are protected and it is against the law to remove artifacts. Today there are First Nations Reserves on Effingham, Keith and Nettle Islands, and advance permission is needed to visit these reserves. For information contact either the Tseshaht band office (250-724-1225) or the Hupaḏasath band office.

Important Note

Parks Canada expects boaters and paddlers to be self-sufficient and to follow Canadian Coast Guard regulations and guidelines. All users of the Broken Group Islands are required to obtain up-to-date weather forecasts before starting out (250-724-1333) as heavy rains and strong winds can develop rapidly and unexpectedly. Marine Charts 3670 (the Broken Group) and 3671 (Barkley Sound) are essential for travel. Tide tables are also mandatory and can be obtained from any major marine supplier on the coast or the Canadian Hydrographic Service. Ask for the Canadian Tide Tables, *vol. 6 (Tofino Tables).*

Important Numbers

Marine Weather Forecasts
250-724-1333

Broadcast on VHF
Channel 21B

Rescue Co-ordination Centre 1-800-567-5111

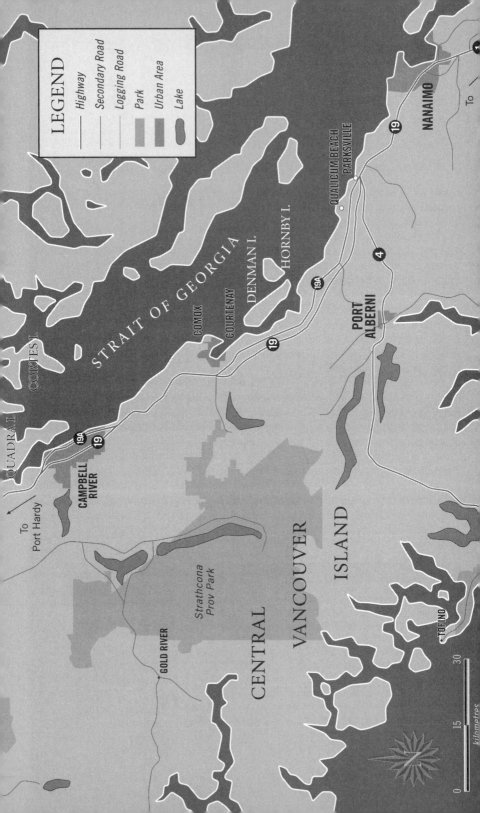

LEGEND
Highway
Secondary Road
Logging Road
Park
Urban Area
Lake

NANAIMO

To

19

QUALICUM BEACH
PARKSVILLE

4

19A

HORNBY I.

DENMAN I.

COURTENAY

COMOX

19

PORT
ALBERNI

STRAIT OF GEORGIA

CORTES I.

QUADRA I.

19A

19

CAMPBELL
RIVER

To
Port Hardy

GOLD RIVER

Strathcona
Prov Park

CENTRAL

VANCOUVER

ISLAND

TOFINO

0   15   30
kilometres

CHAPTER 7
CENTRAL VANCOUVER ISLAND

The Comox Valley

J ust north of Nanaimo is "Beach Country"—the Qualicum Beach–Parksville area. In summer, hundreds of visitors while away the days on miles-long swaths of sun-warmed sand. In spring, wildlife watchers congregate to celebrate as twenty thousand Brant geese stop on the beach for their last rest on their way north. And at any time of year, locals and visitors can happily chase little white balls around the fairways. Farther north are the historic farmlands of the pastoral Comox Valley stretching between the high white Comox Glacier and the sea, while winter skiing and summer hiking in the nearby Forbidden Plateau area draw year-round visitors to Comox and Courtenay. Another short drive north and you're at Campbell River, the Salmon Capital of Canada and one of the biggest tourist service centres on the island. Here the rich and famous have caught trophy fish since the turn of the century, and the lure of eco-tourism and a raft of other outdoor sports—salmon snorkelling, anyone?—are bringing in a whole new contingent of visitors. Jutting from the water along this gorgeous piece of coastline are Denman, Hornby, Quadra and Cortes islands—all accessible by short ferry rides, each with its own special character. Catch a fish, explore a cave, take in a First Nations puppet show, go on a workboat cruise or just sit back and let the splendour of the island coastline work its magic.

Getting to Nanaimo

From Vancouver (Horseshoe Bay) to Nanaimo (Departure Bay) *Drive aboard a BC Ferry at the Horseshoe Bay terminal (just north of Vancouver). 1 hour 35 minutes crossing time; 8 sailings daily year round.*

Limited vehicle reservations accepted on this route.

From Vancouver (Tsawwassen) to Nanaimo (Duke Point) *Drive aboard a BC Ferry at the Tsawwassen terminal (just south of Vancouver). 2 hours crossing time; 8 sailings daily year round.*

For more information about travel aboard BC Ferries, see p. 8

From Victoria *Drive up Highway 1 to Nanaimo (see Chapter 5). The 113-km drive takes about 1 1/2 to 2 hours.*

PARKSVILLE– QUALICUM BEACH

Craig Heritage Park

Highlights

Beaches and wide
tidal sand flats

Great mountains for
skiing and hiking

Swimming and other
water sports

Wildlife viewing

Spelunking

Stunning waterfalls

Lots of golf courses

As you drive north from Nanaimo, you may notice warships tied up across the water. Since 1965 Nanoose Bay has been the site of a Canadian Forces Maritime Experimental and Test Range jointly operated by Canada and the US. Here, unarmed torpedos are launched by ships, planes and submarines, and then retrieved by helicopter or ship. It is the only range facility of its kind on the west coast of North America. The waters off Nanoose Bay were chosen as a site because of their ideal ocean bottom topography. However, Nanoose has also been the focus of dozens of protests against American nuclear submarines being in Canadian waters and the dangers of a nuclear accident.

Carrying on north, the first choice you make is which road to take at the junction of Highways 19 and 19A and Highways 4 and 4A. Both 19 and 19A will take the visitor up-island, but Highway 19A is the scenic oceanside route—the one we recommend. Highway 19 is the new, faster highway that zooms you inland and beyond the Qualicum Beach–Parksville area. Highways 4 and 4A lead to Port Alberni and the West Coast of Vancouver Island (see Chapter 6). Just look for the signs.

The sister communities of Parksville and Qualicum Beach 37 km north of Nanaimo are known for their wide tidal sand flats and sun-warmed salt water. The beaches are heaven for sun worshippers, kite flyers, wildlife watchers and intrepid sand-castle builders. This is also a great area for outdoor recreation in local mountains and waters. Vancouver Island's snow-capped mountains are laced with fishing lakes and hiking trails. There are lots of good camping, swimming and picnicking

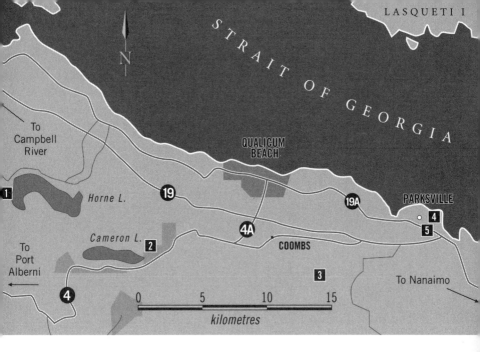

STRAIT OF GEORGIA

QUALICUM BEACH

To Campbell River

Horne L. **19**

1

Cameron L. **2**

To Port Alberni

4A

4

COOMBS

19A PARKSVILLE

4

5

3

To Nanaimo

```
0        5       10       15
|————————————————————————————|
           kilometres
```

spots, and some fine caving, canoeing and biking. And it's all within easy driving distance of Parksville–Qualicum Beach.

A good way to start your visit is with a stop at the **Parksville InfoCentre** (250-248-3613), located on Hwy 19A on the outskirts of Parksville. Right next door is **Craig Heritage Park & Museum** where you can step back into early settler life. Poke into the refurbished heritage buildings that have been moved to the site from elsewhere in the district, including the French Creek Post Office (1886), the Duncan McMillan log

What to See

- ☐ **1** Horne Lake Caves
- ☐ **2** Little Qualicum Falls Provincial Park
- ☐ **3** Englishman River Falls Provincial Park
- ☐ **4** Rathtrevor Beach Provincial Park
- ☐ **5** Craig Heritage Park & Museum

house (1885) and the Knox Heritage Church (1912), and linger over displays of pioneer and Native artifacts in the museum. (Open mid-May to Labour Day, 250-248-6966, or by appointment in off-season, 250-248-3431.)

Stretching from Parksville to Qualicum Beach are the **famous beaches** that have delighted generations of children who've taken home memories of sunny days full of swimming, picnicking and tidepool exploring. The tang of salt blowing on the wind, the raucous cry of a seagull stalking the high-tide line, and a wide, warm stretch of sand are made for holidays. Resorts, restaurants, motels, housekeeping cottages, RV parks, public and private campgrounds, and other tourist facilities all serve sun-and-sea visitors, and local amenities make travel more comfortable all year round.

Parksville and Qualicum Beach are cheek-by-jowl resort-and-retirement communities, but they've taken different approaches to growth. Parksville has welcomed development

Parksville–Qualicum Beach: A Brief History

The Parksville–Qualicum Beach area was once the homeland of the Kwakwaka'wakw people known as the Qualicum. Traditionally, the Qualicums gathered on the shore of the Big Qualicum River in autumn to harvest the chum salmon churning upriver to spawn. But the Qualicum band was nearly destroyed by smallpox in the late 1700s. The young Scots botanist Robert Brown, who sailed past the Qualicum village on a plant-gathering expedition in 1864, noted in his diary that the deadly European disease had wreaked havoc among the local aboriginal people. He reported that their village had been deserted except for three band members who remained alive. Members of today's small Qualicum First Nation (pop. 76), living on a reserve just north of Qualicum Beach, are descendants of the smallpox survivors who intermarried with neighbouring groups.

Europeans began arriving in the 1870s to preempt land for logging and farming. But the area was slow to be settled. It had no natural harbours where boats could land, the rough overland wagon trail from Nanaimo didn't reach Parksville till 1886 and Qualicum Beach till 1894, and the trees were so big that the stumps had to be blasted out of the ground before crops could be planted. Still, hardy pioneer folk did put down roots and build a community.

Nowadays tourism and a large retirement community fuel the engine of the local economy. The population has doubled over the last two decades and is expected to double again in the next two. What attracts so many newcomers is the combination of coastal pleasures away from the noise and bustle of a big city, and a delightfully mild year-round climate—flowers can bloom in January, and golf is a year-round game. Visitors come for the same reasons. The first commercial lodge was built in Parksville in the late 1880s and dubbed the Sea View Hotel. Since then dozens of resorts, lodges, motels and restaurants with the words "sea," "ocean," "beach" or "bay" in their names have sprung up in the Parksville–Qualicum Beach area to accommodate the many visitors attracted by sun-and-sea holidays.

with open arms, but just a few kilometres along the way, at Qualicum Beach, you don't see strip malls and commercial signs. What you do see is lots of greenery. Qualicum Beach has kept the low-key, villagey ambience it has had since the early years of the century when wealthy Europeans flocked to the comfortably elegant Qualicum Beach Hotel. That famous landmark is gone now, but the village is pleasantly homey and very welcoming to visitors. Browse in the artists' studios in the **Old School House Gallery**, explore the **Old Power House Museum**, stroll through specialty shops, enjoy scones or sandwiches in a little tea room or take in a show at the local **theatre**. And the beach that brought in the throngs is still there a few blocks below the village, and still just as inviting.

Rathtrevor Beach Provincial Park

Rathtrevor Beach Provincial Park, just 1.5 km south of Parksville off Hwy 19A, is one of BC's favourite provincial parks. The walk from the parking lot through a cool green Douglas fir forest takes you to unbelievably vast sand flats. At low tide you can walk almost a mile across the hard-packed sand toward the far-distant mainland mountains across the Strait of Georgia. Let the kids splash in the shallow water or pat sand into castles while you stretch out to

watch bright kites zip across the sky. Find out about sea critters at the visitors' centre and watch for family-centred activities led by the park's interpretive staff. (250-954-4600; camping reservations, 1-800-689-9025.)

Rathtrevor Park is also definitely for the **birds**. More than 240 species have been identified here. Look for the big red-crowned pileated woodpeckers in the campground and waterbirds near the beach, especially from February to April when murrelets, loons, grebes and cormorants alight to feed on spawning herring. A big plus for birders is the arrival of some 20,000 Brant geese every April. Parksville–Qualicum Beach is the last stop for these magnificent birds on their way north, and the communities celebrate the event with a three-day **Brant Festival** that includes goose viewing tours, nature talks, photography workshops and children's activities. (For festival information, phone 250-248-3613.)

The sand seems to go on forever at Rathtrevor Beach Provincial Park

Englishman River Falls Provincial Park and
Little Qualicum Falls Provincial Park

If you love waterfalls, pack up a picnic and head for Englishman River Falls Provincial Park just 20 minutes from downtown Parksville. Follow Hwy 4 east toward Port Alberni, take the signed turn south at Errington Rd and follow the signs to the park entrance 9 km south of the turnoff. Then head for the upper end of Englishman River and take the easy forest loop walk from the upper to the lower falls. The river plunges down a wide rock lip at the upper falls and roars downstream to the lower falls to slide under a bridge into a crystal pool. There you can treat yourself to a sweet dip in that oh-so-inviting pool. (250-954-4600; camping reservations 1-800-689-9025.) Want more rough-and-tumble wet stuff? Continue down Hwy 4 toward Port Alberni to mountain-backed Cameron Lake and look for the turnoff at Little Qualicum Falls Provincial Park. Park in the designated lot and walk up the shady trail along Little Qualicum River past the pools of the lower falls to the spectacular double cascade of the upper falls. **Swim** in crisp, clear pools along the river or return to Cameron Lake for a dip. Don't forget your **fishing** pole. Little Qualicum River is known for its rare brown trout (250-752-6305, Reservations 1-800-689-9025).

Englishman River Falls

"Beach Country" could just as well be called "Golf Country." Take your pick of five golf courses in the area. In Parksville, it's the 18-hole public Morningstar Golf Course. In Qualicum, try the 18-hole Eaglecrest Golf Club, 18-hole Glengarry Golf or 9-hole Qualicum Beach Memorial Golf Club. Just minutes north of Qualicum is the new 18-hole Arrowsmith Golf and Country Club. For the nitty-gritty on courses and amenities, check with the Parksville InfoCentre on Hwy19A just south of Parksville (250-248-3613).

Lasqueti Island

Hop aboard the Lasqueti Island foot passenger ferry from French Creek (between Parksville and Qualicum Beach on Hwy 19A) and cruise 17 km across the Strait of Georgia to Lasqueti Island. The population is small—about 400—and islanders like it that way. Development is definitely not on their agenda. There's no car ferry, and islanders have said no to electricity. That makes the quietly rural Lasqueti a great place to **cycle**. Try the 19-km stretch of road from "downtown" False Bay (not much more than a store and a pub) to small but exquisite **Squitty Bay Provincial Park** at the eastern end of the island. There you'll want to stop to enjoy sweeping views of the mainland and Vancouver Island. If it's a clear day, you'll see the blue volcanic peak of Mt. Baker in the far distance. The ferry runs several times a day except for Tuesday (year-round) and Wednesday (off-season). Take Hwy 19A north from Parksville, look for the signed turnoff to French Creek at Lee Rd and follow the road to the ferry dock. For information about Lasqueti Island and ferry schedules, check with the Parksville InfoCentre on Hwy 19A just south of Parksville (250-248-3613) or ask the friendly folk at French Creek Marina and Store (250-248-8912).

The Lasqueti Island ferry is for foot passengers only

Parksville–Qualicum Beach Recreation, Accommodations and Services

Recreation
Bicycle rentals
Kayak/Canoe rentals
Fishing/Boat
charters/rentals
Scuba diving/charters
Golf courses
Hiking
Horseback riding
Spelunking
Birding

Accommodations
Bed & Breakfasts

Inns/Resorts
Hotels/Motels
Campgrounds
RV Parks

Services
InfoCentres
Restaurants
Pubs
Cafés
Banks/ATMs
Grocery stores
Gas/Service stations
Medical clinics

Horne Lake Caves Provincial Park

Up for a down-under **spelunking** day trip to nearby Horne Lake Caves Provincial Park? To get there, take Hwy 19A north from Qualicum, drive 13 km and turn left onto Horne Lake Rd, then follow the road 14 km to the park. Or take Hwy 19, exit at the Horne Lake Rd interchange and follow the signs to Horne Lake Caves. The Main Cave and Lower Main Cave are open all year for self-guided tours. You can squeeze through back-torquing tunnels to eerie mineral formations like the "Toothpaste Room" or the "Cauliflower Room" and marvel at capacious limestone chambers. The Main Cave even has a waterfall at its far end. Or join seasonal on-site

Spelunkers marvel at the sites at Horne Lake Provincial Park

▶ Parksville–Qualicum Beach Annual Events

February
Qualicum Beach Art Show

March
Old School House Gallery Annual Open House
Parksville Music Concert

April
Brant Wildlife Festival
Nanoose Place Spring Craft Sale/Art Show

May
Hammerfest BC Cup Mountain Bike Race
(Englishman River Falls)

June
Jazz Festival

July
Canada Day Celebrations, Parksville
Community Park
Coombs Rodeo
Coombs Provincial Fiddling Jamboree

August
Country & Western/Bluegrass Music Festival

World Croquet Championship
Coombs Fall Fair
Nanoose Days & Teddy Bear Picnic

November
Parksville Christmas Craft Show
(Nanoose Place Community Centre)
Festival of Wines (Island Hall Beach Resort)
Nanoose Place Christmas Craft Fair
Dickens Festival
Festival of Trees
Village Christmas Craft Show
(Qualicum Community Hall)
Lions Christmas Craft Show
(Parksville Community Hall)

December
Sunrise Preschool Kids Fest
Festival of Champagnes (New Year's Eve)

For more information, Parksville InfoCentre
250-248-3613; Qualicum Beach InfoCentre
250-752-9532

cave tours of the spectacular Riverbend Cave. The 1¹/₂-hr **Family Interpretive tour** is a high-octane family adventure, and the demanding 5-hr **High Adventure tour** is for on-the-edge spelunkers determined to get their adrenalin highs. (A rappelling course offered in the evenings is recommended before taking the High Adventure option.) (For information and reservations, call Horne Lake Cave Tours at 250-757-8687.)

Important Numbers

Ambulance **911**
Hospital (Nanaimo) **250-754-2141**
Police emergency **911**
Police non-emergency **250-248-6111**
Fire **911**
Coast Guard **1-800-567-5111**

QUALICUM TO COURTENAY

Oyster count▸

Marshes north of Qualicum

Highlights

Quaint oceanside towns

Quiet beaches

Abundant
marine wildlife

Kayaking and
boating spots

Ocean-fresh oysters

Nearby islands
to explore

Great cycling

Bowser, Deep Bay, Fanny Bay, Buckley Bay, and Union Bay

From Qualicum, the old island highway (Hwy 19A) skims away from Parksville-style development to run through little oceanside towns like Bowser, Deep Bay, Fanny Bay, Buckley Bay, and Union Bay that have kept their old-time character. When it comes to the names of these towns, local stories abound. Bowser was named for flash-in-the-pan BC premier William John Bowser (1915–16), but folks like to think that it had something to do with the bartender dog at the old Bowser Hotel. According to Ripley's *Believe It or Not*, the dog carried beer bottles to customers' tables, took their money and came back with the change. Fanny Bay was probably named for an unknown lady by the captain of the British survey ship *GH Richards*, but its name has been the occasion for many a ribald local joke. Fanny Bay is famous for its oyster farms. Those white shell mounds along the highway are used to seed the tiny oyster sprats that are racked and dunked into Baynes Sound to grow into plumply sea-succulent morsels. The Fanny Bay Inn—known as "the FBI"—is a favourite pub stop for Vancouver Islanders. Just past the FBI at Buckley Bay is the turnoff to BC ferries. This is your chance to island-hop to two offshore charmers, Denman and Hornby islands.

Denman Island

Denman, a low-lying, fertile island, stretches 19 km alongside Vancouver Island. To get there, just hop aboard the BC ferry at Buckley

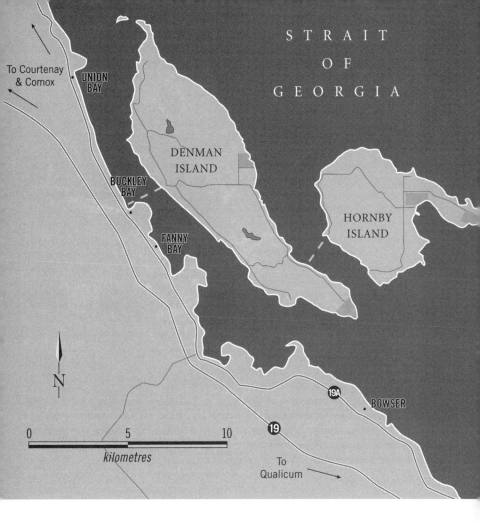

Bay for a quick and scenic 10-minute sailing. Denman is a few minutes away but a world apart. The island's special magic reveals itself to any visitors who want to slip off their Timexes and get in synch with island time. Local pleasures are leisurely and earth-simple—walking for miles on gravel beaches at low tide, biking through a patchwork of farms on less-travelled roads, kayaking a protected cove shot with sunbright ripples, watching an eagle knife into the water and rise with a fish in its talons.

One of the island's attractions is its abundance of wild creatures great and small. Waterbirds and eagles flock to Denman's gravel shores in winter and you could see as many as a dozen eagles perched over the water in the same snaggy tree. Migrating sea lions heave their great bulk up the strait, and deer can be spotted in fields and along the roadside all year round.

When the ferry dumps its load of cars onto the Denman Island dock, many drivers just put their foot to the pedal and career across the island to catch the ferry to Hornby Island. A more leisurely pace—maybe **hiking, biking, scootering or kayaking** around Denman Island—lets you discover the island's quiet delights.

Just a 5-minute walk up the hill from the ferry terminal is **Denman Village**, the centre

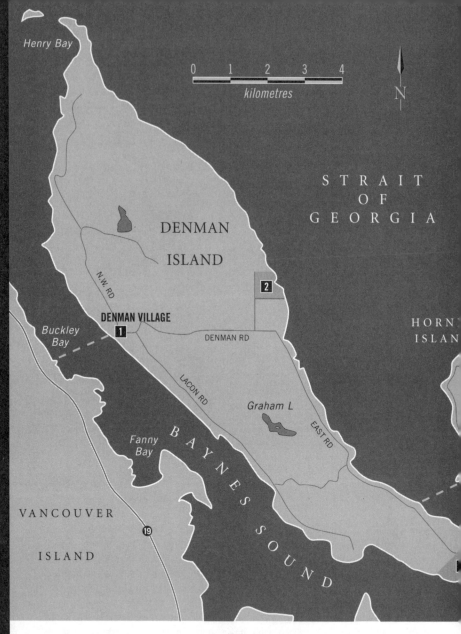

Henry Bay

0 1 2 3 4
kilometres

N

STRAIT
OF
GEORGIA

DENMAN
ISLAND

N.W. RD

2

DENMAN VILLAGE
1

HORN
ISLAN

Buckley
Bay

DENMAN RD

LACON RD

EAST RD

Graham L

Fanny
Bay

B A Y N E S

VANCOUVER

19

ISLAND

S O U N D

What to See

- ☐ 1 Historic Denman Village
- ☐ 2 Fillongley Provincial Park
- ☐ 3 Boyle Point Provincial Park
- ☐ 4 Chrome Island

Getting to Denman Island

From Buckley Bay Drive aboard a BC Ferry at Buckley Bay (on Hwy 19A, 40 km north of Qualicum/20 km south of Courtenay). 10 minutes crossing time; 18 sailings daily year round.

Note: fares collected as return fares. Ships running to Denman (and Hornby Island) shuttle back and forth when traffic is heavy, which may alter sailing times on short notice.

For more information about travel aboard BC Ferries, see p. 8.

for commercial services and the soul of Denman Island life. Even though tourism is not yet a big item on Denman and visitor services are scanty, a stroll through Denman Village makes a great little excursion. It's a small but funky mix of old and new buildings laid out in an easy here-and-there way along North-west Rd. A good starting place is at the turn-of-the-century **Denman Island General Store** (1910) above the ferry terminal at the corner of Denman Rd and North-west Rd. This is the quintessential country store with lots of services all rolled into one small space—a great little café, a post office, a liquor store, gas pumps, groceries, and seasonal scooter and bike rentals. **St. Saviour's Anglican Church** (1914), with its cornerstone milled from Denman's short-lived sandstone quarry, is just across the road. Farther up North-west Rd is the rest of "downtown" Denman, including a local **museum**, a handful of craft shops and gift studios, the **Denman Craft Shop** which features Denman-only artisans, a book shop with large dose of holistic/meditative/alternative lifestyle offerings, a deli market, a sea kayak rental outlet and a light dusting of eateries. There's no pub or motel, but a dozen or so little B&Bs are scattered around the island, four of them within spitting distance of Denman Village. Choices range from a hilltop organic farm with free-range chickens and a sweat lodge for spiritual healing to an ocean-view heritage home half a block from Denman village. Denman Islanders are a friendly lot and many have fascinating personal histories and an intriguing outlook on life. (For the up-to-the-minute scoop on island services, pick up the Hornby and Denman Islands Visitor's Guide at the

Denman Island General Store

263

Fillongley Provincial Park is a Denman "must-see"

Denman Island General Store, phone Denman/Hornby Tourist Services at 250-335-2293, or visit the Denman Island website www.denmanis.bc.ca/features.)

Fillongley Provincial Park

If you ask Denman Island residents what not to miss, the island's two public parks—Fillongley Provincial Park and Boyle Point Provincial Park—are sure to be major picks. The 23-ha Fillongley Provincial Park was once part of the seaside estate of the pioneering couple George and Amy Beadnell, who were known for their warm hospitality. A Latin inscription over their hearth read (in translation): "Here let my friends gather in the red glow of my fireplace." When the Beadnells died, the property was handed over to the province at their request, so that visitors could continue to enjoy their lovely fragment of coastal paradise.

Short easy paths meander along a fern-splashed creek beneath stands of old-growth Douglas firs and giant alders. Walk to the **wide grassy meadow** where the Beadnells' manor once stood in encircling woodlands. The old manor house, bentwood gates, tennis court, greenhouse, lily pond, bowling green and manicured gardens are all gone, but the Beadnells' benevolence still hovers over the place. After viewing the grounds, you can head for the small (10-site) **campground** to pitch your tent right next to the shore or unwrap your sandwiches at the **beachside picnic tables**. This is also a perfect place to start a low-tide saunter along Denman Island's **long gravel beaches**. Stride out in either direction (but avoid stomping through oyster leases flagged with red markers).

To get to Fillongley Provincial Park (250-954-4600, Reservations 1-800-689-9025) stay on Denman Rd as you exit the ferry terminal and follow it across the island. From Denman Rd park signs will direct you left at Swan Rd and then right at Beadnell Rd. The parking lot is by the campground at the end of Beadnell Rd.

Boyle Point Provincial Park

Boyle Point Provincial Park near the Hornby Island ferry terminal doesn't have camping or picnicking facilities, but this 125-ha park does offer several **good trails**. The most popular trail is the 7-km return hike to Boyle Point at the extreme south tip of the island. From the steep bluff at Boyle Point the views are spectacular. You can look down from the cliff over the bright red and white buildings of the Chrome Island light station, and out over miles of islands and ocean. You might catch sight of eagles or turkey vultures soaring on the updrafts over **Chrome Island** or the rubber-shiny heads of **scuba divers** exploring the **wreck** of the British merchant ship *Alpha* not far offshore. On December 16, 1900, the ship was steaming toward Vancouver Island to pick up coal destined for Japan. But hidden in the swirl of a blinding snowstorm were the dangerous rocks of Chrome Island. The ship ran aground and sank, taking the captain and eight seamen to their watery graves. The lure of the ship's scattered remains attracts divers to the shallow waters to the east of Chrome Island. To get to Boyle Point Provincial Park, stay on Denman Rd as you exit the ferry terminal. At the east side of the island Denman Rd kinks south and becomes East Rd. Follow East Rd past the Hornby ferry terminal to the park.

Hornby Island

Even though Hornby Island's population of 800 full-time residents more than triples with the influx of summer visitors, locals are generally a welcoming bunch who don't mind sharing their island with visitors. The Hornby ferry shuttles between Denman Island and Hornby, where the landmark profile of Mt. Geoffrey towers some 330 metres above the ferry terminal.

Hornby Island has attracted a special breed of independent-minded folk whose inventiveness sets the island apart. Potters, artists, weavers, musicians, dancers and writers by the dozen have come to Hornby. The potter Wayne Ngan is perhaps the most famous Hornby artist, but **studios and galleries** around the island hold a treasure trove of intriguing objects. "People here are fundamentally different" says one islander who came in the heyday of the 1960s back-to-the-land movement. "This is a community of rebels and refugees." You can see that creativity in Hornby's famous **hand-built houses** made from inventively recycled found or pre-used materials.

The entrance to Hornby Island's Community Hall

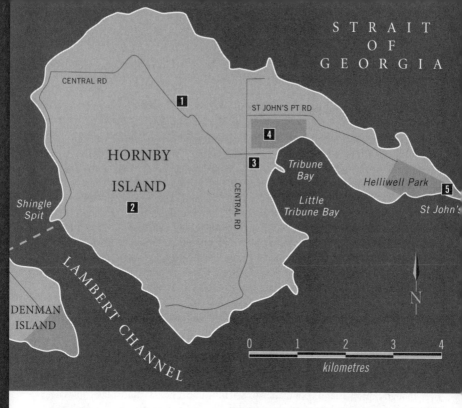

STRAIT
OF
GEORGIA

CENTRAL RD

ST JOHN'S PT RD

1

4

HORNBY

3

ISLAND

Tribune
Bay

Helliwell Park

5

Shingle
Spit

CENTRAL RD

2

Little
Tribune Bay

St John's

DENMAN
ISLAND

LAMBERT CHANNEL

N

0   1   2   3   4

kilometres

Much of the building is a co-operative venture as neighbours swap handiwork and materials—some PVC pipe and plumbing help for a load of manure and gardening expertise, or a handwoven sweater for some accounting work. If creative independence is one side of the coin on Hornby, then community is the other. The hand-built **Hornby Island Community Hall** on Central Road is a striking example of community spirit. It is the heart of community

What to See

- ☐ **1** Hornby Island Community Centre
- ☐ **2** Mount Geoffrey
- ☐ **3** Hornby Island Co-op store
- ☐ **4** Tribune Bay Provincial Park
- ☐ **5** Helliwell Park

cultural activity, including the **Hornby Festival** in August where internationally known writers, musicians, dancers and theatre groups join regional and local talent in a 10-day festival of the arts (for tickets, 1-250-335-2734 or fax 1-250-335-0121).

The other community gathering place is the **Hornby Island Co-op Store** on Central Road. The Co-op is a remarkable community-owned complex where you can get anything from groceries, gas, household goods and hardware to videos and gourmet food. (However, there is no bank machine and no liquor outlet on Hornby.) Ranged around the Co-op in a tree-shaded courtyard are several wood-shingled shops and eateries. You can find very good (and innovative) fast food with a strong vegetarian bent at a couple of little eateries, as well as **bike rentals** and an eye-catching potpourri of **art, crafts, clothes and books**. This is the hub of island life, and its aura is about as earthy and laid back as it gets.

Getting to Hornby Island

To get to Hornby Island, travellers must first take the ferry to Denman Island, cross Denman to the ferry terminal at Gravelley Bay, then catch the ferry to Hornby (Shingle Spit terminal). (See "Getting to Denman Island," p. 263.)

From Dennman Island

Drive aboard a BC Ferry from Denman Island (Denman East terminal). 10 minutes crossing time; 12 sailings daily year round.

Note: *Extra sailings on Fridays only. Ships running to Denman (and Hornby Island) shuttle back and forth when traffic is heavy, which may alter sailing times on short notice. Fares collected as return fares. Fares to Hornby Island can be paid at Buckley Bay terminal or Denman Island terminal. Cash or traveller's cheques only at Denman Island terminal.*

For more information about travel aboard BC Ferries, see p. 8.

One way to get a feel for Hornby is to take the picturesque main route around the island. You'll see every rural sight from sheep grazing in grassy pastures behind split-rail fences, to sandstone-sculpted beaches where sea lions sun themselves on the outer rocks, to wide vistas of the snow-crowned mountains of Vancouver Island. From the ferry terminal, head north along Shingle Spit Rd, which runs along the coast and then turns inland to become Central Rd. Central Rd shimmies past the island's recycling depot, fire hall, medical centre, community hall and school almost up to the deep incision of Tribune Bay on the island's east coast. But just before it reaches Tribune Bay, Central takes a right-angle turn at the Hornby Island Co-op and heads off on a curving south-southwest course to Ford's Cove down the west coast from Shingle Spit.

Inviting side roads lead to half a dozen destinations like Phipps Point, Collishaw Point, Galleon Beach, Tralee Point, and Whaling Station Bay where you can take **great road and/or beach walks**. Unlike smooth-bordered Denman Island, Hornby's edges are ruffled with spits and coves and bays where islanders have staked out their private bits of paradise.

On your way on or off the island, don't overlook another favourite local gathering spot. The pub at Shingle Bay right next to the ferry terminal has great food—including take-out if you're in a hurry. It also has great ocean views and a very welcoming atmosphere, and it's all topped off by the trademark Hornby sod roof.

Hornby Island's Parks

Several of Hornby's most beautiful spots are protected as parks and open to all. The thousand-metre white sand beach of **Tribune Bay Provincial Park** is one of the coast's **all-time best swimming beaches**. This day-use-only walk-in park has picnic and toilet facilities, the waters are safe and warm, and it's just half a kilometre from the Co-op Store down Salt Spray Rd.

Another must-see outdoor spot is **Helliwell Provincial Park**. It's on top of the high bluffs that form an arm of Tribune Bay. The

Tribune Bay's white sand beach

Helliwell Provincial Park, another "must-see"

panoramic views from the carved sandstone headlands are unbeatable. Look down below for passing seals and sea lions, the occasional porpoise and killer whale, and a variety of sea birds. The park includes a **protected underwater area** extending from St. John Point to Lambert Channel. Just off the point is **Flora Island** where **divers** come to trade hard stares with the rare (and harmless) **six-gill basking sharks**. In summer the sharks loll in the warm waters along the underwater ledge at the south end of the island. The park's grassy headlands are backed by stands of cedar, maple, alder, holly and old-growth fir, and looped with trails. An easy 5-km **circle trail** leads from the parking lot along the edge of Helliwell Bluffs and then through the Douglas fir forest. You'll also find **picnic grounds**, **toilets** and a **trail guide** and information shelter in the park. To get there from the four-way stop by the Co-op Store, take St. John's Point Rd north, then east to the parking lot at the far end of the road.

The top of Mt. Geoffrey is also protected in a regional park, and it adjoins great stretches of Crown land. Hike to the top of **Mt. Geoffrey Regional Park** for wonderful views over the Strait of Georgia to Denman Island and Fanny Bay on Vancouver Island. There's a whole slew of other **island hiking trails** to explore, including hikes along the benchlands below Mt. Geoffrey and around the base of the mountain from an old road at Ford's Cove. See Charles Kahn's *Hiking the Gulf Islands* for details, or buy a map at the Co-op Store and ask obliging-looking locals for advice. But hiking is not the be-all and end-all of Hornby Island outdoor action. There are lots of ways to see the island from fresh perspectives—renting an ocean **kayak** or taking a **horseback ride**, chartering a **fishing or sightseeing boat** or trying your hand at **scuba diving**. (For details on recreational services, pick up the Hornby and Denman Islands Visitor's Guide, phone Denman/Hornby Tourist Services at 250-335-2293, or visit the Denman Island website www.denmanis.bc.ca/features). If you plan to stay on Hornby, reserve accommodations or campsites well in advance.

Courtenay

Vancouver Island has another set of twin communities 62 km north of Parksville–Qualicum. Courtenay basks in a wide agricultural valley between the ocean and the imposing white forehead of the **Comox Glacier**. Its sister community of Comox is a few kilometres east on the peninsula that hooks around Comox Harbour. Courtenay was the centre for early logging and farming operations in the Comox Valley, and Comox (originally known as Port Augusta) was the sheltered harbour for ships bringing supplies to these isolated communities before the roads were built. The Comox Valley was a quiet place until recently, and it still has a wide-open rural feel. But the tide is turning. The Courtenay–Comox area is fast becoming a major tourist/retirement community and jumping-off point for outdoor adventure.

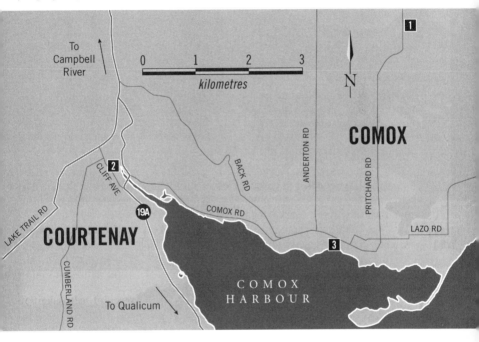

Mt. Washington and Forbidden Plateau

Two big draws to the Courtenay–Comox area are the winter skiing and summer hiking areas in the mountains west of Courtenay: Mt. Washington Resort and the Forbidden Plateau Ski Area. In winter, Mt. Washington Resort is **Vancouver Island's biggest ski facility** where you'll have lots of opportunity to cavort in the thick white stuff, including 42 **downhill**

What to See

- ☐ **1** Comox Air Force Museum
- ☐ **2** Courtenay & District Museum
- ☐ **3** Filberg Heritage Lodge & Park

runs, a **snowboard** park, 40 km of **cross country trails** and even night-lit **snow tubing**. It's a friendly, down-to-earth family and group-outing facility with lots of beginner areas.

Tubing on the Puntledge River near Courtenay

You can rent private condos or stay in the lodge, and a $75-million hotel-condo village is under construction. Forbidden Plateau Ski Area in Strathcona Provincial Park has been in action since days of wooden skis and bear trap bindings. It's a smaller resort with a day lodge, 24 **downhill** runs and a sizable helping of intermediate and advanced **cross country** runs. Experienced **backcountry skiers** can also head for untracked wilderness from the Forbidden Plateau Ski Area. One ski trek is a two-day traverse through alpine meadows from Forbidden Plateau Ski Area to Mt. Washington, and the other is a long two-day trip from Forbidden Plateau up the northeast ridge of nearby Mt Becher.

These two ski resorts continue to draw visitors during the summer. A network of linked **hiking trails** from trailheads at Mt. Washington ski village and Forbidden Plateau ski lodge offer plenty of choices from **easy sub-alpine loops** to lung-bursting backpacks into **deep wilderness destinations**, including the **Mt. Comox Glacier**. One of the most popular short hikes is the loop trail to pretty Lake Helen Mackenzie. The 3-km trail starts at Mt. Washington Ski Area's Nordic Trail parking lot and wends through splashes of purple, pink and yellow wildflowers in Paradise Meadows to the lake. Mt. Washington Resort also runs a **chairlift** so summer visitors can ooh and aah at the spectacular mile-high vista of sea and mountains. "Extreme" **mountain bikers** can buy a lift ticket and rip down steep bike tracks as many times as their bodies can take it. There are also **guided trail rides** for those who want to explore the area on **horseback**. Forbidden Plateau Ski Area also runs a summer chairlift to **alpine hiking** and a **campground** next to the lodge. The lodge has lots of activities, and nearby alpine lakes are known for good late summer **fishing**. (For more information, Mt. Washington Resort at 250-338-1386, fax 250-338-7295, snow phone 250-338-1515, or website www.vquest.com/alpine/, or Forbidden Plateau Ski Area at 250-334-4744 or 250-334-4428.)

Courtenay is the Comox Valley's major service centre and a good home base for local

Cumberland: A Side Trip to Comox Valley History

"Ginger" Goodwin

Just a short drive from Courtenay in the foothills of the Beaufort Mountains is the little village of Cumberland. This **historic mining community** was once the second-largest coal producer in North America. In the 1880s coal baron Robert Dunsmuir bought up all of the rich coal fields in the vicinity and founded Cumberland, naming it after the famous English coal-producing district. Before long some 13,000 workers from all over the globe, including the British Isles, Italy, Hungary, Japan and China, arrived to toil in the maze of coal-dark Cumberland mines. Dunsmuir brought in so many Chinese workers—they were paid far less than white miners and forced to do the most dangerous jobs—that turn-of-the-century Cumberland had the biggest Chinatown north of San Francisco. It was just one of the town's many neighbourhoods separated from each other by class and ethnicity.

The workers' pay was pitiful and conditions were extremely dangerous. Miners crawled on hands and knees through dank underground seams with only caged canaries to warn of deadly methane or carbon dioxide gases. Mining disasters were terrifyingly familiar to every local resident. After a lethal gas leak at Bonanza Number Four, a witness described how the dead bodies were carried to the surface and laid out row after row at the pithead. Nearly 300 miners died in gas explosions between 1884 and 1912. Neglect of worker safety and wage cuts turned Cumberland into a hotbed of labour unrest. Cumberland miners were front and centre in the bitter and often bloody coal strike of 1912–14. One miner named Albert "Ginger" Goodwin was a key player in the strike, and he was seen by authorities as a Russian-style revolutionary and troublemaker. In 1918 Goodwin was shot dead by a bounty hunter just outside Cumberland, and many people believed that the police were behind the slaying. Goodwin's death provoked the Vancouver General Strike. A mile-long funeral procession followed his body down Cumberland's Dunsmuir Avenue to the cemetery where his bones still lie under a stone inscribed "the worker's friend." (To find out more about this important BC character, we recommend the book *Ginger: The Life and Death of Albert Goodwin*, by Susan Mayse.) But Cumberland's days were already numbered. Demand for coal fell off in the 1920s, and the last mine closed in the 1960s. Today little remains of the rowdy coal mining city that was once king of the valley, but Cumberland's Dunsmuir Ave is still lined with turn-of-the-century buildings, recently spiffed up with antique shops and gift boutiques. Coal-dust memories are kept alive in the **Cumberland Cultural Centre and Museum** at the corner Dunsmuir Ave and First St (250-336-2445). To get to Cumberland take Hwy 19 south from Courtenay, turn right at Royston Rd and follow it to Cumberland.

Comox Valley Recreation, Accommodations and Services

Recreation
Bicycle rentals
Kayak/Canoe rentals
Fishing/Boat
charters/rentals
Scuba diving charters
Golf courses
Horseback riding
Skiing
Hiking
(Comox District
Mountaineering Club
250-336-2130 or
250-334-2270)

Accommodations
Bed & Breakfasts
Hotels/Motels
Inns/Resorts
Campgrounds
RV Parks

Services
Travel InfoCentres
Restaurants
Pubs
Cafés
Grocery stores
Banks/ATMs
Major shopping centres
Health care centre

recreation. Along the highway at the southern outskirts of Courtenay is a strip of restaurants and motels. This is the place to find moderately priced eats and sleeps. Farther up the highway around 5th Street is the old and still vital Courtenay town centre, an unpretentious charmer with its heritage buildings, colourful flower baskets, gift shops and super-friendly feel. To get closer to Courtenay's friendly ways, stay in one of its more than twenty B&Bs ranging from fine heritage homes on the waterfront to a verandah-wrapped South African style rancher deep in the forest.

If you want to lap up a little local history, visit the **Courtenay & District Museum** at 360 Cliffe Ave with its displays on fossils, pioneer history and First Nations culture, including a scale model of a Big House and mockups of a pioneer kitchen and blacksmith shop. Its most popular exhibit is a life-sized replica of an **Elasmosaur**. The bones of this ferocious-looking 80-million-year-old marine reptile were unearthed by amateur fossil hunters at nearby Puntledge River. It was the first major fossil find west of the BC Rockies, and the site is now preserved as a heritage site. But you can still try your hand at **fossil hunting** in the Comox Valley. Just ask for directions to hot fossil spots at the museum (250-334-3611). (For more information contact the Comox Visitor InfoCentre, 240 Cliffe Ave, Courtenay, BC V9N 2L3, phone 250-334-3234, email chamber@mars.ark.com, website www.tourism-comox-valley.bc.ca.)

▶ Comox Valley Annual Events

February
Trumpeter Swan Festival

March
Art Auction

April
Comox Valley Snow to Surf Race

May
Empire Days
Brian McLean Annual Mini Sprint Tri-K
Triathlon (Courtenay).
Buskers Fair (Courtenay)

June
Comox Harbour Opening Day
(Comox Marina)

July
Comox Nautical Days (Downtown Comox)
Courtenay Youth Music Festival

August
Filberg Arts & Crafts Festival (Courtenay)

September
Comox Valley Fall Fair

October
Comox Valley Fall Home Show
Comox Recreation Centre

November
Christmas Bazaar

December
Christmas Craft Fair

For more information, Comox Valley
InfoCentre **250-334-3234**

Comox

Comox is best known as a pretty and affordable seaside community. To get to Comox from Courtenay, take Hwy 19 north across the Courtenay River and follow signs right onto Comox Rd. It turns into Comox Ave and runs through the centre of town. The Comox Marina with its new harbourside promenade is just two blocks right of Comox Ave on Port Augusta St. Walk past all those colourful working **fish-ing boats** tied up at the docks. You can sometimes buy **ocean-fresh fish or prawns** straight from the boat deck. Or try **catching your own fish** from the promenade. To spend some time on the water, **charter or rent a boat** and head out to sea. Some of the very best cruising on coast, including **Desolation Sound** and **Princess Louisa Inlet**, is just waiting to be explored.

Important Numbers

Police *911*

Ambulance *911*

Fire *911*

Cumberland Travel InfoCentre *250-334-2427*

Comox Valley Chamber of Commerce
250-334-3234 / fax *250-334-4908*
email *chamber@mars.ark.com*
website *www.vquest.com/cvchamber/*

Otherwise, continue down Comox Ave to **Filberg Heritage Lodge and Park** at Filberg Rd (250-339-2715). The wonderfully rustic Arts and Crafts-style lodge was built of BC native woods by Robert J. Filberg, president of Comox Logging Company. Now the public can enjoy the parklike grounds overlooking the Strait of Georgia. Stroll past colourful flowerbeds, shady rose arbours, a tumbling brook and a **petting zoo** for little folk. Explore the lodge and then indulge yourself in the charming **tea house** just steps from the beach (May–Sept, 250-339-1622). If your visit falls on the BC Day weekend, you're in luck. This is the site of the four-day **Filberg Festival** where up to 140 of BC's top (jury-selected) craftspeople show off their handiwork. (Festival information, 250-334-9242.)

Comox is the home to a major Canadian Forces Base and a large military contingent. Aviation enthusiasts may be interested in the **Comox Air Force Museum** (located on Little River Rd), which contains more aviation memorabilia than any other military museum in Canada. Open seven days a week, June through August, 10 a.m. to 4 p.m.

For those wishing to cross the Strait of Georgia to Powell River (Westview terminal) and the Sunshine Coast, the BC ferry departs from the Little River ferry terminal in Comox (For information 1-800-223-3779).

A bird's-eye view of Comox

NORTH TO CAMPBELL RIVER

Big Mike

The Campbell River

Highlights

Pastoral surroundings

*World-renowned
fishing spots*

*Abundant birds and
marine wildlife*

*Hiking, rock climbing and
back-country skiing*

Canoeing and kayaking

Snowfields and glaciers

*Stands of pristine
rain forest*

From Courtenay the highway winds north through the heart of Comox Valley agricultural country to Campbell River 45 km away. Green pastures stretch under a soft blue sky, dotted with modern farmhouses and sun-shadowed barns. Watch for signs to **roadside stands** where you can buy produce—some of it organic—fresh from the garden. And keep your eyes peeled for a whole different breed of farm animal. **Emus** are being farmed on Vancouver Island—mostly for breeding pairs. But the lean red meat is catching on with cholesterol-wise carnivores, and emu oil is making the headlines as an unbeatable moisturizer and salve for joint inflammation.

It's hard to imagine that this open agricultural land was once dark with centuries-old rain forest. Before the 1890s only a handful of farmers ventured into the dense bush to clear out "stump farms" between Courtenay and Campbell River. But handloggers, then railway logging syndicates, soon set to work. The Comox Logging and Railway Company laid more than 160 km of tracks across the Comox Valley to seize the timber treasure. The old-growth forest was stripped off, the logs were boomed up and towed off to South Island and Vancouver mills. The area around Merville just north of Comox was logged before 1900 and in 1919 was settled by World War I veterans, who with financial assistance from the government tried to turn the rocky, thin-soiled, thick-stumped clear-cuts into working farms. Merville took its name from the Canadians' first field headquarters in France. It was also the boyhood home of BC novelist Jack Hodgins and the inspiration for his *Spit Delaney's Island* and his other popular novels set on Vancouver Island.

Marshland north of Miracle Beach

Miracle Beach Provincial Park

About halfway from Courtenay to Campbell River, when the road sidles toward the sea, you'll see the turnoff to Miracle Beach Provincial Park. Put on the brakes—this is **one of BC's best parks.** A drive through tall sun-dappled second-growth hemlock and Douglas fir trees is a reminder of the pre-logging days when rain forest cloaked the coast (and also a reminder of nature's regenerative powers). Generous **campsites** are snuggled under a canopy of mossy trees, trails loop through the forest, and playgrounds and hot showers make family camping more fun than work. But the star attraction is Miracle Beach. Its name comes from a Kwakwaka'wakw legend about a supernatural stranger who appeared on the beach and miraculously transformed a Native princess into Mitlenatch Island. But the beach itself is magical, if not miraculous. Plunge into the ocean for a **swim,** count all the **tide pool** creatures, or just wiggle into the warm sand and watch the clouds drift toward the blue mainland mountains. The seasonal visitor centre has **nature displays,** and park interpreters give talks on everything from the stars above to the lowly slug. (Camping reservations 1-800-689-9025.)

Oyster River Regional Park

Just up the road is the Oyster River Regional Park and the start of the popular "two-pub walk." Park in the Oyster River Regional Park lot, and quaff a brew at Fisherman's Lodge. Then light out on the trail down the Oyster River and head north along the beach past Woodhus Slough to Salmon Point. If you're a birder, bring your binoculars. **Birds galore** flutter through nine different habitats ranging from seashore to marshland to woodlands. Sharp-eyed birdwatchers have recorded more than 190 species. (For a bird checklist pick up the pamphlet "A Nature Guide to Woodhus Slough" at the Country Junction Market and Deli across the road from the Miracle Beach turnoff.) It's about an hour's walk to Salmon Point Pub. Then settle into a foaming pint and watch all the boat traffic on the Strait of Georgia against a panoramic backdrop of mainland mountains. By the way, your route retraces part of the **turn-of-the-century bush-and-beach trail** linking Courtenay and Campbell River. The trip was a rough two-day slog and many a traveller stopped at Walter and Annie Woodhus's little hotel near Oyster River for hospitality and libations. The hotel is just a memory now, but the tradition of cordiality and good drink lives on. To get to Oyster River Regional Park follow the highway across the Oyster River and take an immediate right turn onto Glenora Rd. Turn right again on Regent Rd and follow it to the parking lot.

Campbell River

Campbell River is just about midway between Victoria and Port Hardy, and it has one foot in the North Island and the other in the South Island. Campbell River is a true North Island community with roots deep in lumbering and fishing. Smack in the centre of town at the waterfront mall is the high rigger "Big Mike," a carved wooden lumberjack swinging from a harness way up a spar pole. Big Mike is an icon of Campbell River's proud century-long logging heritage. Just north of town is the belching red-and-white-striped smokestack of the Elk River Falls pulp and paper mill. After the mill opened in 1952 Campbell River sprouted from a small town to one of Vancouver Island's major communities. Despite industry-wide downsizing, many Campbell River families still make their living directly or indirectly from the North Island forest industry. Commercial fishing is another longtime income source in Campbell River. One look at the forest of fish boat masts behind the downtown government marina breakwater tells the tale. Fishing for a living—however perilous the future may be—is still at the heart of Campbell River life.

But Campbell River is also a South Island town with its eyes fixed on tourism as the way to smooth out the bumps of a roller coaster resource-based economy. It's been a sports fishing resort since 1896 when a visiting British angler published an account of catching nearly twenty spring salmon averaging a staggering 50 pounds. After that Campbell River and its incredible salmon runs were worldwide news. By the 1940s two classic fishing resorts—Painter's Lodge just north of Campbell River and April Point Lodge on Quadra Island—were catering to celebrities from Zane Grey and the King of Siam to Bing Crosby, Bob Hope and Gary Cooper. The town still proudly calls itself "the **Salmon Capital of the World**," and salmon fishing is the major tourist draw. Campbell River operators offer sports fishing services for any budget, from luxury packages for the deep-pockets clientele to independent charters and guides to do-it-yourself boat rentals

▶ Fish Calendar

Chinook/King/Spring	Year-round
Tyee (Chinook over 13.5 kg/30 lbs)	July–September
Coho/Silver	June–September
Pink	August–September
Sockeye	August
Chum	September–November
Steelhead (summer run)	August–October
Steelhead (winter run)	November–April
Trout/Char	Year-round

For sports fishing updates, call Campbell River Tourism at **1-800-463-4FUN** or visit their very informative website at **www.vquest.com/crtourism/**.

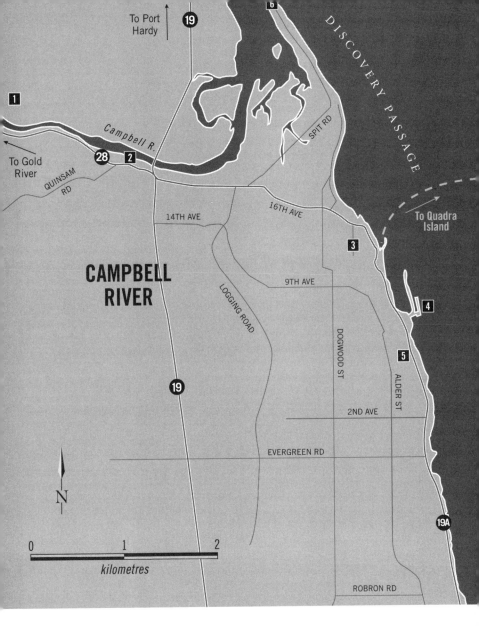

To Port
Hardy
19

To Gold
River

QUINSAM RD

Campbell R.

28 **2**

14TH AVE

**CAMPBELL
RIVER**

LOGGING ROAD

SPIT RD

16TH AVE

9TH AVE

DOGWOOD ST

2ND AVE

EVERGREEN RD

ALDER ST

19

N

0   1   2

kilometres

ROBRON RD

19A

D I S C O V E R Y   P A S S A G E

To Quadra
Island

b

3

4

5

What to See

- ☐ **1** Elk Falls Provincial Park
- ☐ **2** Haig-Brown House
- ☐ **3** Shoppers Row
- ☐ **4** Discovery Fishing Pier
- ☐ **5** Campbell River Museum
- ☐ **6** Tyee Spit

▶ **Campbell River Annual Events**

April
Campbell River Floating Boat Show

May
Storey Creek Mixed Open Golf Tournament

June
World Salmon Guide Tournament
Miracle Beach Sandcastle Competition

July
Canada Day Celebrations
Children's Festival

August
Annual Dog Show
Summer Festival (Nunns Creek Park)
Sea & Cedar Festival
Festivals by the Sea

September
Great Salmon Race

November
Folk Weekend (Strathcona Park Lodge)

For more information, Campbell River
*InfoCentre **250-287-4636***

and public boat launches. Many local marinas welcome boaters, and local custom processors will freeze, can, smoke or vacuum-package your catch.

Campbell River offers many more activities for visitors as well. Local ecotourism, outdoor recreation and historical adventuring industries are expanding. Campbell River is the gateway to **Strathcona Provincial Park**, a huge wilderness park that was preserved at the turn of the century, and which now offers wonderful opportunities for **hiking, rock climbing, backcountry skiing, swimming, sailing, canoeing, camping and lots of wildlife viewing**. The surrounding mountains are full of lakes and rivers, including McIvor, Buttle and Upper Campbell lakes and the Gold and Nimpkish rivers. Anglers go after game fish such as salmon, steelhead, cutthroat trout and rainbow trout.

Discovery Passage, running between Campbell River and Quadra Island, is not just a hot spot for salmon fishing. Its clear, fast-moving, oxygen-rich water is abloom with undersea life like strawberry anemones, wolf eels, octopuses, sponges and corals. A new **scuba diving** spot is the artificial reef created when the decommissioned Canadian destroyer HMSC *Columbia* was deliberately sunk near Maud Island in 1996. The beautiful **Discovery Islands** off Campbell River with their sheltered coves and waterways are prime destinations for **cruising and sea kayaking. Killer whale watching** in Johnstone Strait, **birdwatching** at the Mitlenatch Island bird sanctuary, **black bear tours** to Toba Inlet in breathtaking Desolation Sound are only a few favourite picks among the many ecotourism activities. Campbell River's First Nations peoples invite visitors to **paddle** a great Lekwiltok war canoe through Discovery Passage or take a water taxi to the Kwagiulth Museum on Quadra Island. **Mine, mill, forestry and fish hatchery tours** show off all the modern techniques used in Campbell River's resource industries.

With so much to do in Campbell River, a good first stop is the downtown **InfoCentre** where the staff can suggest activities that suit you to a "T." It's located at 1235 Shoppers Row in the well-marked Tyee Plaza.

In and around downtown Campbell River are several visitor attractions that are well worth a visit. The town has spent millions of dollars sprucing up its waterfront, and further improvements are on the drawing board. So far Campbell River has a new **foreshore park**, eye-catching waterfront stores, restaurants and marinas, and a **shoreline walk** running from downtown south along Discovery Passage to the Discovery Fishing Pier. From the InfoCentre head for nearby Foreshore Park where the Island Hwy (Hwy 19A) jogs west at the light to become Shoppers Row. Take in the views across Discovery Passage to beautifully rugged Quadra Island on the far side. The contemporary life of the coast is written in the marine traffic that hauls through Discovery Passage—commercial fish boats and freighters, tugs with log booms in tow, Alaska-bound barges, cruise ships, speed boats brimming with red-vested sports fishermen, and yachts heading out for adventure. Slide along the walkway south to the **government marina** and check out all the boats along the docks. Then make your way out to the 180-metre **Discovery Fishing Pier** on the far side of the marina breakwater. This is Canada's first-ever saltwater fishing pier, and since the day it opened in 1987 it's been swarming with ever-hopeful anglers of all ages.

Salmon fishermen share Discovery Passage with a cruise ship

Then make your way back north toward the centre of town around **Shoppers Row**. Antique lovers will find some "ye olde" stuff to pique their interest in adjacent streets, and local restaurants and cafés—some a combo of North Island friendly and South Island food-savvy—are good choices for a lunch stop. If you're staying overnight, check out the play at **Tidemark Theatre** across Shoppers Row from the InfoCentre. You can't miss the renovated Art Deco theatre that's a centrepiece of Campbell River culture. Just stepping into the old theatre lobby is a nostalgia trip. For a dose of BC coast history and lore, spend some time at another cultural institution, the Page Eleven Bookstore at 1070A Shoppers Row.

Just south of town at 470 Island Hwy (Hwy 19A) at 5th Ave is another linchpin of local culture, the **Campbell River Museum** (250-287-3103). If the view of Discovery Channel from the lobby's floor-to-ceiling windows doesn't knock your socks off, the sound and light presentation of "The Treasures of Siwidi" will. Its focal point is a collection of brilliant contemporary Northwest Coast masks by Willie Seaweed and members of the Hunt family. The museum also has displays on pioneer history, and changing exhibits. The small museum shop has First Nations arts and crafts and an interesting assortment of books.

The ultimate in Discovery Passage views, however, is found at **Painter's Lodge** off the Island Highway (Hwy 19A) just north of town at 1625 MacDonald Rd (250-598-3366, reservations 1-800-663-7090, or website www.obmg.com). The venerable old fishing resort burnt to the ground on Christmas Eve 1985, but a big new hotel has risen in its place. Oak Bay Marine Group's luxury lodge and conference centre has all the bells and whistles you could ask for—fitness centre, jogging track, swimming pool, tennis courts, elegant dining room, lots of recreation activities and eco-adventure tours and a fishing

The Tyee Club

Shipwright Ted Painter, a pioneer in Campbell River's sports fishing industry and first owner of Painter's Lodge, crafted the classically beautiful little rowboats known as "tyee boats." In 1924 Painter and a handful of dedicated sports fishermen founded the famed Tyee Club. *Tyee* is a Native word for "chief," and a tyee in angling lingo is a chinook salmon weighing 13.5 kg (30 lbs) or more. Tyee Club membership is open to anyone who lands a tyee in strict accordance with club rules—unaided, on a single hook, using a hand-operated reel and 20-lb line from a hand-powered rowboat in the "Tyee Pool" off Tyee Spit. The chal-

lenges of catching a fighting Pacific salmon under such stringent conditions are far greater than ordinary salmon fishing, but to many sports fishers the rewards are that much sweeter. Every year hundreds of dedicated anglers sign up at the little green clubhouse by the Tyee Pool for the chance to join the elite roster of Tyee club members. In 1986 Painter's granddaughter Catherine Painter won the season's Tyee Man Trophy for a 25-kg (55-lb) tyee. But the all-time record belongs to Texan Walter Shutts for a 32-kg (71.5-lb) chinook caught in 1968.

Campbell River's waterfront walkway

centre with everything you need to bucktail for coho, troll or mooch for chinook, or row the Tyee Pool for the mighty tyee. Sink deep into a cushioned chair in the Tyee Pub and watch an indigo sky darken over Quadra Island beyond the crystal curtain of bevelled glass. Just across the water is Oak Bay's new acquisition, the April Point Lodge. A hotel water taxi ferries guests across to what was once the genteel rival of Painter's Lodge in the celebrity fishing lodge trade. The views from **April Point Lodge's** deck back over Discovery Passage to Campbell River, with its backdrop of snowy peaks, is equally pleasing. Even the striped smokestack at Elk Falls Mills looks picturesque in this setting.

Roderick Haig-Brown

The forces of development and conservation have long been in conflict with each other along the coast, and Campbell River has had its fair share of controversy. One of the wisest voices in the fray was Campbell River's beloved writer, outdoorsman, conservationist and judge Roderick Haig-Brown. His 1923 farmhouse beside the Campbell River, Above Tide, is now a BC Heritage Property. People come from all over the world to step into the book-lined study that opens onto a tree-shaded garden running down to the fast-flowing Campbell River. It was here that he wrote the fly-fishing books that made him a modern-day Izaak Walton. Haig-Brown was also an early and ardent conservationist. He wrote movingly about resource management in *The Living Land* and dedicated years to preserving the Campbell River system and assuring the survival of west coast salmon stocks. It is largely due to his efforts that the Fraser River, which runs from east-central BC through Vancouver, was never dammed. His legacy lives on at Above Tide, now the

Campbell River Recreation, Accommodations and Services

Recreation	Resorts
Bicycle rentals	*Hotels/Motels*
Kayak/Canoe rentals	*Campgrounds*
Fishing/Boat charters/rentals	*RV Parks*
Scuba diving charters	**Services**
Golf courses	*InfoCentre*
Adventure tour charters	*Restaurants*
Horseback riding	*Pubs*
Hiking	*Banks/ATMs*
Accommodations	*Gas/Service stations*
Bed & Breakfasts	*Several Grocery stores*
Inns	*Shopping malls*

Roderick Haig-Brown

Haig-Brown House Education Centre. The centre offers tours, retreats and workshops on Haig-Brown's favourite subjects, from conservation, writing and natural history to gardening and fly fishing. The Haig-Brown house is also a B&B where you can enjoy big country breakfasts with generous helpings of homemade jam and fresh fruit straight from the lovingly tended gardens. From the breakfast room you can watch the morning sun play across the grapevines on the old verandah.

To get to the Haig-Brown House, follow the Island Highway (Hwy 19A) to the lights at the intersection with Hwy 19. Follow the directing sign to Gold River (Hwy 28) straight through the stoplight and watch for the small B&B sign to your right at 2250 Campbell River Rd (Hwy 28). (For information on events and B&B reservations, phone 250-286-6646, fax 250-286-6694, or email kdbhbh@oberon.ark.com.)

Just west of the Haig-Brown House on Hwy 28 is the well-signed left-hand turnoff to the **Quinsam River Hatchery** (250-287-9564). Follow the winding road 2.5 km to the hatchery. There you can try the self-guided tour, with loads of information on the life cycle of salmon and an opportunity to see how the hatchery rears and releases about 2 million juvenile chinook and coho a year. Visitor facilities include a picnic site and nature trails.

Less than a kilometre west of the hatchery on Hwy 28 is 122-site **Elk Falls Provincial Park** on the banks of the Quinsam River (250-954-4600, Reservations 1-800-689-9025). In winter you can fish for Quinsam River steelhead right from your riverside campsite, and in summer there are excellent walking trails and cool swimming holes at the Elk Falls day-use area. But the star attraction in these parts is Elk Falls, a foaming cascade of water that tumbles deep into a rocky gorge and then cuts away through a high-walled canyon. This park—only 2 km from downtown Campbell River—is a great base camp for exploring the Campbell River and the North Island.

Discovery Passage and Ripple Rock

The steady parade of marine traffic past Campbell River gives no hint of the dangers awaiting mariners in nearby waters. From the south, stiff winds drive up across the Strait of Georgia, a 65-km stretch of open water, toward the high bluffs of Cape Mudge on the southern tip of Quadra Island. And from the north, tidal rivers of up to 15 knots surge through the constricted passageways of Seymour Narrows, just above Campbell River. The combination of open fetches and narrow waterways creates tidal chaos. "This part of Gulf [Strait] of Georgia forms a sort of playground for the waters," the captain of a British survey ship warned in 1860, "in which they frolic utterly regardless of tidal rules. They relax for a scant ten minutes every six hours when the tide turns." The government built a lighthouse on Cape Mudge in 1898 to warn sailors of the peril, but dozens of ships have

The Haig-Brown House Education Centre carries on the legacy

foundered in the rapids and rough waters.

The single biggest hazard to marine traffic was the infamous Ripple Rock, twin peaks hidden under the water in the middle of the 1 kilometre-wide Seymour Narrows. At low tide the south peak was only 3 metres below the surface and the north peak only 6 metres down. The fierce tidal currents racing through this constricted passage were made a dozen times more dangerous by the huge whirlpools, overfalls and sudden eddies swirling around the treacherous rock. It's estimated that twenty large ships and perhaps a hundred smaller vessels were destroyed at Ripple Rock and 114 lives were lost.

In 1942 a 50-metre drilling barge was anchored over the rock and drillers set about blowing the devil rock out of the channel. Within days the 10-tonne steel cables anchoring the barge were snapped by the awesome currents through Seymour Narrows. The plan was shelved when a whirlpool opened up under nine workers leaving the barge in a boat and sucked them down to their watery graves. In the early 1950s a whole new plan was approved and work began in 1955. Sixty miners working day and night for two and a half years drilled 175 metres down on nearby Maud Island, then tunnelled 884 metres across the seabed to the base of Ripple Rock and bored up 100 metres into each peak.

They packed 34 boxcar loads of dynamite—nearly 1.35 million kg—into a honeycomb of bore holes in the twin peaks. On April 5, 1958 Ripple Rock was blown out of the water in **the biggest non-nuclear blast in history**. Sailors navigating Discovery Passage can breathe a little easier now that Ripple Rock is just a memory.

Important Numbers

Police 911

Fire 911

Ambulance 911

Hospital 250-287-7111

Campbell River & District Chamber of Commerce 250-287-4636 / fax: 250-286-6490

Strathcona Provincial Park

Campbell River is the front door to 253,773-ha Strathcona Provincial Park just 45 minutes west on Hwy 28 (250-954-4600). This rugged wilderness is so spectacular that in 1911 it became the very first park created in British Columbia. Its vast boundaries enclose **snowfields** and **glaciers**, dozens of saw-toothed mountain peaks, including six of Vancouver Island's seven **highest peaks**, and one of the ten **highest waterfalls in the world**, Della Falls. It's spangled with turquoise lakes and alpine tarns and laced with rivers, streams and cataracts. In summer bright displays of heather, lupine, Indian paintbrush and moss campion light up subalpine meadows. In the valleys are centuries-old stands of **pristine rain forest**. Three spectacularly scenic nature conservancy areas covering more than 122,000 hectares have been set aside to preserve undisturbed natural environments. Wildlife is plentiful, including distinctive Vancouver Island species of the Roosevelt elk, the coast black-tailed deer and the Vancouver Island marmot and wolf. Best of all, this spectacular park never seems to get crowded.

Upper Campbell Lake from Strathcona Park Lodge

Strathcona is primarily a wilderness park and is largely undeveloped, except for the privately owned **Strathcona Park Lodge and Outdoor Education Centre** just east of the park boundary at Upper Campbell Lake, and public campgrounds, picnic grounds and boat launches around Buttle Lake. The lodge and education centre is a good place to get lots of information about the park. It functions as an unofficial park headquarters. (The park itself has a ranger station but no visitor centre.) You might even want to tempt yourself with the lodge's famous fresh and healthy buffets or make a reservation for a room or lakeside cabin (250-286-3122 or Super, Natural British Columbia Accommodations, 1-800-663-6000). Its excellent **outdoor education program** has been teaching outdoor skills to people of all ages for more than twenty years, including sailing, rock climbing, back country hiking, canoeing, and whitewater and sea kayaking. The popular "Best of Adventure" program lets novices sample outdoor activities under the guidance of certified instructors. Down on the beach behind the lodge are stacks of multicoloured **canoes** and **kayaks** as well as **sailboats** and **motor boats for rent**, and Upper

Campbell Lake with its encircling mountain peaks just begs to be explored.

A paved road running south from Hwy 28 along the shore of Buttle Lake to the Westmin mine is the only access road to the wild heart of the park. All that wilderness adds up to backpacker heaven. Secluded **Ralph River campgrounds** (76 sites) down the paved road at the south end of Buttle Lake is a favourite with **high country hikers**. But there are also lots of **easy and moderate hikes** in the Buttle Lake area, including eight easy nature walks and short trails and eight more moderate day or half-day hikes. **Buttle Lake campgrounds** (85 sites) just west of the bridge between Upper Campbell and Buttle lakes and south of Hwy 28 is a family-oriented campground with an **adventure playground** and daytime **nature talks**. In July and August friendly Buttle Lake Campground hosts serve up lots of information, brochures and insider tips about local recreational activities. For hiking details, pick up *Hiking Trails III* (1996), published by Vancouver Island Trails Information Society.

It's no wonder that water sports are big at Strathcona Provincial Park. Upper Campbell Lake and Buttle Lake are part of a staggeringly long and lovely lake chain. One of the most popular **canoe trips** is the leisurely three-day 31-km paddle from Buttle Lake Campground at the north end of Buttle Lake to the Ralph River Campground at the south end with overnights at four small marine campgrounds on the lake's western shore. **Rock climbing** is the other sport that's popular for those in the know. Crest Creek Crags has 19 different rock faces ranging from beginner to advanced climbing. Anchors are already in place and a map near the parking area lists all the routes. All you have to do is find a route that matches your skill, crank up your courage, rig up and away you go. But remember to climb with a partner, use a rope and wear a helmet. New climbers can get help from an instructor certified by the Association of Canadian Mountain Guides. Strathcona Park Lodge can point you in the right direction. Crest Creek Crags is near the western park boundary south of Hwy 28. The turnoff is marked with a rock climbing symbol.

Gold River

Drive to the end of Hwy 28 to experience Vancouver Island's stunning west coast and the little forestry town of Gold River, 89 km from Campbell River. Once a remote logging camp, Gold River burst into being as one of BC's newest planned communities in 1967 when a kraft pulp mill was built on the shore of deepwater Muchalat Inlet. Nearby Tree Farm Licence 19 and the **Gold River pulp mill** were the town's major sources of income, but the pulp mill closed in 1999. The closure has been a huge blow to the community, but many residents are looking to recreation in the rugged mountains and gorgeous waterways wrapped around this west coast town to generate an alternate source of income. Gold River is a neighbourly place with a range of visitor services,

The picturesque Gold River

Remote Muchalat Inlet on the west coast

including grocery stores, restaurants, motels and a good helping of B&Bs. Catch a fish and the friendly neighbourhood pub will cook it just the way you like it. **Sports fishing** is still a thriving west coast enterprise, and many local charter outfits take anglers out for steelhead in the winter, halibut in the spring and hefty chinook in high summer. Nootka Sound is a mecca for sports fishers, who can catch cod, red snapper and halibut in outside waters in the morning and angle for salmon in the protected waters of the sound later in the day. (For more information contact the Gold River Visitor InfoCentre at the Village Square Plaza, daily mid-May to late September, 250-283-2202, or browse the website at www.island.net/~goldriv/)

Spelunking in the Upana Caves 27 km from Gold River is an increasingly popular visitor attraction. A well-marked trail connects five caves, including the two-chambered Main Cave with a waterfall at the end of one passage, the marble-smooth Resurgence Cave with its toothy rock outcrops, and the spiralling Corner Cave. For a self-guided Upana Caves tour brochure or for guided caving expeditions, contact the Gold River Visitor InfoCentre (see above).

Coastal Workboat Cruises

Gold River is the home port for the MV *Uchuck III*'s west coast "workboat" cruises. Once a hidden treat for in-the-know travellers, they are fast being discovered. The *Uchuck* is a converted 1943 US minesweeper that is now the coastal workhorse of Nootka Sound and Kyuquot Sound. Depending on the day and time of year, your destination might be historic Yuquot (or Friendly Cove), the ancestral home of the Mowachaht/Muchalaht people of the Nuu-chah-nulth (formerly Nootka) nation. Yuquot was the site of the first contact between BC's First Nations people and European explorers. Captain James Cook sailed into Friendly Cove in 1779 where he was greeted by the great Chief Maquinna of the Mowachahts. This was the beginning of the otter fur trade that brought Europeans from a dozen nations to Vancouver Island. The site of Fort San Miguel in the late 1780s and early 1790s when Spain gave up claims to the Pacific Northwest, Yuquot is now a National Historic Site.

Or you might journey through Nootka Sound and out Esperanza Inlet to the open ocean of Kyuquot Sound and the First Nations village of Kyuquot. Along the way you'll discover the fascinating workaday world of coastal boats as the *Uchuck III* calls in at remote logging camps and fishing ports to pick up passengers and offload cargo— anything from a box of diapers to a brand-new refrigerator. On the way you might see gray whales, killer whales, bears and eagles. These coastal fjords are west coast wilderness at its spectacular best. (For information, Nootka Sound Service Ltd., 250-283-2325, 250-283-2515, fax 250-283-7582, email mvuchuck@island.net, website www.island.net/~/mvuchuck/.)

Quadra Island

Surprisingly rural, almost remote Quadra Island is only a 10-minute ferry ride from downtown Campbell River. Some Quadra Islanders are city folk who need to escape way back in the woods without a house in sight. Others live here for the island's magical tranquillity. For them life is at its best in a quiet cove where the wash of the tide and the cry of gulls are the only sounds breaking the silence. Still others are camper-truck types who want to be up and doing—fishing, hiking and canoeing—right in their own big back yard. And others just like living where they can drive past the stores clustered at Heriot Bay and Quathiaski Cove and know who's at the post office or in the pub from the cars out front.

Kwagiulth mask on display in April Point Lodge

What makes this place so special to Quadra Islanders also makes it ideal for island-hoppers. The north end of the island is a **heavily treed near-wilderness** area. A sheltered **chain of lakes** and a fabulous network of **hiking trails** attracts many visitors. The south end of the island is home to most of Quadra's residents and the site of the island's two villages, Quathiaski Cove and Heriot Bay. The south end has two prime visitor destinations—the Wewaikai Band's wonderful Kwagiulth Museum and Cultural Centre at Cape Mudge Village just north of the lighthouse, and the famous Cape Mudge lighthouse itself at the island's southwestern tip.

Quadra's rumpled shore also attracts lots of saltwater recreation aficionados. Almost half of Campbell River's list of **fishing hot spots** are along Quadra's coast. Some of the region's best **scuba diving** spots are also off Quadra, with sponges, tube worms, crimson

Getting to Quadra Island

From Campbell River

Drive aboard a BC Ferry at the Campbell River ferry terminal (downtown). 10 minutes crossing time; 17 sailings daily year round.

Note: fares collected as return fares.

For more information about travel on BC Ferries, see p. 8.

anemones, wolf eels, nudibranchs and octopus in abundance. Interest in local **sea kayaking** is growing, and Quadra Island has several protected bays, islets and a provincial marine park for exploring.

The BC ferry docks at picturesque **Quathiaski Cove**, where you can still see some of the old fish cannery houses from Quadra's industrial heyday. Just after the turn of the century, W.E. Anderson bought the cannery and hired up to 300 workers every season for his booming concern. Anderson brought in the notorious system of buying fish with the company's metal tokens instead of cash. Fishermen had no choice but to buy supplies from the company store, at hugely inflated prices. Angry fishermen grumbled about the token system, but it was Billy Assu, chief of the Wewaikai band of Cape Mudge, who put a stop to the practice. He kept the Native fleet tied up until Anderson reluctantly agreed to pay fishermen in cash. The Quathiaski cannery burned down in the 1940s, but Quathiaski Cove still wears the weathered charm of a true coastal fishing village.

Quathiaski Cove is also the nerve centre of island life. Within blocks of the ferry dock are three small plazas where you'll find most of the island's services, including a gas station, café, arts and crafts galleries, a bakery, a well-stocked market, a general store, a liquor outlet, a hardware store, a credit union, a realty office and the RCMP office. If you need anything "store-bought" or have a heavy case of the munchies, follow the road straight out of the ferry terminal, swing left on Harper Rd and then right onto Heriot Bay Rd. You'll pass by almost all the nearby stores. In summer there's also a **tourist information booth** and **Saturday farmers' market** with produce, crafts, home baking and other goodies at the Cove Centre. It's on your right just a couple of blocks above the terminal straight past Green Rd.

Cape Mudge Village and the Kwagiulth Museum and Cultural Centre

If you're ready to see what's down the south island's rustic winding roads, exit the ferry terminal and turn right onto Green Rd. The first destination is picturesque **Cape Mudge Village** and the wonderful ceremonial objects of the "Potlatch Collection" at the **Kwagiulth Museum and Cultural Centre**. Some of these items were confiscated by the Canadian government at the turn of the century and returned in the 1970s. The village is on Quadra's west coast about halfway to the southern tip of the island. Unspoiled Green Road, with its canopy of trees and peek-a-boo views of Discovery Passage, is a perfect first encounter with Quadra's tranquil beauty. Take the signed turnoff to Cape Mudge Village and drive south through the village to the museum parking lot. Step through the museum doors and into Kwagiulth life. The three-storey museum is shaped like a spiral seashell to suggest the organic growth and change of Kwagiulth culture

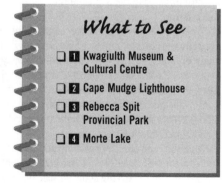

What to See

- [ ] **1** Kwagiulth Museum & Cultural Centre
- [ ] **2** Cape Mudge Lighthouse
- [ ] **3** Rebecca Spit Provincial Park
- [ ] **4** Morte Lake

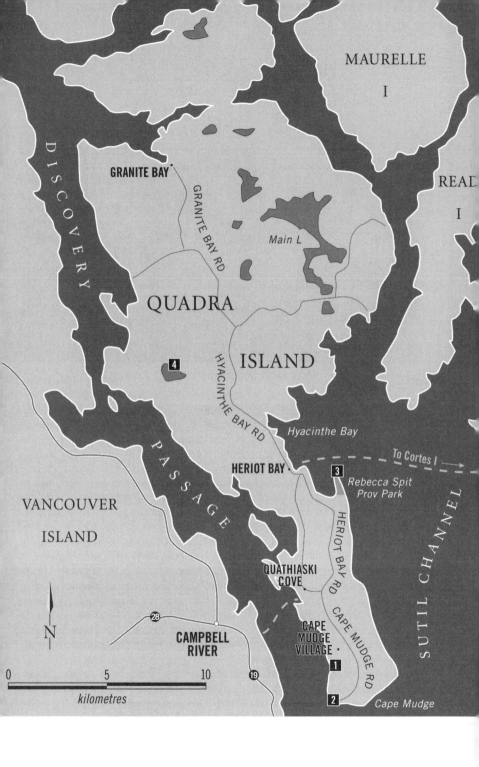

MAURELLE
I

REAL
I

GRANITE BAY

GRANITE BAY RD

Main L

QUADRA

ISLAND

4

DISCOVERY

HYACINTHE BAY RD

Hyacinthe Bay

To Cortes I

HERIOT BAY

3

Rebecca Spit
Prov Park

VANCOUVER

ISLAND

PASSAGE

HERIOT BAY RD

CAPE MUDGE RD

SUTIL CHANNEL

QUATHIASKI
COVE

N

28

CAMPBELL
RIVER

CAPE
MUDGE
VILLAGE

1

0   5   10

19

2

Cape Mudge

kilometres

Quadra Island ferry terminal at Quathiaski Cove

through time. Totem poles and a brilliant array of Kwagiulth masks and other ceremonial property are part of a tradition that extends back to a time known only from stories told orally, and forward to the children of Cape Mudge who are inheritors of the Kwagiulth culture. Historic photographs and contemporary displays on Kwagiulth history and culture round out the displays. You'll find a demonstration of the many ways cedar was used in the "Cedar: the Tree of Life" display, a summer puppet theatre dramatizing Kwagiulth stories, a gift shop and tours to see ancient **petroglyphs** along the shore at low tide. Ask about making a rubbing of a petroglyph at the museum or look for (but don't touch) the original petroglyphs by the seashore.

The real splendour of the museum is the Potlatch Collection of ceremonial regalia, especially the brilliantly carved dance masks. These masks were at the heart of Kwagiulth potlatches, great ceremonies where hundreds or thousands of guests gathered from villages all over the coast to witness the initiation of a dancer, assign an honorary name or celebrate a marriage, a birth or other special occasion. Feasts and lavish gift-giving were part of the event—*potlatch* means "to give" in Chinook jargon—and the host chief's largesse was a measure of his merit and authority. But the core of the potlatch were the songs, rituals and masked dances performed in the flickering firelight of the cedar Big House (for more on potlatches, see p. 324)

Before leaving Cape Mudge village, wander over to the pretty white-steepled **Quadra Island United Church** just across the parking lot. Its carved wall of yellow cedar was designed by the world-famous Haida artist Bill Reid and carved by Jim Hart. The carved emblem of two salmon enclosed in a circle signifies both the traditional fish symbolism of Christianity and the Kwagiulth reverence for the salmon as the staff of life. The cedar design is a hallmark of the church's success in blending Christian beliefs and traditional practices. When the first missionary teacher came to Quadra in 1878, the Wewaikai of Cape Mudge Village were the only Lekwiltok band to build a church. It's been the backbone of the Cape Mudge community for a hundred years. Under its high-pitched roof babies are baptized, couples are married, potlatches take place and the dead are sent to their eternal rest. The church also displays art works from other First Nations artists to signal its all-embracing attitude, and Buddhist services are held here every couple of months. It's truly a church for the whole community.

Cape Mudge and the Cape Mudge Lighthouse

The next stop is the southern tip of Cape Mudge and its famous lighthouse. Return to Green Rd and head south. The road swings east and becomes Weway Rd. At the T-junction with Cape Mudge Rd, turn right and follow the road to the intersection with Joyce Rd, turn right onto Joyce Rd and right again onto Lighthouse Rd, and park by the lighthouse. The white profile of the light station stands guard near the 60-metre bluffs of Cape Mudge, where a beacon has warned mariners of impending danger since 1898. This lighthouse was slated to be automated, but public outcry has put a stop to the plan for the time being.

The cheery red and white light station buildings are perched on one of the most scenic overlooks on Quadra Island. From the lighthouse you can look across the fast-flowing waters of Discovery Passage to Campbell River and the snowy peaks of Vancouver Island. It was from these bluffs that the fierce Lekwiltok confederacy of the Kwagiulth nation launched pirate raids on craft that had the temerity to sail past their stronghold. Several pitched battles took place nearby, and once the Lekwiltoks killed the whole crew of a Hudson's Bay Company vessel that had stopped near Cape Mudge for water. The Lekwiltok raided even farther afield, taking slaves and booty as far south as Puget Sound.

Today you can hike around the rocky beach in front of the light station at low tide and enjoy great views across the surging waters off Cape Mudge. But respect the fact that you are on Wewaikai band land.

At low tide, look closely at the scattering of granite boulders near the high-tide mark for the faintly etched lines of ancient **petroglyphs**. Watch for gulls, cormorants, herons and other shore birds around the offshore rocks, and eagles and ospreys fishing from snag trees. Occasionally a pod of killer whales slices its way up Discovery Passage. A few minutes' hike southwest of the lighthouse takes you to the dramatic **Tsa-Kwa-Luten Lodge** of the Wewaikai Band that straddles the bluff. It is surrounded by 445 hectares of meadow and forest where you can sometimes see black-tailed deer stepping

Cape Mudge lighthouse

Cape Mudge church

daintily through the glades. Stop by for lunch or a drink and enjoy unbeatable views of the southernmost tip of Cape Mudge from the vaulted two-storey cedar-and-glass lobby bar, or make reservations to stay in the lodge or cabins (250-285-2042 or 1-800-665-7745).

Tsa-Kwa-Luten is a Coast Salish word meaning "the gathering place." When Captain Vancouver and the ship's naturalist, Archibald Menzies, ascended the zigzag path up the bluff at Cape Mudge in 1792, they found a large village of nearly 350 Coast Salish people living in 12 large cedar plank houses. The dwellings were strategically situated on the cliff edge for defence against hostile bands. Some sixty years later the Lekwiltok wrested this territory away from the Salish in a series of bloody attacks and built their own village near the bottom of the bluffs.

Rebecca Spit

Long, sandy Rebecca Spit on the west side of Quadra Island just south of Heriot Bay was also the scene of fierce battles between the Coast Salish and the Kwagiulth. A trained eye can still pick out the remains of a Salish defensive trench and other fortifications, but the idea of warfare seems at odds with the magical peacefulness of this lovely hook of land. There's no better place on the island to while away a sunny day than **Rebecca Spit Provincial Marine Park**. To get to Rebecca Spit, return to Cape Mudge Rd and follow it north up the middle of the island to the T-junction with Heriot Bay Rd. Turn right onto Heriot Bay Rd and follow it to the well-marked turnoff to the park. This is a day-use-only park, but the Cape Mudge Band runs the 140-site **We Wai Kay Campsite** at the south edge of the park (250-285-3111). Bring a **picnic or barbecue** fixings and have a great al fresco lunch. Play frisbee on the huge grass lawn or **swim** or boat in the enticing blue water of this protected corner of the island. The **sand beach** is so deliciously long—almost 2 km—that it's hard to resist a sunny stroll along the water's edge. From the tip of the spit you can watch the BC ferries shuttling between Quadra Island and Cortes Island. Then walk back through the dappled light of the Douglas fir forest that shelters the centre of the spit. Rebecca Spit is a great place for **birders**. Depending on the season, you may see anything from chickadees and crows to scoters, mergansers, loons, ducks and cormorants. Bald eagles, kingfishers and great blue herons turn up at any time of the year. If you happen to be on the island during the Victoria Day long weekend, be sure to take in the island's biggest annual event, the May Day festivities. This huge parade and celebration has taken place here every year for more than a century.

Heriot Bay

Heriot Bay, the island's other village centre, is just a few kilometres north of Rebecca Spit on Heriot Bay Rd. The Heriot Bay Inn and Marina (250-285-3322), in various incarnations, has been serving up pub food and suds for a century. It was built and burned down

Quadra Island Recreation, Accommodations and Services

Recreation
Bicycle rentals
Kayak/Canoe rentals
Fishing charters
Scuba diving charters
Hiking
Horseback riding
Accommodations
Bed & Breakfasts
Inns
Resorts
Campgrounds
RV Parks
Services
Restaurants
Cafés
Grocery stores
Credit Union/ATM
Service station

so many times that its history is hard to trace, but the old white inn on Heriot Bay is a charmer. Its beer parlour was the haunt of thirsty loggers and fishermen while a more genteel clientele took tea under the flower baskets on the hotel's wide verandah. The inn still has the feel of a come-one come-all place where everyone has a comfortable niche in the bar or restaurant or out on the seaside porch. This is a great place to wait for the **Cortes Island ferry** that docks within shouting distance of the pub. For boaters there's also a **government dock and marina**. You'll also find the belly button of island life—the post office—and a couple of **craft shops** with local art works. From Heriot Bay you can continue west past the mall and loop south onto West Rd, which takes you down the west side of the island to the village shops at Quathiaski Cove and the ferry terminal. Or you can backtrack south down Heriot Bay Rd to Quathiaski Cove. To the left, on Smith Rd, there is access to two great local walks—**the Haskin Farm Trail** and the **Kate Dubois Trail**. Inquire locally for up-to-date information and access points. From Smith, turn left on to Quadra Loop and call in at the **Drahanchuck Studios & Gallery** (157 Quadra Loop, 250-285-3160). This beautifully crafted gallery/residence is festooned with exotic orchids and the lovingly landscaped

Rebecca Spit Provincial Marine Park

Important Numbers

Fire **911**

Police **911**

Ambulance **911**

Hospital (Campbell River) **250-287-7111**

Coast Guard Emergency **1-800-567-5111**

Medical clinics **250-285-3663**

Campbell River and District Chamber of Commerce
Travel InfoCentre **250-287-4636**

grounds lead a to-die-for view over Sutil Channel. Umbrellas are thoughtfully provided for visitors strolling the property in wet weather.

If South Island **hikes** have sharpened your appetite for outdoor adventure, you've got a treat in store. The North Island is riddled with **trails and old logging roads**. The **Morte Lake Trail**, with several routes, offers the reward of a sandy beach and a cool plunge. The **Chinese Mountains trails** are steep and rugged in places but the panoramic views at the top are worth it. A trail guide pamphlet to the Morte Lake and Chinese Mountains trails is available at the information centre and local outlets.

There are other great trails on Quadra Island, and energetic Quadra Islanders are busy developing new trails. The **Visitors' Map of Quadra Island** by Hilary Stewart, available at local outlets, is a good bet for identifying additional trails and logging roads. Local hiking and conservancy groups are also gold mines of useful information. For more information phone Quadra Island Conservancy and Stewardship Society, the Quadra Island Recreation Society (250-285-3243) or the Recreation Officer, Ministry of Forests, Campbell River Forest District (250-286-9300). Or pick up *Hiking the Gulf Islands* by Charles Kahn or *Hiking Trails III* (1996), published by Vancouver Island Trails Information Society.

For more information about Quadra Island, contact the Campbell River InfoCentre (250-287-4636), or pick up the brochure and map "Quadra: Gateway to the Outer Islands" at Vancouver Island InfoCentres and aboard BC ferries. A Quadra Island tourist information booth is open from mid-June to early September at the Cove Centre just above the ferry terminal. For accommodations, contact the Campbell River InfoCentre or Super, Natural British Columbia Accommodations (1-800-663-6000).

Cortes Island

Cortes Island is the "back of beyond" — even farther off the beaten track than Quadra Island. But its remoteness has meant that this island is still unspoiled by development. A Vancouver newspaper writer raved about Cortes's quiet beauty back in 1925: "Every bay on the 15-mile long island presents a vista of beauty, where one feels the desire to erect a summer home. There are lovely prospects of sea foliage at every turn. An ideal peaceful place to forget the cars and noise of the city." Mercifully, the island remains little changed more than seventy years later, and its sandy

What to See

- ☐ **1** Whaletown
- ☐ **2** Squirrel Cove
- ☐ **3** Gorge Harbour
- ☐ **4** Manson's Landing Provincial Park
- ☐ **5** Hague Lake
- ☐ **6** Smelt Bay Provincial Park

READ I

WEST REDONDA I

SUTIL CHANNEL

LEWIS CHANNEL

CORTES

2

WHALETOWN RD

WHALETOWN 1

ISLAND

← To Quadra I

GORGE HBR RD

3

SEAFORD RD

MARINA I

MANSONS LANDING 4

5

Smelt Bay

SUTIL PT RD

N

6

TWIN IS

0   2   4   6

kilometres

Sutil Pt

Getting to Cortes Island

From Quadra Island

Drive aboard the BC Ferry at the Heriot Bay terminal on Quadra. 45 minutes crossing time; 6 sailings daily year round.

Note: fares are collected as return fares. Cash or traveller's cheques only.

For more information about travel on BC Ferries, see p. 8.

beaches, beautiful coves and bays and quiet lakes are remarkably unspoiled. Yet Cortes Island is just a 45-minute ferry hop from Quadra Island.

Cortes is a small island community, and visitors come for its natural beauty, not its amenities. Depending on who's counting, 500 to 750 people live on Cortes Island year round, mostly on the drier south end. So visitor services are sparse, and many are open only in season.

Cortes has two summer festivals, **Cortes Days** and a **Salmon Festival**, a handful of restaurants and cafés, **kayak, scooter, bike and car rentals, boat charters** and **plane charters**, and a regular charter bus between most Cortes Island accommodations and Campbell River. You can even book **guided tours** to nearby **Mitlenatch Island Provincial Marine Park**, an island **wildlife sanctuary** that has been called the "Galapagos of Georgia Strait" for its huge colonies of nesting seabirds. It is also a great place for spring and summer wildflowers. Cortes Island's wealth of protected coves and bays have made it a favourite stopover for boaters cruising in beautiful Desolation Sound. You'll find docks and general stores at Whaletown, Squirrel Cove, Cortes Bay, Gorge Harbour and Manson's Landing to serve the ocean-going crowd.

Rural Cortes Island

A kayaker takes a break at Von Donop Inlet on Cortes

Cortes also has a few resorts and B&Bs. Probably the best known is **Hollyhock Seminar and Holiday Centre**, where guests come for relaxation and spiritual healing in peaceful seaside surroundings. The kitchen is a favourite for its fine, mostly vegetarian cuisine. (Phone ahead for a lunch or dinner stop, 800-933-6339 or 250-935-6578.) Several B&Bs also get high marks from departing guests, including Blue Heron Bed & Breakfast (250-935-6584), just a hop and a skip from the beach. Our personal favourite is Fairhaven Farm Bed & Breakfast, a tastefully updated turn-of-the-century log home in a pastoral setting where good books, great farm breakfasts, and lots of extra little touches are thoughtfully provided (250-935-6501). (For more information, contact the Campbell River and District Chamber of Commerce Travel InfoCentre, 250-287-4636, or Super, Natural British Columbia Accommodations, 1-800-663-6000.)

The ferry docks at Whaletown. Make your way around to the **Whaletown General Store** for a Cortes Island map with updated **tourist information**. And yes, there once were hundreds of whales in these waters. Captain Vancouver described the sight when he sailed past Cortes Island: "Numberless whales enjoying the season were playing about the ship in every direction." But European whalers arrived in the mid-1800s and the carnage

Cortes Island Recreation, Accommodations and Services

Recreation
Kayak rental
Fishing/Boat charters
Scuba Diving
Hiking
Interpretive tours
Parks

Accommodations
Bed & Breakfasts
Motels
Cabins/Resorts
Hostel
Campground

Services
Restaurants
Cafés
General stores
Gas stations
Credit union (No ATM)

began. One whaler named Dawson set up a whaling station at Whaletown in 1869. By 1871 only a few whales had escaped the mass slaughter, and Dawson's whaling company closed.

Gorge Harbour is another of Cortes Island's beautiful bays. The tall cliffs rise up at the narrow entrance to the harbour, the site of a skirmish between Kwagiulth raiders sweeping down from the north and the Coast Salish who lived on Cortes Island. Legend has it that the Salish sent boulders crashing down onto the enemy canoes trying to attack through the narrow opening at Gorge Harbour. A pictograph celebrating the Salish victory was painted on the cliff face. Gorge Harbour Marina just off Whaletown Road is the spot where sleek yachts rock gently on the tide while the crew enjoy a delectable meal at the Old Floathouse Restaurant perched above the harbour (250-935-6631).

Nearby **Manson's Landing Provincial Marine Park** is a pleasant place to enjoy a lazy afternoon. The park was named for Michael and John Manson, two brothers who arrived here to settle in the 1880s. John Manson's son Nick, gazing out to sea from the family property over islands scattered like rough emeralds in the Strait of Georgia and across to the far-distant blue mountains, described his father's arrival on Cortes: "He was twenty-one when he came out on this bank and saw this view and said: 'This is where I'm going to put down my tent pegs.' And he lived here for the rest of his life." Unlike the whaler Dawson, the Mansons were conservationists dedicated to protecting Cortes Island's natural bounties. In 1973 Manson's Landing Marine Park was established to safeguard the **white sand beach and lagoon**. Pack a picnic and enjoy whiling away a few hours strolling the sandy spit or wandering down nearby forest paths. Manson's Landing is one of several places where it's legal to harvest shellfish (other places are Squirrel Cove, Smelt Bay and the beach south of the government wharf at Gorge Harbour) but check the regulations, and avoid clam and oyster leases (posted with red concrete blocks).

Not far away is Hague Lake, a **favourite local swimming hole** with an inviting sand beach. (Make sure to read the posted warnings about swimmer's itch.) You can hike there from a trail that starts at Manson's Landing. The **Hague**

Cortes ferry

Lake Regional Park also has several new but as yet unmarked trails through the forested lands around Hague Lake and Gunflint Lake. Inquire locally for up-to-date information on trails and access points. Farther south off Sutil Point Road is yet another park, the 16-ha **Smelt Bay Provincial Park** (250-954-4600, Reservations 1-800-689-9025). This beautiful park has 22 **campsites** and a stretch of **sandy beach** that is perfect for beachcombing. Behind it is a rolling green rise of land thought to be a Salish defensive fortification.

Important Numbers

Police 911

Fire 911

Ambulance 911

Hospital (Campbell River) 250-287-7111

Doctor 250-935-6718 / 250-935-6734

Coast Guard Air Marine/Emergency 1-800-567-5111

Campbell River and District Chamber of Commerce Travel InfoCentre 250-287-4636

Sunset at Smelt Bay

Much of Cortes is still Crown land, and a big chunk of private land is owned by the giant lumber company MacMillan Bloedel. Even though Cortes has been logged, big sections of the island are covered with mature second-growth trees. If you enjoy taking backroads through dense green forests with here-and-there coastal views (and if you don't mind sections of good gravel road), then circle around the east side of the island and up to beautiful **Squirrel Cove** at the edge of Desolation Sound. Its protected waters and splendid scenery make this spot a popular anchorage for boaters. Squirrel Cove has been the hereditary homeland of the Coast Salish, and it is now a reserve of the Klahoose Band. Stop to savour the beauty that makes Desolation Sound a boater's paradise before heading back for the ferry.

CHAPTER 8
THE NORTH ISLAND

The log sorting and booming grounds at Beaver Cove

The "North Island" between Campbell River and Cape Scott is as rough-hewn and rural as the south end is urban and citified. Logging trucks slam down the highway, fresh clear-cuts patch the mountainsides, RVs and dented pickups are the vehicles of choice, photos of local folks with their trophy fish and bucks are tacked up in cafés and fishing fleets bob on the tide from Campbell River to Winter Harbour. The North Island's brawny, resource-rooted life has its flip side. Carved cedar logger's boots stuffed with nasturtiums brighten a suburban garden. Beautifully polished wood burls do duty as hanging planters. A wonderful "totem pole" of fantastic metal critters made from recycled logging equipment stands beside a cable-wrapped café.

Always give logging trucks the right of way

Chainsaw-carved wooden sculptures perk up municipal parks all along the coast. Once you've taken the time to discover its rugged beauty, you'll see why North Islanders treasure their place. But they're happy to welcome visitors, too. The locals here have a genuine warmth—there always seems to be time for a friendly wave or a bit of conversation, even for perfect strangers.

The rugged North Island is a wilderness playground. It is crisscrossed with logging roads that give hunters, anglers, campers, canoeists and backcountry hikers and mountain bikers access to real deep woods recreation. Two of the most popular visitor destinations are **Schoen Lake Provincial Park**, a spectacular lake under the summit of Mt. Schoen where canoeists and hikers can find spectacular wilderness, and **Cape Scott**, the wild surf-swept coast at the northwest tip of the island. As well, windsurfers flock to long and blustery **Nimpkish Lake**, divers marvel at the fecund sea life off Port Hardy, and spelunkers scramble to explore the fantastic cave world of the **Quatsino Limestone formation**.

Getting to Campbell River

The tour of the North Island begins at Campbell River. Getting there from the Mainland (Vancouver or Sunshine Coast) involves taking a ferry over to Vancouver Island then finding transportation north to Campbell River.

By Ferry to Nanaimo

Vancouver (Horseshoe Bay) to Vancouver Island (Nanaimo/Departure Bay)

Drive aboard a BC Ferry at the Horseshoe Bay terminal (just north of Vancouver). 1 hour 35 minutes crossing time; 8 sailings daily year round. Limited vehicle reservations accepted on this route.

Vancouver (Tsawwassen) to Vancouver Island (Nanaimo/Duke Point)

Drive aboard a BC Ferry at the Tsawwassen terminal (just south of Vancouver).

2 hours crossing time; 8 sailings daily year round. Limited vehicle reservations accepted on this route.

By Car from Nanaimo

Drive up Highway 19 or 19A to Campbell River (see Chapter 7). The 153-km drive takes 2 to 2^1/$_2$ hours.

By Ferry to Comox

Sunshine Coast (Powell River/Westview) to Vancouver Island (Comox/Little River)

Drive aboard a BC Ferry at the Westview terminal (Powell River).

1 hour 15 minutes crossing time; 4 sailings daily year round.

By Car From Comox

Drive up Highway 19 or 19A to Campbell River (see Chapter 7). The 33-km drive takes half an hour.

BC Ferry Information (Schedule and Fares):

Greater Victoria **250-386-3431**

Fax Victoria **250-381-5452**

Elsewhere in **BC 1-888-BCFERRY (223-3779)**

Out-of-Province **250-386-3431**

Web site **www.bcferries.bc.ca**

Port McNeill (Alert Bay–Sointula) Ferry **250-956-4533**

For Reservations on Mainland/Vancouver Island Routes:

Within BC **1-888-724-5223**

Outside BC **604-444-2890**

Wildlife is plentiful, a naturalist's dream. The North Island's four-footed residents include black bears, beavers, wolves, cougars, black-tailed deer and Roosevelt elk. Viewing killer whales off **Robson Bight** is one of the biggest tourist attractions in the area. The sight of these awesome black-and-white leviathans breaking out of the water has delighted thousands of whale watchers. But whales aren't the only marine mammals that live along the North Island for at least part of the year. There have always been plenty of harbor seals, and porpoises, sea lions, humpback whales and gray whales are all making strong comebacks after some sparse years. Schools of Pacific white-sided dolphins— sometimes 400 at a time—have recently started appearing in Johnstone Strait, which runs along most of the east coast of the North Island. These speedy little ocean acrobats often keep company with whales, flipping into the air and racing in tandem through the water to the delight of wildlife watchers.

The highway is peppered with rest areas, lookouts, parks and hiking trailheads perfect for serendipitous stops. Feel free to pull over, stretch and take a sniff of piney-fresh air. Or stay to enjoy outdoor fun. Some of the most popular pulloffs are the historic **Seymour Narrows and Ripple Rock Rest Area and Trailhead** overlooking the swirling waters of Seymour Narrows (see p. 283), **Roberts Lake and Rest Area** with its swimming, hiking, canoeing and excellent trout fishing, **Schoen Lake Provincial Park** with its scenic canoeing and stunning wilderness hiking. Watch for the blue and white trailhead signs emblazoned with a hiker icon, scattered at irregular intervals along the highway—including McNair Lake, Dalrymple Creek, Klaklakama Lakes, and Nimpkish Lake. North Island trails are ideal for adventurers who love getting back to nature's basics. (For details on North Island hiking trails contact the Campbell River InfoCentre at 1235 Shoppers Row, Tyee Plaza, 250-287-4636.)

Smaller communities like Telegraph Cove, Port McNeill, Port Hardy and Zeballos are known for their colourful histories and their knack for making visitors feel right at home. Two of the North Island's most intriguing historic communities are on beautiful islands accessed by BC ferry from Port McNeill—the old Finnish utopian fishing village at Sointula (Malcolm Island) and the still vibrant First Nations community at Alert Bay (Cormorant Island). Other towns have their own zesty tales to tell. Taking side trips down paved or gravel roads to places like Sayward or Woss, Zeballos or Telegraph Cove, gets you right down to the North Island's fascinating logging, fishing and mining roots. Larger communities like Port McNeill and Port Hardy are geared up for visitors and can offer services, accommodation and outdoor adventures from sports fishing, scuba diving, kayaking and windsurfing to wildlife viewing, golfing and forestry tours. And Port Hardy is the southern terminal for BC Ferries Northern Cruises through the spectacular Inside Passage.

A tug at work at Kelsey Bay

Campbell River to Sayward and Kelsey Bay

North of Campbell River, Hwy 19 narrows to two lanes and veers away from the coast. Within a few kilometres, "civilization"—schools, gas stations, roadside bungalows, hobby farms—starts to disappear. Towns are few and far between, so make sure to get gas and check under the hood in Campbell River.

As you drive north through second-growth forests, you can feel the raw edge of the logging industry that still keeps this area alive. You pass a huge pulp and paper mill complex, a beehive burner, a shake and shingle factory. Logging trucks flash by loaded with giant cedars whose shredded bark flaps in the wind. Through a fringe of trees you catch a glimpse of a beautiful bay that is half-filled with a huge log boom.

On a bright day the dense North Island forest ranges from delicate lime alders to deep hunter green conifers. Wisps of cloud hang lazily across snow-patched peaks, and lakes and rivers glimmer through a fringe of trees. Tall pink fireweed and cheerful white daisies clustered along the roadside are a colourful hemline accent to the cloak of the forest. (Look for a delightful roadside honey stand where you can buy honey produced by local fireweed-flitting bees.) The blue mountains that line the horizon call out to the wilderness adventurer, promising solitude in every direction.

Side trips off Hwy 19 let you see what makes the North Island's smaller communities tick and get a taste of the North Island's special brand of raw beauty. The first side trip is to Sayward and Kelsey Bay. Look for the signed turnoff to Sayward Junction 64 km north of Campbell River. Just after you've turned right onto Sayward Rd, look to your left for the great local truck stop called **Charlie's Place**. The smell of sizzling onions and the sight of a sweet little lady tucking into a plate-sized burger and haystack of fries tells you that you've got the right place. If you like old-style diners where real people eat generous portions of real stick-to-the-ribs food, this is it. When you've had your fill of food, check out the book racks. They're crammed with regional books from coast histories to four-wheeling guides that give you more windows into the world of the BC coast.

Just down the road is another favourite eatery, the **Cable Café**. "Cable" is the right

Honey stand south of Sayward

Mt Hkusam is steeped in Native lore

descriptive word. The café is wrapped in 26 tonnes of old logging cable! The great folk-art logger's totem pole of recycled machinery stands next door, and lots of rusted logging equipment is hunkered down in the greenery around the café. A sign by the door says "Welcome to the herd," and the folks inside mean every word of it. It's a friendly place where locals sit at the counter shooting the breeze, and diners debate which of the café's famous dozen-plus pies to order. (If in doubt, go for the bumbleberry.)

From the highway it's a 10-km drive through quiet semi-suburbs and the idyllic wide-open farmland of Salmon Valley to the town of Sayward and the wharf at Kelsey Bay. Along the road are signs for **home-based arts and crafts, smoked salmon and fruit** for sale. The new home-front shops are part of the North Islanders' determination to protect their future from uncertainties of forestry and commercial fishing. Ditto for the **Coral Reef Pub** on the Sayward Rd. Built by a local commercial fishing couple hedging their economic bets, the pub is a popular spot for Sayward loggers to unwind after work.

Railroad logging came to this valley about 1904, and forestry has remained the primary local industry. Sayward, still the division headquarters for MacMillan Bloedel's forestry operations, has the feel of a tidily modern company town. It sits in a pretty river valley cradled by mountains in the Vancouver Island Range. To see what an uncut forest looks like, ask for directions in Sayward to the **White River Forest**. The trees are so magnificent that loggers refused to cut them down. The most eye-catching peak in the area is the dramatic hump of 1,671-metre-high **Mt. Hkusam** with its perpetual crown of mist. To the Kwakwaka'wakw people, the valley's first inhabitants, it was known as Hiatsee Sakelekum, "where the sea lion's breath gathers at the blowhole." They believed that the mist at the mountain's summit was the vapour of a sea lion's breath rising through a tunnel in the heart of the mountain. To many Sayward residents the misty cloud is known affectionately as "Oscar," and a community BC Day weekend festival in honour of the mountain is called Oscar Daze. The biggest local event, however, is the **Sayward Logger**

Logging on the North Island

Forestry has changed since the early days. At one time logging companies started falling trees at one end of a valley and kept going right through to its head, then moved on over to the next valley—without a thought for the future. Salmon- and trout-rich creeks were damaged and logging roads caused massive landslides. But the cut-and-run mentality has changed over the years, and so have the rules. Clear-cuts are smaller, care must be taken with fish-bearing streams, roads must be built sensitively and removed after logging. Single-species forests are no longer the ideal method of silviculture and three seedlings are planted for every tree harvested. Still, the debate over "managed forests" is charged. The forest industry claims that today's reforestation practices will sustain our forests, but biologists and environmentalists argue that clear-cutting and plantations cannot re-create the dynamic ecosystems of the original forests. Meanwhile, the trees are growing back. While almost the entire landscape in this area of the island has been logged over the years, there are few if any places where forests are not growing again.

Those interested in logging history should stop at the fascinating little **Link and Pin Logging Museum** near Roberts Lake about 30 km north of Campbell River (daily June to late September). You'll see photographs of the early days of the North Island and lots of old logging tools like handsaws, jiggers and stamp hammers. For a look at forestry at the turn of the millennium, sign up for tours by the island's major forestry companies at the **North Island Forestry Centre** just south of Port McNeill.

Forest tours are a popular draw on the North Island

Sports in late June where loggers gather to test their muscles and skills against other heavy-duty competitors.

Even though lumber is king in the Salmon Valley, commercial and **sports fishing** are also major draws. Drive past Sayward to beautiful little Kelsey Bay a few kilometres down the road and you'll see the Kelsey Bay wharf, the town's doorway to the world where coastal ferries once called in to off-load passengers and freight before a road was built into Sayward. Now Kelsey Bay is the harbour for commercial fishing, sports fishing and **whale watching tours** in the area. (Check with the Sayward Tourist Association, 250-789-9015 for information on whale watching charters and other local services.) You can also see the forestry giant MacMillan Bloedel's high-tech dryland log sorting operation where logs are made up into floating booms to be towed south.

Schoen Lake Provincial Park

North of Sayward on Highway 19 is the turnoff to **Schoen Lake Provincial Park** (phone 250-954-4600). From the road you can see the beautiful 5-km-long sliver of Schoen Lake reflecting the profile of towering Mount Schoen. This is one of the most beautiful camping spots on all of Vancouver Island. You can tent in one of the park's 10 car camping spots or park at the campground, launch a canoe and paddle to a wilderness campsite down the lake. Try fishing for small but succulent lake trout or take one of the mountain trails near the lake. One trail leads to Nisnak Meadows where subalpine flowers brighten the meadows in late sprint and summer. Another trail is a demanding climb up Mount Schoen with a payoff of panoramic views of the surrounding mountains. This region is known for its wildlife. Nature lovers may spot black-tailed deer, black bears, beavers, cougars and Roosevelt elk. For more information on trails in the Schoen Lake area, phone the park at 250-954-4600 and/or see *Hiking Trails III* (1996), published by the Vancouver Island Trails Information Society.

Woss

North between Sayward and Port McNeill is the broad, majestic Nimpkish Valley, where some of the biggest trees in the world once grew. It's been a major source of North Island timber since the first years of the century, and it's still a "working forest." Canadian Forest Products (Canfor) harvests some 1.25 million cubic metres of wood from the Nimpkish forests and replants about 1.5 million trees every year. The Nimpkish Timber Company started railway logging in the Nimpkish Valley with two locomotives and 10 km of track back in 1917. In 1944 Canfor's founders took over logging operations in the Nimpkish Valley, and today Canfor is one of the world's major railway logging operations with over 100 km of track, 500 rail cars and four locomotives.

A locomotive on display at Woss

It's also one of the world's last railway logging operations—a living legacy of early "locie" (locomotive) logging. Logging railway buffs can take a trip down memory lane to see historic **steam locomotives** like old Engine No. 113, as well as the Grey Ghost Coach on sidings by Canfor's division headquarters in the little town of Woss. "Locie" 113 was the largest logging engine in the world when it was built in 1920. Often Canfor's working diesel electric locomotives and equipment are also sitting on the sidings, and it's a great chance to have an up-close encounter with modern railway logging operations. Woss also has visitor services including a motel, service station, tackle and groceries, and a neighbourhood pub. And just 3 km from Woss is Canfor's scenic sandy-beached campground beside the big, clear Woss Lake. In fact Canfor welcomes visitors to use its seven wilderness campgrounds and more than 1,000 km of logging roads (except where closures are posted). Stop at the Canfor office in Woss for maps and up-to-date information on campgrounds and road conditions.

Little Hustan Cave Regional Park

About 23 km north of Woss is the well-signed turnoff to Little Hustan Cave Regional Park and the old gold mining town of Zeballos on Vancouver Island's wild west coast. The park is a 21-km drive down the gravel road to Zeballos. Follow the signs to parking, then hike the short trail to see pools with water-carved boulders, limestone arches and the cathedral-sized cave entrance. This cave is easily accessible and gives inexperienced spelunkers a sample of the vast underground labyrinth of the region's karst (limestone) formations which range from huge amphitheatres covered in stalactites to rock faces streaked like bacon or curdled like cottage cheese, to slick limestone passages plunging into the bowels of the earth. Vancouver Island has a thousand caves (only 239 have been officially mapped) and it's a black paradise for experienced cavers. Spelunking can be dangerous, too, so make sure you have the right equipment and experienced spelunkers on any caving adventure. To book an in-depth cave exploration, contact Mountain Line Tours and Travel (250-956-4827, fax 250-974-8162), call the Port McNeill InfoCentre (250-956-3131) or contact the Strathcona Park Lodge (250-286-3122, fax 250-286-6010—tours on selected dates). Call ahead to find out what clothing and footwear are recommended and to check that the level of activity is suitable. Caving can be an easy family affair or as physically demanding as mountain climbing, including rappelling down shafts and wiggling through narrow passages.

Zeballos

At the end of the 42-km gravel road is the former gold-mining centre of Zeballos. This picture-pretty little town is nestled in rugged conifer-green mountains at the head of Zeballos Inlet. It has only about 260 residents but a surprising number of amenities including a pub and hotel, motels, B&Bs, an RV park, liquor store, groceries, a campsite, boat and scuba diving charters and the delightful little Zeballos Museum on Maquinna Ave. (For more information, contact the tourist information booth at the Zeballos Museum, 250-761-4070, the Zeballos Village Office, 250-761-4229, or the Zeballos Board of Trade, 250-761-4270).

Prospectors have roamed the mountains around Zeballos ever since the Spanish discovered gold in the 1700s. (Zeballos is named for the Spanish explorer Ciriaco Cevallos.) Old Spanish records show that by the time the Spaniards gave up their claim to the Pacific Northwest, nearly $800,000 worth of placer gold had been shipped out of Vancouver Island's west coast. But it was in the 1930s that gold in them thar hills brought the first big influx of gold-diggers to this isolated corner of the west coast. At first, prospectors mined by hand in the hills above Spud Creek. They packed the ore out on their backs, slip-sliding down a muddy mountain trail to the river where the ore sacks were barged out to a smelter in Washington state. The first gold bullion was produced in Zeballos in 1938, and over the next five years more than $13 million worth of gold bricks were shipped down Zeballos Inlet. The town prospered, and residents still joke that in its heyday the streets were paved with gold (quite literally—mine tailings with traces of gold had been used to build the roads). The gold was all played out by 1948.

During the Second World War the region's fine spruce was in high demand for building strong, light aircraft frames for Mosquito bombers. After the war, the Tahsis Company began acquiring more tree farm licences and expanding its logging operations around Zeballos. Logging breathed new life into the near ghost town when the Tahsis Company picked Zeballos as its company headquarters in the 1970s.

Forestry is still the engine of local economy, and Western Forest Products is the town's main employer. But the area's excellent **sports fishing** draws lots of visitors. Salmon, halibut, snapper, ling cod and crabs are the main saltwater catches. Steelhead and rainbow trout in nearby lakes challenge freshwater anglers. Zeballos is also a jumping-off point for nearby **Nootka Sound** and **Kyuquot Sound** on Vancouver Island's remote and wildly beautiful west coast. Travellers can book **boat trips** in Zeballos to explore the fjords and waterways around **Nootka Island**, and kayakers and boaters can launch from **Fair Harbour**, a 35-km trip by unpaved road from Zeballos, to explore **Kyuquot Sound** and **Brooks Peninsula Provincial Park** (250-954-4600), where lovably clown-faced sea otters have made a comeback. They were hunted to near-extinction in the late 1700s. In the 1960s and 1970s Alaskan otters were introduced to the BC coast and a colony of sea otters 900 strong is now well established. For would-be prospectors all that glitters just might be gold. There's **gold panning** in many nearby streams and rivers. And for expert **spelunkers** there are innumerable caves waiting to be discovered in the region's dead-giveaway karst formations—the surface limestone that is a clue to eroded limestone formations just under the surface.

Nimpkish Lake and the North Island Forestry Centre

Make your way back to Highway 19, where the highway runs along the shore of the long and lovely Nimpkish Lake for nearly 20 km. The peekaboo views of the lake through a fringe of trees are spectacular. The shimmering sliver of lake lies in a deep valley with mountains rising steeply on the other side. Fragments of drifting clouds hook over snow-patched peaks and a dusty gold light plays in and out of the clouds. Nimpkish Lake is one of the few places where **windsurfers** can enjoy a true backcountry experience. From spring through fall, hot air rises off the lake and cool ocean air slips in above the lake. These "thermals" create winds up to 30 knots during the middle of the day. It's heady stuff for expert windsurfers who hook

Nimpkish Lake

themselves into harnesses and tack and jibe in front of the wind. The tiny community of Nimpkish Valley, 11 km past the Zeballos turnoff, has a few services for visitors (gas station, store and RV campground), and it's the site of the Nimpkish Speed Slalom Weekend.

Just beyond the north tip of Nimpkish Lake is the well-signed North Island Forestry Centre just down Beaver Cove Road off Hwy 19. Stop by for logging maps and **forestry industry information**, or sign up for **guided tours** by Western Forest Products and MacMillan Bloedel. The popular 6- or 8-hour tour takes you to old-growth and second-growth forests and a dryland sort. You may also get to visit a **fish hatchery** or watch a logger fall a tree. (Tours run Tuesday to Friday, early July to early September. Advance booking advised: 250-956-3844, fax 250-956-3848.)

Beaver Cove and Telegraph Cove

The turnoff for the North Island Forestry Centre is also the turnoff to Beaver Cove and Telegraph Cove. If you make just one side trip on the North Island, go to Telegraph Cove. You'll see the real working North Island at the historic log sort and booming ground at Beaver Cove and step into a perfectly preserved close-to-the roots 1920s coastal village at picturesque Telegraph Cove. The opening of a great new pub and restaurant guarantees a relaxing jaunt. Telegraph Cove is also the bar-none best place to go **whale watching** at Robson Bight.

Drive down the gravel road 13 km to the fascinating **Beaver Cove log sort**. (By the way, the last 6 km is real logging road!) Canadian Forest Products (Canfor) trains still ferry payloads of logs to this historic booming ground. From a pullout on the bluff above Beaver Cove you can watch all the hustle and bustle at Canada's biggest dryland log sort where Canfor crews sort, scale and boom 1.4 million cubic metres of Nimpkish Valley logs a year. See huge-jawed grapple loaders snatch up mouthfuls of logs as if they were tooth-

Telegraph Cove

A sperm whale jaw bone at Telegraph Cove

picks and send them sliding down a chute into the salt water. Watch the acrobatic little **sidewinder tugs** tipping from side to side at perilous angles to nudge the logs into booms. Farther out, a giant 2,000-horsepower harbour tug waits to take the huge log booms on their seven-day journey to Vancouver mills. A big Canfor display explains all the action at the log sort and touts Nimpkish forest recreation and the company's forest management practices.

Just 2 km past the wide arc of Beaver Cove is Telegraph Cove. This **historic boardwalk village** standing on stilts over the jade green harbour is a little gem of a coastal settlement. Cedar boardwalks run between the lovingly preserved old cottages painted bright shades of red, blue, green and chocolate brown. Colourful flower boxes brighten the boardwalk. Here and there nasturtiums climb up a fishnet draped against a sun-warmed wall. Each house bears a plaque with fascinating snippets about its former owners. Read about folks like Colin Armitage, who floated an old shack from Beaver Cove to house his new bride, and Thomas Yui, who was mysteriously murdered aboard a China-bound ship. Some of these houses are still residences, and others are available for rent to visitors. At the far end of the boardwalk are little gift shops and an art gallery tucked in historic buildings, as well as a new pub and restaurant. The marina in front of the boardwalk is alive with boats bobbing on the waves. A backdrop of evergreen forest behind the cove and coastal islands beyond the wharf make this one of the prettiest little corners on the coast. One hillside has been scarred by development for a condo complex, but most recent additions near the cove—a 125-site campground, restaurant, tackle shop, public washrooms and showers—fit right in. The Killer Whale Café and Old Saltery Pub building,

Relic of the past at Telegraph Cove

made of re-milled boards from the village's former saltery, stands on stilts overlooking the marina as if it has been there forever. Sit between the huge windows and the round copper fireplace in the pub and sip a foaming "designer" beer or order up west coast foods like Thai curry or crab cushions on the waterside deck.

Telegraph Cove was the site of the northernmost station of telegraph line strung from tree to tree up the coast in the early 1900s. By the 1920s a salmon saltery and sawmill had been built here. The sawmill supported ten or twelve families at Telegraph Cove for sixty years. Today tourism is the lifeblood of the village. Pleasure craft stop by for supplies before heading up or down the coast. **Sports fishers** bound for the excellent fishing grounds in Blackfish Sound tie up at the marina. A tackle shop beside the marina offers all kinds of tackle and bait—squid, salmon strips, octopus, minnows and anchovies—and promises lots of tips and fish stories. Cars and tour buses disgorge excited whale watchers into the parking lot. At the end of the boardwalk they'll board boats and head down to Robson Bight in search of killer whales. (For more information and reservations, phone Telegraph Cove Resorts Ltd, 250-928-3131, fax 250-928-3105, or 1-800-200-4665.)

A log railway is still used at Beaver Cove

Whale Watching at Telegraph Cove

Robson Bight (Michael Bigg) Provincial Park is an **ecological reserve** about 20 km south of Telegraph Cove, accessible only by boat. It's here that killer whales (orcas) stop to rub their bellies on the gravel beaches—maybe to scrape off parasites or maybe just because it feels good (see killer whale box, pp. 154–57). The ecological reserve is off limits to hikers and whale watching craft, but whales can be seen from just beyond the park boundaries and as they swim along the shore. Some 30,000 whale watchers visit Robson Bight every year in hopes of seeing the rubbery black dorsal fins slicing up the strait, or a shiny black-and-white orca leap from the water in a flurry of sea foam. The best time for whale sightings is from mid-July to mid-September, when about 200 killer whales in 16 pods swim in and out of the waters of Johnstone Strait. To make sure that these magnificent animals are not disturbed, whale watching charter vessels and kayakers obey special guidelines and stay at least 100 metres away from the whales. This is one of the world's best places to see killer whales. On a really good day, you may see a hundred whales or more belonging to four or five different pods. Many boats are equipped with sonar so you can hear the whales calling to each other as they swim. You're likely to see other wildlife too, including humpback, gray and minke whales as well as porpoises, harbor seals, sea lions and Pacific white-sided dolphins. And no matter what, island-studded Johnstone Strait is a perfect setting for a coastal cruise. (For information about whale watching tours, contact Stubbs Island Whale Watching at Telegraph Cove, 250-928-3185, 250-928-3117, fax 250-928-3102, or toll free 1-800-665-3066; or call local travel infocentres at Sayward, 250-789-9015; Port McNeill, 250-956-3131; or Alert Bay, 250-974-5213.

Port McNeill

Port McNeill, the second largest community on the North Island, is just 20 minutes from Telegraph Cove. To get to Port McNeill go back to Hwy 19 and follow it north about 10 km to the well-signed turnoff. This tidy modern community is a major hub for North Island services including gas stations, grocery stores, a bank, restaurants, hotels and B&Bs. As the "port" in its name suggests, Port McNeill also has a first-rate municipal marina for yachts and sailboats as well as **fishing and whale watching charters**. The town advertises that its downtown merchants will go that extra mile for visitors. This in not just PR bumpf. We found Port McNeill to be one of the friendliest and most service-oriented towns on Vancouver Island. Diane Hitchcox, the owner of Roseberry Manor B&B, goes out of her way to pamper guests in her Victorian-collectible-filled home. She thinks of every detail, from a pillow chocolate and a split of wine at bedtime, to fuzzy robes and slippers, to pull-out-all-the-stops gourmet breakfasts. Ask her anything you want to know about North Island adventuring—she knows. And all that hospitality comes straight from the heart.

The town's longtime mayor-by-acclamation, Gerry Furney, is also known for his big heart. He recently rescued an eighty-six-year-old visitor who mistakenly turned up for a fishing expedition a month early. Furney took him in tow, got his lost baggage sorted out, found him a place to stay in nearby Port Hardy and made sure his boat's skipper would make the appointed rendezvous. Thanks to Furney and other caring North Islanders in Port Hardy—a town that rivals Port McNeill in the friendliness department—the visitor had the time of his life in the month before his fishing charter boat arrived. Gerry Furney is also known island-wide as an outspoken pro-logging man. In fact some folks at Port McNeill don't even talk about logging. It's "tree farming" to them. Not pillaging the forests, but forest stewardship through harvesting and replanting. Port McNeill bills itself as a "tree farm community." It's pride and joy is the **world's largest burl**—a 22-tonne "tree wart" found by MacMillan Bloedel surveyors at the base of a 351-year-old giant spruce

A restored steam donkey at Port McNeill

Nimpkish River

near the Benson River. The famous burl, measuring 13.5 metres in circumference, is on display just off Hwy 19 a few kilometres north of Port McNeill by MacMillan Bloedel's Division offices. More tributes to the community's logging history are displayed in the pleasant downtown harbourfront park, including a huge log, an old "**donkey engine**" from pioneer logging days and a three-panel colour display on reforestation.

Port McNeill has been a forestry town since 1939 when Pioneer Timber lost most of its Malcolm Island timber supply in a devastating forest fire set by three island youngsters. The company just barged its bunkhouses over to Port McNeill, heaved them up on land above the high-tide mark and set up shop again in nearby forests on Vancouver Island. You can still see some of the original bunkhouses above the shore on Beach Drive. Today four major forestry companies operate out of Port McNeill. Western Forest Products has its offices downtown, and can supply you with local logging road maps, up-to-date travel information and tips on off-road adventuring to popular nearby fishing and swimming destinations like O'Connor, Keogh and Benson Lakes. (For more information, contact Port McNeill InfoCentre, Box 129, Port McNeill, BC V0N 2R0, 250-956-3131.) Downtown Port McNeill is also the **BC Ferries terminal** for service to two offshore communities, Sointula on Malcolm Island, and Alert Bay on Cormorant Island. With their distinctive histories and special coastal charm, Sointula and Alert Bay are great day trip destinations.

Sointula (Malcolm Island)

The 25-minute BC ferry sailing from Port McNeill to Sointula on Malcolm Island is a voyage into the past. Malcolm Island is steeped in history. It was colonized at the turn of the century by a group of Finnish utopians. The community soon broke into factions and the colony disbanded, but many of the founders stuck it out on "Harmony Island." They maintained their ideals and put deep roots into Sointula's thin soil, building a new community rich in personal independence and co-operative spirit. With the 1960s "back to the land" movement, a different kind of counterculture added its own imprint. The result is a gentle, orderly island wrapped in winter mists and lit with summer sun—still very much a place of harmony. Hints of its unique history just add to its natural pastoral splendour.

Sointula's utopian history is written right across the village above the BC Ferries dock at **Rough Bay**. The whitewashed two-storey **Sointula Co-operative Store** has stood proudly above the dock since 1909. It was built by volunteer labour and is still run co-operatively by the island community. It is the longest continuously running co-op in Canada. The **Finnish Organization Hall** high on a hill above the village is another reminder of the resilience of the Finnish utopians. Once upon a time the rafters echoed to the rousing voices of pro-labour activists. Today fewer Malcolm Island folk are ardent unionists, but islanders still gather at the old hall to celebrate a birth or a marriage, to mourn a death, or to dance the night away. Clustered along the shore on either side of the Co-op Store are high, squared-off cedar plank homes reminiscent of Finnish country farmhouses. Behind the neat picket fences with their old-fashioned roses and mossy apple trees, you can glimpse the occasional sauna built more than eighty years ago. Ranged down the pebbly beach of Rough Bay to the left of the dock are weatherbeaten boat sheds on stilts over the water, looking just as they did at the turn of the century. The fleet of modern trollers and gillnetters tied up behind the island breakwater is solid

Fishboats at a buying station in Sointula

testimony that fishing is still the economic backbone of Sointula. Stroll into the village and you'll meet people with family names like Tynjala, Siider, Vuorela and Pakkalen, along with the greying grandparents who were once sixties hippies, North Islanders commuting to jobs on Vancouver Island, and summer people from Vancouver and the USA.

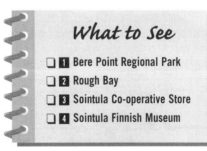

What to See

- ☐ **1** Bere Point Regional Park
- ☐ **2** Rough Bay
- ☐ **3** Sointula Co-operative Store
- ☐ **4** Sointula Finnish Museum

Sointula's services are clustered in the village above the ferry dock. To get a feel for the place, take a walk left down First Street. Start at the Co-op Store, the heart of island life. It does duty as grocery store, hardware and dry goods store. In summer you can buy produce fresh from **Lansdowne Farm**. The notice board outside the front door is a gather-and-gossip spot for locals catching up on the latest island buy-and-sells and local events. The rest of the village to the left along First Street is easy to take in—a gift shop, gas station, liquor store, the funky waterfront café, a hotel/pub/credit union, the post office, library and medical clinic. You can also **rent sea kayaks** or arrange **fishing and whale watching charters**. Just ask at any local establishment. It's a friendly place where people nod and wave at newcomers, and hitching rides is standard practice. At the end of the village by the tennis courts is a thrift store, senior centre and the Sointula Museum all rolled into one small building. The one-room **Sointula Finnish Museum** is stuffed with pioneer artifacts donated by Malcolm Island folk—cups and saucers, lamps and shoes, fishing lures, a record player, a wheelchair, the town's original telephone switchboard. Scattered amongst the flotsam of island life are signs of its anarchist origins—photographs of Stalin, dusty tracts with titles like *Notes on Guerrilla Warfare*, a mural of a fierce-looking Lady of Liberty leading workers to the promised land. Don't overlook the inspiration for the museum, the giant coffee grinder, which in the 1930s sent the delicious aroma of fresh-ground coffee drifting through the Co-op Store. An antique collector nearly escaped with it a few years back. That's when the women of Sointula swung into action and started the museum, with the old coffee-pot-shaped grinder as its proud first possession.

If you're feeling footloose and fancy free, walk past the museum toward the west end of Rough Bay about 3 km from the ferry dock. On the right side are more colourful Finnish houses with prettily fenced gardens and a scattering of homey B&Bs. On the left are the old cedar-grey boat sheds in varying states of repair standing on stilts over the rocky beach. The silvery sheds draped with green fishnets are a photographer's delight, especially when the late afternoon sun lights up the old wood. Sprinkled here and there among the boat sheds are a few cottages, marine ways and government wharves where

you may catch sight of Sointula's commercial fleet in action. You can walk to the tidal flats at the end of Rough Bay and watch the shorebirds stalking the shallow water. The road ends just beyond the tidal flats in a dense green forest.

The interior of Malcolm Island is thickly covered with second-growth forest and crisscrossed with logging roads. The unprotected north shore is

Rural scene on Kaleva Road

mostly uninhabited. If you wish to venture into the interior, the dockside art gallery sells logging road maps. Many of these roads are in rough shape—the logging industry has slowed down—but the gravel road to **Bere Point Regional Park** is a happy exception. It's maintained by the local district and perfectly drivable. The road leads through scraggy alder and second-growth cedar forest to Bere Point on the wilder north coast bordering Queen Charlotte Strait. Bere Point Regional Park has 8 campsites above the wide sweep of gravel beach. There are picnic tables, pit toilets and a boat launch for camper-top boats. (Bring your own water.) The park is a favourite getaway for islanders and the only public camping on the island. Whales sometimes swim past the shore and seiners work the waters in August. To get to Bere Point Regional Park from the ferry dock, turn left down First St and watch for the right turn onto Bere Point Rd just past Ocean Bliss B&B. Less than 1 km later the paved Bere Point Rd gives way to a gravel logging road. Watch for the red hand-lettered signs at major junctures directing you to the campground. It's about a 5-km drive from the Sointula ferry dock.

Kaleva Road—the island's one major paved road—is a great place to drive, cycle or walk. It starts just to the right of the ferry dock and runs east for about 9 km, hugging the island's gentle southern shore. The road leads past colourful shake-roofed houses in well-tended gardens. A few dogs keep a lazy eye on the road from their properties.

The island cemetery is on your right just outside town and worth a stop. Compared to other pioneer grave plots, this neat and tidy cemetery surrounded by hedging is a miracle of order. The past has not been abandoned. Buckets of daisies, marigolds, petunias and foxgloves brighten the graves of beloved family members.

Scan the trees over the water for a pair of resident eagles whose eerie twittering is the only sound that breaks the calm. Then head down the road, winding through pastures edged with wild berry brambles and past old weather-greyed cottages and newer hobby farm homes. Here and there you'll see a whimsical touch—a roguish wooden chicken over a gatepost or a mini-herd of llamas below a guest lodge.

There are plenty of pull-off spots where you can get down on the shelving gravel beach and walk to your heart's content. This is the place to let yourself be enveloped by the island's pervasive sense of calm and domestic order. The traffic is light and generally unobtrusive—a quiet woman in long skirt and sturdy shoes cycles by, a farm truck ambles homeward, an old VW Bug with a kayak over its roof heads for a quiet cove. There's no real destination down Kaleva Road: let personal whim take you as far as you feel like going.

Important Numbers

*Police **911***
*Fire **911***
*Ambulance **911***
Police non-emergency
250-973-6531

Alert Bay (Cormorant Island)

Cormorant Island is just 45 minutes by ferry from Port McNeill or 35 minutes from Sointula, but it seems a world away from its neighbours. No place on Vancouver Island retains such a strong presence of Kwakwaka'wakw (Kwakiutl) First Nations heritage. The Kwakwaka'wakw are made up of 15 Kwak-wala-speaking groups living along the northeastern coasts of Vancouver Island and on the nearby mainland. The 'Namgis, one of the most powerful of the Kwakwaka'wakw peoples, moved from their traditional Vancouver

Alert Bay

Island home on the salmon-rich Nimpkish River across the strait to Cormorant Island in the 1870s to work in the salmon saltery.

The bustling little village of Alert Bay takes up most of Cormorant Island. One main road runs along the island, and a good pair of walking shoes will get you just about anywhere else you want to go. Most of the island's establishments—restaurants, hotels, pubs, stores, laundromats, bank machine, sports fishing and whale watching charters, marina and fuel docks—are located on the main drag.

What to See

- ☐ **1** World's 2nd tallest totem pole
- ☐ **2** U'Mista Cultural Centre
- ☐ **3** 19th-century Anglican Church
- ☐ **4** Gator Gardens
- ☐ **5** Nimpkish Burial Grounds

To scout out most of Alert Bay's services turn right from the ferry dock down Fir Street. A good first stop is the **Alert Bay InfoCentre** at 118 Fir St, where you can pick up a map and local brochures (250-974-5213). The free pamphlet called "Your Guide to Historic Alert Bay" is a handy guide to the sites.

Cormorant Island was Kwakwaka'wakw territory for centuries before the Europeans arrived, used mainly as a summer home and food-gathering area, and as a burial ground.

Nimpkish Burial Grounds

Modern settlement of Cormorant Island can be traced back to two early entrepreneurs called Huson and Spencer who built a salmon saltery on the island in the 1870s. At first they hired Native labourers from around the mouth of the Nimpkish River (on Vancouver Island across from Comorant Island). But whenever celebrations were held at other villages on the coast, their workers left for days at a time, which was bad for production. In 1878, to secure their work force, they persuaded the Anglican missionary at Fort Rupert to move to Cormorant Island. The missionary arrived and organized the building of a church, school and sawmill for Native parishioners. Once the mission was relocated, many Kwakwaka'wakw families moved here as well, and Huson and Spencer had secured a steady supply of Native workers. Later an Indian agency, an RCMP station, a salmon cannery, a hospital and a Native residential school were all built at Alert Bay, and two communities—Native and non-Native—grew side by side for over a hundred years.

A quick drive or an easy 10-minute walk up the hill from the InfoCentre is **Gator Gardens Ecological Park**. Don't be put off by visions of a Florida-style tourist trap. It's actually the Northwest Coast equivalent of the Florida everglades, where three boardwalk nature trails traverse a marshland. Ghostly cedar snags, pines and hemlocks draped in "witches' hair" moss thrust up through trailing wisps of mist. Ravens swoop through the air, eagles perch high up snag trees and migratory birds flit through the undergrowth. Fleshy skunk cabbage leaves push up from muddy banks and white bunchberry flowers and pink-flowered salal brighten the forest floor. The walk takes less than 45 minutes and is suitable for kids. Huson and Spencer accidentally created this eerie, other-worldly marshland when they dammed a river to accumulate fresh water for their salmon saltery.

If you backtrack down the hill and carry on down Fir Street past the InfoCentre, you'll come to the **'Namgis Burial Grounds**, one of the few remaining places on the coast where totems stand untouched on their original site. Some of the poles date back to the nineteenth century while others have been raised in recent years. Look for Kwakwaka'wakw ancestral family crests, including frog, grizzly bear, thunderbird, eagle, raven and giant halibut. (These grounds are sacred, so please stay outside the fence.)

Just past and around the corner from the burial grounds is the 1920 Nimpkish Hotel and Pub. It was built on the 'Namgis reserve in 1920, but the government refused to license a beer parlour and hotel on reserve land. So its owners loaded the structure onto a barge and towed it down to the white community at the south end of the island. Stop in for a pint and watch Alert Bay's avid chess players try to stump their opponents.

Retrace your route and drive or walk north past the ferry dock to the **U'Mista Cultural Centre**. This first-rate museum and cultural showcase is a must-see for anyone interested in Northwest Coast art and culture. The centre's permanent display is the impressive **Potlatch Collection**. The word *u'mista* is a Kwakwala word for people taken in slave raids by enemy groups and then returned to their communities. The return of the treasured potlatch objects from museums in eastern Canada is seen as a special kind of u'mista. The collection, displayed in the subdued half-light of the main gallery, is haunting. It is impossible not to feel the beauty and power of these ceremonial objects, including intricately woven cedar bark headgear, coppers (each with its own history of ownership) and the hereditary masks (raven, bear, eagle, wolf and others) representing the First Ancestors of the Kwakwaka'wakw Nations. These are not just museum pieces but the living heritage of the Alert Bay Native community: the cultural centre is dedicated to forging links between the

Gator Gardens

Kwakwaka'wakw people's past, present and future. (For information, U'mista Cultural Centre, 250-974-5403, email umista@north.island.net.)

On the hill behind the U'mista Centre is the **world's second tallest totem pole** with the many-rayed Sun Mask at its narrow tip (the new Commonwealth pole in Victoria is now the tallest). It was raised in 1972 to celebrate the tribes of the Kwakwaka'wakw First Nations. In spite of decades of systematic repression, Kwakwaka'wakw culture is alive and well in Alert Bay. Come experience Northwest Coast Native culture for yourself. Non-Natives are welcome at the 'Namgis Indian Reserve.

Alert Bay Recreation, Accommodations and Services

Recreation	Campground
Bicycle rentals	RV Park
Boat charters	**Services**
Dive charter	Places to eat
Hiking trails	(Pubs, restaurants)
Tennis courts	Credit union (No ATM)
Bowling alley	Gas station
Accommodations	Grocery store
Bed & Breakfast	Art gallery
Inns	Post office
Resorts	Hospital

Important Numbers

Police **911**
Fire **911**
Ambulance **911**
Hospital **250-974-5585**

Port Alice

Back on Vancouver Island, the next major turnoff north of Port McNeill is to Port Alice. Look for the well-signed turnoff to the left. Port Alice, a logging and pulp mill town, is tucked under the cedar-covered mountains at the head of **Neroutsos Inlet** in **Quatsino Sound** just 30 minutes from the highway. Port Alice was named for Alice Whelan, whose sons built the first pulp mill on Neroutsos Inlet in 1917. Today's pleasantly contemporary planned community was re-sited 7 km from the original village in 1965 to become BC's first instant municipality.

The Potlatch

Potlatches were complex ritual celebrations of important events in Kwakwaka'wakw life—marriages, naming of children, transfer of honorary names or privileges. During the potlatch the songs, masked dances and rituals belonging to the host's family were performed as a way of confirming and enhancing the position of the host chief and his family. Witnesses to the event were honoured with feasts and gifts. The higher the chief's status, the more elaborate the gifts. The potlatch was at the very heart of Kwakwaka'wakw culture: it defined social, economic and kinship relationships among families and affirmed each individual's place in the community and in the wider scheme of creation. White missionaries, Indian agents and a few Christianized Indians who opposed the religious and cultural life of the Native people naturally opposed the potlatch as a central element of that cultural life, and in 1884 the Dominion government passed a law banning the potlatch. Many Kwakwaka'wakw and other Natives resisted the law. Many chiefs, elders and their allies pressured government to revoke the law, and some communities held potlatches in secret. Matters came to a head in 1922 after the famous five-day "Christmas Potlatch" on the remote Village Island, to celebrate the marriage of 'Namgis chief Dan Cranmer. Thousands of dollars in gifts were given to three hundred guests. Soon afterward forty-five people were charged under the anti-potlatch law. In return for suspended sentences, whole villages were forced to surrender their potlatch regalia. Twenty men and women refused and were sent to Oakalla Prison. Meanwhile the Alert Bay Indian agent crated up hundreds of ritual objects, including twenty coppers and scores of masks and rattles, and shipped them off to the National Museum of Ottawa. Some objects were given to other museums. Potlatching continued, but on a smaller and less lavish scale. In 1951 the anti-potlatch law was quietly dropped from the books and a new era began as the Kwakwaka'wakw First Nations began to revive their beleaugered cultural heritage. In the mid 1970s Canadian museums agreed to return many potlatch treasures to the Kwakwaka'wakw, and by 1980 the Potlatch Collection was back home in the newly built Kwagiulth Museum and Cultural Centre on Quadra Island (see pp. 288, 290) and the U'Mista Cultural Centre at Alert Bay. Tears of bitterness and joy greeted the ancient masks and treasures when the U'Mista Cultural Centre was formally opened in 1980.

Today Port Alice is a base for outdoor adventure and for exploring the Quatsino Sound area by boat. The town has visitor services including stores, restaurants, a bank, RV sites and campgrounds, a golf course, a marina and a boat ramp. Kayakers use it as a launch spot for paddling the sheltered waters of Neroutsos, Holberg and Rupert inlets or venturing into the open Pacific Ocean past Quatsino Sound. The **fishing** and **swimming** are excellent in nearby Alice Lake and Victoria Lake, and canoeists can tour both lakes with just a short portage. Popular off-roading excursions include the **exotic karst formations** known as Devil's Bath, Eternal Fountain and Vanishing River, and trips to **wilderness campsites** nestled in soaring forests by prime fishing or **boating** locations. (Pick up current logging maps at the North Island Forestry Centre south of Port McNeill or contact the Port Alice InfoCentre at Quatsino Chalet, 1061 Marine Dr. Open year-round Mon to Fri, 250-284-3318.)

Port Hardy

Port Hardy is the next major stop north of the Port Alice turnoff, and lies at the end of Hwy 19. With more than 5,000 residents, this is the biggest community on the North Island. It is spread across an open green hillside above Hardy Bay, and got its prosperous start on paycheques from mining, logging and fishing. In recent years North Island resource industries have endured slowdowns. The huge open pit **Island Copper Mine** closed down, and commercial forestry and fishing are edging downward. This plucky community's answer has been to accentuate the positive. Port Hardy still celebrates its resource roots in the annual Filomi Days in mid-August. ("Filomi" is short for the historic industries of fishing, logging and mining.) But it's also looking to tourism, the other cornerstone of the community's economy, to carry it into the twenty-first century.

Its setting on Hardy Bay is charming, its history is colourful and it is a great jumping-off point for BC ferries cruises through the splendid Inside Passage to Prince Rupert, Bella Coola or the Queen Charlotte Islands (Haida Gwaii). Just east and north of Port Hardy is a wildly beautiful (and accessible only by boat) rain coast on the open Pacific Ocean where hardy adventurers can venture into true wilderness. Port Hardy is also in "King Coho Country." Here, between July and November, anglers regularly hook giant **northern coho salmon** weighing in at 9 kg, and at other times of the year they catch other species of salmon, halibut, ling cod and snapper. For the ultimate in wilderness fresh- and saltwater fishing, there's **fly-in fishing** to remote destinations like Rivers Inlet, Milbanke Sound and Tweedsmuir Park. Port Hardy is also the place where many of BC's professional **scuba divers** take a bus driver's holiday to super-hot diving spots. If this is your avocation, you can go eyeball to eyeball with curious wolf

Carrot Park with the Government Wharf in the background

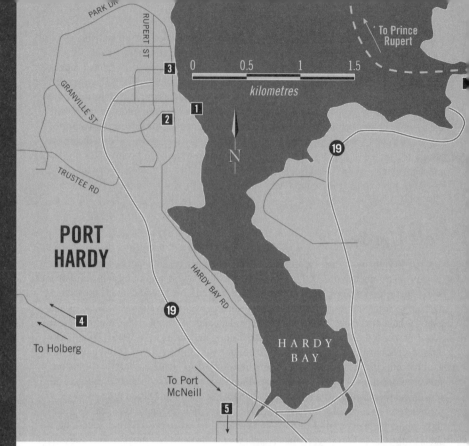

PORT
HARDY

To Holberg

To Port
McNeill

HARDY
BAY

To Prince
Rupert

kilometres

N

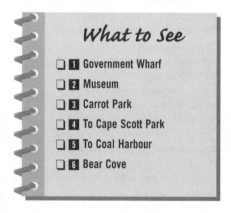

What to See

- ☐ **1** Government Wharf
- ☐ **2** Museum
- ☐ **3** Carrot Park
- ☐ **4** To Cape Scott Park
- ☐ **5** To Coal Harbour
- ☐ **6** Bear Cove

eels at Hunt Rock, explore the cornucopia of Gorgonian corals at Berry Inlet, drift along the colourful undersea wall at Browning Pass or search for undersea wrecks. Today there are many more places around Port Hardy to hike and cycle, and the kayaking is great. You can even book **Native cultural kayak expeditions** in Johnstone Strait and **Quatsino Sound** or choose your own dropoff spot around Bella Bella, Namu and Hakai Pass straight from the car deck on BC Ferries Discovery Coast sailings (see Chapter 9). You'll enjoy golfing at the challenging **Seven Hills Golf Course** at Port Alice—built partly by local volunteers—even if sweeping views of the North Island mountains distract you from your game.

As the biggest tourist centre on the North Island, Port Hardy covers all the bases. You'll find a full range of services, including more than 400 hotel and motel rooms, full shopping facilities, banks, two marinas and three campsites. Because Port Hardy is the

The Carrot Highway

Before the paved highway was completed in 1979, North Islanders used to bump up and down a rutted logging road to get back and forth to Campbell River. In the 1970s Port McNeill and Port Hardy folk joined forces to put on a good-natured publicity campaign to get a paved road for the North Island. Down in Port McNeill, Mayor Gerry Furney staged a tongue-in-cheek golf tournament on "the world's longest golf course" with the logging road as the course and the potholes as the putting greens. The Port McNeill village council handed out Road Survival Kits containing a can of beans, a fish hook and line, a toilet paper roll and a stamped envelope addressed to the Department of Highways. Up in Port Hardy people pinned on buttons addressed to the highway minister, asking, "Do you carrot all?" The "Carrot Highway" campaign was a success, and by 1979 a paved road ran right up to the top of Vancouver Island. Port Hardy built **Carrot Park** and unveiled a giant carrot sculpture to celebrate its victory.

southern terminal for BC Ferries Northern Cruises through the Inside Passage, accommodations and campgrounds are usually booked solid during July and August. In fact, the Northern Cruises are so popular that BC Ferries had to beg Port Hardy folk to make more room for ferry passengers. Quite a few locals in this very hospitable community opened their homes as B&Bs and set up a shuttle bus to take overnight guests to the **BC Ferries Bear Cove terminal**. But the town is still crammed to the gills in peak season, so book well ahead of time. (For reservations, contact North Island Reservations and Information, 250-949-7622, or Super, Natural British Columbia Accommodations, 1-800-663-6000.)

To get to the downtown business district just take Hwy 19 as it swings to the right toward the water and follow it until the road ends at Hardy Bay. Market St is the main road that runs along the bay, and most of the town's services are within a four-block radius of the waterfront. The Port Hardy InfoCentre is on Market Street not far from the Seagate Hotel (250-949-7622, daily early June to late Sept; Mon–Fri off-season.) It's a good place to get the details on local services and attractions. History buffs will want to visit the nearby Port Hardy Museum and Archives for displays on Kwakwaka'wakw culture, European exploration and pioneer history (7110 Market St, 250-949-8143; Tues, Thurs, Sat afternoons). A pleasant sea walk runs north from the business district between Market St and Hardy Bay. This is the perfect end-of-the day stroll when the far-distant mountains darken to silhouettes beneath the ruddy glow of late-evening clouds.

For a slice of real Port Hardy, try downing a pint at the rough-and-ready **Seagate Hotel** pub at the head of the wharf right in the heart of Port Hardy's business district. It's a real fishermen, loggers and locals bar—the kind of place where you want to be careful about staring at fellow patrons too intently.

If you wonder what it's like going to sea in one of those fish boats tied up at the wharf, pick up Edith Iglauer's award-winning book *Fishing with John*. Iglauer is a former *New Yorker* writer who met a BC fisherman named John Daly, and moved to the west coast to marry him. In her book she describes days and nights aboard John's cramped wooden salmon troller, the *MoreKelp*. She fell in love with the life and people of this enchanted place, as have many readers of her classic book, which is now being made into a feature film.

Bear Cove and Fort Rupert

Bear Cove just south of Port Hardy was actually the first place settled by non-Natives in this area. In 1849 the Hudson's Bay Company built **Fort Rupert** to mine coal at nearby Suquash. To stake their claim as fur trade middlemen and to establish a treaty requiring the HBC to pay for exploiting coal on aboriginal land, four Kwakiutl tribes of the Kwakwaka'wakw Nation moved to Fort Rupert and built their huge cedar longhouses just outside the fort's palisades. Relations between the HBC and the Kwakiutl were tempestuous and the coal was poor, so the HBC sold its holdings to the fort's last chief factor, Robert Hunt. Hunt was an interpreter and collaborator with the famous anthropologists Franz Boas and Edward Curtis. Hunt's wife Mary Ebbetts was a Tlingit noblewoman and the daughter of Chief Shaiks of Alaska. The couple stayed on at Fort Rupert to run the company store and founded a proud family lineage. Their beautiful great granddaughter Margaret Frank was the princess bride in Edward Curtis's 1914 ethnographic film classic, *In the Land of the War Canoes*. Today many of their descendants, including Henry Hunt and Tony Hunt, are renowned Native artists. Calvin Hunt, son of hereditary Chief Thomas Hunt, and his wife Marie Hunt have organized a dance troupe called the **Copper Maker Dancers** to pass on Kwakiutl songs and dances to the next generation. They have performed across North America and in Europe and Australia. The Hunts also run **The Copper Maker**, a carving studio and workshop featuring fine masks, totem poles, prints and jewellery by Hunt family members in Fort Rupert Village. This popular gallery is just 10 minutes south of Port Hardy. Take the turnoff to Beaver Harbour Rd, then turn right at T'sakis Way and drive into Fort Rupert Village (114 Copper Way).

The Discovery Coast ferry leaving Bear Cove

Coal Harbour, Quatsino Sound

Fort Rupert Village also boasts an impressive new **Big House** and Fort Rupert's original chimney. It survived a fire that destroyed the HBC fort in 1889. Just beyond the turnoff to Fort Rupert Village, Beaver Harbour Rd runs along behind **Storey's Beach**. This long, sandy beach is popular with swimmers and sand castle builders. And the rugged 7-km **Tex Lyon Trail** bordering the beach is equally popular with adventurous hikers. This challenging trail runs along the seashore and up rocky bluffs through a spruce, cedar and hemlock forest to Dillon Point and a payoff of panoramic views over Queen Charlotte Strait. The hike starts at the **Beaver Harbour Park** boat launch and takes about 2 1/2 hours each way. Beach sections of the trail can disappear under high tides, so check the tide tables before setting out. (For more information, contact the InfoCentre, 250-956-3131, or the Port Hardy InfoCentre on Market St, 250-949-7622.)

Coal Harbour

For a short jaunt out of Port Hardy, take the well-signed turnoff from Highway 19 on the southern outskirts of town to the historic west coast town of Coal Harbour. Coal Harbour, on the shores of Holberg Inlet, is just 20 minutes from Port Hardy. The short road to Coal Harbour is probably the narrowest portion of Vancouver Island, where the "west coat" is just minutes from the "east coast." Its name comes from the coal veins discovered back in

Port Hardy Recreation, Accommodations and Services

Recreation
Bicycle rentals
Golf course
Fishing charters
Dive charters
Recreation centre

Accommodations
Bed & Breakfasts
Inns
Resorts
Campgrounds

RV Parks

Services
Travel InfoCentre
Places to eat
(Restaurants, pubs, fast food)
Banks
Gas stations
Grocery stores
Galleries/Studios

1859. But the town's real claim to fame is as "A Whale of a Town." It was the site of the last whaling station on the BC coast which finally shut down in 1967. Now it's a quiet seaside village circled around the government wharf on Quatsino Sound. The view from the wharf with float planes dropping into the inlet and eagles flapping up into the misty blue sky is a classic coastal

Important Numbers

Emergency (Fire/Police/Ambulance) **911**
Environmental Emergency **250-666-6100**
Search & Rescue **1-800-567-5111**
Travel InfoCentre **250-949-7622**

scene. A 4-day Native cultural kayak expedition up Quatsino Sound leaves from Coal Harbour (250-949-7707) and a water taxi runs to the out-of-the-way hamlet of Quatsino where you can see an old-time coastal settlement and go beachcombing, hiking or berry picking. Tiny Quatsino has a historic church and graveyard and Eagle Manor, a refurbished 1912 hotel where you can get a great lunch if you call ahead.

Cape Scott Provincial Park

On the remote northwest tip of Vancouver Island is the untamed raincoast wilderness of 21,849-ha Cape Scott Provincial Park. The 23-km stretch of surf-battered sand beaches and rocky headlands is one of Vancouver Island's most spectacular coastlines. Looking for an outdoor adventure that's way off the beaten track? Come to Cape Scott and sling on your backpack. This magnificent park can be travelled only by way of hiking trails, which wind through a 500-year-old rain forest with a proliferating understorey of moss, ferns and salmonberry. Eventually the trails take you to miles of surf-swept beaches on the wild Pacific Ocean. Step onto a beach to find the footprints of a mink or wolf in the wet sand or to see a black bear padding quietly into the forest fringe. This is a place for the truly adventurous.

The Cape Scott trails are also studded with reminders of its fascinating history. In the late 1890s, Danish homesteaders from the American midwest arrived to try to establish a colony. It was a brave attempt: the far corner of Vancouver Island was stormy, foggy and supremely isolated with no harbour, no steamer service and no nearby settlements. But to Rasmus Hansen, a Danish halibut fisherman from Puget Sound, Cape Scott was so beautiful that he was determined to found a farming and fishing Eden. A band of settlers, armed with a promise from the government in Victoria that a good road would be built to Cape Scott, arrived by sea in 1897 and began clearing homesteads at the head of Hansen Bay. But the promised road never materialized, and the land proved better for pastures than farming. The colony was abandoned by 1907. A second wave of Danish settlers arrived in 1908, but by 1930 this settlement too had given up.

The wagon roads carved by the Danes through the tangled rain forest are now the park's hiking trails. Heritage markers along the trails and beaches point out the remains of the turn-of-the-century settlements, including tumbledown cabins, sun-bleached driftwood fence posts, cedar planked "corduroy roads" and a cougar trap built by the Jensen children that actually caught a cougar for a few minutes!

To get to Cape Scott Provincial Park, take the turnoff for Holberg 3 km south of Port Hardy. The paved road soon becomes a gravel logging road. Follow this road about 46 km to tiny Holberg (a former military base), where the road forks. Take the well-signed San Josef Main fork and follow the logging road another 18.5 km to the Cape Scott Provincial Park parking lot. Here you'll find the trailheads for both the San Josef Bay Trail and the Cape Scott Trail, as well as a small but fine Western Forest Products campsite in a grove of soaring Sitka spruce. San Josef Bay is a popular destination for a day hike. It takes about

Sea stacks at San Josef Bay

an hour to walk down the well-graded 2.5-km trail through a wildlife marsh of giant ferns, salmonberries and skunk cabbage to San Josef Bay, where there's an expanse of sandy beach so wonderfully flat and wide that a jumbo jet could make a comfortable landing. At the north end, a rock outcropping with beautifully twisting wind-stunted trees adds the perfect finishing touch to a picturesque setting.

To explore all of this huge wilderness park, you would need a good week to hike along the 23.6-km Cape Scott Trail and offshoot trails. It runs northwest from Holberg Inlet to the Cape Scott lighthouse, Fisherman Bay and Hansen Lagoon. The start of the trail is a legendary muddy quagmire through the Quatsino Rain Forest. But the pleasures ahead are worth the first hard slog—Sitka spruce trees arching to a canopy 50 metres above the ground, the wide surf beach and multicoloured tidepools at Nels Bight, the windswept grasses and turquoise water of Guise Bay, warm-water swimming and fine fishing at Eric Lake, the fascinating remains of the Danish colony at Hansen Lagoon, a tidal wave of bird life during the spring and fall migrations, and the pleasure of standing under the tall white lighthouse at Cape Scott on the very tip of Vancouver Island.

Some words of warning: Cape Scott Provincial Park is a 2-hour drive down a heavily used logging road, so exercise caution or travel after working hours. Make careful advance preparations and bring good equipment, especially wet weather gear. Storms accompanied by heavy wind and rain are likely even in high summer, and getting emergency help is difficult in this deep wilderness area. For a Cape Scott Provincial Park brochure, contact BC Parks, 250-387-4550, or stop by Vancouver Island InfoCentres. For more detail, pick up *Hiking Trails III*, published by Vancouver Island Trails Information Society.

CHAPTER 9

THE NORTH COAST

Prince Rupert's impressive Butze Rapids

T he North Coast's spectacular geography of up-thrusting coastal mountains, deep-tongued fjords and island-spattered waters have kept major settlement at bay. The coastline is barricaded from an approach by land behind ramparts of snow-bright mountain peaks—so difficult that only two roads from BC's interior have been pushed down deep river valleys to the sea.

The sea has always been the region's highway to the outside world, and it's still the lifeline to the tiny settlements between Vancouver Island and the Alaska border. Hundreds of islands and islets form a labyrinth of sheltered navigation channels. They're part of the huge north–south ocean corridor between Puget Sound and Alaska known as the Inside Passage, where tugs towing barges, stout commercial fishboats, high wedding-cake cruise ships, and sleek pleasure craft all weave in and out of the tangled channels.

A giant cedar in the Queen Charlotte Islands

Despite thousands of years of human habitation, the North Coast still seems an untamed wilderness, where a footprint is more likely to be animal than human. Little has changed since the early 1790s when English and Spanish mapmakers traced out the intricate coastal fretwork north of Port Hardy. An occasional small hamlet, the cheerful solidity of a lighthouse, the greying cedar skeleton of a turn-of-the-century cannery or the wide scar of a mountainside clear-cut are the few reminders of human presence in this ancient rain coast. Eagles flap out of trees to scan the sea for prey, and the occasional bear

Getting to Port Hardy from the Vancouver Area

Note: The following travel information assumes that visitors to the Mid- and North Coast will be travelling via ferry from Port Hardy. If you are planning to begin your coastal adventures from Prince Rupert or the Queen Charlotte Islands, see the travel information in the Prince Rupert and Queen Charlotte sections of this chapter.

From Vancouver

Drive aboard the BC Ferry from Tsawwassen terminal (just south of Vancouver). Ferry runs to Duke Point terminal, just south of Nanaimo. 2 hours crossing time; 8 sailings daily year round.

Or: Drive aboard the BC Ferry from Horseshoe Bay terminal (just north of Vancouver). Ferry runs to Departure Bay terminal at Nanaimo.

1 hour 35 minutes crossing time, 8 sailings daily, year round.

From Nanaimo

Drive up Hwy 19 to Port Hardy (see Chapters 7 & 8). The 391-km drive takes 5–6 hours.

From Victoria

Drive up Hwys 1 and 19 to Port Hardy (see Chapters 5, 7 & 8). The 502-km drive takes 7–8 hours.

For more information about travel aboard BC Ferries, see p. 8.

---

stalks the shore of a protected cove. Whales, porpoises or sea lions can appear out of nowhere to leap and plunge in the deep green water.

Three BC ferry routes thread through this remote wilderness. The **Discovery Coast Passage Route** angles north and east from Port Hardy through the region known as the Mid-Coast to Bella Coola. It is a place where the great Northwest wilderness remains a stronghold of coastal wildlife. Formerly the preserve of private yachts and cruisers, travellers can make stopoffs at small Native communities and former logging and cannery settlements. Kayakers can arrange dropoff and pickup straight from the ferry deck to paddle this unforgettable wilderness to their heart's content.

The **Inside Passage Route**, BC Ferries' popular 15-hour daylight cruise from Port Hardy to Prince Rupert, follows Alaska-bound ships up the spectacular forest-green

BC Ferries' Queen of the North

fjordland that has made this a hugely popular summer cruise destination. Passengers can overnight at Prince Rupert and sail back to Port Hardy the next morning or make connections to the Alaska Marine Highway ferries. Another popular option is to drive across the mountains to the interior of the province and down to Vancovuer.

Prince Rupert is also the departure point for BC Ferries' **Queen Charlotte Islands Route**. The ferry sails southwest 100 km across the open sea of Hecate Strait. Expect the unexpected, where "magical" is the only word many visitors can find to describe these rugged volcanic islands.

These three ferry routes are your ocean highways to adventure.

A Brief History of the North Coast

The first sea voyagers ventured down the North Coast from the Bering Strait after the last ice age retreated some 10,000 years ago. The ancestors of today's First Nations peoples— including the Tlingit, Haida, Tsimshian, Nuxalk, Heiltsuk and Kwakwaka'wakw—settled on the North Coast, canoed to salmon fishing streams and berry-picking grounds all along these intricate waterways and built winter villages up storm-sheltered inlets. Captain George Vancouver mapped the Inside Passage in the 1790s, casually sprinkling the European names of friends, crew members and the Lords of the Admiralty over dozens of islands and bays, while rival Spanish explorers added their own piquant names to the mix. In the late 1800s homesteaders' cabins, floating logging camps and canneries appeared in small coves and bays. Coastal steamships carried passengers and freight to far-flung North Coast communities. But the smaller logging and cannery operations started shutting down as the lumbering and fishing industries became increasingly mechanized and centralized in larger centres to the south. Coastal workers drifted away to find jobs elsewhere, and by the end of the 1950s the welcome whistle of coastal steamers was just a memory. In 1966 the BC Ferries began to knit up the coast again with the first vital marine link between Vancouver Island and Prince Rupert. Today three major ferry routes tie small North Coast communities to the outside world.

Historic photo of the Haida village at Yan, Queen Charlotte Islands

THE DISCOVERY COAST PASSAGE ROUTE TO BELLA COOLA

Queen of Chilliw.

Traditional Native canoe

Highlights

Rich First Nations
culture

Spectacular fjords and
jagged mountains

Kayaking, canoeing
and boating

Adventure touring

Remote camping

Sport fishing

It's a summer morning in Port Hardy, and BC Ferries' Bear Cove terminal is awash with activity as some 300 passengers and 115 vehicles load up for the Discovery Coast passage to Bella Coola. On the jam-packed car deck of the *Queen of Chilliwack*, drivers are squeezing out of campers and cars and heading toward the beckoning smells of fresh coffee and bacon sizzling on the cafeteria grill. Outdoorsy types in bright blue and yellow waterproof jackets hover over sleek sea kayaks stowing backpacks and dry sacks. Upstairs on the passenger deck walk-on travellers stake out comfy recliner chairs under the windows while excited youngsters call out to report their new finds. "Hey, Mom, they've got showers!" "Look at the TV sets up in that corner. Can we watch movies?" "You said we could set up a tent. Where should we put it?" In the licensed lounge, a quiet, pony-tailed Native artist—guest speaker of BC Ferries—begins laying out paints, brushes and a drum skin. Later dozens of people will stop to chat and watch as an elegant red-and-black Tsimshian eagle motif takes shape on the tautly stretched hide. As the ship leaves the dock, a crew member begins making intercom announcements about shipboard services and activities— where to sign up for shore excursions, how to rent cots, blankets and pillows, where to meet for a sea shanty singalong with the crew and a barbecue on the ship deck. A good-natured bustle and spirit of fun and camaraderie sets this voyage apart—it's an adventure for old and young, one and all.

The Norwegian-built *Queen of Chilliwack* has been comfortably refitted with passenger enjoyment in mind, but it's a "working boat" in the proud tradition of the old coastal steamers.

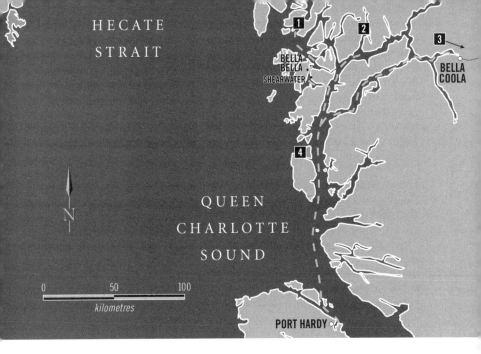

Expect airline-style recliner seats instead of stateroom beds, and a cafeteria instead of a restaurant.

For non-locals the Discovery Coast Passage Route is a once-in-a-lifetime chance to walk ashore at the *Chilliwack*'s ports of call and meet the people—Native and non-Native—who know the ruggedly beautiful coast's many moods and secrets. Shore excursions are short—1 to 3 hours long—but they're the stuff of longtime memories. You can also make arrangements for a stopover

What to See

- [ ] **1** Klemtu
- [ ] **2** Ocean Falls
- [ ] **3** To Tweedsmuir Provincial Park
- [ ] **4** Hakai Recreation Area
- [ ] **5** Fitz Hugh Sound

to enjoy **adventure-touring** on your own before catching another sailing. The communities offer services from **fishing charters** and boat rentals to adventure tours. Kayakers and boaters can arrange with BC Ferries for dropoffs and pickups and explore this rugged kingdom of **mountainous islands** and **knifing fjords** under their own steam. Popular sea **kayaking** and **boating** destinations are the new 124,000-ha **Hakai Recreation Area** midway between Port Hardy and McLoughlin Bay (Bella Bella) and the legendary salmon fishing grounds of Hakai Passage, the galaxy of unspoiled islands between Bella Bella and Ocean Falls, and the 91,000-ha Fiordland Recreation Area where deep Mussel and Kynoch Inlets are girded by towering coastal mountains. For information on the marine recreation areas, contact BC Parks, Cariboo Region, 250-398-4414.

Keep in mind as you're planning your trip that what stops the *Queen of Chilliwack* makes on its way to Bella Coola—if it stops at all—depends on the day. You'll need to match up your intended stops and dates of travel.

McLoughlin Bay (Bella Bella/Waglisla)

It's a 10-hour sail to the first stop at McLoughlin Bay on Campbell Island. The new ferry terminal is about 3 km from Bella Bella, also called Waglisla, the largest community on this part of the coast and home to about 1,500 members of the **Heiltsuk First Nations band**. Bella Bella got its start when the Heiltsuk settled around Fort McLoughlin, a Hudson's Bay Company trading post built in 1833. In recent times, the Heiltsuk have worked at logging and fishing, and the band maintains a few tourist services in Bella Bella itself. But band members want to make sure that village life is not disrupted by too many visitors.

McLoughlin Bay has been okayed for tourism, and Frank and Kathy Brown offer **waterfront camping** and transport to **kayakers** and **campers** to remote spots as well as lots of opportunities for visitors to see, in their words, "the land and sea through the eyes of our ancestors," including sea charters, interpretive walking tours and Heiltsuk heritage and eco-canoe tours. You can look at handcrafted items and photographs and sample fried bread at the **Browns' Interpretation Centre**, hand-built in traditional "Big House" style from recycled material—trusses from a grandmother's house, plank siding milled from beach logs, and a floor of fine white and purple sand (the purple comes from broken sea urchin shells left by a recently closed fishery). The Browns have been active in the cultural revival of coastal First Nations and they're delighted to share their culture with visitors.

Ferry passengers rave about the **hour-long paddle trip** in the 7-tonne traditional Heiltsuk canoe *Glwa*. After stepping gingerly into the rocking canoe, rearranging the rocks for ballast and getting a few tips from Frank on how to paddle, they're off across the Lama Passage to Shearwater, where they reboard the ferry. (For information, contact BC Ferries or SeeQuest Development Company, 250-957-2611.)

Shearwater

This non-Native community of 125 people on Denny Island 5 km (45 minutes) from McLoughlin Bay is the next port of call. The Heiltsuk camped at Shearwater before relocating around Fort McLoughlin in the mid-1800s, and a fish plant operated here from 1919 into the 1930s. But Shearwater's real claim to fame was as a Second World War air force base with 600 people, two hangars, barracks and mess halls, big guns and scanning towers, and flying boats patrolling for Japanese submarines. The **old cannery**—now a B&B—is still there, and so is the big hangar. But the **old RCAF base**, bought by Andy Widsten just after the war, has been transformed by his son into a major marina and fishing resort complete with a 22-room hotel and a pub/restaurant, the Fishermen's Bar & Grill, overlooking Shearwater harbour. Most government services are in Bella Bella, but Shearwater has **guided fishing charters, fishing tackle, kayak, canoe and mountain bike rentals** as well as **B&Bs**, **campgrounds** and **RV parks**. Still tranquil Denny Island, described by a local as one of the last outposts, is far, far from the madding crowds. (For more information, contact BC Ferries or Shearwater Resort, 604-270-6204 or toll free 1-800-663-2370.)

Klemtu

Four hours by ferry from Shearwater is the Native village of Klemtu on Swindle Island. Tidy rectangular houses rim a horseshoe-shaped bay backed by a **deep green rainforest** ruffle of mountains. A narrow boardwalk on stilts joins the two halves of the village, and a dock juts into the still, green water where Native canoes are sometimes tied up at the dock alongside aluminum commercial fish boats. Klemtu, an alcohol-free village, is home

Sunset at the dock at Shearwater, Denny Island

to about 500 people, mostly Tsimshian-speaking Kitasoo with a leavening of Heiltsuk speakers. The people of Klemtu have always made their living from the sea. Now that the fisheries are declining, they've embraced tourism and have a **couple of B&Bs** and a **campground** as well as a band store and band café. You might see the floating A-frame Floathouse Inn at the Klemtu dock or it might be at nearby Princess Royal Island, home of the rare Kermode bears. While Klemtu locals climb aboard to have dinner "out" in the ferry cafeteria, you can take a 2- to 2^1/$_2$-hour cultural walking tour past the fish processing plant and old cannery to the salmon hatchery and then to the carving shed to watch local artisans at work. The tour ends with a feast of smoked and barbecued salmon, herring roe, rice, clam fritters and seaweed followed by traditional **Kitasoo clan dances and songs** at the church hall. Many returning passengers are wowed by the warmth of the people and their glimpse into the world of the Kitasoo. (For more information, contact BC Ferries or Klemtu Tourism Information, 250-839-2346.)

Ocean Falls

Seven hours from Klemtu at the far end of beautiful Cousins Inlet, a white tumble of water cascades down a dam into the sea. Off to the right is the harsh yellow line of a silent pulp mill. To the left is a scattering of mostly empty buildings—a clutch of weathering houses from the 1920s and 1930s, apartment buildings from the 1970s and 1980s, where trees grow through abandoned carports, and the partially restored **Heritage House** where British royalty and Canadian prime ministers were once wined and dined. Near the centre is the tall pink-and-white courthouse and the nail-bitingly narrow wharf where the "flying doctor" is landed by helicopter. This is the modern near-ghost town of Ocean Falls. Thanks to abundant hydropower and huge timber stands, this pulp-and-paper town was once the largest community on the Mid-Coast with more than 3,000 residents,

a **big hotel**, a **movie theatre** and a **department store**, a **town orchestra** and an **Olympic-sized pool** that spawned several international swimming champions. The mill closed in 1980 but about a hundred friendly, nature- and isolation-loving people live in the Martin Valley subdivision. A walking tour of the townsite where alders, evergreens and tangled blackberries are silently reclaiming the earth, is a fascinating insight into how quickly nature asserts itself. **Link Lake** above the

The BC Ferry at Ocean Falls

dam is locally famous for **trout fishing** and sweet drinking water. On the way back to the ferry, stop at the yellow floating café called The Shack for homemade deli treats and ice cream. (For more information, contact BC Ferries or Ocean Falls Improvement District, 250-289-3813.)

Bella Coola

The last whistle sounds for the 5-hour sailing up the slivered fjords of Dean and Burke channels to Bella Coola on North Bentinck Arm and BC Ferries' mainland terminal. Bella Coola lies cradled at the mouth of the broad Bella Coola river valley between angling mountain peaks wreathed in cotton-batting clouds. The valley home is shared by the Coast Salish Nuxalk people at Bella Coola and descendants of nineteenth-century Norwegian settlers 15 km inland at Hagensborg, who were reminded of the deep blue fjords of the old country. For centuries the Nuxalk travelled the "Great Road" (now the Nuxalk–Carrier Grease Trail) from Dean Channel, carrying the much-prized grease of the eulachon fish to trade with interior tribes. With the help of Nuxalk guides, the famous explorer Alexander Mackenzie walked down the same trail to the coast in 1793. The first non-Native to cross North America, he mixed grease and vermilion to paint a memorial on a big rock in Dean Channel. (The ferry sometimes pulls under Mackenzie's Rock on its way to Bella Coola where a scrawled re-inscription reads "Alexander Mackenzie, from Canada, by Land, the Twenty Second of July, One Thousand Seven Hundred and Ninety Three.") In the late 1860s the Hudson's Bay Company built a trading post here, but today only the house of John Clayton, a former HBC clerk, is still standing.

At Bella Coola the ferry docks alongside a jumble of fishing and pleasure boats as well as sports fishing charter boats. Just up the road is the low-key village of Bella Coola, where houses are randomly tucked into the bush along the Bella Coola River. It has basic accommodations, restaurants and general store and a splendid setting where eagles and bears sometimes appear along the soaring mountainsides to scour the river for fish. In the village centre, the small **Bella Coola Museum** housed in a nineteenth-century surveyor's cabin displays objects linked to its Norwegian and Hudson's Bay Company past. **Scenic tours, fishing and hunting charters** as well as **alpine, horseback and fly-fishing trips** from Bella Coola can be arranged, and the village's unofficial greeter, Darren Edgar, is happy to take

Approximate Distances

From Bella Coola to Williams Lake 465 km
From Williams Lake to Vancouver 540 km
From Williams Lake to Whistler 660 km
From Whistler to Vancouver 123 km

folks to see nearby Thorsen Creek petroglyphs. (For more information, contact BC Ferries or the Bella Coola Tourist Office, 250-799-5268.)

Tweedsmuir Provincial Park

Just a 45-minute (51-km) drive east of Bella Coola is the west entrance to Tweedsmuir Provincial Park (250-398-4414). At 994,246 ha, this is easily **BC's biggest provincial park**, with a spectrum of climates, vegetation and animal habitats from multi-coloured lava formations to high Coast Mountain peaks to deep coastal fjordlands. Campgrounds are at the bottom of "the hill" at Atnarko River (28 sites) and Fisheries Pool (14 sites). Fishing is a big draw in the park. The Dean River is a favourite haunt of fly fishers and the Bella Coola and Atnarko rivers lure steelhead, trout and salmon fishers. (Watch for bears along the rivers.) Tweedsmuir is a true wilderness park where you'll need to take along good supplies and maps if you hike into the backcountry. A popular trek crosses through the park, the historic Nuxalk–Carrier Grease Trail (Alexander Mackenzie Heritage Trail). (For details and maps, see John Woodworth's *in the Steps of Alexander Mackenzie*.) Alternatively, arrange park tours with Bella Coola outfitters or stay at historic Tweedsmuir Lodge (1950) near the park entrance and sign up for guided tours (250-982-2402).

A Circle Tour through the Chilcotin–Cariboo Region to Vancouver

From Bella Coola many visitors brave "the hill" and head on a circle tour through BC's Chilcotin–Cariboo Country to Vancouver. The Chilcotin–Bella Coola Highway (Hwy 20) runs from Bella Coola 456 km through Cariboo country ranchland to Williams Lake in the BC Interior. Until 1953 a 60-km gap in the road meant Bella Coola residents had no link other than a steep pack horse trail to the rest of the province. In 1950 folks on both sides of the gap got together and helped finish the road themselves. The completed Highway 20 was dubbed the "Freedom Road." But be prepared with good tires and brakes—freedom has its price. About 120 km of road is still gravel-surfaced, and "the hill"—an infamous 20-km stretch of narrow, switchbacked gravel road with a grade up to 18 percent—requires strong nerves and extra caution. An excellent reference on the highway and its interesting history is Diana French's *The Road Runs West* (Harbour Publishing).

The highway rises from the Bella Coola Valley past sky-scraping Coast Mountain peaks with names like **Stupendous Mountain**, **Matterhorn Peak** and **Thunder Mountain**, through the rolling ranchland of Cariboo Country to Williams Lake, known as "Stampede Town" for hosting one of BC's biggest rodeos. From Williams Lake travellers can follow Highway 97 and the Trans-Canada Highway (Hwy 1) down the mighty Fraser River to Vancouver, or take Highways 97 and 99 for a sybaritic stop at the ski and luxury resort town of Whistler before heading into Vancouver. (For information on Highway 20, call the Ministry of Transportation & Highways, Central Cariboo Office, 250-398-4510. For more information about travel possibilities, contact Super, Natural British Columbia Reservation and Information Service, p. 8.)

The action-packed Bella Coola Rodeo

THE INSIDE PASSAGE ROUTE TO PRINCE RUPERT

Bald eagle

Highlights

*Beautiful weaving
channels and fjords*

*Largest temperate rain
forest on earth*

*Snowy mountain peaks
and waterfalls*

*Wildlife viewing
(grizzly bears and wolves)*

*Plenty of
shipboard amenities*

*Friendly and helpful
crew members*

The BC Ferries *Queen of the North* sails 274 nautical miles through the spectacular Inside Passage from Port Hardy to Prince Rupert. The 15-hour day trip is one of North America's great travel bargains. The ferry sails the same waters as the luxury cruise ships—but at nothing like cruise ship prices—and you can take your car along.

The *Queen of the North* is a "ferry-liner"—a hybrid ferry boat and cruise liner. You won't find all the bells and whistles of a cruise ship, but it is the flagship of the BC Ferries fleet. You'll find a licensed lounge, buffet, cafeteria, telephones, movies, elevator and rentable dayrooms or, if you're making the round trip, overnight cabins. There's also a West Coast Artists and Speakers Series where you can find out more about the BC coast, its culture and peoples.

But the real treat is outside. Slip into a deckside chair and drink in the sights. After navigating open Queen Charlotte Sound, the *Queen of the North* ducks behind **Calvert Island** and threads up **Fitz Hugh Sound** and **Seaforth Channel** and past **Princess Royal Island**. Then it squeezes through dramatically narrow **Grenville Channel** before sailing past

What to See

- [ ] **1** Grenville Channel
- [ ] **2** Princess Royal Island
- [ ] **3** Seaforth Channel
- [ ] **4** Hakai Passage
- [ ] **5** Fitz Hugh Sound
- [ ] **6** Koeye Valley

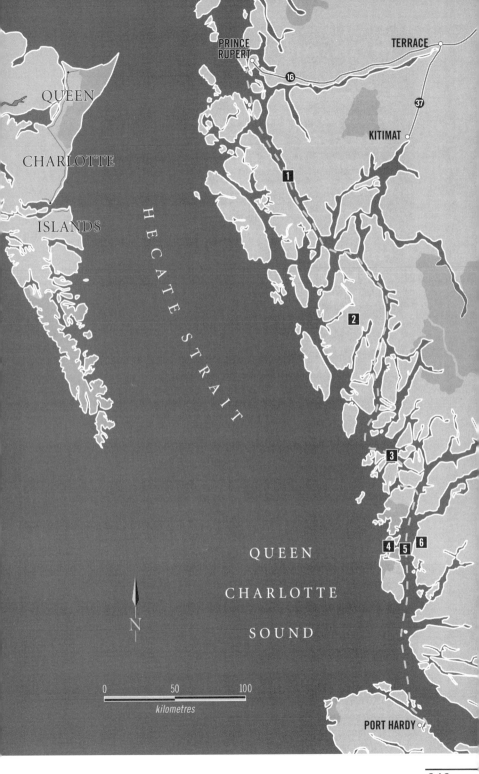

QUEEN

CHARLOTTE

ISLANDS

H E C A T E   S T R A I T

QUEEN

CHARLOTTE

SOUND

PRINCE
RUPERT

TERRACE

16

37

KITIMAT

1

2

3

4 **5** **6**

N

PORT HARDY

| | | |
0   50   100
kilometres

The remote lightstation at Boat Bluff

the mouth of the Skeena River and into Prince Rupert. The scenery is a **kaleidoscope of channels, islands, snowy mountains, waterfalls and fjords**. The wilderness between Fitz Hugh Sound and Seaforth Channel is the heart of the vast region now being called the **Great Bear Rainforest**. The name is really a battle cry for the fight of conservationists to bring to world attention the largest intact temperate rain forest on earth. This 3.2 million-hectare rain forest—it's double the size of the Serengeti, five times the size of Banff National Park—cloaks the coastal wilderness from the top end of Vancouver Island to the Alaska border. It has some eighty **untouched river systems**, and it is dense with old-growth trees and rich with wildlife—especially **grizzly bears** and **wolves**. And it is under threat of clear-cut logging.

Ian and Karen McAllister were the first to bring widespread attention to the ecological significance of this "forgotten"—and unprotected—coast. They set out to chart and photograph all the intact river valleys between Bute Inlet and the Alaska border and to assess bear and wolf populations in the region. Their book *The Great Bear Rainforest: Canada's Forgotten Coast* (Harbour Publishing) is a moving account of their experiences and a passionate plea for protecting the Great Bear Rainforest. For Ian McAllister, the long journey to protect this vast region began in the Koeye Valley near Fitz Hugh Sound in 1990. He writes, "Everywhere in the Koeye valley there were signs of bears—where they had lain down in beds of moss under big old trees, and where they had walked on trails worn deep into the forest floor by hundreds of generations of bears moving between their favourite fishing spots and the cover of forest. The tracks of wolves and bears crisscrossed the riverbanks, and the soil of the estuary had been ripped apart by bears digging up roots. Out in the river the salmon were so thick it looked as if we could walk across the water on them. One evening I sat on a piece of driftwood with my feet wrapped in the sand, staring out toward the open Pacific. Fitz Hugh Sound was calm as glass and it looked as if the sun was being lowered into the hollow of Hakai Pass solely for my bene-fit. The rear paw print of a grizzly bear lay fresh in front of me, intricately etched into the moist sand...I knew from that moment forward a large part of my time was going to be devoted to tracking that shy monarch of the rainforest, the maker of these great tracks, and trying to understand how its fate and the fate of the wilderness rainforest were joined."

The BC Ferry Queen of the North travelling the Inside Passage

PRINCE RUPERT AREA

Native carvir

Government docks

Highlights

Gateway to northern
destinations

Gorgeous mountain setting

Rich maritime history

Eco-adventures (including
grizzly bear watching)

Airtours and heli-rafting

Sport fishing

Ferries to Alaska

Connecting highways
to Vancouver

I n Prince Rupert the *Queen of the North* docks at an industrial dock area festooned with bright white lights. Behind the terminal a hill rises dark against a starry sky. It's an oddly attractive scene—a kind of mechanical fairyland—and a fitting introduction to the working character of Prince Rupert. This small city is a major Pacific coast port and the centre of the North Coast's ocean-going transportation network. Many passengers and vehicles leaving the *Queen of the North* will take another BC ferry to the Queen Charlotte Islands or board an Alaska Marine Highway ferry for ports of call on the Alaska coast. Legions of freighters also sail into Prince Rupert terminals to take on loads of lumber, wood pulp, coal and golden prairie grain bound for the USA, Mexico, England, Japan and Korea. Prince Rupert is also the nerve centre for the North Coast's major air and land transportation links. Commercial airlines take off for scheduled flights to Vancouver and other destinations from busy Prince Rupert Airport on Digby Island. Float planes rumble out of the harbour trailing veils of sea water on their way to smaller coastal settlements in BC and Alaska. The Yellowhead Highway and the Via Rail railway link parallelling the highway are Prince Rupert's overland access to the BC Interior and North America. From Prince Rupert you can go north to Alaska, south to Vancouver or east to Jasper and Banff.

But Prince Rupert is not just a gateway to other destinations. This city of 18,000 people may be small by south coast standards, but it has several definitely-worth-a-stop visitor attractions, including **one of BC's best small museums**, a **railway museum**, a **restored**

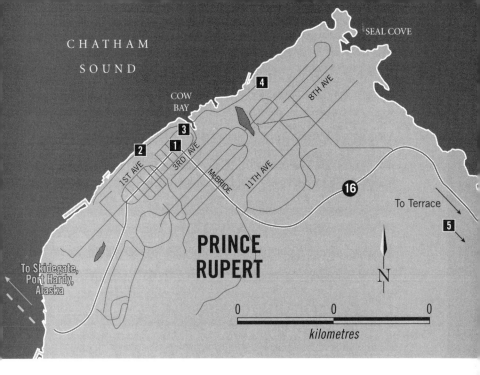

SEAL COVE

CHATHAM
SOUND

COW
BAY

4

8TH AVE

3

2

1

1ST AVE

3RD AVE

McBRIDE

11TH AVE

16

To Terrace

5

PRINCE
RUPERT

To Skidegate,
Port Hardy,
Alaska

N

0   0   0

kilometres

cannery village, a historic waterfront area and a whole spectrum of **harbour tours**, **fishing charters** and **eco-adventure expeditions** (grizzly bear watching, anyone?). Prince Rupert is rainy but mild year round. Even on rainy days the city's harbour-and-mountain setting can be a graceful medley of slate blues, silvers and luminous greys. But on a clear day when sea-green islands are layered against blue water, deeper blue mountains and blue, blue sky, it's hard to imagine a prettier setting.

What to See

- [ ] **1** Chatham Village Longhouse/ Museum of Northern BC
- [ ] **2** Kwinitsa Station Railway Museum
- [ ] **3** Pacific Mariners Memorial Park
- [ ] **4** Eagle Bluff
- [ ] **5** To North Pacific Cannery Village Museum

Downtown Prince Rupert

To get to downtown Prince Rupert, exit the ferry terminal and follow the Yellowhead Highway (Hwy 16) into town where it becomes Second Avenue. This is the heart of the tidy downtown laid out in a grid on flat land between Rupert Harbour and a stack of sugarloaf hills. Most services lie in a nine-block area bounded by First and Third avenues and by First and Ninth streets. The downtown has a 1950s feel to it—slightly dated buildings and no mega-malls. Many of the commercial buildings along Third Avenue actually date back to the city's early days, including the **Art Deco City Tel building** (1930), the **Capitol Theatre** (1925), where vaudeville acts once packed in the crowds, and the **Spanish Renaissance-style Besner Building** (1924) built by the Prohibition bootlegger Ollie

▶ ## The City of Prince Rupert: A Brief History

Prince Rupert was the brainchild of Charles Hays, an American railway magnate. He dreamed of building a port city to rival Vancouver and to steal its thriving Asian trade. Prince Rupert Harbour was deep and ice-free all year, it was several hundred kilometres closer to Asia, and it was at the heart of North Coast resources. Hays brokered a deal with the Canadian government to build a transcontinental railroad—the Grand Trunk Pacific Railway (GTP)—all the way from Moncton, New Brunswick, to Prince Rupert Harbour. And he commissioned the young architect Francis Rattenbury (see pp. 98–99), who had designed so many of Victoria's splendid buildings, to draw up plans for imposing train stations all along the route. The finest was to be Rattenbury's dazzling hotel in Prince Rupert. A frenzy of land speculation began in 1910, and a year later all the trees on the rocky swampland had been cut down, streets were hacked through solid rock, wooden planking was laid over the spongy muskeg, and a raw frontier town with houses, taverns, churches, hotels and brothels sprang into life. The foundation for Rattenbury's opulent 450-room hotel was being dug when the unfortunate Hays went down with the *Titanic* in 1912. Hays' dream of a North Coast metropolis died with him.

The railway down the Skeena River to Prince Rupert was completed in 1914, but five years later the Grand Trunk Pacific Railway went bankrupt. The new Canadian National Railway emerged to pick up the pieces of the shattered GTP empire and run a transcontinental rail service. However, it wasn't until the 1960s that Prince Rupert began to develop as a commercial harbour. Today Prince Rupert's bustling waterfront coal, cargo and grain terminals seem to vindicate Charles Hays' dreams of building a major Pacific Rim port.

Prince Rupert's magnificent harbour

Besner. Besner was such a popular local figure that when he was convicted of bootlegging and taken to the dock to be transported by ship to a Vancouver jail, the townspeople accompanied him with a torchlight parade and the local pipe band skirled him on his way. (Ask at the Prince Rupert InfoCentre about downtown heritage walking tours.)

Prince Rupert is the North Coast metropolis where folks from smaller places come to do their Christmas shopping, buy big-ticket items like cars and freezers, and enjoy lights that are brighter than back home. The city has full tourist facilities, including more than a **dozen motels** and **nearly 20 B&Bs, banking, restaurants, cafés** and **pubs, craft and gift shops**, an **18-hole golf course**, a **great aquatic centre** and the **fine Performing Arts Centre**. Prince Rupert merchants also pride themselves on hometown friendliness. Here you'll get service with an honest-to-goodness smile.

The Chatham Village Longhouse

The best place to start a visit is at the Chatham Village Longhouse, home to the **Prince Rupert Information Centre** and the must-see Museum of Northern BC in its fine new premises. To get there, continue on Second Avenue to McBride Street. Turn left and look for the unmistakable modern glass-and-cedar longhouse at First Avenue and McBride. (McBride ends at First, just to the right of the longhouse.) Prince Rupert has always been a crossroads of Native cultures, and today it is home to the largest group of First Nations peoples in BC. People of Tsimshian, Haida, Nisga'a, Gitksan and Haisla ancestry live and work in Prince Rupert. The Chatham Village Longhouse, a blend of contemporary and traditional Native coastal architecture, was built by the North Coast Tribal Council of the Tsimshian, Haida and Nisga'a Nations to demonstrate the modern-day vitality of ancient Pacific Northwest cultures.

Sport Fishing, Ecotouring, Hiking

At the Prince Rupert Information Centre inside the Chatham Village Longhouse (open year-round, 250-624-5637), you can get maps and all kinds of helpful information on everything from accommodations to hiking trails to ferry schedules. Ask about fishing charters, heli-adventures, whale watching trips, archaeological tours of the harbour and grain port tours on Ridley Island, downtown heritage walking tours, self-guided Prince Rupert totem pole walks, Prince Rupert museums and golfing.

Sports fishing charters are right at the top of the list for many visitors. From late April to late September fishing for the likes of prawn, crab, rock fish and halibut often pays off in "bragging-rights" catches. It's not unusual for an angler to land a 14-kg halibut, and a lucky few pull in 27-kg specimens. Prince Rupert calls itself the "**Halibut Capital of the World**," and halibut in the water or served up on a plate is one of Prince Rupert's very best offerings. (For harbour tours and fishing charters, contact Prince Rupert InfoCentre, 1-800-667-1994.)

The newest visitor attraction is **ecotourism**. Helicopter and seaplane operators offer combination air/land/water tours for close encounters with eagles, orcas, seals, otters, wolves, mountain goats and waterbirds in a range of wilderness destinations. Try remote lake and river fishing or **heli-rafting**, or take scenic **air tours** of the wonderfully convoluted coastline. Scenic **boat excursions** to unspoiled fjords and rain coast islands are also popular. One hot item is a tour of the new **Khutzeymateen Grizzly Bear Sanctuary** 45 km north of Prince Rupert in rugged Khutzeymateen Provincial Park, where these shaggy giants can be spotted feeding on salmon and sedge grass in the inlets and estuary. The Khutzeymateen Valley is accessible only by boat or plane.

The visitor information centre also has details about local **hiking trails**. The

Kinsmen's Linear Park is a system of 10 nature trails right in and around Prince Rupert, ranging from a short, pleasant forest stroll to a 2-km hike. Just 6 km east of Prince Rupert on the Yellowhead Highway (Hwy 16) are three more trailheads. The 4.8-km Butze Rapids Trail leads to views over the **reversing tidal rapids** of Butze Rapids. The Grassy Bay Trail runs east through meadowland and then circles back to connect with the Butze Rapids Trail. The Mount Oldfield Meadows Trail passes through flower-bright meadows and a natural bonsai forest stunted by soil and climate. A more rigorous day-hike trail continues up to Mount Oldfield.

Museum of Northern BC

One of BC's best community museums is also housed in the Chatham Village Longhouse. The Museum of Northern BC (250-624-3207) is a great place to get a sense of the North Coast and its human history. Tsimshian historians, teachers and artists work with museum staff in creating databases, collecting oral history and publishing books. Museum displays tell the story of 10,000 years of First Nations habitation as well as the history of aboriginals' relations with the fur-trading Hudson's Bay Company and nineteenth-century missionaries, and the life of Prince Rupert's pioneers.

The museum also has changing exhibits in its new **Maritime Gallery** and **Art Gallery**. In summer it offers a number of popular excursions and tours. One favourite is "A Sail Through Time," a harbour tour to First Nations **archaeological sites** and Metlakatla. Another is "Dig It! The Past Through Archaeology," a hands-on program featuring the chance to **dig for authentic artifacts**. The museum also has a gift shop featuring First Nations art and crafts.

Kitty corner from the longhouse is the museum's carving shed where First Nations artists create beautiful objects from cedar, argillite and silver. Artists keep their own hours, but afternoons and evenings are good bets for finding someone at work.

Chatham Longhouse

Human history on BC's North Coast began thousands of years ago. After the last ice age receded, the earliest ancestors of today's Native peoples began trekking across the Bering Strait from Asia. Archaeological digs reveal evidence of flourishing pre-contact cultures finely attuned to the natural environment. By the time of European contact, the northwest coast had the largest indigenous population anywhere in Canada. The ancestors of the Tsimshian occupied the Prince Rupert area at the mouth of the Skeena River for at least 5,000 years. In the winter the Tsimshian peoples lived in nine great cedar longhouse villages near Prince Rupert Harbour and at Metlakatla on Venn Passage. In summer they canoed up the Skeena—sometimes called the "River of Mists"—to summer camps to fish for salmon. (The word *tsimshian* means "going into the river of mists"—that is, going up the Skeena River.)

The Tsimshian were also at the crossroads of aboriginal sea and land trade routes and became the greatest tradespeople of the region. They bartered for otter furs from the Haida of the Queen Charlotte Islands, native copper from the Tlingit of southern Alaska, and slaves and dentalium shells from the Kwagiulth of Vancouver Island and the northern Gulf Islands. They carried eulachon (candlefish) oil up the Skeena River "grease trail" to trade for furs with the Gitksan and Athabascan-speaking peoples of the BC Interior. When the Hudson's Bay Company cornered the lucrative North Coast fur trade market in the 1830s, HBC chief trader John Frederick Kennedy married a Tsimshian chief's daughter, and the Tsimshian continued as major players in the coastal trade. However, not long afterwards the thriving Native populations on the North Coast were decimated by smallpox and tuberculosis, diseases brought by the Europeans. Today BC First Nations are rebuilding their cultures. The Chatham Village Longhouse and the Carving Shed across the street are both symbols of that renewal.

Kwinitsa Station Railway Museum

The Museum of Northern BC operates another small but intriguing satellite museum, the Kwinitsa Station Railway Museum (open daily June–mid September, 250-627-1915 or 250-624-3207). It's located in a pleasant new park on the waterfront across from the VIA Rail Station about three blocks west of the Chatham Village Longhouse. Drive west on First Avenue, turn right down the hill on Bill Murray Drive and look for the old-time station by the tracks. The railway museum is housed in the old Kwinitsa train station, which was barged from its original site 70 km up the Skeena River. Step inside to discover the lively history of Prince Rupert's growth from a mere muskegy twinkle in Charles Hays' eye to BC's most important North Coast city. The emphasis is naturally on its railroading past. You'll find out about the days when the "mixed rail train" shuttled freight from the Canadian interior and a plain caboose with wood bench seats and a pot-bellied stove gave small comfort to its passengers. The Canadian National Railway (which took over the bankrupt Grand Trunk Pacific Railway's lines) also ran luxury passenger trains with dome cars so that passengers from the posh Prince Line of steamships could marvel at the wild Skeena River country where mountains dive straight down into the broad Skeena River Valley. The museum features replicas of a line worker's bunkhouse and a railway agent's office and family living quarters.

Pacific Mariners Memorial Park

No matter where you go in Prince Rupert, you're never far from the sea. Pacific Mariners

Pacific Mariners Memorial Park

Memorial Park on First Street right next to the Chatham Village Longhouse was dedicated in 1990 to the region's **marine heritage**. The idea was sparked by the loss of all hands aboard the Prince Rupert dragger *Scotia Cape*. The memorial park features a bronze statue of a mariner and Japanese fisherman Kazuki Sakamoto's boat *Kazu Maru*. Sakamoto disappeared at sea, but his boat was later found washed up on the Queen Charlotte Islands. Brick walls surrounding the park inscribed with the names of people who "lived and loved by the sea" or "lost their lives at sea" are a reminder of the bounties and the hardships of a seafaring life. Every year as part of the Seafest celebrations, newly inscribed bricks are added to the walls.

Cow Bay

Cow Bay is a 3-block (5-minute) walk or drive east of Pacific Mariners Memorial Park, and it is the "up" side of seafaring life. Head east on First Ave West to Manson Way, jog left one block to Cow Bay Rd and follow Cow Bay Rd east along the waterfront to Cow Bay with its delightful jumble of old waterfront warehouses, marinas and fishing supply stores, gift shops, cafés and cappuccino bars in historic buildings circling the bay. Cow Bay was called Vickersville until 1909 when a Swiss immigrant named Nehring decided to take up dairy farming. He brought milk cows into the bay by boat, then had them heaved overboard to swim for land. It's been Cow Bay ever since then.

Cow Bay is spiffier these days, but it hasn't lost a jot of authenticity or true local friendliness. Venerable old **Smiles Seafood Café**, named for the light-up smile of its early owner, Dolly Nelson, has been serving up fish and chips to happy customers for sixty years. The waterfront Breaker's Pub in the renovated 1940s Prince Rupert Fisherman's Co-op building is a favourite hangout for good pub food, a sociable drink and a game of pool or darts. Don't miss the Cow Bay Café right on the dock with super-close views of the marina from its floor-to-ceiling windows (reservations recommended, 250-627-1212). Simplicity and respect for food are the by-words here. The cuisine rivals the best of

Vancouver restaurants, and it's served up in a small café where loyal locals and out-of-town visitors swap enthusiastic comments about the tantalizing fare across the cozy tables. Several years ago its owner, Adrienne Johnston, stepped into the café and smelled the wonderful cooking. "It just smelled right," she said. "I thought, wow, someone cooks the way I cook!" She took a job and worked happily alongside the former owner, refining and simplifying her own ideas about cooking. When he was ready to sell it, she bought it. You'll say "wow," too, when you step in the door and sniff the mouth-watering aroma of fresh foods prepared with love.

Just beside the café on the wharf is the Eagle Bluff Bed & Breakfast (250-627-4955, 1-800-833-1550). Originally a cannery building, it was later towed down Tuck Inlet and set on stilts overlooking the harbour. It did service as a hair salon, electric and marine supply and taxi company before being remodelled as a cozy B&B, where from the bedroom window you can see boats at the yacht club tilting on the tide.

▶ Prince Rupert Annual Events

February
All Native Basketball Tournament

March
Children's Festival

May
BC Annual Jazz Dance Competition

June
Seafest
Seafest First Nations Event
Ladies', Men's & Seniors' Jubilee Golf Tournament

July
Canada Day
Cow Bay Days (Cow Bay)

September
Duffers Golf Tournament

For more information, Prince Rupert Visitor Information Centre 250-624-5637, 1-800-667-1994

Eagle Bluff

To walk off any extra girth you picked up at Cow Bay's many tempting eateries, head east on Cow Bay Road for some **eagle viewing**. Cross the bridge and stroll along George Hills Way to the public boat launch 5 minutes away. Just behind it is Eagle Bluff, where as many as a dozen eagles at once swoop in and out of the trees. A popular **seawalk** starts at the end of the road where local joggers and dogwalkers get their salt-air exercise. This is just one of several nature walks and hiking trails in the area ranging from short, gentle wooded strolls to energetic 2-km hikes. (Maps and directions are available at the Prince Rupert Information Centre.)

The North Pacific Cannery Village Museum

This museum is a 30-minute (20-km) drive south of Prince Rupert at the mouth of the Skeena River just beyond Port Edward. It is situated on the site of the oldest standing cannery in Canada, dating back to 1889. The cannery closed its doors in 1981 and was declared a **National Historic Site** in 1985. It's now being restored as a living museum of BC's historic salmon fishing and canning industries. Step back into pioneer days when self-sufficient cannery villages dotted the North Coast near the region's

Cannery museum at Port Edward

Alaska Marine Highway
(Prince Rupert–Alaska)

The Alaska Marine Highway Ferry sails north from Prince Rupert along Alaska's spectacular Inside Passage to Skagway with calls at Ketchikan, Wrangell, Petersburg, Juneau and Haines on most sailings. Passengers can drive off at each port and reboard the next sailing. The one-way sailing time from Prince Rupert to Skagway (789 km) is a leisurely 36 hours. Vehicle and stateroom reservations are recommended.

Alaska Marine Highway Reservations/Information:

Canada 1-800-665-6414

USA 1-800-642-0066

website www.dot.state.ak.us

VIA's Skeena Railway Tour
(Prince Rupert–
Prince George–Jasper)

VIA Rail offers a 2-day all-daylight scenic rail trip between Prince Rupert and Jasper with an overnight stop in Prince George aboard the Skeena, affectionately nicknamed the "Rupert Rocket." The Skeena travels from the coastal rain forests through wide ranching country to the world-famous Rocky Mountains and its final destination at Jasper. It makes eight scheduled stops at places like Terrace, Burns Lake and Smithers with 72 optional flagstops at smaller communities like Loos, Cedarvale and Usk. The trip takes about 19 hours—12 hours from Prince Rupert to Prince George on the first day and 7 hours from Prince George to Jasper on the following day. Passengers can disembark at Prince George for connecting service between Prince George and Vancouver aboard BC Rail's Cariboo Dayliner (1-800-663-8238). Advance reservations are recommended. Passengers are responsible for arranging overnight accommodation in Prince George.

VIA Rail Information/Reservations

Canada 1-800-561-8630

USA 1-800-561-3949

website www.viarail.ca

rich salmon grounds. During fishing season, hundreds of workers arrived to live in cannery housing, shop at cannery stores and fish for the company on the nearby fishing grounds or butcher and pack the salmon in the factory. They were of many different backgrounds—British managers, Scandinavian fishermen, Japanese boat builders, Chinese and First Nations cannery workers. The North Pacific Cannery Museum has exhibits showing the evolution of cannery work from the early days when everything was done by hand under primitive working conditions to the introduction of a mechanized butchering machine (the "Iron Chink") and can-making factory to a reform line. Other exhibits depict the boats and nets used in the salmon fishery from the time of sails and oars to their replacement by gas-powered engines. Still other exhibits tell the stories of Chinese, Japanese and First Nations workers who lived in ethnically separate "villages" around the cannery. Stroll the plank boardwalk to see the managers' tidy white houses, the cannery store, the bunkhouses, mess house and office. Watch demonstrations of rope making and net mending, and stop to eat in the Cannery Café. In summer, cannery tours start with a popular live heritage show, "The Skeena River Story." Restoration is ongoing.

To get to the cannery museum, follow Hwy 16 east from Prince Rupert about 10 km to the junction with Skeena Dr. Turn right and follow the road another 10 km to the cannery village. Open daily 9–6, mid-May to mid-Sept; off-season by appointment (250-628-3538).

Travel Adventures
from Prince Rupert

As the transportation hub of the North Coast, Prince Rupert is a perfect jumping-off point for further adventure. The busy Prince Rupert Airport on Digby Island has daily scheduled flights between Vancouver and Prince Rupert. There is also daily float plane service to outlying communities including Ketchikan, Alaska, as well as charter float planes and "flightseeing" tours to deep wilderness destinations. Between the BC Ferries and Alaska State ferry systems, travellers can sail to ports of call all the way from Washington to Vancouver

Approximate Rail Distances

From Prince Rupert to Terrace 143 km
From Prince Rupert to Prince George 724 km
From Prince Rupert to Jasper 1,110 km
From Prince Rupert to Vancouver 1,543 km

Island, the Queen Charlotte Islands, the Yukon and Alaska. Many ferry passengers bring their vehicles on board to combine ferry and car excursions. The famous Yellowhead Highway (Hwy 16) starts in Prince Rupert and runs 143 km up the spectacular Skeena River to Terrace. Beyond Terrace you can pick the route that suits you best—east on the Yellowhead Highway to Jasper and then south on Hwy 93 to Banff, north on the Cassiar and Alaska Highways to the Yukon and Alaska, south on Highway 97 through Cariboo Country to Vancouver or off to dozens of other vacation destinations in the BC Interior. VIA Rail runs the passenger train *Skeena* on a route that roughly parallels the Yellowhead Highway on its 1,160-km run from Prince Rupert to the Canadian Rockies. For people who love riding the rails, this daytime-only rail excursion is a scenic favourite.

Prince Rupert Recreation, Accommodations and Services

Recreation
Bicycle rental
Kayak/Canoe rentals
Fishing charters
Boat charters/tours
Eco-adventure tours
Whale watching tours
Tennis courts
Hiking trails
Golf course
Swimming pool/
Racquet centre

Accommodations
Bed & Breakfasts
Hotels/Motels
Campgrounds
RV Park
Hostel

Services
InfoCentre
Places to eat (Restaurants, pubs, cafés)
Banks/ATMs
Grocery stores
Gas/service stations
Hospital
Airport

Important Numbers

Police Emergency **911**
Police Non-emergency **250-624-2136**
Fire **911**
Ambulance **911**
Hospital **250-624-2171**
Air/Marine Emergency **1-800-567-5111** or cellular **311**
Prince Rupert Visitor Information Centre **250-624-5637** (open year-round)
email **prtravel@citytel.net**

Kitimat

Located 62 km south of Terrace on the north end of Douglas Channel, Kitimat is a unique community, a company town built by the Aluminum Company of Canada (Alcan) to house its large workforce. Built over a three-year period in the early 1950s, Kitimat is a carefully designed model town with alphabetical street names and pretty suburban homes. Kitimat is also one of the most multicultural communities in northern BC. Many of Alcan's original workers were recruited from Europe. Over a dozen languages are spoken in Kitimat today and almost a third of the town's 12,000 citizens are of Portuguese descent. Kitimat's economy revolves around three industrial plants: the Alcan aluminum smelter (250-639-8259), the Eurocan pulp and paper plant (250-639-3597), and the Methanex/Pacific Ammonia facility (250-639-9292). All three operations offer free public tours in the summer.

Visitors who are more interested in nature than industry will revel in the pristine beauty of Douglas Channel. **Natural hot springs, fjords, and waterfalls** are all part of the channel's scenery. Moore Creek Falls and Humphrey Creek Falls offer visitors an up-close look at two of Kitimat's most **spectacular waterfalls**. The channel is also home to a variety of wildlife including orcas, eagles and sea lions. If you want an educational perspective on Kitimat's natural surroundings, take a tour of the **Kitimat River Hatchery** (250-639-9888), where you can feed salmon fry and learn more about salmon conservation. Ever seen a 50-metre tall tree? Kitimat boasts the province's **largest Sitka spruce tree**, a 500-year-old wonder that contains enough wood to frame nine houses.

If outdoor recreation is your main interest, you'll find lots of things to do in Kitimat. Douglas Channel and nearby Kitimat River are heaven for **sports fishing** enthusiasts and there are many private charter boat companies in Kitimat ready to take fishermen to all of the best spots. Enjoy hiking? There are plenty of scenic **hiking trails** in the Kitimat area in such places as Coho Flats, Hirsch Creek Canyon, Robinson Lake, Clague Mountain and Mt. Elizabeth. **Cross-country skiers** will be delighted by Kitimat's heavy snowfall and by the community's excellent ski trails. **Onion Lake Ski Area**, located 28 km north of Kitimat, offers 25 km of set tracks. Skiers can also visit the **South Hirsch Touring Area** or try out the set tracks at the **Hirsch Creek Golf Course**.

Kitimat Centennial Museum

No trip to Kitimat would be complete without a visit to the Kitimat Centennial Museum (250-632-7022). The Museum has exhibits on everything related to Kitimat's history and geography, from examples of Haisla artwork to chronologies that trace the development of Alcan's smelter. Visitors can also view displays on the area's wildlife, plant life and geology, sealife of Douglas Channel, early settlement and the building of the 1950s town of Kitimat, and local art. Guided tours of the entire museum are available all year round.

Kitimat Recreation, Accommodations and Services

Recreation
Bicycle rentals
Fishing/Boat charters
Golf course
Numerous hiking trails
Cross-country skiing

Accommodations
Hotels/Motels
Resort
Campground/RV park

Services
InfoCentre
Restaurants
Pubs
Cafés
Grocery stores
Shopping malls
Banks/ATMs

The Haisla First Nation and Kitlope Valley

While the community of Kitimat is less than fifty years old, the area has a long history of human settlement. Douglas Channel has been home to the Haisla people for many years. The Haisla were called *Kitamaat* by neighbouring Native bands. The word means "people of the snow" and is an appropriate name for a community that receives 361.5 cm (12 feet) of snow annually. The Haisla village of Kitamaat, located on the eastern shore of Douglas Channel, 11 km across the inlet from the city of Kitimat, is well worth visiting. **Native carvers** and craftsmen have erected beautiful **totem poles** in the village, and the new Haisla school has won praise for its striking architecture. Kitamaat is also the place to go to learn about the Kitlope Valley, the **world's largest expanse of intact coastal rain forest** (317,000 ha).

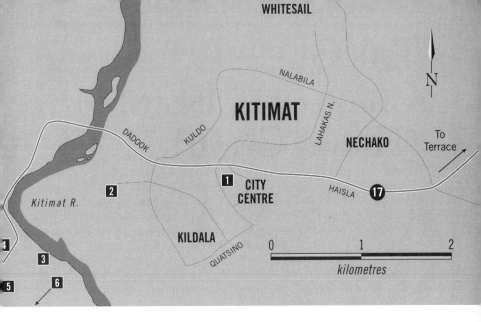

Located 100 km southeast of Douglas Channel, the Kitlope Valley is very isolated and can only be approached from the water although **ecotours** can be arranged through Kitamaat's Nanakila Institute (250-632-3308).

Lakelse Lake Provincial Park

Just 25 km south of Terrace along Highway 37 is the Lakelse Lake Provincial Park (250-847-7320), a 354-ha land reserve made up of cedar, hemlock and Sitka spruce forests. The park contains an impressive array of wildlife including moose, wolves and cougars. Birdwatchers will be delighted by the large number of birds at Lakelse Lake; the park is home to majestic bald eagles, ospreys and trumpeter swans, a species that was once threatened with extinction. Because of the delicate wildlife in the area, wilderness camping is not permitted although there is plenty of camping at designated campsites. Lakelse Lake is an excellent place for trout fishing and hosts several salmon and steelhead runs. Visitors interested in outdoor recreation can go **canoeing** or **windsurfing**, or try hiking the park's 2-km Nature Trail. Those who want to enjoy the wilderness without enduring the rigours of camping can stay at nearby Mount Layton Hot Springs Resort, a popular tourist destination with **hot mineral pools** and waterslides.

What to See

- ☐ **1** Kitimat Centennial Museum
- ☐ **2** Giant Spruce Tree
- ☐ **3** Kitimat Fish Hatchery
- ☐ **4** Eurocan Pulp & Paper
- ☐ **5** Methanex/Pacific Ammonia
- ☐ **6** To Alcan Aluminum Smelter

Important Numbers

Ambulance **250-632-5433**
Hospital **250-632-2121**
Police **250-632-7111**
Fire **250-639-9111**
Kitimat Chamber of Commerce and InfoCentre **250-632-6294**
email **gguise@sno.net**
website **www.sno.net/KCOC)**

THE QUEEN CHARLOTTE ISLANDS (HAIDA GWAII)

Haida carving

Sac Bay, Moresby Island

Highlights

Beautifully rugged scenery

Richly diverse wildlife

Vibrant Haida culture and history

Swimming, fishing, kayaking and boating

Endless emote beaches

Old growth temperate rain forest

A s the sun drops below the horizon in a last burst of flaming orange and ruddy pinks, BC Ferries' *Queen of Prince Rupert* is about to set off on its 8-hour journey from Prince Rupert to the Queen Charlotte Islands (Haida Gwaii). A hundred kilometres southwest across Hecate Strait the sun is still hanging bright in the evening sky over the Queen Charlottes. Long, long ago the Queen Charlotte Islands were known by their Haida name *Xhaaidlagha Gwaayaai*, "Islands at the Edge of the World." The name evokes the lonely splendour of these razor-backed volcanic islands, cut off from the mainland eons ago by a rising sea. Now muffled in sea mist, now lashed by storms, now dazzling in a deluge of silvery sunlight, the Queen Charlottes' volatile

What to See

- [ ] **1** Rose Spit
- [ ] **2** Agate Beach
- [ ] **3** East Beach Trail
- [ ] **4** Port Clements
- [ ] **5** Rennell Sound
- [ ] **6** Tlell
- [ ] **7** Queen Charlotte City
- [ ] **8** Gray Bay
- [ ] **9** Cumshewa Inlet
- [ ] **10** Lyell Island
- [ ] **11** Nunsting (Skung Gwaii Island)
- [ ] **12** Kunghit Island

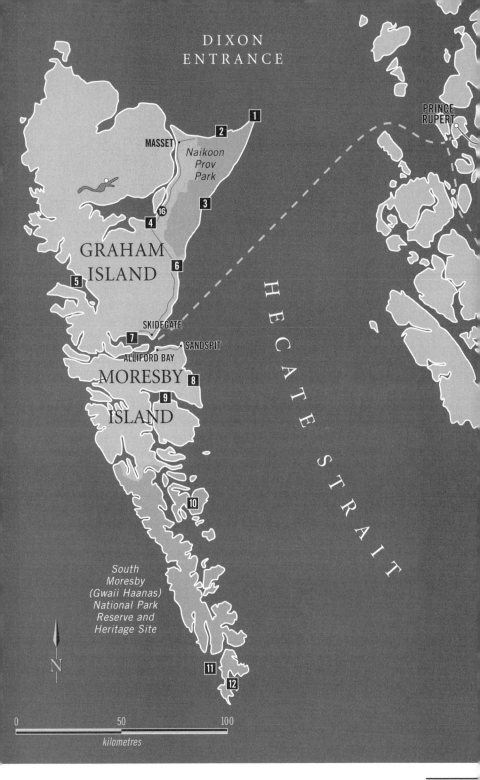

DIXON
ENTRANCE

PRINCE
RUPERT

1

2

MASSET

*Naikoon
Prov
Park*

3

16

4

GRAHAM
ISLAND

6

5

H
E
C
A
T
E

S
T
R
A
I
T

SKIDEGATE

7

SANDSPIT

ALLIFORD BAY

MORESBY

8

9

ISLAND

10

*South
Moresby
(Gwaii Haanas)
National Park
Reserve and
Heritage Site*

N

11

12

0   50   100

kilometres

Huxley Island shrouded in mist

beauty is a haven for seekers of nature's last wild places.

This mountainous wedge of some 200 islands and islets covers almost 10,000 square kilometres. The largest islands are Graham Island, at the north end of the archipelago, and Moresby Island, just south of Graham. Almost all of the islands' 6,000 residents live in the six towns on Graham Island and in the town of Sandspit on the north end of Moresby Island. Most of the other islands—the homeland of thousands of Haida less than two centuries ago—are now uninhabited. The southern third of the archipelago, including south Moresby Island, is a spectacular rainforest wilderness known by its Haida name Gwaii Haanas, "Islands of Wonder." The subject of a worldwide storm of environmental controversy in the 1980s, Gwaii Haanas is now protected inside the boundaries of the Gwaii Haanas National Park Reserve and Haida Heritage Site.

The Land and the Climate

Perched in the Pacific Ocean many miles from the nearest landfall, the Queen Charlotte Island archipelago is known as a temperate rainforest climate. From mid-May to mid-September the weather is cool but comfortable (16–25°C) and fairly dry. August is the warmest month, but the rainy season can start in mid-August. The storm-pelted west coast of the Charlottes is the wettest place in Canada, with as much as 400 cm (13 feet) of rain in one year. The sheltered east coast gets a quarter of that amount.

But to say "temperate and rainswept" is to miss the crucial defining element of the Queen Charlottes' weather—changeable. Hurricane-force winds gusting up to nearly 200 km/h are not unusual on the west coast. Dark rain-bellied clouds can hurtle across the sky, then unexpectedly the clouds can part and a halo of sunshine crowns the rough green spine of an island. Ferocious winds and strong currents can combine to send monster waves 35 metres and higher slamming against the shore. But when the winds suddenly drop, the water smoothes to a glassy sheen.

The "Canadian Galapagos"

The Queen Charlottes are so extraordinarily rich in marine animals and wildlife that they are known as the "Canadian Galapagos." Scientists believe that ice-free pockets of plants and animals called "refugia" escaped the ravages of the last ice age, so that "endemic" species distinct from their mainland cousins evolved on the Queen Charlottes. Among them are 7 subspecies of mammals, including the largest black bear in North America (*Euarctos americana carlottae*) and the deer mouse, dusky shrew and pine marten, as well as the Steller's jay, hairy woodpecker, saw-whet owl, stickleback fish and three species of beetles. Plants found nowhere outside the Queen Charlottes include subspecies of saxifrage, alpine lily, willow and some mosses and liverworts. For naturalists this isolated archipelago is not just a marvellous Darwinian showcase but a dream laboratory for studying evolution.

> ## Planning your trip

It's important to plan your trip and book accommodations, rentals and any charters and tours well ahead of time. Graham Island services are limited, and demand is high in the peak summer months. You won't find five-star hotels or restaurants or shopping malls on Graham Island, but Queen Charlotte City and Masset have basic services, and some services are available in Tlell, Port Clements, Skidegate Reserve and Old Massett. You can get good food at several local cafés and restaurants and a good night's sleep in comfortable motels and cabins. B&Bs can be delightfully quirky and often serve up scrumptious food. Graham Island has a range of private, provincial park and BC Forest Service campgrounds, and Masset has an RV park.

Queen Charlotte Island stores have limited stocks, and prices are higher because everything has to be shipped from the mainland. But local business folk are very friendly and helpful to "off-islanders," and they appreciate visitors' patronage. The Haida communities of Skidegate Reserve and Old Massett also welcome people to visit shops and studios. They ask only that visitors respect residents' privacy as well as culturally important objects and sacred places such as heraldic (totem) poles and cemeteries.

Getting to the Queen Charlottes Aboard BC Ferries

It's easy enough to get to the Queen Charlottes on float planes or scheduled airline flights out of Prince Rupert or Vancouver. But for many summer visitors and Queen Charlottes residents, a sea voyage on BC Ferries' *Queen of Prince Rupert* is just the ticket. This trusty workhorse of the ferry fleet makes the 8-hour shuttle between Prince Rupert and Skidegate on Graham Island during the summer months. In the off-season, the *Queen of the North* shifts onto the Queen Charlotte Island Route.

The *Prince Rupert* is the sturdy, older sister of the more glamorous *Queen of the North*, much loved by Queen Charlotte Islanders as their main link to the outside world. Nearly everything that comes here, from cars, appliances, furniture and marine supplies to fresh meat and produce, is delivered to the Charlottes from the *Prince Rupert's* cavernous car deck. The old ferry is also the local sea bus, ferrying Islanders to visit friends on the mainland or go to school in the south, to shop or do business in Prince Rupert or just to make

Getting There

To the Queen Charlotte Islands via the Prince Rupert

Drive aboard the BC Ferry at the Prince Rupert terminal. The ferry sails to Skidegate (Graham Island).

8 hours crossing time; 6 sailings weekly in summer, 3–5 sailings weekly off-season.

To North Moresby Island via the Prince Rupert

Drive aboard the BC Ferry at Skidegate (Graham Island). The ferry sails to Alliford Bay (North Moresby Island).

20 minutes crossing time; 12 sailings daily.

a getaway when the Islands feel a pinch too small.

And the *Prince Rupert* is not without its creature comforts. Passengers can while away their time in the deep-backed chairs of the passenger lounge, settle into the cafeteria or the licensed lounge, or plunk down on the outer decks to enjoy the salt-tangy sea breeze. Kids crowd into the video arcade, and Tilley-hatted tourists browse the gift shop for that special something to take back home. People who think a voyage across open water is an invitation to sleep can rent cabins and snooze their way across the strait.

Hecate Strait is the largest stretch of open sea in the whole ferry system. In foul weather this dangerous crossing merits its hellish name, but the final sweep up Skidegate Inlet to the ferry dock on the southeast tip of Graham Island is a picture-perfect introduction to the Queen Charlottes. The dock at Skidegate is tucked into a quiet cove where drifting mist sifts down the forest-mantled shoulder of Graham Island, born of a volcano. The hill above the dock shades from grey to forest green in the half-light of morning. A road at the top of the dock hugs the nips and tuckings of Graham Island's southern shore. From Skidegate the road runs west to Queen Charlotte City and east to Skidegate Reserve. South across the inlet from the Graham Island ferry terminal is the rough profile of Moresby Island.

A Choice of Destinations from Skidegate

At Skidegate you can take another ferry south to north Moresby Island, or head up Graham Island.

North Moresby is reached by a 20-minute car ferry ride across Skidegate Inlet to Alliford Bay. From Alliford Bay you can go to the village of Sandspit or the boat launch at Moresby Camp. Both are popular jumping-off places for adventuring by boat or plane in Gwaii Haanas National Park Reserve and Haida Heritage Site. Or you can head down the logging roads of north Moresby Island for some great off-road getaways, from beach camping to forest hiking and fishing. (See pp. 380–89 for more on this destination.)

Your other choice is to explore Graham Island. Graham Island has only pockets of the Queen Charlottes' legendary virgin rain forest—logging and human habitation have taken their toll. But it still has a cloak of second-growth conifer forests as well as great sweeps of wild beaches and miles and miles of sand dunes, marshlands and woodlands in Naikoon Provincial Park. Delkatla Wildlife Sanctuary is home to a multitude of resident and migratory birds, and eagles, deer, bears and other wildlife are plentiful right across Graham Island. Plenty of off-road recreation, from semi-wilderness camping to fine lake and river fishing, can be found down logging roads.

Approximate Driving Distances from Skidegate

To Queen Charlotte 4 km

To Skidegate Reserve 2 km

To Tlell 43 km

To Port Clements 65 km

To Masset 103 km

To Old Massett 107 km

To Sandspit 17 km

The Haida Homeland

The Queen Charlotte Islands are also known as Haida Gwaii, meaning "the Islands of the Haida." The archipelago has been the Haidas' homeland since their sea mammal-hunting ancestors first paddled these waters after the last ice age, some 6,000 to 10,000 years ago. On these shores they found rich food sources and huge cedar trees that they used in making everything from lodges, clothing and utensils to carved bowls and boxes, elegantly designed canoes, sublime ceremonial masks and a bristling of carved poles fronting their villages. As recently as two centuries ago, thousands of seafaring Haida lived in some four dozen major villages and other small villages strung along sheltered beaches throughout Haida Gwaii. In Gwaii Haanas alone, traces of Haida presence have been found in more than 500 places.

Skidegate, circa 1900

Sometimes called the Vikings of the Pacific Northwest, the fierce-looking Haida warriors with their painted faces and tattooed bodies, plunging through the water in their great canoes, were the masters of the northwest coast, raiding villages from Alaska to Washington state for slaves and goods. The proud, indomitable Haida developed one of the world's outstanding aboriginal cultures—a complex society and unique art forms reflecting an abiding and respectful relationship with land, sea and sky.

The arrival of European fur traders was a further spur to their cultural ascendancy. The new wealth from trade triggered even greater displays of artistic prowess in the form of heraldic pole raisings, house construction, lavish potlatching, and the crafting of exquisite ceremonial objects graced with geometric imagery of Eagle, Raven, Grizzly, Moon, Beaver, Killer Whale, Sea Wolf and other beings, depicting the mythic relationships among all living creatures and between Haida peoples of different families and clans.

But European trade also brought the terrible sword of disease, especially smallpox and tuberculosis. Whole villages were cut down by disease, and a population of tens of thousands of Haida were reduced to a few hundred souls by the late nineteenth century. The few survivors left their far-flung villages and regrouped at the Haida villages of Skidegate and Old Massett on Graham Island where missionaries offered succor. But the missionaries and the Canadian government also pursued a harsh policy of cultural assimilation. Haida children were forced into boarding schools, where they were punished for speaking their own language, and forbidden to recognize traditional family and clan relations or to make art in the Haida tradition.

The Haida culture staggered, but never died. The roots were too strong. In the modern-day Haida communities of Skidegate Reserve and Old Massett, potlatches, pole raisings and ceremonial storytelling and dancing have come back among the people. Traditional Haida objects from ceremonial button blankets and beautiful cedar masks to ocean-going cedar canoes are once again being crafted by master Haida artists. The Haida are also major players in the islands' commercial fishing and forestry industries.

Exploring Graham Island

You might start by taking a left from the ferry dock and driving west along Skidegate Inlet to Queen Charlotte City (just minutes away) for visitor information and any last-minute supplies and services. Then you can backtrack and drive the road up the east side of Graham Island to Masset, just over 100 km from Skidegate. You'll pass through a loose beading of communities—the Haida Gwaii Museum, the Haida's Skidegate Reserve, the eclectic ranching and home-crafts community of Tlell, forestry giant MacMillan Bloedel's "company town" at Port Clements, the commercial fishing village and former Canadian Forces base at Masset, and the other Haida village of Old Massett. Stops at these small communities will give you a good sampling of island life.

This paved highway—actually an extension of the Yellowhead Highway (Highway 16)—is also the road to outdoor adventure. It takes you to either entrance to Naikoon Provincial Park, covering almost the whole northeast corner of Graham Island and containing everything from lowland bogs to stunted cedar forests to huge stretches of sand dunes and wilderness beaches. Between Port Clements and Queen Charlotte City a warren of logging roads take you to semi-wilderness camping and fishing. And just at the outskirts of Masset is the Delkatla Wildlife Sanctuary, a haven for more than a hundred species of migratory and resident birds. On Graham Island wilderness still prevails—and it's just off the road.

A visitor soaks up the majesty of the Queen Charlotte Islands

BILL REID, HAIDA ARTIST

Raven and the First Men

Bill Reid was one of the central figures in the contemporary revival of Haida arts. As Bill Holm, art historian and Reid's longtime friend, wrote for a 1974 retrospective exhibit of Reid's art at the Vancouver Art Gallery, "Bill found the dry bones of a great art and, shamanlike, shook off the layers of museum dust and brought it back to life." Born to a Scottish-German American father and a Haida mother in Victoria in 1920, Reid grew up thinking of himself as a white Canadian. It was the sight of two gold bracelets made by Reid's great-uncle Charles Edenshaw, the legendary Haida artist, that changed his life. Reid gave up a career as a Toronto broadcaster to become a master carver, creating works ranging from exquisite jewellery, bowls and boxes to soaring poles and dugout canoes and massive bronze and cedar sculptures. His masterwork is the 5-tonne *Spirit of Haida Gwaii*, a 6-metre-long bronze canoe overflowing with creatures of Haida mythology—Seawolf, Raven, Eagle, Grizzly, Dogfish Woman, and Mouse Woman, among others. Reid described the canoe's passengers as "symbols of another time when the Haidas, all ten thousand of them, knew they were the greatest of all nations." The black bronze casting, known as *The Black Canoe*, graces the Canadian Embassy in Washington, DC. It is considered one of the most distinguished artworks in the US capital. The green casting, known as *The Jade Canoe*, is the jewel of Vancouver's new international airport.

Reid died in 1998, at the age of seventy-eight. The Haida canoe *Loo Taa*, accompanied by several hundred mourners wrapped in ceremonial button blankets, carried his ashes on the two-day journey from Skidegate Reserve to a bluff overlooking the sea at his mother's ancestral village site of Tanu in Gwaii Haanas. It was the first Haida ceremony in Tanu since a handful of smallpox survivors left the village for Skidegate more than a century ago.

The Haida Gwaii Museum

For a great introduction to the Queen Charlottes, check out the Haida Gwaii Museum (250-559-4643). You'll find a fine sampling of Haida culture—old and new—artfully displayed in this warm, sunlit cedar building. The heart of the museum is the fine collection of historic Haida objects, ranging from a century-old frontal pole from Alder House in Skedans (Gwaii Haanas), a raven headdress recently repatriated from the Smithsonian Institution, a carved dogfish mortuary board, woven spruce-root baskets and painted cedar boxes. The museum also holds the world's largest collection

Haida cemetery at Skidegate Reserve

of Haida argillite carvings, a glossy black slate found only at a secret site on Graham Island. Look for art works by modern master Haida artists Bill Reid, Robert Davidson and others. To get to the museum, turn right from the ferry terminal and carry on for 2 km. The museum is located on the western edge of the Haida reserve of Skidegate.

Next to the museum is a building in the style of a traditional Haida longhouse. This is the administrative office of the Haida Gwaii Watchmen. When visitors began to discover Gwaii Haanas in the 1970s, the Haida worried about the potential destruction of sacred Haida village sites. For several years Haida volunteers spent summers as watchmen in the ancient villages to protect them from harm. Today Haida Gwaii Watchmen are official site guardians at five locations in Gwaii Haanas National Park Reserve and Haida Heritage Site (see pp. 387–88).

Queen Charlotte City

Queen Charlotte City is just a couple of kilometres west of the ferry landing. Known in the early days as "the townsite," Queen Charlotte City is the farthest thing imaginable from either a planned town or a city. It lounges along the road above Skidegate Inlet until it widens to two or three blocks around the harbour. This is the heart of town. It thins out again west of the harbour and tails out completely at MacMillan Bloedel's maintenance shop. This shop marks the end of town and the start (or end) of logging roads to Rennell Sound, Juskatla and Port Clements (see p. 372). "Charlotte," as it's known locally, is not exactly picturesque. But there's something pleasing about this easygoing, narrow-gauge town strung out along Skidegate Inlet.

Queen Charlotte City sprang up around a lumber mill, and logging and commercial fishing have been the economic mainstays. Recent downturns in forestry and commercial fishing have taken a big bite out of local incomes. The community is split over how to manage resources in the future, and debates rage over forestry jobs versus environmental protection, the competing rights of the commercial and sports fisheries and Native land claims. Despite troubled economic times, Queen Charlotte still has the friendly air of a small frontier town and visitors are made to feel at home. This is the service centre for southern Graham Island and the **administrative headquarters for the Queen**

The wharf at Queen Charlotte City

Charlottes, including Parks Canada and the BC ministries of forests, the environment, and fisheries and oceans, among others. This is a good place to pick up tourist information, lay in supplies, get any useful government information, and enjoy shopping and good food. You might even make local lodging or nearby **campgrounds** a base for exploring the island. There's never much more than a hundred kilometres between Queen Charlotte City and anywhere else on the Island you might want to visit.

When you get near the town centre, take the first left as you enter the heart of town to the bright new Queen Charlotte **Visitor Information Centre** on the waterfront at Wharf Street (250-559-8316). You'll find lots of information about Graham Island and Gwaii Haanas National Park Reserve and Haida Heritage Site. There's an impressive video introducing visitors to Haida Gwaii and a big relief model of the islands, as well as **marine charts and topographic maps and logging road maps** for trip planning. Staff can give you information on travel in the islands, charters and adventure expeditions, hiking, fishing, camping and lots more. They also give the **mandatory orientation sessions** for Gwaii Haanas visitors twice daily from May through September (see pp. 387–89).

From the information centre you can walk the whole downtown area in a few minutes. This is a good chance to pick up **last-minute supplies**, including a fishing licence and tackle. Don't pass up the chance to tuck into some good home cooking at any of several local restaurants. The decor may not be fancy, but the food is fresh, tasty and inexpensive. Just ask a local to point you in the right direction. There are also gift shops and stores specializing in Haida arts, crafts and books. Although the best Haida art is mostly sold in galleries in Vancouver and Victoria, you can find work by up-and-coming Haida artists at good prices. To get a feel for local life, try the pub near the government wharf where loggers and fishermen—Haida and non-Haida—like to settle in for a drink. Then check out all the boats at the dock. Queen Charlotte City is home port for a big commercial fishing fleet and for a number of **fishing charter operators**. From spring through fall, salmon, halibut and crab fishing in the waters around the Queen Charlottes are magnets for sports fishing enthusiasts. Charter vessel operators also provide service ranging from **kayak mother-shipping** to luxury **sailing** in Gwaii Haanas (see p. 387–389).

Queen Charlotte can also be your home base on Graham Island. It has 3 motels and a handful of B&Bs—that's a big number on the Charlottes—and 2 **campsites** down the logging road west of town. Just past the pavement on the main drag is Haydn Turner Park, a community-run campground with 15 campsites, including some walk-in beach sites, and pit toilets. About 5 km west of town on Honna Forest Service Road is the Kagan Bay Forest Service Campground. It has 6 sites on beautiful Kagan Bay, picnic tables and pit toilets. **Kayakers** can go for a paddle in the sheltered bay, and hikers can take the trail up to the alpine meadows on Sleeping Beauty Mountain. A trail map is posted at the trailhead.

Also west of town is the gravel logging road that heads up-island as far as Rennell Sound and Port Clements (see p. 372).

Skidegate Reserve

To get from Queen Charlotte City to Skidegate Reserve and the east coast of Graham Island (and Tlell, Port Clements, etc.), backtrack down the paved road and past the ferry terminal at Skidegate. The Haida community of Skidegate Reserve, about 6 km east of Queen Charlotte, is wrapped around a long stretch of beach at the entrance to Skidegate Inlet. On the hillside behind the beach are the modern suburban-style homes of the Skidegate band. Skidegate Reserve doesn't have many services, but it does offer a sense of contemporary Haida culture. Several Haida artisans well known for **carvings in wood, stone and precious metals** have studios or carving sheds in Skidegate Reserve. You can stop by the Skidegate Band Council Office just above the beach to ask about **visiting artists at work** (open weekdays, 250-559-4496).

From the band council offices, stroll east a block up the road to the old cemetery on a gentle slope above the water. Beyond the wonderful carved cedar gateposts are stone monuments, some topped with angels, others with bears or ravens, ranged across the hillside with dottings of smaller wooden crosses here and there. (Be sure to ask at the band council office for permission to enter the cemetery.) For a longer walk, head for the wooded hills above Skidegate Reserve. The trailhead of the brand new 1.5-km **Spirit Lakes Trail** starts just across the road from the George Brown Recreation Hall. The wide, easy trail runs through stands of old-growth forest to two small lakes surrounded by eerie grey tree snags. Legend has it that the far lake was inhabited by a sea monster named Wasko who swam up a tunnel from Skidegate Inlet. Along the trail look for ancient "culturally modified trees" where strips of cedar bark were once peeled off for making Haida baskets and other household objects.

Queen Charlotte City/Skidegate Reserve Area Recreation, Accommodations and Services

Recreation
Kayak rentals/transport
Kayak charters/mother-shipping
Air charters
Charter vessel tours
Fishing charters
Eco-adventure tours
Tennis courts
Hiking trails
Backroading

Accommodations
Bed & Breakfasts
Hotel
Motels
Campgrounds

Services
InfoCentre
Places to eat (Restaurants, pub, cafés)
Credit union/ATMs
Grocery stores
Laundromats
Gas/Service stations
Car rentals
Galleries
Gift shops

Important Numbers

Hospital emergency (Queen Charlotte City) **250-559-4506**
Hospital non-emergency **250-559-4300**
Medical clinic **250-559-4447**
Police **250-559-4421**
Fire **250-559-4488**
Queen Charlotte Visitor Information **250-559-8316**

Balance Rock

Just beyond the last houses of Skidegate Reserve as you head north up the highway is the locally famous ice-dropped boulder known as Balance Rock. (Watch for an unmarked parking pullout on the right with a path down to the **beach**.) The hefty chunk of elliptical rock perches on an unbelievably small stone base. People just can't help prodding at the rock to figure out how all that weight can balance on that tiny stone pedestal. The beach itself is a tranquil place of gravel and slabs of grey stone backed by alder and conifers. It's easy to get sidetracked by peering into the **tidal pools** to look for scuttling crabs and other intertidal life, or easing up the beach in search of an artful twist of driftwood.

The East Coast:
Skidegate Reserve to Tlell

From Skidegate Reserve the highway runs up the coast to Tlell about 40 km away. There aren't any services between Skidegate and Tlell, and chances are you'll hardly see a soul on the road. To

Balance Rock

your left as you drive are forests broken by an occasional overgrown clearing. To your right is a beach that changes gradually from gravel to stone, with scallops of rocky headlands behind a light fringe of trees. When a panorama of freighters and tugs plowing through the white-capped breakers of Hecate Strait is too good a photo-op to pass up, just pull off. The world is your oyster, shared only by silky black ravens strutting along the tideline, and bald eagles hovering in the air like monarchs surveying their kingdom. Once you're on Graham Island, it's clear why every Haida family marked its lineage with either the Eagle or Raven crest.

Tlell

The government opened up the east coast of Graham Island for homesteading in the early 1900s, and its gentle contours lured pioneers to the Tlell area with the promise of fertile farms. But the soil was sometimes thin and the weather fickle. Some pioneers still managed to grow fine vegetables, and others like the ex-Klondike prospector William Duncan bolstered their farm incomes by building sluice boxes on the beach and processing placer gold. But the lack of nearby markets and the onset of the First World War curtailed hopes of prosperity. Little is left of the old homesteads besides overgrown fields and abandoned gardens where a few gnarled apple trees or a tall stand of foxgloves are reminders of pioneer dreams.

A few ranchers still run **Hereford cattle** on grasslands near Tlell. In the 1970s, "flower children" and back-to-the-land craftspeople moved in. Now parents and pillars of the little community, they run an eclectic mix of home-based craft shops and studios.

But keep a sharp eye—Tlell is easy to miss. To off-islanders, it looks like the town-that-isn't. Instead of a village centre, you'll see a scattering of handmade signs pointing to turnoffs. If you don't take at least a couple of serendipitous turnoffs in Tlell, you'll miss a big swatch of the Island's funky enterprises where you can get great **cappuccino, crystals and gemstone jewellery, vintage clothes and fibre collectibles, local artworks, hand-thrown pottery and driftwood sculptures**. Look for Riverworks Farm Country Store right on the highway, where you can get **fresh-laid eggs and organic foods**.

From Tlell it's about a 30-minute drive to Queen Charlotte and about a 40-minute drive to Masset, so you can use the "village" as a base for exploring the island. Tucked hither and yon are a handful of cottages and B&Bs, including Cacilia's B&B (Hltunwa Kaitza) cozied up against the sand dunes in a sun-dappled forest where Sitka black-tailed deer browse (250-557-4664). The Tlell River House is the local hotel/restaurant/pub overlooking the beautiful Tlell River (250-557-4211). Naikoon Provincial Park's Misty Meadows **Campground** has 30 sites nestled in spruce-covered sand dunes just inland from the beach (1-800-689-9025). Primitive camping is also permitted throughout the park.

Naikoon Provincial Park (South)
Graham Island's best area for outdoor recreation is big Naikoon Provincial Park, 73,325 ha stretching all the way up the island's east coast, from Tlell to the north coast and up long, narrow Rose Spit. The low-lying park encloses a host of microclimates from boglands and lakes to cedar and lodgepole pine forests to more than a hundred kilometres of beaches and the **longest stretch of sand dunes** in all of British Columbia. The park has two entrances—one near Tlell and the other northwest of Masset. The park headquarters is just north of Tlell where the road begins to angle inland towards Port Clement. Misty

A black bear forages in marsh grasses

Meadows Campground is north of headquarters, just beyond the bridge over the Tlell River. Both are well-signed from the road.

The Sand Dunes of Naikoon Provincial Park

Naikoon Provincial Park's famous sand dunes lie just above the beach stretching up Hecate Strait. At the high tide line, stacks of weathered logs—escapees from log booms being towed through blustery Hecate Strait—lie like giant matchsticks along the beach, and behind them the sand dunes rise like wind-sculpted waves. On the crest of the dunes, beach grasses, sedges and wild strawberry anchor themselves against wind and shifting sand with a spread of shallow roots. Farther inland is a fringe of shrubs and conifers. You can walk for an hour or more through a sand dune landscape that rivals Cape Cod for beauty and is populated by eagles, not by other people. An occasional line of fence posts or an almost invisible cabin tucked into the trees are the only signs of human habitation. The best public access is from a trailhead at the Misty Meadows Campground picnic area. The trail leads south along the coast through the forest fringe. You'll reach the first dunes in about 15 minutes. Be sure to pick out landmarks from your entry point. One stretch of sand dunes looks remarkably like all the others.

The East Beach Trail (Naikoon Provincial Park)

If miles and miles of beach and sand dunes and a blissful absence of other footprints is your idea of paradise, head north from Misty Meadows Campground along East Beach. Word is getting out and this is becoming a popular hike. But it's still a wild beach where you can spend hours or days in perfect solitude. The East Beach hike is a **true wilderness adventure** for experienced hikers who are well equipped for all kinds of weather. This area is not patrolled, and hikers can't be rescued by sea.

The 94-km East Beach hike takes 4 to 7 days. Parks Canada recommends hiking south to north to get the strong prevailing southeasterly winds and driving rain at your back and to keep the sun out of your eyes. The trail starts at the picnic area on the northwest side of the Tlell River bridge, just north of the campground. It runs without any elevation change right along beautiful East Beach from Tlell to Rose Spit. To the east is an open expanse of sea and shifting clouds. To the west are sand dunes and high sand cliffs crowned by spruce forests. A few rivers flow into the sea and are good places for wilderness camping. But you'll need to carry water—these rivers are either tidal flow or else they drop under the beach on their way to the sea. You'll also need tide charts so you can make the river crossings at low tide. At the north end of the beach you can either cut across the Cape Fife Trail to Tow Hill or hike all the way to Rose Spit at the very tip of Graham Island. These trail exits are close to Naikoon Provincial Park's Agate Beach Campground where you can leave a vehicle or arrange a pickup. For more information, stop by the Naikoon Provincial Park headquarters just south of the Tlell River bridge (250-557-4390).

The Pesuta Shipwreck Hike

If a shorter, family-style jaunt is better for you than a 6-day wilderness hike, try the Pesuta Shipwreck Hike along the start of the East Beach Trail. It takes you to the wreck of the log barge *Pesuta*. On a raw December day in 1928, the tug *Imbrecaria* was towing the barge when a sudden gale-force storm tossed it into the shallows and snapped the towline. The *Pesuta* was flung onto the beach and soon held fast by drifts of sand. The 16-km (3 1/2- to 4-hour) round-trip hike to the shipwreck runs through a fragrant spruce forest along a ridge above the Tlell River to the river mouth. From there, head north across the gravel beach to the *Pesuta* site. The beach is a good place to look for agates, sea sponges and pet-rified wood.

Fishing the Tlell River
The Tlell River bridge is a great place to angle for the big ones on a renowned salmon and steelhead stream. Steelhead run up the river from February through April, trout fishing for cutthroat and Dolly Varden is good in the spring and summer, and coho salmon run from early September to mid-October. From September to the end of June cutthroat trout fishing is catch-and-release. Many fishermen head down Beitush Road, which runs along the south bank of the river, to find their fishing spots. At the end of the road is the Tlell River House where you can rent boats, book fishing charters or celebrate a good day on the river with a hearty dinner and a foaming pint.

Tlell to Port Clements
North of the Tlell River bridge the highway slants inland 22 km to Port Clements. It's a pleasant trip through stunted forests and occasional clearings. About halfway to Port Clements you can take the right-hand turn down to Mayer Lake about 1 km away for **swimming, fishing and boating**. A raw clear-cut on the outskirts of town is a reminder of this town's primary reason for being. Most residents make their living at MacMillan Bloedel's nearby Juskatla headquarters, and this place has the air of a company town.

Port Clements sits on Masset Inlet, a long waterway that slices deep into north Graham Island. Its founder, Eli Tingley, intended to call the townsite Queenstown but astutely switched to Port Clements, in honour of Herb Clements, the local Member of Parliament, in 1914. Clements returned the favour by getting a government wharf built for the town on Masset Inlet. In the First World War, Port Clements was the supply centre for logging camps that hauled out the giant spruce trees used to build the famous Mosquito bombers, and it's remained a forestry town. It does have a few tourist services, including **lodging, eateries, and a couple of diving charters**. And thanks to the efforts of Queen Charlotte Islands historian Kathleen Dalzell and others, it also has the **Port Clements Historical Museum**. To find out more about Port Clements' pioneer and early logging history, stop by the small, volunteer-run museum on the main road into town (45 Bayview Dr, open afternoons daily July–August; weekend afternoons off-season, 250-557-4576).

Haida Canoe
One attraction near Port Clements is a roughed-out but unfinished old Haida canoe—abandoned, according to some tellers, when its carver was struck down by smallpox. Traditionally, a Haida carver walked the forest to find a tall, straight cedar tree. After selecting and felling a mighty old cedar, the carver gave thanks to the tree for its sacrifice. The first year the carver rough-shaped the log and then left it in the woods to season over the winter. The next year the men of the village hauled the canoe to the ocean and float-ed it down to the beach. There the inside was hollowed out and the outside shaped and smoothed. Water was poured into the canoe and red-hot stones dropped into the water, so that the whole canoe could be steam-bent into its final elegant curves. Then the prow and stern pieces were attached and the surface charred and rubbed to bring the cedar oils to the surface. Finally, the canoe was given its name and could set out to sea.

To get there, take Bayview Drive from Port Clements south along the shore of Masset Inlet. The paved road quickly turns to gravel and leads toward Juskatla and MacMillan Bloedel's Queen Charlotte Division office. It's about a 13-km drive. Look for the marked trailhead on the east side of the logging road. Park and walk down the short trail.

Hikers will find endless opportunities on the Islands

Port Clements to Queen Charlotte City on Logging Roads

You can follow MacMillan Bloedel logging roads from Port Clements all the way down the centre of Graham Island right back to Queen Charlotte, 68 km (2 hours) from Port Clements. The route continues past the Haida Canoe trailhead to Juskatla and along the Yakoun River, known for its fine **steelhead fishing**, then past Marie Lake where you'll find a Massett Band Council **salmon enhancement facility** and a **wilderness camping** spot. The mainline logging road ends just west of Queen Charlotte City where you pick up the paved road back into town.

The logging roads are well maintained and can be driven in a reliable car. But be sure to fill up with gas and have a spare tire, drive carefully with your headlights on, obey all posted signs, always expect a logging truck around the next corner, and pull off and stop if you do see a logging truck approaching. If you plan to travel on MacMillan Bloedel's roads during working hours (weekdays, 6:30 a.m. to 5:30 p.m.) check in at the Juskatla Division Office just past the Haida Canoe trailhead, or phone 250-557-4212. You can also pick up a Recreation Map/Guide (check for any recent changes) or sign up for a **Forest Tour** (May–Sept) to see how MacMillan Bloedel manages its working forests.

A Side Trip to Rennell Sound

An offshoot logging road south of Marie Lake runs to Rennell Sound on Graham Island's wet and wild west coast. The turnoff is about 45 km south of Juskatla, and the road runs across a low alpine pass and down switchback turns to make a last super-steep (18–24 percent grades) descent to Rennell Sound. This long aquamarine inlet is popular for **fishing, boating, scuba diving and beachcombing** for Japanese glass fishing floats. It also has two BC Forest Service **campgrounds** with a total of 10 walk-in wilderness beach campsites. At Five Mile Beach you'll find rocky **tidepools** with mussels, abalone, turban snails and just possibly the tusk-shaped dentalium shells that once served as currency among coastal aboriginal groups. Three well-marked **trails** along Riley, Gregory and Bonanza creeks lead to **beautiful beaches**. The 2-hour return Riley Creek Trail starts at a trailhead marker 6 km past the campground. It is a pleasant, well-marked trail that runs through an **old-growth forest** of hemlock, cedar and spruce down to the beach. About 3–5 km past the Riley Creek Trail are the trailheads for Gregory Creek Trail (just before the Gregory Creek bridge) and the Bonanza Creek Trail (a left turn just past the Bonanza Creek bridge). Both are easy 10-minute walks to surf-pounded beaches looking over the Pacific Ocean.

Tlell/Port Clements Area Recreation, Accommodations and Services

Recreation	Services
Dive charters	Places to eat
Hiking trails	(Restaurant, pubs,
Fishing	snack bars)
Backroading	Grocery stores
Accommodations	Laundromat
Bed & Breakfasts	Car rental
Lodges	Gas
Cabins	Galleries
Campgrounds	Gift shops

Important Numbers

Ambulance *1-800-461-9911*

Medical Clinic *250-557-4478*

Police *250-626-3991*

Fire *250-557-4355*

Port Clements Village Office *250-557-4295*

Port Clements to Masset

From Port Clements it's an easy drive through rolling woodlands to Masset 45 km away. If the weather's good, stop for a **picnic and swim** at **Pure Lake Provincial Park** about halfway along the route. It's a pretty little lake tucked in among salal and stunted conifers. Then it's on to Masset at the north end of Masset Inlet. The town sits on a tongue of lowland between the narrow inland thrust of Delkatla Inlet and Masset Inlet. Wrapped around Delkatla Inlet is the **Delkatla Wildlife Sanctuary**, where thousands of migratory birds settle to rest and feed. A causeway over the southern end of the Delkatla Inlet leads west from the highway to the Masset townsite and its harbour.

Masset is the biggest community on Graham Island and the only significant service centre other than Queen Charlotte City. Masset has always been a fishing and logging town, and there's a seasonally busy fish canning and freezing plant nearby where Masset's commercial fishermen unload their catches. Until recently, Masset was also the site of a Canadian Forces satellite tracking station known locally as "The Circle." This hush-hush spy station was originally built to keep track of Soviet military manoeuvring. The big Masset base, complete with houses, schools, mess halls, a hospital, a 9-hole golf course, a curling rink and a fully equipped recreation centre was once home to more than 600 military personnel and their families. When the Canadian government "downsized" its military, the Masset base was all but eliminated. Now just over a dozen people still work for CFS Masset, and the local economy is definitely feeling the pinch.

On the south edge of Masset just past the big "Welcome to Masset" sign is a summer tourist information centre (open daily June–late August, 250-626-3982; year-round phone 250-626-3995). You can get the nitty gritty on local attractions and services, including maps of Masset and Old Massett showing local services and artists' homes/studios. Masset also has **fishing and sightseeing charters**, a handful of restaurants and cafés, a neighbourhood pub called Daddy Cool's, groceries, a credit union and ATM machine, a **golf course**, seaplane service from Prince Rupert, car rentals, a 22-unit **RV site**, a **campground** and even **llama trekking** in nearby Naikoon Provincial Park.

It also has a sprinkling of accommodations from lodges and B&Bs to a 33-unit motel with restaurant and lounge. David Phillips' Copper Beech House B&B is doubtless the best-known B&B among off-islanders. Phillips' turn-of-the-century cottage is perfectly situated by the wharf at Masset Harbour to catch the silvery sea-light all year. An enormous copper beech spreads towards the water from the leafy English-style garden enclosing the cottage. In the 1930s this was the home of a British bride named Marjorie Fish. She planted her Haida Gwaii paradise with trees of her childhood—two red hawthorns, a white hawthorn, mountain ash, a giant chestnut tree, a laburnum twined around a sturdy oak. Phillips has added plantings of herbs, which he uses to flavour delectable food for his guests.

Larger than life in a luxuriant beard and caftan and surrounded by one young helper in an Italian cycling jersey and another in a plumed hat, Phillips has created his own small universe in this far north coast outpost. The open-handed warmth at Copper Beech House is reflected time and again elsewhere in this community. Just look a little puzzled or lost, and someone will appear at your elbow to help you find your way. Smile and you'll get a smile back—it's that kind of place.

Old Massett

The present-day Haida village of Old Massett is just minutes (2 km) north of Masset near the mouth of Masset Inlet. It stretches along grassy flats just back of a long shallow beach. The village—sandwiched between two roads along the beach—is just a block wide and 5 blocks long. At the north end is the old graveyard, its memorials oddly forlorn in the tall grass. Old Massett was once the site of three older Haida villages—Atewaas, Kayang and Jaaguhl. It was a refuge for Haida from outlying villages during the smallpox epidemic.

North Beach rock formations

Haida button blanket

Now Old Massett is home to the **Council of the Haida Nation**. Visitors are welcome to browse in the **Haida Arts and Jewellery Shop** next to the longhouse community building, and stop by shops of **artists** who sell their work from their homes. Locally produced art includes Joyce Bennett's **button blankets**, Golly Hans' **cedar hats**, Christian White's **argillite carvings**, and **jewellery and prints** by Reg Davidson. You can also visit the **carving sheds** of several well-known carvers, including Jim Hart's Carving Shed and Chief Edenshaw/Morris E. White Haida Canoe and Carving Shed. To find out more about visiting local artists, ask at the Old Massett Village Office in the large community hall on Eagle Rd (weekdays, 250-626-3337). If you want to enter or take pictures of the old and new cemeteries, ask for permission at the village office.

The village also has 6 **heraldic (totem) poles**, all raised in the last two decades. The first pole to be raised stands in front of the Anglican Church. It was carved by Old Massett's world-famous artist Robert Davidson, whose art is rooted deep in the soil of Haida Gwaii. His father and grandfather encouraged him to carry on the tradition of his great-grandfather, master Haida carver Charles Edenshaw. But there were only a few carvers in Haida Gwaii and almost no artifacts remaining—no poles, only 2 Haida boxes in all of Old Massett. Davidson had to uncover his heritage in southern BC where he took art courses, apprenticed to Bill Reid and haunted Vancouver museums.

For Davidson, the lack of local art was a measure of all that had been taken away from the Haida elders—culture, beliefs, identity. When he was just twenty-two years old, Davidson decided to carve a pole so that the elders "would shine one more time." His father, Claude Davidson, felled a tree and Davidson started carving in May 1969 with the help of his fourteen-year-old brother Reg. He based the pole's design on faded old photographs of village poles. Some people in the community regarded the idea of a pole raising as un-Christian. (The old poles had been cut down after the village chief was baptized in the early 1880s.) But when the day came for the pole raising, the whole village turned out to celebrate.

As the first pole to be raised in Old Massett Haanas in almost half a century, it was a powerful and lasting symbol. "It was the reawakening of our souls, our spirits," wrote Davidson in *Eagle Transforming: The Art of Robert Davidson*. "It was the reconnection with the values that still existed, with some of the innate knowledge that was demonstrated on that day." Today five more poles have been raised in Old Massett, Haida elders are teaching the younger generations old stories, songs and dances, and contemporary Haida artists are creating works that reflect their remarkable artistic heritage. As the noted art historian George F. MacDonald wrote in 1989, "Those great traditions in sculpting in wood, bone, and precious metals are also rapidly developing in directions hardly expected five years ago...A younger generation of artists led by Robert Davidson is ... making the world aware of the serene beauty of Haida art. The future of Haida culture looks immensely brighter towards the close of the century than it did at the beginning."

Delkatla Wildlife Sanctuary

From Masset, it is just a stone's throw to a nature lover's heaven—the Delkatla Wildlife Sanctuary. This 553-ha tidal marshland is directly on the **Pacific flyway**. Each spring **millions of birds** migrate up the Pacific coast to nesting grounds in the Arctic, and each fall they head back south. The sanctuary's wetlands, grassy meadows, ponds and saltwater mudflats attract hundreds of migrating waterfowl as well as resident birds. At least **140 species** have been identified at Delkatla, among them a few unexpected vagrants blown in by Pacific storms, such as the rare Aleutian tern and wood sandpiper. An impressive number of birds arrive every year, including black-bellied plovers, saw-whet owls, mallards and pintails, sharp-shinned hawks, green-winged teal, tree swallows, short and long-billed dowitchers, and cedar waxwings. Trumpeter swans—once endangered but now making a remarkable comeback—winter over at Delkatla, and elegant sandhill cranes stalk the marshland and court their mates in spring. (A checklist of birds is available at

Delkatla Wildlife Sanctuary

most Queen Charlotte Islands visitor information centres, and birding tours of the Delkatla Wildlife Sanctuary can be arranged by phoning/faxing 250-626-5015.)

Even to uninitiated birders, the medley of bird calls as you walk the sanctuary trails, and the sight of birds rising and dipping from the three viewing towers, is well worth the trip. You might also spot **deer** or the island's famous **black bears** in the deep grass of bordering meadows.

To get to Delkatla Wildlife Sanctuary, follow Tow Hill Road (the eastward extension of Hwy 16) past the causeway into Masset. Turn left onto Cemetery Rd and drive 1.1 km to the parking lot. Alternatively, you can take marked trails from Trumpeter Drive right in the town of Masset. Trumpeter is the first right turn past the causeway into town.

Naikoon Provincial Park (North): Tow Hill and Rose Spit

Masset is the self-proclaimed northern gateway to Naikoon Provincial Park. This section of the park lies along the pulsing waters of Dixon Entrance at the north end of Graham Island. Miles of surf-hammered beaches stretch along Dixon Entrance all the way to Rose Spit at the far northeast tip of the island. The park's name comes from this long sandy point of land. To the Haida, Rose Spit was a sacred place known as *Nai-Kun*, or "the long nose of Nai." About halfway along is the **towering basalt pillar** called Tow Hill, whose rounded brow is the most dramatic landmark in this low-lying region and a must-see for visitors.

To get to Naikoon Provincial Park, follow Tow Hill Road east 25 km past the Masset Airport, the Dixon Entrance Golf Course, the former Canadian Forces base and a scattering of beachfront homes along Dixon Entrance. About halfway to the park, the road turns to gravel and winds through an **other-worldly rain forest** where still brown pools reflect eerie moss-hummocked trees and fallen logs.

Agate Beach Campground

About 23 km from Masset is the park's Agate Beach Campground. This popular campground is named for the translucent, wave-tumbled **quartz stones** that gleam all along the beach in front of the campgrounds. The beach is a treasure trove for youngsters, who can spend hours searching for just the right agates. Anglers can **fish in the surf** from a nearby rocky headland, and if the surf's not up, inflatable boats can be launched to jig for bottomfish. The Agate Beach Campground has 41 campsites, a picnic shelter and a parking lot.

Tow Hill

At the far end of Agate Beach, about 2 km east of the campground, is Tow Hill. You can hike the beach to Tow Hill or drive 2 km past the campground to the parking lot at the Tow Hill picnic grounds beside the Hiellen River. A **delightful trail** from the picnic grounds wends its way from the river to Tow Hill. It's a very easy 15-minute trail through grasslands brightened with wildflowers and deep greenery patchworked with ferns and ancient lichen-covered logs. This is the place to experience that magical odd green light of a Northwest Coast rain forest.

The path ends on a huge basalt outcropping right under the towering stone brow of Tow Hill. This imposing cliff was formed by fire and ice. First a volcano heaved molten lava up through cracks in the earth's crust. The lava cooled and then cracked into a fluted basaltic pillar of stone. Then a glacier plowed gravel up against the landward side of the stone pillar and plucked away the bedrock on the seaward side, leaving behind a classic inclined landform known as a *roche moutonne*. The scene at the foot of Tow Hill is spectacular. The surf kabooms against rough, water-darkened volcanic rock. At mid-tide, spouts of water explode skyward through the famous **Blow Hole** in the rocks—known locally as "the gun." Legend has it that the blow hole is all that remains of a whale that beached itself and was turned to stone.

From the foot of Tow Hill you can follow a marked trail up to the cedar-covered top of the hill. Or backtrack up the trail from the picnic grounds and take the well-marked fork where a short trail leads up Tow Hill. It's a steep climb, but affords **unbelievable views** of the long crescent of Agate Beach 100 m below your dizzying perch.

North Beach and Rose Spit

On the other side of Tow Hill is the long stretch of hard-packed sand known as North Beach. It ends in the curved talon of Rose Spit. Rose Point at its very tip is the turbulent meeting place of Hecate

> ## Masset Annual Events
>
> **May**
> Masset Harbour Days (Masset)
> **June**
> Hospital Day (Queen Charlotte City)
> Skidegate Days (Skidegate Reserve)
> **July**
> Canada Day (Port Clements)
> Music Festival (Queen Charlotte City)
> **August**
> Fall Fair (Tlell)
> Community Days (Queen Charlotte City)
>
> For further Information, Queen Charlotte Visitor Information Centre **250-559-8316**

Tow Hill

Strait and Dixon Entrance. Many boats have foundered in the fierce currents swirling around the spit. To get to North Beach and Rose Spit, cross the bridge over the Hiellen River right by the parking lot at the Tow Hill picnic grounds. A public road runs north along the riverbank to North Beach. You can **hike the beach** all the way to Rose Point 17 km from the parking lot.

Long North Beach is backed by a haystack of sun-bleached driftwood and wind-sculpted sand dunes. It's a great place to enjoy the tang of sea kelp and salt spray, dig for succulent **razor clams**, build sand castles or **beachcomb** for shells, sponges and glass fishing floats, or take the whole day to hike or **mountain bike** to Rose Spit. Cars and dune buggies are also allowed on the beach, but 4-wheel-drive vehicles equipped with winches are recommended. Many a vehicle has been trapped in the deep sand and carried away by the tide.

Rose Spit, with its wide meadow of surf grass, is lush with plants and a haven for birds.

Masset/Old Massett Area Recreation, Accommodations and Services

Recreation
Fishing charters
Boat charters
Float plane flights/charters
Recreation centre
Golf course
Llama tours
Hiking trails
Birdwatching

Accommodations
Bed & breakfasts
Motels
Cabins
Lodges

Campgrounds
RV park

Services
Restaurants
Pub
Cafés
Credit Union
ATM
Grocery stores
Gas
Service stations
Car rental
Galleries
Gift shops

Important Numbers

Ambulance **1-800-461-9911**
Hospital (Masset) **250-626-4711**
Doctor **250-626-4702**
Police **250-626-3991**
Fire **250-626-5511**
Masset Village Office **250-626-3995**
Masset Tourist Information Centre **250-626-3982**

Look for the rare sea mertensia, the purple blush of lupins, and the bright pink tumble of wild strawberries. More than a hundred species of birds flock to the spit—peregrine falcons, gulls, ducks, sandhill cranes, eagles and more. In 1971 Rose Spit was declared an ecological reserve to protect its plants and animals and keep it unchanged for scientific studies. Rose Spit is also a Garden of Eden for the Haida people—the place where the humans appeared on earth. As the story goes, after the great flood covering the earth subsided, Raven was flying over Rose Spit. He heard muffled squeaking from a giant clamshell on the beach and flew down for a closer look. He cracked open the clam with his sharp beak, and coaxed out the naked little creatures huddling in the shell. These were the ancestral Haidas, the first people in the world.

The Cape Fife Trail

The Cape Fife Trail also starts just across the Hiellen River bridge from the Tow Hill picnic grounds parking lot. It runs across the Argonaut Plain to Fife Point on Hecate Strait 10 km away. The trail passes through a lowland rain forest and open woods. About halfway along, the rain forest gives way to meadows, muskeg and stunted pines. The trail ends at the sand dunes of East Beach at Fife Point. From Fife Point you can make a loop by hiking north along East Beach to Rose Spit and returning down North Beach to the parking lot. The Cape Fife Loop is a 2- to 3-day **wilderness trip** of 21 km. Alternatively, from Fife Point you can hike south along East Beach to the mouth of the Oeanda River 10 km away and then back track to the parking lot.

Sandspit and North Moresby Island

On your way down the road from Masset to southern Graham Island, you can hop on a little BC car ferry at Skidegate for a trip to north Moresby Island, a mountainous island just south of Graham Island across Skidegate Inlet. The northern half of the island is an active logging area with a scattering of remote logging camps. The southern half is part of the Gwaii Haanas National Park Reserve and Haida Heritage Site (see pp. 384–89). Most of this big, rugged island is accessible only by boat or chartered plane, but on the northern tip is a short paved road running northeast along Skidegate Inlet to the village of Sandspit and the Sandspit airport. A twist of logging roads also loops through the northwest corner of the island. Sandspit is primarily a jumping-off point to the BC mainland and Gwaii Haanas, a service centre for visitors to the site and the headquarters for TimberWest logging operations. But birdwatchers swear by the grassy spit near the airport for sightings of all manner of waterfowl and shore birds, and off-the-beaten track types like to rumble onto north Moresby Island logging roads for some fine backwoods camping at Gray Bay and Mosquito Lake, and salmon, steelhead and trout fishing in local streams and beautiful Skidegate and Mosquito lakes.

Sandspit

Its name says it all. The little village of Sandspit is strung along a grassy, windswept spit overlooking Shingle Bay about 13 km northeast of the ferry dock at Alliford Bay. A paved road—the only paved road outside Graham Island—leads to Sandspit and the airport, seaplane dock and small craft harbour. Until Gwaii Haanas was created, this was basically a logging town. Sandspit has basic services, including a handful of B&Bs, a few restaurants, a motel and an RV site, car rentals, grocery stores, tackle, camping gear, **kayak rentals and transport, and fishing and eco-adventure charters**. You can even get in a round of **golf** at the Willows Golf Course. But be sure to book lodging, equipment rentals and Gwaii Haanas transportation and charters well ahead of time. Sandspit services are limited and demand is high in peak summer months.

A good first stop is the **Sandspit Visitor Information Centre** at the airport terminal, open daily May–September. This attractive centre has lots of displays, information and useful handouts, including a Gwaii Haanas marine route planning area with **charts and topographic maps**, and a VHF radio for **marine weather forecasts**. The **mandatory orientation session** for Gwaii Haanas visitors is also given each day by park reserve staff (see box, p. 383).

Canoeists exploring at Skung Gwaii

Driving the Logging Roads of North Moresby Island

If you plan to drive logging roads to Moresby Camp or elsewhere, ask the Sandspit Visitor Centre staff for forest recreation maps and information about active logging areas and closures. You can also get maps and travel advice from the TimberWest Forest Office/Information Centre on the paved road into town. The TimberWest centre offers free half-day **forest tours** twice a week from mid-May to mid-September. Once you've decided when and where you want to go backroading, be sure to check in with the Sandspit Visitor Centre or TimberWest. North Moresby Island is an active logging area, so please make sure not to have a close encounter with a monster logging truck. The best times for travel are weekends, or between 6 p.m. and 7 a.m. weekdays.

North Moresby Island Logging Road Circle Tour

This circle tour, from Sandspit to the Alliford Bay ferry dock—known hereabouts as "the Loop"—is a fine way to spend a day. The 60-km trip takes about 2 1/2 hours without stops. Add another hour or so if you take the side trip to Mosquito Lake, Pallant Creek Hatchery and Moresby Camp. From Sandspit take Copper Bay Road east and then south past the golf course 11 km to Copper Bay. The road threads along Hecate Strait through thick stands of beautiful second-growth forest to Copper Bay. Copper River empties into this shallow bay, and the **salmon fishing** attracts anglers from August to October. There's a handy boat launch at Copper Bay and a scattering of fishing cabins where Haida from Skidegate Reserve stay when they're busy netting and smoking salmon.

From Copper Bay the logging road runs inland along the Copper River valley where fishers cast for **trout, steelhead and salmon**. A few kilometres from Copper Bay (about 21 km from Sandspit) is the signed left-hand turnoff at Spur 20 leading down to a lovely 20-site **campground** at sandy Gray Bay. Gray Bay is popular for **salmon fishing** and **body surfing** for those who don't mind goosebumps from the freezing cold water.

Gray Bay is also the start of the **Cumshewa Head Trail**. Just walk south along the beach and you're on your way to user-built Cumshewa Head. It runs mostly through forest above the shoreline from Gray Bay to Cumshewa Head on Cumshewa Inlet. The trail

climbs over rocky headlands and sometimes dips down to gravel or cobble beaches. There are three possible destinations along the Cumshewa Head Trail, ranging from a leisurely 3-hour round trip to a demanding 3-day backpack. For a short hike, take the Crabapple Marsh Loop Trail. This 3-hour loop takes you through a marsh, stands of **old-growth Sitka spruce** and out onto the beach. For a day trip, hike to Gitz Cove and back, about 7 hours. For a challenging backpack of one or two overnights, hike all the way to Cumshewa Head and back. For more information, see *Queen Charlotte Islands' Cumshewa Head Trail* by John F. Wood (Western Canada Wilderness Committee, 1990).

From the turnoff to Gray Bay the main route continues along the north

A creek flows through an ancient forest

shore of **trout-filled Skidegate Lake** through beautiful second-growth Sitka spruce and hemlock forests. Watch for the turnoff to Mosquito Lake, the Pallant Creek Hatchery and Moresby Camp on Cumshewa Inlet. Mosquito Lake (about 44 km from Sandspit) was used as a log sort. It was named after the Second World War Mosquito bombers that were built from the Sitka spruce harvested in the surrounding forests and then dumped into Mosquito Lake for sorting. A **boat launch** and an 11-site BC Forest Service **campground** at Mosquito Lake attract **trout fishers**. Down the road 2 km toward Moresby Camp is the **Pallant Creek Hatchery** where visitors can see juvenile chum from February to April, juvenile coho from March to June and watch salmon spawning mid-September to October (250-559-8695). From the hatchery it's a 2-km jaunt to Moresby Camp, an abandoned logging camp with 7 **campsites** and a boat launch. As the closest water access to the northern border of Gwaii Haanas National Park and Haida Heritage Site some 50 km south, it's a popular launch for Gwaii Haanas-bound **sea kayakers** and boat tour groups and for anglers heading to **salmon fishing** in Cumshewa Inlet. Return to the Mosquito Lake turnoff and follow the road north through heavily logged hills toward Alliford Bay. You'll pass TimberWest's dryland log sort at South Bay where over 2 million board feet of logs are sorted and barged down to Vancouver each year. Just a few kilometres past the log sort the road forks. Both forks lead to Alliford Bay, but the left fork running closer to the water is the more scenic route. During the Second World War, Alliford Bay was the site of a Royal Canadian Air Force station where reconnaissance planes scanned the sea for Japanese invasion forces. You can end your north Moresby Island circle tour at the Alliford Bay ferry terminal or swing east on the paved road to Sandspit.

Louise Dover Memorial Trail

Between Alliford Bay and Sandspit is a favourite local hiking trail. It was developed by Sandspit residents and named in honour of Louise Dover, a respected Haida elder. The trail runs south from Shingle Bay on Skidegate Inlet along Haans Creek. Then it loops back north through the forest and rejoins the original trail leading back to the trailhead. The main creek-and-forest loop, which is flagged with blue and yellow ribbons, takes about 2 hours return. This trail passes through fern-splashed lowlands and stands of giant cedar and

Sandspit/North Moresby Island Area Recreation, Accommodations and Services

Recreation	Campgrounds
Kayak rental/transport	RV park
Kayak mother-shipping	**Services**
Dive charters	InfoCentre
Fishing charters	Airport
Eco-adventure charters	Restaurants
Float plane tours	Snack bar
Helicopter tours	Grocery stores
Charter vessel tours	Taxis
Birdwatching	Gas
Backroading	Service stations
Hiking trails	Car rentals
Golf course	Gift shop
Accommodations	
Bed & Breakfasts	
Motel	

Important Numbers

Ambulance **1-800-461-9911**

Hospital (Queen Charlotte City) **250-559-4506**

Hospital (non-emergency) **250-559-4300**

Health care clinic **250-637-5403**

Police **250-559-4421**

Fire **250-637-2222**

Sandspit Visitor Information Centre **250-637-5362**

Gwaii Haanas National Park Reserve and Haida Heritage Site **250-559-8818**

Sitka spruce. Look closely at the **old-growth cedars** to see where the Haida stripped off bark for making clothes and baskets. You can extend your hike by taking side trails, flagged with orange ribbons. The parking area for the Louise Dover Memorial Trail is 9.5 km east of the Alliford Bay ferry dock just past the bridge over Haans Creek. The sign for the trailhead is about 40 metres west of the bridge.

Gwaii Haanas National Park Reserve and Haida Heritage Site

The astoundingly beautiful islands of Gwaii Haanas National Park Reserve and Haida Heritage Site were outside the public eye until the 1980s when environmentalists and forestry companies squared off over the rain forest. Moresby Island and Lyell Island were already a patchwork of raw clear-cuts where ancient forests had once cloaked the mountainsides. In 1974 a logging company filed for permission to start logging in the heart of south Moresby Island. Two local residents, the burly, bearded Haida artist Guujaaw and the American expatriate Thom Henley, vowed to protect the fragile wilderness. They drew up the South Moresby Wilderness Proposal, demanding that all land south of a line drawn across Moresby Island just above Lyell Island be saved from the saw bite of "progress."

To the Haida this region was their ancient homeland of Gwaii Haanas, "Islands of Wonder," where tens of thousands of Haida once lived in villages on its many protected bays and inlets. Even though most Haida people lived in Skidegate and Old Massett, they were always tied to the old villages by family histories and to the land by ancestral heritage. The ancient Haida villages were not "abandoned," but powerful and sacred places. The islands and lapping seas of Gwaii Haanas were not a lost legacy but a living one.

To environmentalists, the ancient temperate rain forests and fecund waters of Gwaii Haanas were a precious natural heritage. Gwaii Haanas was one of the earth's most prolific places, rich with plant and animal life, including **species found nowhere else on the planet**. But it was also a vulnerable ecosystem, in which the death of a single species spelled disaster for a dozen more. Logging would surely destroy that fragile balance, and the world would be forever poorer for it.

Spectacular Windy Bay, Lyell Island

Skung Gwaii (Anthony Island), part of the UNESCO World Heritage Site

Protests heated up when logging was proposed for Burnaby Island in the early 1980s, and matters came to a head when new cutting was okayed on Lyell Island in 1985. There, seventy-two young Haida in lumberjack shirts and war paint stood shoulder to shoulder with Haida elders resplendent in ceremonial button robes to stand down logging trucks. Their arrest and trial captured the imagination of the world. Millions of people—among them singers Bruce Cockburn and Pete Seeger and major US environmental groups— pledged support for the proposed new wilderness area. Logging was halted in 1987, and discussions about the new protected area began. After several years of talks, Canada and the Haida Nation signed an agreement to jointly "safeguard Gwaii Haanas as one of the world's great natural and cultural treasures" in 1993. The Gwaii Haanas National Park Reserve and Haida Heritage Site became a reality.

Gwaii Haanas covers a secluded, storm-swept archipelago of 138 islands in the southern half of the Queen Charlotte Islands, including the southern half of Moresby Island as well as Lyell, Kunghit and Burnaby Islands and Skung Gwaii (Anthony Island). The San Christoval range runs down Gwaii Haanas archipelago. Its rugged peaks—some over 1,200 metres high—shelter the eastern shore from rain and gales. But the western shore is open to the full fury of Pacific storms. As the wettest place in Canada, the west coast of Gwaii Haanas receives more than 400 cm (160 inches) of rain per year. That's four times the rainfall on its more protected east coast. Winds sometimes blow up to 200 km/h, sending towers of foaming surf crashing against the steep mountain flanks. The east coast is less vulnerable to the Queen Charlottes' notoriously volatile wind and weather, and a maze of islands, channels, inlets and bays offer harbour in bad weather. But it lies on the lip of notorious Hecate Strait, and frontal systems can hammer the east coast from the southeast and southwest. In fact the Coast Guard considers small craft warnings to be in effect at all times on Gwaii Haanas's eastern shores.

Nunsting: UNESCO World Heritage Site

At the once-great village of Nunsting (formerly Ninstints), tilting greyed cedar poles stand in a sun-dappled clearing above a shingle beach. These are the world's finest array of still-standing Haida mortuary poles—all more than a hundred years old. For visitors Nunsting is a touchstone, an inspiration, a place to step back into the ancient world of the Haida. For the Haida people it is a sacred site, especially honoured and respected as the last resting place of their ancestors.

Nunsting is on tiny Skung Gwaii (Anthony Island) at the southwest tip of Gwaii Haanas. It was the main village of the Kunghit Haida, who once numbered in the thousands, but who were struck down by plagues of smallpox and tuberculosis. Only a few

Mortuary poles

Kunghit Haida survived into the twentieth century. Their monuments—mortuary poles, house frontal poles and massive house timbers and frames—were left to the mercy of wind and weather. Efforts to preserve this unique and fragile place began at the turn of the century when Charles Newcombe studied the village site shortly after it was abandoned. For sixteen years starting in 1897, Newcombe made maps and notes, took photographs and collected artifacts. The last of the hereditary Kunghit leaders named Nunsting ("He Who is Equal to Two")—a cultivated man accomplished in carving silver, gold, argillite and cedar—worked with Newcombe to make a record of Kunghit history and traditions for posterity. Thanks to their efforts, we have a rich record of the village and its history.

But it wasn't until after the Second World War that serious efforts were made to protect the remains of the village site. In 1957 Wilson Duff, curator at the Provincial Museum of BC, with the permission of the Skidegate Haida, led an expedition to remove eleven of the best-preserved poles. The University of British Columbia's Museum of Anthropology still houses seven Nunsting poles, including a mortuary pole, interior poles and frontal poles. Because of ongoing theft and vandalism, a few Haida re-occupied Nunsting in the late 1970s to watch over the site. Nunsting was declared a UNESCO World Heritage Site in 1981 for its historical value not only to the Haida people but "to the history of mankind." A Haida Watchman now protects this remarkable site for future generations.

The Nunsting poles have been stabilized and carefully cleared of undergrowth and destructive mosses. But they will not stand above the beach forever. Instead they will be allowed, according to Haida custom, to return to earth as their makers intended. From their decay will spring new life, new growth. New poles, like the ones in Skidegate and Old Massett, will be raised as the spirit of the carvers is passed from one generation to the next. They too will be allowed to return to the earth in the elemental cycle of creation, decay and regeneration.

Visiting Gwaii Haanas

This rugged wilderness has no road access and almost no services. The only way in is by air or sea. Float plane and helicopter operators fly into Gwaii Haanas, and more than four dozen Gwaii Haanas charter boat operators offer a range of tours from half-day power-boat tours to week-long kayak and sailing expeditions. Boaters and sea kayakers are allowed to explore Gwaii Haanas independently, but most visitors take guided tours with licensed Gwaii Haanas operators (see p. 389). No matter how you travel, you'll need to plan well ahead of time. Your best bet is to get the Gwaii Haanas National Parks Reserve and Haida Heritage Site information package (250-637-5362). It has almost everything you'll need to know, including lots of information for sea kayakers and an up-to-date list of licensed Gwaii Haanas tour operators. You can also find information and lists of tour operators on the park reserve's website. For general information on the Queen Charlotte Islands, including maps and services, contact the Queen Charlotte City Visitor Information Centre, 250-559-8316.

Where you go and what you do depends on how and why you choose to travel in Gwaii Haanas. But for most visitors, the dream is the same—to find their own elemental connection with this rainforest world of earth, sea and sky. As Bill Reid once wrote of Gwaii Haanas, "There is nowhere more worthy of the care and reverence due the sacred places of the earth than this."

Exploring Gwaii Haanas as an Independent Visitor

The number of visitors to the park is limited to protect fragile natural and cultural features. Independent visitors must make advance reservations to travel in the park or obtain standby space at the Queen Charlotte Visitor Information Centre. Reservations are strongly recommended since only 6 standby spaces a day are available on a first-come, first-served basis. Advance reservations can be made starting February 1 by calling Super, Natural British Columbia (see p. 8). A reservation fee ranging from $15 per person to $60 for a group is charged. Visitor fees are also collected by Super, Natural British Columbia. In 1999, the fees were $10 per day or $60 for 6–14 nights, and $80 for the season. Visitors aged 17 and under are admitted free. Independent visitors must also take a 90-minute orientation session at either the Queen Charlotte Visitor Information Centre or the Sandspit Visitor Information Centre.

Independent Sea Kayaking in Gwaii Haanas

Most independent visitors are sea kayakers who paddle down the spectacular east coast wilderness. Some set off from Queen Charlotte City or Sandspit, but many launch at Moresby Camp on Cumshewa Inlet, located down a logging road about an hour south of Sandspit (see p. 383). The paddle from Moresby Camp to the northern boundary of Gwaii Haanas takes about 2 days if the weather holds. Otherwise, you can arrange to be transported with your kayak and equipment to a dropoff in Gwaii Haanas. The Queen Charlotte City and Sandspit Visitor Information Centres can provide information about kayak rentals and transport, and the Gwaii Haanas visitor package lists licensed Gwaii Haanas transport operators (250-637-5362).

Paddlers are encouraged to travel in small groups to minimize the impact on the environment and maximize their wilderness experience. There are no campgrounds in Gwaii Haanas. Instead the park encourages no-trace random beach camping below the tideline. Only 12 people at a time are allowed ashore within sight and sound of each other. Visitors are asked not to camp at a number of sensitive cultural sites and bird nesting areas. Haida Watchmen live at half a dozen old Haida villages in summer as site guardians—K'una

Skedans

(Skedans), T'anuu (Tanu), Hlk'yaah (Windy Bay), Gandl K'in (Hotspring Island) and Skung Gwaii (Anthony Island). Their symbol—three human figures in tall hats facing in three directions—is taken from the carved figures atop many Haida poles. These carved figures were the watchmen who guarded the village from harm, just as today the Haida Watchmen keep the old village sites safe from vandalism and overuse. They also provide basic information and emergency assistance. Even though it's not part of their job description, the Watchmen are generally proud to share their remarkable culture with visitors.

A word of warning—independent sea kayaking in Gwaii Haanas is not for the novice. The weather changes in the blink of a eye, winds can veer and shift to near-hurricane velocity without warning, exposed areas are subject to powerful ocean currents. Services are almost nonexistent and rescue can take 2 hours or more even in good weather. Self-reliance, good judgment, advance planning, the right equipment and plenty of experience in ocean paddling and wilderness survival are essential. The Gwaii Haanas visitor package (250-637-5362) has all the information you need to decide if you've got what it takes to paddle Gwaii Haanas and to help you arrive prepared for your adventure. It includes details on access, services, maps and charts, equipment checklists, recreation, camping, route planning and reference materials. If you have any doubts, it's best to go with a Gwaii Haanas tour operator.

At anchor in Anna Inlet

Exploring Gwaii Haanas with a Tour Operator

Most Gwaii Haanas visitors opt for guided tours. More than 50 commercial operators fly or sail into Gwaii Haanas. So far there is no park access for the physically challenged, but operators do cater to all different ages and abilities from youngsters and spry seventy-year-olds to super-fit outdoor adventurers. You have a choice of air charters, helicopter excursions, kayak charters and kayak mother-shipping as well as powerboat and sailboat charters and tours. Tours range from half-day excursions to 1- or 2-week-long adventures, from float plane fly-ins and luxury sailboats with private cabins and onboard naturalists to small, single-kayak expeditions through the outer reaches of Gwaii Haanas. Most sailing vessels have inflatable boats for shore excursions and kayaks for some independent exploring.

Guided visitors don't need to make reservations because tour operators work under the quota system. Tour operators also collect the visitor fees and arrange for the mandatory orientation session.

Carved figures of watchmen

FOUR-WHEELING
ON THE BRITISH COLUMBIA COAST

Mark Bostwick

The temptation to leave British Columbia's highway system and explore some of the province's many side paths, back roads and logging trails may be irresistible. For many it is the lure of a secluded lake, or the chance to poke around a tumbledown cabin or watch a bald eagle stalk its prey. Others seek to refresh their souls in solitude, or savour the satisfaction of discovering what lies beyond the next ridge, or simply to scramble over a particularly rough patch of road. Most British Columbians live clustered in towns and hamlets along the main transportation corridors, and until recently the backcountry has been treated as part of the common wealth of the community, public domain rather than real estate. Thus it is possible to drive beyond fenceposts through a landscape where the lakes have no cottages and the sky above a distant ridge is the only limit.

The highways, byways and backways of BC are part of a hierarchy. Street signs are for roads in towns and the occasional road to a ranch or farm. Most of these roads end up at someone's house, with the usual gate and barking dog, but some continue up side valleys once the pavement ends. Signposts disappear, telephone lines shrink from two lines to one to none. The road surface gets rougher, the curves tighter, and eventually what began as a street becomes a Forest Service road or a logging company mainline.

Provincial Forest Service roads are usually well marked with a sign (e.g. Copper Creek Forest Service Road). Typically these are old mainline logging roads upgraded in response to heavy use or the demands of fire protection, and they are usually graded at least once a year. Some are wide with gravel surfaces, others are narrower and made of pounded dirt. Many a Forest Service road parallels a stream and ends near the headwall of a valley. Side paths and skid roads lead to logging cuts or cattle pastures above the valley floor. A Forest Service road leading to a provincial recreational area (usually a lake) are almost always passable by an ordinary automobile; access to primitive backcountry campsites often requires four-wheel drive capability. Do not expect to find country stores, gas stations or even a house with a telephone along the way.

Next in the hierarchy are mainline logging roads. Mainlines were engineered with one central purpose: getting cut timber out of valleys and to the mill as expeditiously as possible. There is no universal designation system as there is in the USA. A mainline logging road may be identified by a name, a number or nothing at all. It may well have a series of kilometre markings, but zero may be at the start of the road, at the junction of the highway or even at the centre of the nearest town. Mainline roads follow the valley bottoms and are like the trunks of large trees: the branches are secondary roads that lead to logging patches on the slopes of surrounding hills. So if you keep coming to forks, it suggests you are heading toward the end of a road; if you find your route being joined by other roads, it suggests you are heading out toward civilization. Such tracks may extend 50 or 60 km up a long valley, or be as short as 3 or 4 km. Networks of logging roads are not usually connected to each other in BC, although serious four-wheelers spend many weekends every summer searching for these elusive passageways.

Logging roads are maintained only during active logging. Once the allowable cuts have been harvested, the roads are deactivated and gradually deteriorate or grow over.

Before vacating an area the logging company normally cuts shallow ditches across the road to improve drainage. The backcountry explorer should be careful to watch for these and ease vehicles over them gently. Many of the more obscure logging roads, especially those lined by sheltering trees, remain derivable for decades before alder and new seedlings reclaim them. The combination of new growth, washouts and collapsed bridges announce the end of a road's recreational use. So do arbitrary road closures and privatization. The wider, more modern roads built to current government and environmental standards tend toward dust, mudholes and a washboard surface after a couple of years. They can be hard on shock absorbers.

Backcountry exploration should always be tempered by caution. The very fact that large parts of BC remain wild and sparsely populated should remind the traveller that help is not likely to be just around the corner. Always be on the lookout for logging trucks; they are the kings of the road in the bush and must be given the right of way in all instances. Before starting up a logging road, look for a recent posting stating that the area is being actively logged. Get out of the car and check the dirt for the big tire prints of logging trucks. A scattering of green twigs or small branches is a clue that the logging rigs have come down the road recently. Watch for dust plumes in the distance and find a place to pull off the road so that the big rig coming your way can pass. If you meet a logging truck on the road, get out of the way and remember that the logs hanging off the rear sweep a wide swath on the outside corners. If a logging truck—or any other vehicle—catches up to you from behind, pull over and let it by. The locals are more familiar with the road and deserve the courtesy of going ahead.

If the really old, worn logging and mining trails appeal to you, take a few additional precautions: a full gas tank, warm clothes, a shovel, compass, map and guidebook and anything else you may need if you get stuck miles from nowhere. Watch out for ditching, deadfall, soft shoulders and decayed bridges. Typical obstacles include ruts, small mud-holes, exposed rock and fallen trees, all of which require driving slowly, in low range. In some places the brush makes old paths into blind alleys, so watch for the hidden pothole or jagged rock. Remember that Pacific storms lose little force when they hit the coast, and it is a notorious understatement to say that the coast of BC has a rainy climate.

If you intend to camp, take a map identifying the campsites. Experienced four-wheelers in BC usually tote a water can rather than trusting the purity of local streams. Plan an early camp, and if you see fresh bear scat on the track into the campsite, take it as encouragement to find another spot. Bears can be a nuisance; don't mess with them. Cougars have been known to attack small children although they are usually quite shy. Wolves are less dangerous than some family pets. For most campers, mosquitoes and blackflies are the most wicked creatures in the bush. Keep small children away from rushing streams, always douse the campfire, and leave a spotless campsite in the morning.

It is possible to travel for days in the backcountry without meeting anyone. But if you park in the middle of even the smallest, most obscure path, it is guaranteed that someone will come along and want to get past you. It is equally bad manners to drive off the trail or rip up any field or meadow. Always leave a gate the way you found it and respect all No Trespassing signs, including those installed by First Nations. Fishing licences and campground stickers are obligatory: in BC forest wardens get around in four-wheel-drive vehicles and can easily check out the smallest ponds.

All this precautionary preaching is mostly a reminder of common courtesy, which will make your trip and everyone else's more pleasant. Generally, the watchword in British Columbia is definitely "tread lightly," and those who adhere to the backcountry code deserve the rewards.

Old-timers will tell you that the most exquisite enjoyment is often found early in the morning or near dusk. The long summer days and short northern nights may mean getting up early or going to bed late in order to indulge in the best. Drive slowly and quietly along a backcountry lane just after dawn, the best time to see an old black bear ambling along the trail or a doe and her fawn grazing in a thicket. Dusk arrives with a chorus of birdsong that gradually wanes as the lake becomes a bowl of shimmering mercury. Listen to the loons exchange endearments until at last only a lonely owl is awake to cheer the canopy of stars.

Enjoy the midday in a leisurely fashion. Don't pass by that little clearing by the old log bridge—it's probably perfect for a picnic lunch off the tailgate. Indulge your aesthetic needs with a visit to a riot of wildflowers in an old clearcut. Watch for the rusted relics of obsolete mining equipment. Stop from time to time just to listen to the wind or watch the cloud formations.

Some suggested reading to assist backcountry travellers: The *British Columbia Recreational Atlas*, 4th edition (BC Ministry of Environment) contains maps of mainline logging roads, identifies provincial recreation areas, makes suggestions for wildlife viewing, and much more. The *Backroad Mapbook* Series, Vols. I and II, 2nd edition (Mussio Ventures) has tracings of most major and many minor logging roads. *The Four-Wheeler's Companion: The Off-Road Guide to Southwestern BC*, 3rd edition and *Four-Wheeling in the BC Interior* (Mark Bostwick, Harbour Publishing), and *Four-Wheeling on Southern Vancouver Island* (David Lee, Harbour Publishing) describe the best local backroad trips from easy to super-challenging, with lots of photos, maps and four-wheeling tips.

ACKNOWLEDGEMENTS

Creating a comprehensive guide to BC's fabulously long and fascinating coast and its great communities, large and small, is by its very nature a collaborative effort. We'd like to thank all the people who made this book possible by contributing photographs and insider information and recommendations and by inspiring us with their enthusiam for this wonderous place. In particular, a tip of the hat to the helpful folks at InfoCentres, provincial parks, and Chambers of Commerce everywhere we travelled. Special kudos to Laura Serena of Tourism Vancouver, the Ucluelet Chamber of Commerce, Jean McIntosh of the Alberni Valley Museum, Charles McDiarmid of the Wickaninnish Inn in Tofino, Nancy J. Turner of the University of Victoria, Tammy Rayner of the Village of Masset Economic Development Office, Michele Deakin and Gilbert Parnell of the Gwaii Haanas National Park Reserve and Haida Heritage Site, Barb Brittain of the Pacific Rim National Park Reserve, BC Ferries, Kelly Widsten of the Shearwater Marine Group, Penny Sopel of the Oak Bay Marine Group, and especially to Steve Dennis of Seaside Adventures in Tofino for his remarkable generosity with photographs and information about BC's wild west coast and to Jennifer Echols for her many fine Vancouver photographs. Thanks, too, to good friends and great travel companions/photographers Sarah Eaton and Lynn Katy, who took up where Allison left off.

No book is ever born without enormous backroom efforts by its publishers. Here's to the hard-working people at Harbour Publishing: project editor Peter Robson, managing editor Mary Schendlinger, editor Derek Fairbridge and designer Martin Nichols.

Above all, thanks to Eric Boyum and Trish Smyth of Ocean Adventures Charter Co, not only for the inspired photographs of Gwaii Haanas but for their deep love and abiding reverence for this all-too-fragile coast and its creatures. No one who sails with Trish and Eric aboard the *Ocean Light* in the Gulf Islands or the Land of the Spirit Bear or the Haida homeland of Haida Gwaii can fail to be touched by the magic of BC's West Coast.

—Diane Eaton

This book is a product of an enormous amount of hard work by all the people mentioned above and I would also like to add a personal thank you to Diane for the tremendous experience and privilege of discovering the BC Coast. I would like to dedicate my contribution to this publication to Fred and Joan Hess for their unwavering support of me both personally and professionally.

—Allison Eaton

INDEX

Page numbers set in bold-face type indicate maps.

Coast, 64, 70, 75, 83, 86, 87; Vancouver Island: Nanaimo to West Coast, 216, 232, 240, 245, 249; Vancouver Island South, 182, 183, 185, 188, 191, 199, 207

English Bay, 23, 31

Englishman River, 256

Englishman River Falls, 256

Entrance Island, 204

Eric Lake, 331

Esquimalt Harbour, 107, 112, 113

Esquimalt Lagoon, 113

Esquimalt & Nanaimo Railway (E&N), 111, 180, 184, 216

European exploration, 12–13, 227, 228–29, 335. *See also* Hudson's Bay Company (HBC)

F

Fair Harbour, 309

False Bay, 257

False Creek, 31

Fanny Bay, 260, **261**

farmers' markets: Central Vancouver Island, 288; Gulf Islands, 133, 149, 164; Vancouver & area, 32, 33, 42; Vancouver Island: Nanaimo to West Coast, 212, 230

ferry service: Alaska Marine Highway, 354; BC, 8; to Campbell River, 302; to Cortes Island, 296; to Denman Island, 263; Discovery Coast Passage route, 334, 336–41, **337**; to Gabriola Island, 201; to Galiano Island, 171; to Gulf Islands, 122; to Hornby Island, 267; Inside Passage route, 334–35, 342–45, **343**; to Mayne Island, 141; to Nanaimo, 101, 209, 251; to North Moresby Island, 362; to Pender Island, 161; to Port Hardy, 334; to Quadra Island, 288; to Queen Charlotte Islands, 361–62; Queen Charlotte Islands route, 335; to Salt Spring Island, 127; to Saturna Island, 151; to Sointula (Malcolm Island), 318; to Sunshine Coast, 56; to Thetis Island, 189; to Vancouver & area, 101; to Victoria & area, 95, 101

festivals: Central Vancouver Island, 255, 266, 273, 292, 296; Gulf Islands, 142; North Island, 305; Sunshine Coast, 66, 84; Vancouver & area, 34, 35, 39, 42, 53; Vancouver Island: Nanaimo to West Coast, 215, 233; Vancouver Island South, 199; Victoria & area, 94, 98, 105, 118

Fife Point, 380

First Nations sites and culture: BC, 12; Central Vancouver Island, 253, 254, 272, 275, 278, 280, 286–87, 287, 288, 290–91, 292, 298, 299; Gulf Islands, 129, 130, 132–33, 140, 158, 159, 165, 173; North Coast, 335, 338–39, 340, 349, 350, 351, 354, 356–57, 361, 363, 364, 365, 366, 367, 368, 372, 375, 376–77, 380, 382, 384, 385, 386; North Island, 303, 305, 320–23, 324, 327, 328; Sunshine Coast, 65, 67–68, 73, 74, 84, 88; Vancouver & area, 25, 26, 30, 37–38, 42, 43, 45, 48, 49, 52; Vancouver Island: Nanaimo to West Coast, 214–15, 216, 221, 222, 223, 227, 228–29,

235, 236, 240, 241, 244, 249; Vancouver Island South, 178, 181, 182–83, 184, 188, 196, 198, 200; Victoria & area, 98, 100–101, 103, 106, 108, 118

Fisherman Bay, 331

Fitz Hugh Sound, 342, 344

Flora Island, 268

Florencia Bay, 223, 226–27

Florencia Beach, 227

Flores Island, 240, 241

Fort Langley, 28, 43–44

Fort McLoughlin, 338

Fort Rupert, 328–29

Fort Victoria, 103

Frances Island, 217

Fraser River, 28, 43–44, 45, 138

French Creek, 257

Friendly Cove, 286–87

Fulford, 136

Fulford Harbour (Salt Spring Island ferry terminal), 126–30, 136

Furney, Gerry, 314, 327

fur trade, 12, 43, 95, 241, 287, 328, 350, 351

G

Gabriola Island, 200–207, **201**

Galiano, Mt., 175

Galiano Island, 121, 123, 147, 168–75, **169**

Galleon Beach, 267

galleries. *See* art galleries

Gambier Island, 58

Gandl K'in, 388

Ganges, 124, 128, 131–34, 136

Ganges Harbour, 136

Garden Bay, 71, 72–73

Garden Bay Lake, 74

gardens, public: Vancouver & area, 25, 31, 38, 39; Victoria & area, 97, 98, 113–15, 117

Geoffrey, Mt., 265, 268

Georgeson, Henry "Scotty," 145

Georgina Point, 144

Gibson, George, 60

Gibsons, 58–63, **61**, 64

Gitz Cove, 382

Goldie Lake, 47

Gold River, 278, 285–86

gold rush, 12–13, 28, 29, 103, 138, 226–27, 308–9

golf: Central Vancouver Island, 257; Gulf Islands, 136, 158, 161, 167; North Coast, 349, 356, 374, 375, 381; North Island, 303, 325, 326; Sunshine Coast, 64–65; Vancouver & area, 52, 53; Vancouver Island South, 184, 204; Victoria & area, 94, 106

Goodwin, Albert "Ginger," 271

Gordon River, 242

Gorge Harbour, 296, 298

Gorge Inlet, 107

Gorge Waters, 107

Gorge Waterway, 97, 98

Gowlland Point, 163

Graham Island, 360, 361, 362, 363, 364–80